Keep this book. You will
need it and use it throughout
your career.

The LODGING and FOOD SERVICE INDUSTRY

Fourth Edition

Educational Institute Books

10/98

The LODGING and FOOD SERVICE INDUSTRY

Fourth Edition

Gerald W. Lattin, Ph.D., CHA

Contributing Authors: **James E. Lattin** *and* **Thomas W. Lattin**

EDUCATIONAL INSTITUTE

American Hotel & Motel Association

Disclaimer

...ccurate and authoritative information in regard to the subject matter covered. It is sold with the understanding that the publisher is not engaged in rendering legal, accounting, or other professional service. If legal advice or other expert assistance is required, the services of a competent professional person should be sought.
—*From the Declaration of Principles jointly adopted by the American Bar Association and a Committee of Publishers and Associations.*

The authors, Gerald W. Lattin, James E. Lattin, and Thomas W. Lattin, are solely responsible for the contents of this publication. All views expressed herein are solely those of the authors and do not necessarily reflect the views of the Educational Institute of the American Hotel & Motel Association (the Institute) or the American Hotel & Motel Association (AH&MA).

Nothing contained in this publication shall constitute a standard, an endorsement, or a recommendation of the Institute or AH&MA. The Institute and AH&MA disclaim any liability with respect to the use of any information, procedure, or product, or reliance thereon by any member of the hospitality industry.

©1998
By the EDUCATIONAL INSTITUTE of the
AMERICAN HOTEL & MOTEL ASSOCIATION
2113 N. High Steet
Lansing, Michigan 48906

The Educational Institute of the American
Hotel & Motel Association is a nonprofit
educational foundation.

Printed in the United States of America
  2 3 4 5 6 7 8 9 10 03 02 01 00 99 98

Library of Congress Cataloging-in-Publication Data
Lattin, Gerald W.
  The lodging and food service industry/Gerald W. Lattin;
  contributing authors, James E. Lattin and Thomas W. Lattin.—
  4th ed.
    p. cm.
  Includes bibliographical references and index.
  ISBN 0-86612-169-2
  1. Hospitality industry. 2. Hospitality industry—Vocational
guidance. I. Lattin, James E. II. Lattin, Thomas W. III. Title.
TX911.L297 1998
647.94'023—dc21   98–6590
                                                         CIP

Editor: Priscilla J. Wood

Contents

Preface

THE OBJECTIVES AND PURPOSE of this book are to provide an introduction to the lodging and food service industry, to explain the complex interrelationships involved in the business, and to stress the variety of career opportunities available. In this fourth edition, we continue to provide coverage that is international, thus reflecting the globalization the industry has undergone during the past few years and is continuing at a rapid pace. To my knowledge, this is the only hospitality industry textbook encompassing a global approach. People who are certain to benefit from this text include those working in the industry, those entering or thinking of entering the industry, hospitality program educators, career guidance counselors, hospitality industry suppliers, and, of course, hospitality students.

Books are not written singlehandedly. I am grateful for the very able assistance of my co-authors: Mr. Tom Lattin, President and COO, Patriot American Hospitality; and Mr. Jim Lattin, General Manager, Park Ridge Hotel and Conference Center, Valley Forge, Pennsylvania. I wish to thank my panel of international experts for their learned input and advice on the industry worldwide. The panel members are: Mr. Rodolfo Casparius, CHE, Nation's President Emeritus of the Mexican Hotel and Motel Association; Mr. Olivier Friedli, former Vice President, Swissôtel, Ltd.; Mr. Fred Mosser, President, Wingate Inn; and Mr. Leo Claus, owner/operator of several restaurants in the Netherlands. Special thanks are due the industry executives who contributed the Insider Insights, a key feature of the fourth edition.

A round of kudos to Dr. Bjorn Hanson, Industry Chairman—Hospitality, Coopers & Lybrand, and Mr. John Norlander, recently retired President and CEO, Carlson Hospitality Worldwide, fearless prognosticators of what our industry will be like in the twenty-first century.

Special thanks are due Dr. Jack Ninemeier, School of Hotel, Restaurant and Institutional Management, Michigan State University, for his input in the chapters dealing with food and beverage management, and to the staff of the Educational Institute for all their efforts.

This book is dedicated to Jean Lattin, my bride of 54 years, and to the students, lodging and food service staff members, teachers, trainers, and other professionals of the hospitality industry, one of the greatest and finest industries in the world. Our industry deals with people—those employed and those served by the many hospitality operations throughout the world—and it is this fact that makes hospitality careers so fascinating and rewarding.

—Gerald W. Lattin
Founding Dean
and Dean Emeritus
School of Hospitality Management
Florida International University

About the Authors . . .

| Dr. Gerald W. Lattin | Thomas W. Lattin | James E. Lattin |

Dr. Gerald W. Lattin, now retired from his administrative duties, continues to impart his knowledge, wisdom, and 50+ years of industry experience to students while serving as distinguished professor at universities here in the United States and overseas. He also continues to offer his expertise to the industry through his consulting firm, Dr. G. W. Lattin and Associates.

During his long and varied hospitality career, he served as administrator and faculty member at three of the nation's most prestigious hotel and restaurant schools. He was a faculty member and Associate Dean at Cornell University's School of Hotel Administration for 25 years; founding dean of Florida International University's School of Hospitality Management for 12 years; and Dean of the Conrad Hilton College of Hotel and Restaurant Management, University of Houston, for 4 years. Noted throughout the industry for combining practical experience with classroom theory, Dr. Lattin has taught many of today's industry leaders.

Dr. Lattin has served as President and Chairman of the Council on Hotel, Restaurant and Institutional Education (CHRIE) and has written three textbooks as well as numerous articles for the trade press. He has organized and taught hospitality seminars on every continent of the world except Antarctica. He has served on the boards of leading corporations and hotels and has participated actively in hotel, restaurant, travel, and club associations.

With more than 30 years of operational and development experience in the hospitality industry, Thomas W. Lattin is President and Chief Operating Officer of Patriot American Hospitality, Inc., the nation's second largest hotel real estate investment trust (REIT). Since its inception and subsequent initial public offering in 1995, Mr. Lattin has directed all aspects of the company's strategic acquisition efforts, from identification of desirable properties, through the due diligence and negotiation processes, which resulted in the company's tripling the size of its rooms portfolio in less than two years. Mr. Lattin's expertise enabled the company to realize significant financial increases over the five consecutive quarters since it became a public company. The innovative independent multi-lessee structure created and implemented by Mr. Lattin is credited for accelerating the company's acquisition efforts, which have resulted in a substantial increase in value for Patriot American's shareholders.

Mr. Lattin has served as senior vice president of Paine Webber Inc., as a partner in Cooper & Lybrand's National Hospitality Consulting Group, and as a national partner of Laventhol & Horwath. As president of Texas-based Mariner Corporation, he was instrumental in developing the company from 2 to 25 hotels in seven years.

He holds bachelor's and master's degrees from Cornell's School of Hotel Administration, and is a certified public accountant. He has lectured at his alma mater as well as at the University of Houston, Michigan State University, Florida International University, and the Centre de Internationale de Glion in Switzerland. Mr. Lattin is a frequent contributor to *Hotel & Motel Management* magazine and has published papers in the *Cornell Hotel and Restaurant Administration Quarterly*. He serves as a director of the Foundation for Research and Education in Hospitality Technology, Inc.

James E. Lattin is currently General Manager of the Park Ridge Hotel & Conference Center in suburban Philadelphia. He also serves as Area Director of Operations for HEI Hotels, a subsidiary of Starwood Lodging Corporation.

Mr. Lattin's career in hospitality management spans over 25 years and includes executive positions with Marriott, Doubletree Hotels, the Pacific Islands Club in Guam, as well as HEI Hotels. His experience includes positions in North America, Asia, and Australia.

He has served as guest lecturer at major schools of hospitality management both nationally and internationally. Mr. Lattin holds a Bachelor of Arts degree from Hamilton College, Clinton, New York, and a Master of Arts degree from Florida Atlantic University in Boca Raton, Florida.

Part I

The World of Hospitality

Chapter 1 Outline

Why People Travel
Where People Travel
Economic and Other Impacts of Tourism
Ecotourism/Adventure Travel

The Travel and Tourism Industry in Perspective

In OUR STUDY of the hospitality industry, we will focus on two of its important segments: lodging and food service operations. But first we need to learn something about the larger enterprise of which hospitality is a part: the travel and tourism industry. What is the travel and tourism industry? What different businesses does it comprise?

The travel and tourism industry includes a vast range of businesses that have one thing in common: providing products and services to travelers. Businesses offering transportation, accommodations, food, drink, shopping, entertainment, recreation, and other hospitality services are all part of the travel and tourism industry.

Many of these businesses also provide products and services to people from the community as well as travelers. Few food service enterprises could be successful without significant business from community members, while lodging properties usually rely on the traveling public to a greater extent. In this respect, hospitality operations are like retail stores, sporting events, or local festivals—all cater to both the traveling and non-traveling public. They are all "partners" in the travel and tourism industry.

Exhibit 1 is an overview of the travel and tourism industry. Note that the industry is divided into five general categories, according to the services offered. Lodging operations offer sleeping accommodations. Food and beverage operations offer food and beverage service. Transportation services enable tourists to travel to a destination. Retail shops of all sorts, ranging from roadside markets to vast shopping malls with hundreds of stores, offer travelers almost every product imaginable. Finally, a variety of business and entertainment activities are available to the traveling public. There can be considerable overlap in these categories—for example, many lodging operations have food and beverage services, gift shops, and recreational activities on site, and some offer limited transportation services. Likewise, cruise ships and resorts could reasonably be listed under all five categories.

Second only in size to transportation services, the hospitality industry comprises the lodging and food and beverage operations from the categories in Exhibit 1. In addition, there is another segment of food and beverage service typically classified as part of the hospitality industry that does not cater to the traveling public. Institutional (nonprofit) food services are offered in health care and educational facilities, in business offices and industrial plants, in the military, in correctional facilities, in seminaries, and by charitable organizations. These institutional food

Exhibit 1   Overview of the Travel and Tourism Industry

Travel and Tourism Industry				
Lodging Operations	**Food and Beverage Operations**	**Transportation Services**	**Retail Stores**	**Activities**
Hotels	Restaurants	Ships	Gift Shops	Recreation
Motels	Lodging Properties	Airplanes	Souvenir Shops	Business
Motor Hotels	Retail Stores	Autos	Arts/Crafts Shops	Entertainment
Resorts	Vending	Buses	Shopping Malls	Meetings
Camps	Catering	Trains	Markets	Study Trips
Parks	Snack Bars	Bikes	Miscellaneous Stores	Sporting Events
Pensions	Cruise Ships	Limousines		Ethnic Festivals
Motor Homes	Bars/Taverns			Art Festivals
				Cultural Events
				Seasonal Festivals

service operations use the same management principles as those used by their commercial counterparts.

Why People Travel

The travel and tourism industry is growing quickly. Contributing to this growth is the fact that many people have more leisure time available, and they often see traveling as an attractive leisure time activity. People travel more as their average work week decreases, as their amounts of vacation leave and holiday time increase, and as their real income and disposable income levels increase. For example, people working in professional occupations and those over 55 years of age are more likely to travel.

Comfortable, convenient, and fast travel as we know it today has come into being only since the 1940s. However, people have always traveled. Prehistoric nomadic tribes traveled, seeking food or safety. Throughout history, people have traveled in order to fight wars, to spread ideological, religious, or political views, and simply to explore unknown areas. The "modern" era of travel began almost 3,000 years ago when money became a popular medium of exchange. Traders and other businesspeople began to travel in efforts to discover and bring back products to sell in their own lands.

Today, travel is commonplace in the lives of many people, especially Americans. Many businesspeople think nothing of flying from Chicago to New York City for a business meeting and returning the same day. Vacation packages offered by airlines and hotels provide great incentives for businesspeople to mix business travel with pleasure or for families to take annual vacations which would have been "dream" vacations only a few years ago.

Insider Insights

J.T. Kuhlman
President
Inter-Continental Hotels
Miami, Florida

Talent, languages, long hours, and a willingness to pack bags often are just some of the ingredients necessary to succeed as a manager in the international hospitality industry. In today's increasingly competitive market, with more people traveling internationally for business and pleasure every year, enthusiasm and old-fashioned hotelier skills are no longer enough. As companies become more global in terms of the people they recruit, the markets in which they operate, and the customers they serve, ambitious employees will need to equip themselves with the business skills and professional skills necessary to run highly complex, global operations.

Certainly, there can be no compromise on the basics—the successful general manager of a hotel should, first and foremost, be a great hotelier. General managers tend to develop their careers by experience, typically following an operational education in, for example, food and beverage, with an apprenticeship building on the educational area. As they rise in the ranks and gain responsibility, a broader business education is usually ad hoc and often dependent on opportunity and personal interest.

The focus in the past has been on delivering a quality product, and service staff and managers were selected primarily on their ability to achieve this objective. The challenge of the future is to maintain all the skills of being a fine hotelier while combining them with the business skills necessary to run a major asset like a hotel.

Today a hotel can be worth $100 to $200 million—large enough to be listed as a separate company on most stock exchanges around the world. To manage such a large asset, a general manager must possess a high level of business skills: the financial skills necessary to manage the assets, the marketing skills needed to position and promote the product, and the leadership skills needed to motivate, communicate, and set goals for a large, labor-intensive organization.

Climbing the career ladder often entails making big sacrifices. You must be prepared to uproot yourself and your family every two or three years to move to a different country, not always of your choice. This may require learning a new language or acquiring new skills. You will be expected to work long, often irregular, hours, including holidays and weekends. Time spent with your family may be scarce and often subject to last-minute changes. To succeed in this business, you will need perseverance, tolerance, and an ability to think clearly and bounce back in sometimes difficult circumstances.

If you have read this far and are still interested in pursuing a career in the international hotel industry, then you are probably the type of go-ahead person this industry needs. The work is certainly challenging, but the rewards can be equally tremendous. With the opportunity to travel extensively and work in many countries around the world, the hotel business offers the chance to experience a wide range of different jobs and acquire an impressive catalog of skills.

(continued)

Insider Insights *(continued)*

Compensation and benefits are highly competitive, and career prospects can offer enormous responsibility at an increasingly early age. As the general manager of a hotel, you will effectively be running your own business—with all the financial and operating problems and rewards that such an entrepreneurial challenge entails—conceivably before you are 40.

After starting work in the international field, I realized that I needed a solid foundation; so, at the age of 27, I went back to school and graduated from Florida International University in 1975. Over the years, I have had the opportunity to work in many different countries around the world. I have met wonderful people and have become a local citizen of many fascinating cultures.

Despite the usual highs and lows common to the development of all careers, I can honestly say that there has never been a day in my career that I have regretted choosing this challenging and exciting profession. I hope this will be true for all of you.

Furthermore, pleasure travel is not just for the rich or near-rich anymore. This is due in part to the widespread use and acceptance of credit cards. Credit cards allow people to charge some or all of their vacation—transportation, accommodations, food, even souvenirs—and to pay for it later, either all at once or a little at a time. In addition, credit cards provide an easier means to handle vacation spending. They are more secure from theft than cash. They are more convenient than traveler's checks, which often have to be ordered from the bank one day and picked up on another. For these reasons, both business and pleasure travel have increased dramatically.

One writer has suggested that there are both internal and external motivating factors which influence the desire to travel.[1]

Internal factors, which motivate one by creating an internal desire to travel, are referred to as "push" elements. For example, some people see travel as a means to maintain or improve their health; spas and health resorts may be destinations for these individuals. People also travel out of curiosity; they wish to experience new people, places, and cultures. Likewise, the desire to participate in or view sports is an important motivator for many. Obviously, some people travel for pleasure. For others, spiritual or religious concerns provide an incentive. Professional and business needs can motivate travel decisions. The desire to visit one's friends, relatives, and/or homeland is another travel incentive. Even prestige—traveling for the purpose of impressing others—is a common reason for travel. When people want to be among the "first" to visit an exotic destination or to view sights made famous because of current news events, prestige may be a factor in their travel decisions.

External factors, or "pull" elements, attract travelers to specific areas once their desire to travel has been generated. A destination's culture, history, and tradition are attractions to many travelers. Geography, wildlife, entertainment, cuisine, and climate are other major attractions. Some people travel to view architecture. Some people travel to shop. Many destinations are known for certain goods; for example,

The Hawaiian Islands are among the most popular visitor destinations in the world. Pictured here is Waiakea Resort Village at Hilo on the island of Hawaii.

Hong Kong suits, Irish crystal, Mexican leather. Others shop for collectibles as a hobby. Some prefer to travel just for the sake of travel and may "collect" countries in much the same way that others collect postage stamps.

Some travelers enjoy the travel more than the destination. Cruise ships, first-class air travel, and chartered bus trips are examples of travel modes that emphasize pleasurable transportation. Some people travel primarily because they enjoy preparing for a trip (such as learning about a country before visiting it) or because they enjoy the memories of a trip after it has concluded.

There are many other factors affecting where and why people travel. Consider, for example, the increase in travel when airfares decrease or when airlines wage price wars in their competition for business. Pleasure travel is often dominated by cost concerns; more people will travel to places that give them the best value for their vacation dollars. People traveling for business usually do not have this flexibility. They are traveling for business-related purposes and must be at a specific destination at a specific time.

Some attention should be given to reasons people do not travel. There are people who cannot afford to travel. There are people who do not travel for psychological reasons—they feel uncomfortable in strange surroundings and

Walt Disney World's Magic Kingdom in Orlando, Florida, is one of the most famous theme parks in the world. (Photo courtesy of the Walt Disney Company, copyright 1991)

have security-related concerns that reduce their travel interests. Some feel they do not have time to travel. Owners and managers of small businesses frequently cite this reason. Others do not travel because of family circumstances. They may, for example, be responsible for a family member who is ill, or they may have small children who make traveling an inconvenience. People with disabilities may be frustrated with barriers that prevent them from enjoying some travel destinations.

Factors like these can reduce travel, because people facing such obstacles may not realize that many businesses in the travel and tourism industry are willing and able to meet their needs. For example, many lodging operations have weekend packages that allow guests to "escape" without leaving their own community. Campgrounds and mobile homes provide opportunities for people with young children to enjoy a relatively inexpensive family vacation. More and more, tourism operations are working to accommodate the needs of people with disabilities. The Americans with Disabilities Act has accelerated the elimination of barriers frustrating people with disabilities.

People travel for a wide variety of reasons. Catering to the wants and needs of such a diverse traveling market requires a significant variety of businesses. For example, some hotels cater to the very rich, while others are marketed to people seeking clean, inexpensive accommodations. Retail shops, transportation companies, and other tourism-related businesses offer products and services that differentiate among tourists based upon the reasons they travel and the needs they experience as they travel.

Where People Travel

Where do travelers go? We have stated that pleasure travelers usually have more leeway in making their travel plans than those needing to conduct business. This added discretion means that tourists can reject locations that do not meet specific requirements. Business travelers often cannot do this, though we should note that many businesses decide to locate in areas that are attractive in their own right.

The requirements imposed by tourists on prospective destinations fall into five basic categories.[2]

- Natural resources—A destination must have natural resources available for visitors. Examples of natural resources that may be important to travelers include climate, geography, plants and animals, access to water, beauty of the surrounding area, and other factors that make the natural environment pleasing and hospitable.

- **Infrastructure**—The infrastructure consists of underground or surface construction necessary to service travelers and tourists, as well as the local population. Examples include systems for water, sewage, gas, electricity, and communication. Highways, airports, railroads, parking lots, lighting systems, boat and dock facilities, or any appropriate combination of these services must typically be available (though some travelers may enjoy more exotic destinations that lack these basics).

- **Superstructure**—The superstructure consists of major above-ground facilities which are serviced by the infrastructure and which help make a destination attractive. Hotels, shopping and entertainment centers, museums, and other attractions are examples of superstructure.

- Transportation and related equipment—The physical means for travel, such as automobiles, airplanes, boats, or trains, must be readily accessible.

- Hospitality resources—The cultural wealth of the destination is often important to the success of the tourism industry in that community. The spirit of hospitality shown by the government, businesspeople, and area residents is

Egypt and the picturesque Nile River are popular destinations for those who like to visit exotic places. Above is the Aswan Oberoi, situated in the winter resort of Aswan on Elephantine Island in the Nile. (Photo courtesy of Oberoi Hotels International)

very important. Cultural resources such as the area's arts, literature, music, and drama frequently contribute to tourism success within a specific area.

Lodging and food and beverage operations are an integral part of a destination. The traveling public needs places to eat and sleep. Most tourists will not go to a destination lacking hospitality facilities. Many tourists specifically want to experience accommodations and cuisine characteristic of an area. For example, thatched-roof huts on a Polynesian island and a temple atmosphere in India may be among expectations of travelers to those destinations. Similarly, travelers may expect fresh seafood in a gulf-coast restaurant and prime steak in a hotel dining room in Omaha or Denver. Decor, table appointments, and employee uniforms also frequently reflect the area within which the hospitality operation is located.

Economic and Other Impacts of Tourism

The tourism boom worldwide has been amazing. Tourism is now the world's largest industry with sales of $3.6 trillion, which is 11 percent of the world's gross domestic product. One of every nine workers worldwide is currently employed in tourism. The World Tourism Organization predicts 700 million travelers by the year 2000—twice the number of travelers in 1985—and more than one billion people by 2006 generating $7.1 trillion in tourism receipts.[3]

Exhibit 2   Tourist Accommodations Worldwide

Region	Accommodations	Increase 1980-Present	Market Share 1980-Present	
Europe	10,870,000	27%	52.4%	45.7%
N. America	6,892,000	30%	32.4%	28.8%
Caribbean/Central South America	1,516,000	25%	7.1%	6.4%
East Asia/Pacific	3,180,000	350%	4.7%	13.4%

Source: World Tourism Organization, June 1997.

An important factor in international tourism is **globalization**. This refers both to the increasing ease with which people can travel all over the world, and to the trend of major corporations, such as large hotel chains or franchise restaurants, to expand their operations into countries all over the world. Globalization is having a particularly strong impact on developing countries, where new tourism can quickly and significantly affect the local economy.

Statistics on the number of tourist accommodations (beds) worldwide are shown in Exhibit 2. The four geographical areas listed account for 95 percent of the world's tourism. Although all four of the areas show increases in number of accommodations, three experienced a loss in market share. Only the East Asia/Pacific region increased its market share as well as its number of accommodations.

In the United States, according to February 1997 Travel Industry Association of America statistics, tourism ranks among the top three employers in 42 of the 50 states. It is the number-one source of jobs in 17 of these states. Tourism generates approximately $440 billion in annual sales. It directly employs 6.6 million people and, indirectly, 8 million, with an annual payroll of $120 billion. Also worth noting is the fact that tourism generates over $60 billion in federal, state, and local taxes. Moreover, tourism, unlike heavy industry and exporting, offers an opportunity to earn money with significantly less depletion of natural resources.

The hospitality industry benefits directly from tourism, and other parts of the economy benefit as a result. This is called the **ripple effect**. Though some economists disagree over the extent of the ripple effect, all agree that the hospitality industry can help other businesses in an area. Some authorities estimate that for every tourist dollar spent in lodging properties, three tourist dollars are spent elsewhere in the community.

In 1996, foreign visitors to the United States spent $80.1 billion. The five major destination states were Florida, California, New York, Hawaii, and Nevada, in that order. The top five cities drawing international visitors were New York City, Los Angeles, Miami, Orlando, and San Francisco. That same year, American tourists traveling abroad spent $60.6 billion. Their major destinations were Canada, Mexico, Japan, Germany, and France.[4]

Worldwide, France has been the number-one tourist destination for several years. Exhibit 3 shows the world's top ten tourist destinations and the annual

Exhibit 3   The World's Top Ten Tourism Destinations

Country	Tourist Arrivals
France	61.5 million
United States	44.8 million
Spain	41.3 million
Italy	35.5 million
China	26.1 million
United Kingdom	25.8 million
Mexico	21.7 million
Hungary	20.7 million
Poland	19.4 million
Canada	17.3 million

Source: World Tourism Organization, June 1997.

Exhibit 4   The World's Top Tourism Spenders

Rank	Country
1	United States
2	Japan
3	Germany
4	United Kingdom
5	Italy
6	France
7	Canada

Source: World Tourism Organization, 1996.

number of tourist arrivals to each. Several notable changes have occurred in this ranking during the past four years. Spain dropped one spot, having been replaced by the United States, which formerly occupied the third highest position in the ranking. China, Mexico, and Poland ranked in the top 10 for the first time, replacing Austria, Germany, and Switzerland.

The world's top tourism spenders are shown in Exhibit 4. United States citizens are currently the biggest spenders, although the Japanese are increasing their spending at a faster rate each year and may take the lead soon.

The United States is also the top tourism earner in the world, as shown in Exhibit 5. Maintaining this ranking is very important to the American hospitality industry.

Given the amounts involved, it's no wonder that governments at all levels—from the national to the municipal—are actively promoting travel and tourism (see

Exhibit 5   The World's Top Ten Tourism Earners

Rank	Country	Share of Worldwide Receipts
1	United States	15.1%
2	Spain	6.6%
3	France	6.5%
4	Italy	6.3%
5	United Kingdom	4.9%
6	Austria	3.5%
7	Germany	3.1%
8	Hong Kong	2.6%
9	China	2.4%
10	Switzerland	2.3%

Source: World Tourism Organization, May 1997.

Exhibit 6   Spending by National Governments to Promote Tourism

Rank	Country	Amount
1	Australia	$87,900,000
2	United Kingdom	$78,700,000
3	Spain	$78,600,000
4	France	$72,900,000
5	Singapore	$53,600,000
6	Thailand	$51,200,000
7	Netherlands	$49,700,000
8	Austria	$47,300,000
9	Ireland	$37,800,000
10	Portugal	$37,300,000

Source: World Tourism Organization, *Hotels*, May 1997.

Exhibit 6). Some smaller countries have used their tourism income as a pathway to modernization. Unfortunately, the amount of governmental promotion and economic support in the United States is smaller than an industry generating such dollar figures might understandably expect. From 1990 to 1996, the U.S. federal government spent between five and six cents per capita per year to promote foreign tourism to the United States, an amount that stands in stark contrast to the $85 per capita spent by the Bahamas. In part to compensate for the relative lack of federal support, some states have developed their own tourism promotion campaigns aimed at foreign visitors. Many cities focus downtown revitalization efforts on remodeling existing hotels or constructing new ones.

In 1991, over 50 U.S. companies in the travel and tourism industry joined together to form the Travel Coalition, which created a $6 million promotion aimed at getting people who were war-shocked and recession-weary to start traveling again. The Travel Coalition participants came from competing airlines, hotel companies, rental car companies, and major tourist attractions—rivals cooperating in a common effort.

For a number of years, leaders from hospitality and other industries have appealed to Congress and the President to substantially increase the funding to promote foreign travel to the United States. Until recently, the U.S. Travel and Tourism Administration served as the federal government's instrument to promote travel to the United States. With an annual budget of only $15 million, it was not very effective. In spite of repeated appeals to increase the funding to $70–$80 million annually, Congress failed to authorize the increase. In 1996, the U.S. Travel and Tourism Administration was abolished.

In 1996, a White House Conference on Tourism was held in Washington, D.C., with tourism industry and government officials in attendance. From the conference came a recommendation that a U.S. National Tourism Organization be created in the private sector with a governing body consisting of 48 members appointed by major national trade organizations in the travel and tourism industry. For example, the American Hotel & Motel Association has five members. Briefly stated, the duties of the U.S. National Tourism Organization are to:

1. Increase the U.S. share of the global tourism market.

2. Develop and implement a coordinated national travel and tourism policy.

3. Advise the President, Congress, and the domestic travel and tourism industry of the implementation of the travel and tourism policy.

4. Operate promotion programs outside the United States in conjunction with the domestic industry.

5. Establish a data bank.

6. Conduct market research.

The immediate challenge for the USNTO is to halt and reverse the downward trend in the U.S. share of the global market. The market share has already decreased by one-sixth since 1993; unless positive action is taken, the United States could lose up to 26 percent of its market share of world travel receipts by the year 2000.

International travelers are extremely important to the hospitality industry. These travelers stay in hotels twice as long as domestic travelers—7 nights versus 3.6 nights. They use hotels with twice the frequency of U.S. travelers. International vacationers are an extremely attractive market. They have an average stay of just under three weeks and per capita spending six times higher than their American counterparts. Currently about 10 percent of all U.S. hotel demand is generated by

Insider Insights

Cindy Rushmore (with David C. Engledrum)
President
HVS Eco Services
Mineola, New York _____

As the travel and tourism industry continues to grow, especially with regard to eco-sensitive regions of the world, the hospitality industry has the resources, the responsibility, and the incentive to be at the forefront of the environmental conservation movement. HVS Eco Services was formed in 1993 to help the industry take the lead in this regard.

Emerging technologies are making eco-sensitivity both affordable and lucrative. Recycling infrastructures are expanding (accepting more materials), more and more environmentally sustainable products are becoming available, and energy- and water-saving equipment is cutting back on both the cost and consumption of natural resources. Besides, consumers are increasingly demanding that companies be more environmentally aware. This applies to the hospitality industry as well. For hotels and lodging facilities to remain competitive, they are going to have to prove to the guests that they are making environmentally sound decisions.

HVS Eco Services' mission is to develop cost-effective, practical programs to heighten a property's level of environmental responsibility in a manner that enhances the guest experience, improves employee morale, and cultivates community relationships. Toward this end we have tailored distinctive, property-specific environmental programs for more than 50 lodging properties throughout the world, from budget and downtown hotels to conference centers, sprawling luxury resorts, and ecolodges. We have demonstrated to our clients—which include major hotel ownership and management companies throughout the United States and abroad—that environmental protection practices are not only essential for the hospitality industry, they are also feasible, profitable, and enjoyable.

Programs range from the fundamentals of hotel environmentalism—comprehensive waste reduction and recycling efforts, the installation of water and energy-saving devices, and the establishment of responsible operating procedures—to more unique initiatives such as archaeological preservation efforts, interactive guest seminars, charitable fundraisers, and nature programs.

Moreover, we have led the hospitality industry into the cooperative world of environmentalism by fostering community partnerships. The Hyatt Regency Scottsdale, for example, donates broken shards of Coleca China from its kitchens to a local community college's art department, and has created the Hopi Learning Center to educate guests about the region's Native American culture. Turnberry Isle Resort & Marina is known for its creative reuse and recycling, donating such diverse materials as strawberry baskets, milk jugs, six pack rings, tennis balls, towels, and furniture parts to organizations like the Miami Rescue Mission, the Fort Lauderdale Art Institute, and the Wildlife Care Center. We design such

(continued)

Insider Insights *(continued)*

creative environmental solutions because they benefit everyone involved: the
hotel, the employees, the guests, the community, and the environment.

To date, HVS Eco Services has orchestrated the diversion of approximately
50,000 cubic yards of waste to recycling and reduction, trash that would have been
destined for the already overburdened landfills. It has saved hotel owners
hundreds of thousands of dollars while preserving precious resources such as
water, coal, oil, and trees.

Savings depend on the location of each individual property, as dictated by the
pricing structure in each area, the recycling infrastructure available, the equipment
at each property, and the area's water and energy costs. Nevertheless, typical
savings from comprehensive solid waste management (including recycling, reuse,
and donation programs) range from 30–70 percent of annual hauling costs, with a
low initial investment. For example, we designed a comprehensive recycling
program for a four-star resort in Santa Monica, which saved 69 percent in hauling
costs, and one for a first-class, suburban Palo Alto, California hotel, which saved
30 percent.

The best conservation measure, however, is employee awareness, because
paybacks are immediate. By instituting a formalized and committed educational
program, a property can reduce its solid waste, energy, and water costs by up to
an additional 10 percent. Our emphasis on education is reflected by the more than
5,000 hours of training we have conducted for hotel staff, environmental groups,
and students at universities such as Cornell University, New York University, and
Johnson & Wales.

It is crucial for lodging executives to realize the overwhelming support
environmental initiatives enjoy among their employees. Based on the results of an
employee environmental survey of more than 2,000 employees which HVS Eco
Services has distributed and tallied to gauge employees' environmental opinions,
for the most part, hotel employees want a variety of environmental programs, are
willing to sacrifice to make them work, are eager to learn about ways to help, and
are teeming with ideas about how best to implement such initiatives.

Approximately 92 percent of those responding indicated a desire for their
property to increase its environmental performance; even more impressively,
roundly 94 percent of the respondents indicated that they would be willing to
change the way in which they work to make the hotel more environmentally
responsible. It is important to note that these results were consistent across the
range of property types and locations; employees at a four-star oceanfront in
California responded similarly to those at an economy, suburban hotel in New
Jersey, and at a business-class Delaware hotel.

To shape its environmental consultation, HVS Eco Services culled the expertise
from a broad spectrum of resources: the environmental building and design
knowledge of the Rocky Mountain Institute, the hospitality know-how of the
Cornell University School of Hotel Administration and the American Hotel &
Motel Association, and the insight into energy, water, solid waste, and other
environmental matters from such groups as The Ecotourism Society, certified
utility consultants, state and federal government agencies (the EPA, for example),
and private architectural and engineering firms.

(continued)

Insider Insights *(continued)*

These reputable hospitality and environmental experts also assisted in helping us develop a set of standards for our ECOTEL® Certification program, a third-party rating system which evaluates and endorses lodging properties based on their environmental performance in the following areas:

- Solid Waste Management
- Water Conservation
- Energy Management
- Employee Education & Community Involvement
- Legislative Compliance & Native Land Preservation

Those properties that demonstrate a superb level of environmental sensitivity are awarded the ECOTEL Certification designation. We provide these member properties with marketing and public relations assistance, as well as a network by which to freely exchange ideas and program innovations. Guests, in turn, are provided with a legitimate tool by which to make an environmentally responsible choice.

The lodging industry is slowly learning that environmental sensitivity is critical to its continued prosperity, that it is both ethically and finally the right thing to do. It is our job to the get the word out and to provide hoteliers with the tools to reach their environmental and economic goals. It is a job we relish.

---

international travelers. Industry experts predict that this figure will increase to 14 percent by the year 2000.

For many years, the U.S. economy suffered from a tourism gap. Exhibit 7 shows that the United States has enjoyed a positive tourism balance of payments only since 1989. This means that instead of contributing to the balance of payments deficit, tourism now helps to reduce it. (The balance of payments is the difference between the amount of money that leaves a nation and the amount that enters it. When the amount that leaves a nation exceeds the amount that enters it, it is called a balance of payments deficit.)

What influences travel to and from the United States? The major influence on foreign travel to the United States is the strength of the dollar in the international market. As the dollar weakens, foreign travelers can buy more dollars for their money, and travel to the United States increases. Conversely, when the dollar strengthens, foreign travelers get fewer dollars for their money, and travel to the United States decreases. The strength of the dollar abroad does not seem to significantly affect U.S. travel to foreign countries. One factor that may affect U.S. travel to other countries is the threat of terrorism. For example, in 1985, several acts of terrorism aimed at travelers significantly reduced travel abroad by U.S. citizens and was a boon to the U.S. travel market through part of 1986. A similar trend occurred in 1991 after the invasion of Kuwait by Iraq.

Exhibit 7   U.S. Tourism Balance of Payments

Year	U.S. Travel Abroad Payments (in billions)	Foreign Travel to U.S. Receipts (in billions)	Balance of Payments (in billions)
1985	$31	$21	−$10
1986	$32	$25	−$ 7
1987	$37	$29	−$ 8
1988	$40	$38	−$ 2
1989	$42	$43	+$ 1
1990	$47	$52.3	+$ 5.3
1991	$52	$59.3	+$ 7.3
1992	$54.1	$64.8	+$10.7
1993	$56.3	$68.8	+$12.5
1994	$58.1	$73.4	+$15.3
1995	$60.2	$79.7	+$19.5

Source: U.S. Travel Research Center Data.

Tourism affects both the businesses that cater to tourists and the community in which the tourist destination is located. Any analysis of the advantages and disadvantages of tourism must consider both perspectives. Such an analysis may yield conflicting recommendations. Those people and businesses who would benefit from tourism would obviously favor it. Those likely to be negatively affected would oppose it.

Consider a hotel development. On the one hand, there are landowners who will gain from the sale of property to the hotel, the local governmental agencies that may benefit from increased tax revenues, the suppliers who will profit from the sale of products and services to the hotel operation, and the local labor force that will gain from employment in the operation. All of these groups are likely to support the development.

On the other hand, the people living in a potential tourist area must consider how a significant influx of tourists might affect local cultural traditions. What if the hotel does not permit local citizens access to beaches and other areas of natural beauty that they have always enjoyed? What if the most important and highest paying positions in the hotel are given to management staff who reside outside of (and therefore remove their incomes from) the area?

Environmental awareness is another important concern. It is increasingly apparent that tourism can cause serious environmental consequences to an area, especially a relatively pristine or unusual area that attracts tourism. In his book *Tourism, A Community Approach,* Peter Murphy writes, "A paradox of tourism is that the industry carries within itself the seeds of its own destruction. Successful development can lead to the destruction of those very qualities which attracted visitors in the first place."[5]

Further evidence of this mounting concern was revealed when CBS's *60 Minutes* news journal devoted a large segment of its April 5, 1992, program to the environmental hazards of tourism.

Ecotourism is low-impact tourism that avoids harming or destroying the natural or normal environment. It is a relatively new approach to promoting enjoyment, as well as protection, of the environment.

Clearly, the travel and tourism industry has significant economic, social, cultural, and environmental impacts on a community. These must be carefully managed so that the benefits to a community outweigh the potential disadvantages. The hospitality industry is in the vanguard of efforts to provide this enlightened management.

Today the hospitality industry is very much involved in the environmental conservation movement. Ms. Cindy Rushmore provides a comprehensive description of this involvement in her Insider Insight featured in this chapter.

Ecotourism/Adventure Travel

Ecotourism has been defined as responsible travel to natural areas that conserves the environment and sustains the well-being of local citizens.

Ecotourism/Adventure travel grew at a rate of 20 percent annually between 1990 and 1996. Since 1996, it has grown about 11 percent annually. Currently, Eco/Adventure travel accounts for 12–15 percent of world tourism. The U.S. Travel Data Center estimates the size of this market to be as large as 43 million persons in the United States alone.

Chase Burritt of E&Y Kenneth Leventhal provides some interesting data on this concept. "In the United States:

a. More than $110 billion is spent annually on Eco/Adventure travel.

b. The Eco Traveler spends an average of $350 per day and takes several 5 day trips per year.

c. In 1998, 80 million people are expected to seek an adventure activity.

d. Eco/Adventure travelers seek products that respect the environment and destinations that provide a wilderness setting.

e. Educational and cultural tourism is growing. Experiences at cultural attractions and learning/study programs are increasingly popular with both new and experienced ecotourists."[6]

Ecotourists form an attractive market for the resort segment of the industry, especially for resorts located in unique and undisturbed environments.

Further evidence of the impact of ecotourism is its presence on the Internet. The Eco-Source site provides areas to learn more about ecotourism, find topical news, discover upcoming events, and query experts in the field. When the site first opened, it was getting 4,000–5,000 "hits" per month. Today, the hits are in the 24,000–26,000 per month range. The founding partners report receiving E-mail from more than 40 different countries.

Endnotes

1. Lloyd E. Hudman, *Tourism: A Shrinking World* (Columbus, Ohio: Grid, 1980), pp. 35–60.

2. This discussion is loosely based upon Robert W. McIntosh and Charles R. Goeldner, *Tourism: Principles, Practices, Philosophies,* 4th ed. (Columbus, Ohio: Grid, 1984).

3. Travel Industry Association of America, February 1997.

4. AH&MA brochure.

5. Peter Murphy, *Tourism: A Community Approach* (New York: Cambridge University Press, 1985), p. 32.

6. "A Return to Motels," *Lodging,* April 1997, p. 50.

Key Terms

ecotourism—Low-impact tourism that avoids harming or destroying the natural or normal environment; a relatively new approach to promoting enjoyment, as well as protection, of the environment.

globalization—A worldwide perspective; an environment in which people are traveling all over the world with increasing ease, and major corporations, such as large hotel chains or franchise restaurants, are expanding their operations into countries all over the world.

infrastructure—The underground or surface construction necessary to service travelers and tourists, as well as the local population. Examples include systems for water, sewage, gas, electricity, and communication; highways, airports, railroads, parking lots, and lighting systems.

ripple effect—The indirect benefits of tourism that non-tourism parts of the economy receive as a result of direct benefits to the tourism industry.

superstructure—The major above-ground facilities which are serviced by the infrastructure and which help make a destination attractive. Hotels, shopping and entertainment centers, museums, and other attractions are examples.

Review Questions

1. In addition to lodging and food service operations, what businesses are part of the travel and tourism industry?

2. What does the term "institutional food service" mean?

3. What role have credit cards played in expanding the travel industry?

4. Can you describe the effect on travel to and from the United States as the U.S. dollar grows stronger or weaker compared to other currencies?

5. What are some arguments that may be used to oppose the expansion of tourism in a community or geographic area?

6. What does the term "infrastructure" mean?

7. What are some common internal factors that cause a desire to travel?

8. What is ecotourism, and how is it likely to affect global tourism?

9. How does the ripple effect work?

10. What is the Travel Coalition? Who formed it and why?

Internet Sites

For more information, visit the following Internet sites. Remember that Internet addresses can change without notice. If the site is no longer there, use a search engine to look for additional sites.

Travel and Tourism

American Hotel & Motel Association (AH&MA)
http://www.ahma.com

The American Society of Travel Agents (ASTA)
http://www.astanet.com

International Hotel & Restaurant Association (IHRA)
http://www.ih-ra.com

National Tour Association, Inc. (NTA)
http://www.ntaonline.com

Smith Travel Research
http://www.str-online.com

Travel and Tourism Research Association (TTRA)
http://www.ttra.com

Travel Industry Association of America (TIA)
http://www.tia.org

Travel Web Sites
http://www.yahoo.com/recreation/travel

World Tourism Organization (WTO)
http://www.world-tourism.org

Travel Publications

Journal of Travel Research
http://bus.colorado.edu/BRD/JTR.HTM

Travel Leader Services
http://www.travelleader.com

Travel Management Daily
http://www.tmdaily.com

Travel Trade
http://www.traveltrade.com

Travel Weekly
http://www.traveler.net

Ecotourism

The Adventure Travel Society, Inc.
http://www2.csn.net/ats

EarthWise Journeys
http://www.teleport.com/~earthwyz

The Eco-Source
http://www.podi.com/ecosource/index.html

The Ecotourism Society
http://www.ecotourism.org/data.html

Green Hotels Association
http://www.greenhotels.com

Travel Source-Eco Tours
http://www.travelsource.com:80/ecotours/index.html

Chapter 2 Outline

Careers in the Lodging Industry
     Entry-Level Positions
     Skilled-Level Positions
     Managerial-Level Positions
     Where to Start
Careers in the Food Service Industry
     Diverse Opportunities
Education for Hospitality Management Careers
The Nature of Hospitality
     Communication
     Turnover
     Demands and Rewards

2

Career Opportunities

THE HOSPITALITY INDUSTRY provides career opportunities for people of almost every age, experience, and education. Like all businesses, it has characteristic advantages and disadvantages that should be carefully considered by anyone contemplating a hospitality career. Its primary advantages are interesting work, good opportunities for advancement, generally excellent working surroundings, social contact, security, and stability of employment. Most positions lack the monotony associated with assembly-line work, offering instead frequent opportunities to meet and serve all segments of the public. For those with managerial, executive, and ownership aspirations, the industry ranks high in opportunity among all American businesses.

Careers in the Lodging Industry

In this chapter, we will use the term "hotel" to represent all types of lodging properties (hotels, motels, motor hotels, resorts, etc.), except when specifically noted otherwise. It is sometimes difficult to distinguish hotels from motels and motels from motor hotels, even though it is generally accepted that they *are* somehow different.

It is difficult to imagine a multi-billion-dollar industry that produces a commodity that is intangible—service to people; but that is an accurate description of the hotel business. The very essence of hotelkeeping is people interacting. Because of this, hotels cannot follow the lead of many other industries and become automated, eliminating the human element wherever possible. True personal service cannot be mechanized or automated. Technologies are being instituted to speed up routine tasks, but the human element remains the determining element of the hospitality business.

Anyone considering a career naturally weighs both its advantages and disadvantages. The frequent interactions with others may seem like an advantage to some people and a disadvantage to others. One type of interaction takes place between different staff members. There may be several separate departments operating in a hotel, requiring frequent communication among staff members to coordinate their activities.

Another type of interaction is between staff members and the guests being served. Of course, not all hotel positions provide guest contact, but those that do bring the employee into contact with people from all walks of life. Guests will include the wealthy and the poor, the famous and the notorious, the engaging and the obnoxious, the cooperative and the difficult. Each guest offers the employee an opportunity to learn more about human nature and presents challenges to provide

Insider Insights

Jorgen H. Hansen, CHA
Senior Vice President, South Region
Hilton Hotels International ——————————————————————————

Since my very first day in the hospitality industry, I can never recall having regrets about going to work. I can only attribute this to the always-changing conditions, the ever-present challenge, and the many varied experiences which each day contains. During my years working back of the house, I was amazed by the international staff I had the opportunity of working with—the creative and artistic performance by chefs, cooks, and pastry chefs, and the ever-changing pace. In the front of the house, what intrigued me was the constant change of guests and the multitude of their needs, tastes, backgrounds, and attitudes. Here I experienced firsthand the reward of satisfying a guest.

As I moved into a management position, the industry took on a new dimension for me. Besides service and food preparation, I now had to focus on budgets, compliance with statutes under which the hotel industry operates, preparation of forecasts, and performance of administrative functions to assure that the hotel, besides being a hostelry known for its services and quality of operation, also made economic sense for its owners.

Being successful in the hotel industry does not necessarily mean becoming a general manager, but rather working in the capacity that gives the greatest personal satisfaction day in and day out. The many young people who have entered our industry in hotels in which I was involved were always advised that they should become involved in departments in which they thought they had the most strength and could best contribute; that they should concentrate on their day-to-day achievements and not on future career moves and strive to build a solid background of expertise in at least two areas of our industry. Furthermore, they should realize that the world doesn't stand still and neither does our industry; continuing education is necessary to keep abreast of new developments. Most important, they should have a good attitude toward other people, have respect for each job position, associate with people willing to share their expertise and knowledge, and make it their own.

The last few decades have seen many new developments in our industry, not only in the way hotel reservations are transmitted, in computer applications to front office operation, in energy conservation, and in strategic planning of sales and marketing functions, but also in the growing awareness of our guests for quality.

Increasingly competitive market conditions will continue to demand better and more sophisticated services of each hotel to attract its fair market share. In contrast to yesteryears, we are no longer competing to serve the guest who travels the highways and routes on which our hostelry may be located. We are competing for business as a destination, whether it be for leisure, cultural, or business travelers; and competing not only with other national destinations, but often with the world at large.

With more leisure time, longer vacations, increased competition, and growing world commerce, the future of the hotel industry is bright, challenging, and offers a wealth of opportunities for people who like people.

service that will enhance the guest's stay. Employees not only have direct responsibility for guest service, they also have the benefit of witnessing the guests' satisfaction and of personally receiving approval for a job well done.

From the standpoint of working conditions, a hotel offers a clean, safe, pleasant environment. And when we consider the potential for advancement, hotel managers and division and department heads traditionally have worked their way up through the ranks; the industry is one that lends itself to academic training, but also one in which there is no substitute for experience.

In the short space of one chapter, it would be impossible to list and discuss all the jobs in the lodging industry. Instead, representative jobs on three different skill and training levels have been selected. The first level comprises the unskilled and semi-skilled jobs which require no previous experience or specialized preparation; these are entry-level positions. The second level comprises skilled jobs, which require experience or specialized training. The third level comprises supervisory, executive, and managerial positions, which require the greatest amount of experience, training, and education.

Entry-Level Positions

Individuals with a high school education or less and no hotel or related experience are most likely to start their hotel careers with an entry-level job. Every department has at least one entry-level job classification. Starting here does not hinder one's ability to advance in the organization; a large number of today's hotel managers and executives began at this level. The experience and skills gained can help employees advance to the skilled level of hotel work.

Exhibit 1 lists some representative entry-level jobs. The exact tasks performed by employees in these and related positions will vary according to the specific needs of the property. Some properties, especially small ones, will not require staff for all of these positions.

Skilled-Level Positions

Employees at the second level, the skilled jobs, come from a variety of sources. Some are employees who moved up from entry-level jobs. Others are people who have learned a skilled trade in another industry and sought similar employment in a hotel. Some are graduates of the growing number of technical schools and junior colleges that offer hotel training, and others come from business schools or specialized high school training courses.

Let's look more closely at skilled-level positions, the staff members who fill them, and where they come from. A person with a desire to work in food preparation might consider a school that trains cooks, bakers, and other food service personnel; graduates of these programs are in great demand by hotels and other food service operations. People with military training in food service can usually find employment in hotel kitchens. Though their number is declining, some hotels operate apprentice training programs in food preparation, and acceptance into such a program is an excellent start toward a successful career in hotel food preparation.

For those interested in employment as bookkeepers, accounting clerks, secretaries, or accountants, training at a reputable business school is a good start. The

Exhibit 1   Representative Entry-Level Positions

Front Office
Bellperson
Apprentice telephone operator
Porter

Housekeeping
Housekeeper
  (room attendant, maid)
Supply clerk

Food Preparation
Vegetable preparer
Kitchen helper
Pantry helper
Storeroom helper
Warewasher
Steward

Engineering
Plumber's helper
Electrician's helper
Oiler's helper

Marketing
Clerk

Secretarial/Clerical (needed for several
  departments)
Clerk
Typist
File Clerk

Food and Beverage Service
Busperson
Barback
Counter server
Runner

Food Service Office
Checker
File clerk

Accounting
Checker
File clerk

skilled-level jobs in the dining and banquet departments depend almost entirely on experience. The usual way to advance is to begin at an entry-level job and move up through the ranks, for example, from busperson to food server to captain to head food server. Mixology, or bartending, is taught at some vocational schools, although many bartenders are former food servers. Likewise, front desk agents and reservation agents might come from the ranks as bellpersons or from technical schools.

Training for some jobs may need to be obtained outside the hotel industry. For example, plumbers, electricians, carpenters, painters, and upholsterers are frequently union members who have completed apprenticeship programs. Anyone seeking employment in these areas should consult either the local unions or contractors employing these trades. Most applicants for such hotel positions attain journeyman status in their trade before seeking hotel work.

Exhibit 2 lists (in no particular order) some representative skilled-level jobs encompassing different levels of responsibility, prestige, and salary.

Managerial-Level Positions

Training, experience, and individual initiative are the keys to attaining managerial-level (executive, managerial, and supervisory) positions. Many of these positions are offered to college-trained people, but opportunities will always be available for

Exhibit 2   Representative Skilled-Level Positions

Front Office
Front desk agent
Reservations agent
Telephone operator
Bell captain

Housekeeping
Assistant housekeeper
Floor housekeeper (supervisor)

Food Preparation
Baker
Roast cook
Garde-manger
Vegetable cook
Fry cook
Saucier

Engineering
Plumber
Electrician
Oiler
Upholsterer
Carpenter
Painter

Marketing
Sales representative

Secretarial/Clerical (needed for several
    departments)
Secretary
Administrative assistant
Accounting clerk
Bookkeeper
Receptionist
Accountant

Food and Beverage Service
Wine steward
Food server
Beverage server
Host/hostess
Captain
Headwaiter/headwaitress
Bartender

Food Service Office
Secretary
Accounting clerk
Bookkeeper
Receptionist
Accountant

Accounting
Accounting clerk
Bookkeeper
Accountant
Food and beverage controller
Night auditor
Cashier

qualified employees who have worked their way up through the organization. Many division-head jobs are filled by those who excel in the performance of activities in skilled-level positions.

Young people considering a hospitality management career should give serious consideration to college training. Many colleges and universities now offer a four-year course in hotel management. While specialized college training is recommended, it is not mandatory; college graduates with a wide variety of majors find hotel employment every year.

Hotel school graduates learn a large amount of technical knowledge and typically receive some practical experience during their college program; however, few are ready for a manager's job upon graduation. A hotel school graduate must go through a **management internship**, or supervised training at a job site, before engaging in actual practice. The length and nature of this training program can vary widely, depending on the size and type of hotel; the training, experience, and

Insider Insights

William H. Edwards, CHA
Vice Chairman & Director, Emeritus
Hilton Hotels Corporation ───────────────────────────────

I was born and raised in Muskegon, Michigan. Upon my graduation from high school in the mid-1930s, I promised myself that I would continue my education at the University of Michigan. This was during the great depression, and circumstances required that I work my way through college. I did not see this as a hardship, but rather an opportunity, requiring that I manage my time and priorities and exert every effort to be productive. The discipline I learned there has remained with me through my entire career.

My career in the lodging industry began in 1937 at the Grand Hotel, Mackinac Island, Michigan. Working two summers during college at the Grand Hotel convinced me that lodging was my future.

I graduated from the University of Michigan, majoring in economics and marketing. After that, I attended the University of Pittsburgh Law School. I got a position as assistant manager at the William Penn Hotel in Pittsburgh, working evenings and attending law school during the day.

When I was halfway through law school, Pearl Harbor was attacked, and I was called into the service. The U.S. Navy sent me to the Midshipman Training School, where I graduated as a commissioned officer. My active duty was four years in minesweeping.

Shortly after I joined the William Penn Hotel, the Statler Hotel Company took over management of the hotel. After the war, the Statler Company sent me to the Detroit Statler, where I served as assistant manager, sales manager, and resident manager.

Perhaps the most significant break in my career came late in 1954 when the Hilton Hotels Corporation acquired the Statler Company. Hilton was a growing company, presenting new opportunities to many people. I was moved to the Hilton executive offices as assistant general sales manager and given the responsibility of writing a sales manual that would merge the Hilton and Statler sales operations into one—combining two systems with very different approaches.

In time, I became a vice president, and then a senior vice president. In 1971, I was elected to the Board of Directors and made executive vice president of operations. Later I served as president of the Hilton Hotels division. When I retired a few years ago, I was vice chairman of the Hilton Board of Directors.

As I look over my 46 years in the lodging industry, I am struck by the amazing technological advances in the industry. Tasks that were previously done manually, such as taking reservations, bookkeeping, and preparing reports, are now done using computers in many operations. Computers have greatly improved the speed, accuracy, and efficiency of the people performing these tasks and made the lodging operations that use them much more efficient. Since the computer will certainly continue to play a major role in the lodging industry, it's important to become familiar with computer applications in the industry.

A career in the hospitality industry can be very demanding, especially in terms

(continued)

Insider Insights *(continued)*

of the time commitment. If you enjoy working with people, it can be a very rewarding career with plenty of chance for advancement.

As you progress in your hospitality career, I encourage you to be active in your local community and involved in your industry. As a past president of the American Hotel & Motel Association, a past national chairman of the Travel Industry Association of America, and a past director on the Board of the National Restaurant Association, I can assure you that I learned a great deal by my involvement.

All of us have certain strengths and certain weaknesses in our job skills. I recommend trying to discover your weaknesses and work on improving yourself in those areas, both on the job and through continuing education courses, until you feel confident your weaknesses have been overcome. The American Hotel & Motel Association's Educational Institute and the National Restaurant Association's Educational Foundation both offer highly regarded courses to satisfy continuing education needs and to help people keep up with the latest technology and trends in the hospitality industry.

If you choose a career in the hospitality industry, you will be choosing to join a growing industry with expanding opportunities for talented managers and staff.

interests of the graduate; the graduate's ability; and the availability of opportunities for advancement.

What types of jobs do hotel school graduates find? Large chain operations usually have management training programs for which they recruit college graduates. A trainee may spend up to one year in the program (actual training time varies), during which time he or she gains experience in several departments. Some hotels allow a management trainee to specialize in one specific department. Upon completion of the program, the graduate is assigned to a management job in the hotel and begins the climb to increased managerial and executive responsibilities.

Hotels without chain affiliations are also eager to hire hotel school graduates. If the hotel does not have a formal training program for managers, the graduate will usually start in a position such as steward, assistant manager, sales representative, food and beverage controller, receiving clerk, accountant, assistant food and beverage manager, or restaurant manager.

Many college graduates, armed with four years of theoretical and technical knowledge, become impatient when told they need experience before assuming high-level positions of responsibility. They do not realize that, though intellectually capable, they generally need more hands-on experience before assuming managerial positions. The crucial management skills of understanding, motivating, and directing people can best be developed through experience. It is vital that graduates understand and accept this situation, or their assets of enthusiasm, ambition, and confidence may gradually be replaced by disillusionment, lethargy, and dissatisfaction.

Exhibit 3   Representative Managerial-Level Positions

Front office manager	Executive assistant manager
Controller	Convention manager
Executive housekeeper	Sales manager
Catering manager	General manager
Executive steward	Auditor
Food and beverage manager	Resident manager
Banquet manager	Chief engineer
Chef	
Executive chef	**Typical Multi-Unit Positions**
Food production manager	Director of training
Catering director	Vice president, finance
Restaurant manager	Vice president, real estate
Beverage manager	Director of franchising
Purchasing director	Area supervisor
Human resources manager	Regional director
Credit manager	

Some representative managerial-level positions are listed in Exhibit 3. In addition to the usual management positions, multi-unit companies may have area, district, regional, and/or corporate-level management.

Where to Start

People entering the industry frequently wonder whether it is better to begin their careers in a small or large hotel, with an independent or chain operation, or in a particular position. What branch of hotel operation is the best to start in after graduation? Where you start is probably less important than how well you work and whether you make the most of opportunities.

Early on, it is important to learn something about all phases of hotel operation. You may prefer to work first in those departments you know least about. Then, with some exposure to all areas, you can begin to focus on your areas of interest.

You should not worry about starting in a different department or in a different type of hotel than someone else. People have risen to the top from virtually every position in a hotel. Initiative is what counts in the end. You should get on the job and give it the best you have. While doing so, evaluate your present work, consider your past experiences, develop a new job goal, and begin working to attain it.

Security, independence, a comfortable home life, respect, dignity, and the sense of accomplishment that comes from a job well done—you can attain all these running any size property in any location. What's important is to work hard at all aspects of your job, take advantage of opportunities that arise, and develop and adhere to a career management plan.

Nonetheless, there are some differences between a large and small property you should consider when you seek your first position. Typically, you can learn the basics of all phases of operation through hands-on experience more quickly in a small operation. This is because a staff member in a small hotel is likely to perform a variety of tasks that would be divided among several staff people in a large property. A manager with unit-wide responsibilities must be a generalist, so a broad range of experience may be gained more quickly in a small property.

Cooperation among all levels of staff is important to achieve success in the hotel business. An important difference between small and large properties relates to coordination of activities. In both cases, the staff must work as a team. But in a small property, the hotel manager can personally supervise each employee. In a larger operation, the hotel manager may oversee several levels of supervisors, who each direct a group of staff members, who may in turn supervise other staff.

In a large hotel, there are more divisions or departments, and the operations within them are more complex than in a small hotel. Thus, graduates have a chance to observe a wider variety of activities, a more structured system of communication among divisions, and a greater reliance on technology. In addition, the staff of a large hotel typically includes a wider range of jobs than are found in a small hotel, and staff members are able to become very skilled and experienced in their defined job duties. The opportunity to work with highly skilled people in a wide range of jobs is one of the major advantages of training in large hotels.

A successful hotel manager must have self-confidence. Many potentially fine executives, when placed in high-level positions too quickly, ruin their careers in the process. In a large property, advancement typically comes when the staff member is ready for it. By contrast, a smaller property may need to expand the job duties of its relatively few staff members more quickly. This is an advantage to the individual who is ready to take on more responsibilities, but it can be a serious problem for those who are less prepared.

Managers encounter a tremendous variety of problems in a large hotel. The challenge of resolving these problems is considered an advantage by some people and a disadvantage by others. Many of the following conditions are associated with working in a large hotel:

- One must learn to manage large groups of employees.

- Communications among the staff are complicated by the larger size of the organization.

- A manager can become "lost" in a large company.

- The pace of activities is faster; there is more demand on personal energies in a large property.

- Participation in community activities is not possible as soon, nor as completely, as in a smaller organization.

For those aspiring to own their own business, there are advantages to both large and small hotels. In a small property, you can advance more quickly through the organization. You will be able to make decisions—and see their results—without having to deal with an elaborate bureaucracy. At a large property, you can interact with more managers and learn from their insights and experiences, and you gain exposure to more sophisticated systems and procedures.

Insider Insights

Hans Weishaupt, CHA
—a retired general manager
living in Switzerland

Throughout my 40 years in the international hotel business, I have always played on what I call my "Swiss advantage," which embraces the qualities I have gained from growing up in Switzerland.

A big advantage is the social standing that hotel work carries in Switzerland. To work in a hotel is a respected endeavor. It is an officially certified trade that must be acquired through a regulated apprenticeship, whether it is in the area of service, the kitchen, or the front office. It is considered a career choice, not something one does while waiting for something better to come along. A hotel manager is treated with great respect, since the hotel industry is recognized as an important contributor to the economy of Switzerland.

Another advantage is growing up with a close exposure to several languages and cultures. No one who lives in tiny Switzerland can avoid meeting people who speak another language or come from another cultural background. Swiss people learn early on to understand and respect these differences. To be comfortable and confident with people from a variety of linguistic and cultural backgrounds is a big advantage in international hotels.

Growing up in Switzerland also teaches one a respect for the pecking order, a sense of loyalty, pride in a job well done, and a desire to strive to exceed people's expectations—all qualities that employers really appreciate!

Someone with these qualities in his or her rucksack has a certain advantage in climbing the rocky cliffs of employment in the international hotel business. However, while these qualities make for a good follower, a dependable doer, and a desirable employee, they do not make for a pioneering mover and shaker, a visionary innovator, or an entrepreneurial spirit.

I find it amusing when accolades are showered on the Swiss for our standard-setting, pioneering role in the international hotel business. Americans are especially generous in appraising us this way. As someone who has the "Swiss advantage" and also has had the viewpoints of academia, operations, and the executive suite, I have a different perspective.

Looking at how hotelkeeping on an international scale came about, I find that we Swiss were supporting players. It was in the United States that Ellsworth Statler lifted hotelkeeping from a local, individually operated enterprise to a structured, nationwide business operation. Statler introduced concepts of management, control, human relations, and sales that permitted the operation of a chain of large, multi-unit hotels. Sadly, even in the United States, this pioneer and innovator who shaped hotelkeeping into a major industry has never been properly recognized for his genius and achievement. It was another American who had the courage and foresight to apply Statler's concepts as the basis for hotel expansion abroad. Conrad Hilton launched and set the standards for the international hotel industry with his hotel chain, which ultimately spanned the world.

It was also in the United States that the business principles and skills needed for the successful operation of these large operations were fully recognized.

(continued)

Insider Insights *(continued)*

Americans were the first to establish courses in hotel administration at institutes of higher education—courses which culminate in academic degrees.

While I am not eager to give up the Swiss advantage and the accolades that come with it, I do feel that recognition should be given to those who really formed the principles of international hotelkeeping—those whose ideas lifted simple innkeeping to a complex industry that spans and bonds the world.

Careers in the Food Service Industry

As mentioned earlier, both hotelkeeping and food service provide career opportunities for people of almost every age, experience, and education. Like hotelkeeping, food service offers interesting work, excellent chances for advancement, social contact, stable employment, good working conditions, and average or better earnings.

Employment in the food service industry also offers excellent opportunities to use initiative, express ideas, and earn the satisfaction that comes from serving other people.

The jobs in the food service industry can also be classified as entry-level (unskilled and semi-skilled) positions, skilled-level positions, and managerial-level positions. Preparation and training for these levels is very similar to that already discussed for the job levels found in the hotel industry. Examples of jobs at each level in the food service industry are included in Exhibits 1, 2, and 3.

As is true in the hotel business, training, experience, and individual initiative are the keys to success in executive and managerial positions. Many of these jobs are filled with graduates of college hotel and restaurant management programs. However, there are many people today with little or no formal education who hold responsible high-level positions. Food service operations are similar to hotel properties in that some managerial positions are filled by the promotion of successful skilled-level staff. Still, people considering management careers in the food service industry should think about college training, since it can give them a competitive edge.

College graduates entering the food service industry have the same ambitions, skills, knowledge, and impatience as those entering the hotel industry. They also must be willing to gain the hands-on experience necessary to move into executive-level positions and should not expect to step directly into a top-level job.

Diverse Opportunities

Too often, applicants consider food service jobs only in hotels and restaurants. This is unfortunate. There are many different segments in the food service industry worth considering. Excellent opportunities exist for staff at all job levels in department store food service; airline in-flight food service; school, college, and university food service; hospitals and nursing homes; city and country clubs; business and industry; parks and recreation; and the military services (which employ civilians to manage clubs and other food and lodging functions). And then there is **fast-food service**, which includes commercial establishments that offer drive-through and/or counter service to customers.

Fast-Food Service. If there is a mystery in the food services, it has to concern fast foods. Fast-food service is the single largest segment of the food service industry. Fast-food service has lots of job opportunities available at every level. However, few students consider these jobs, and even fewer educators and educational institutions address this segment in their classes. Why is this?

Some students, believing that fast-food operations lack status, prefer positions in hotels and expensive restaurants. Others say that fast-food operations do not provide significant challenges. Still others maintain that the fast-food industry offers little opportunity to use the technical skills and procedures they have learned in college.

In truth, responsibility comes quickly to new employees in fast food who demonstrate interest and ability, and that responsibility is increased as rapidly as each employee can handle it. It is not uncommon for a recent graduate to become a unit manager within six to nine months after joining a company, responsible for a small business averaging sales of $750,000 or more per year. Graduates who perform well will typically move beyond the unit manager level within 12 to 14 months. In no other area of the hospitality industry does responsibility come so quickly or in such large proportions.

Perhaps those students who sense a lack of status in fast-food careers perceive fast-food corporate headquarters as somehow less sophisticated or less professional than other corporations. Nothing could be further from the truth. Their methods, practices, and procedures typically make use of the very latest technology; they are often far more sophisticated and advanced than similar offices in other hospitality industry corporations.

Do fast-food salaries compare favorably with salaries in other areas of the hospitality industry? Indeed they do! As one proceeds from unit manager and enters the corporate ranks, one's salary will invariably exceed the average for similar positions throughout the industry. People aspiring to careers in food service should consider all segments of the industry. Fast food is an exciting and growing element which provides challenges and opportunities for people who are willing to consider this "forgotten" segment of a vast industry.

Consider these comments from Robert Nugent, president of Jack in the Box. Speaking at a career conference at Washington State University in the fall of 1990, he said: "A lot of people don't realize it, but fast food is a great career. A student graduating from a hotel school is quickly ahead of retail and banking people in career opportunities and salaries. Within a year, he or she can be a fast-food manager making $28,000 per year—more than a bank branch manager makes. Within five years, the fast-food manager could be making $40,000 per year."

Management Companies. Like the fast-food operations, **contract management companies** often suffer from longstanding, misguided prejudice. Management companies often contract their services to **institutional food service** operations, which provide meals in a closed, non-commercial environment, such as a hospital, school, or correctional institution. Beliefs persist that institutional not-for-profit operations are low paying and don't make use of new technology. However, the truth is that institutional food service operations—with menu, purchasing, and marketing systems—are as sophisticated as any operations in the commercial segment. Unfortunately, most hotel and restaurant school graduates have limited exposure to this segment because few of their teachers have any background with a management company.

Employment with a management company offers excellent hours, a high degree of responsibility very quickly, a good salary, and excellent opportunities for advancement. Since management company personnel use the same basic management principles practiced by effective officials in any type of food service operation, people with experience in these companies can freely move to other segments of the industry. Employment opportunities in contract management present an excellent career choice.

Education for Hospitality Management Careers

A great many changes in the ways people prepare for careers in food service have occurred over the years. It used to be most typical for people to start in entry-level positions, work their way up to skilled positions, and then move up to management positions. Future cooks and chefs entered apprenticeship programs and moved up to higher positions as they gained experience. Cooks moved to different organizations in order to learn specific skills from a particular executive chef. Food servers became captains, maîtres d', and restaurant managers. Some chefs and restaurant managers even joined the entrepreneurial ranks and opened food service operations of their own.

Over the years, formal education has played an increasingly prominent role in preparing people for careers in food service. Apprenticeship programs and opportunities have generally decreased in number, although the American Culinary Federation, a professional association of chefs, has developed an apprenticeship program for its members. Just when industry leaders were expressing grave concern over the shortage of trained cooks, bakers, and chefs, a new form of training came to the rescue. The Culinary Institute of America began a program to prepare people for careers in the culinary arts. When the Institute moved into its present facilities in Hyde Park, New York, education in the area of food preparation came into its own. More recently, Johnson & Wales University initiated its culinary program. Both institutions found themselves with many more applicants than spaces available. Junior colleges offering hotel and food service programs began to proliferate across the country. Today, these programs prepare students for technical positions in food production and middle management positions in other areas of the industry.

There has also been a significant increase in the number of four-year colleges and universities that offer programs in hospitality industry management. A continuing demand for trained personnel means readily available employment opportunities for graduates of these programs.[1]

Not all of the education for industry positions takes place in formal class-rooms. Some employees in the hospitality industry have the necessary intelligence and ability to move up in the industry, but, for a variety of reasons, cannot attend an institute or college. Fortunately for them, the Educational Institute of the American Hotel & Motel Association offers educational packages that may be completed while the employee continues to work full time. The Educational Institute, a non-profit educational foundation, is the largest educational resource center for the hospitality industry in the world. Besides producing textbooks, videotapes, seminars, and other resources for use in schools and on the job, the Institute offers individual courses and certification programs to those who meet educational and experience requirements. The highest certification is the Certified Hotel Administrator (CHA). The Institute also offers programs resulting in the following designations: Certified Food and Beverage Executive (CFBE), Certified Rooms Division Executive (CRDE), Certified Engineering Operations Executive (CEOE), Certified Hospitality House-keeping Executive (CHHE), Certified Human Resources Executive (CHRE), Certi-fied Hospitality Supervisor (CHS), and Master Hotel Supplier (MHS).

The Nature of Hospitality

People interested in careers in the hospitality industry must take a close look at the nature of hotel and food service work. To enjoy a hospitality career requires techni-cal knowledge and skills, a friendly personality, and a commitment to providing quality customer service.

Communication

Because the hospitality industry requires frequent interactions with people, job candidates must demonstrate solid communication skills. Employees at every level need to communicate well; the ability to handle difficult guests or direct staff while maintaining good employee relations requires effective, tactful communication.

Getting a job interview usually requires applicants to "sell" themselves in a well-written **résumé** and concise **cover letter**. A résumé is a formal written presen-tation of an individual's work experience, skills, and education. A cover letter ex-plains what specific job is being sought and reiterates the applicant's relevant experience for the job. Job candidates should think of their résumés and cover let-ters as sales tools to get them interviews, where they will have the opportunity to complete the sale by persuading the employer to hire them. It is vital that these sales tools be as well-written and persuasive as possible. Industry executives agree unanimously that the great majority of applicants do not effectively promote them-selves in their résumés and cover letters. These applicants often fail to get inter-views and therefore lose employment opportunities. A great number of books on résumé and cover letter writing are available to help job candidates today.[2]

The interview itself is another place where good communication skills are impor-tant. The main purpose of a résumé is to get an interview; the main purpose of an inter-view is to get a job offer. Applicants should demonstrate an ability to understand and answer questions articulately, while displaying a friendly, helpful demeanor. Applicants should also discuss their skills, education, and experience that make them especially suited to a job. Finally, job candidates can display their skills in communication and courtesy—another trait essential for successful hospitality employees—by sending a brief thank-you note to the interviewer following the interview.

Turnover

As is the case in many professional fields, the turnover rate of new graduates entering the hospitality industry is significant. One reason for this seems to be that many people are attracted to the hospitality field without really knowing what they are getting into. Once employed, they discover that the job is not what they expected. They dislike the long hours, low pay rates, and physical labor associated with beginning jobs. They recognize too late that they must work weekends, evenings, holidays, and at other times when most people are not required to work.

Partly to alleviate this turnover problem, most college and university hospitality programs now require **student internships** in the industry prior to graduation. By giving students on-the-job experience before they graduate, student internships help students gain an understanding of the industry and its job requirements and demands. They learn what to expect in their first post-graduation jobs. If their internship work experiences are unsatisfactory, they may realize, before committing themselves to several years of study, that the hospitality industry is not for them. In addition, some of the turnover could be avoided if students were better informed about the range of opportunities available in some of the other, less visible segments of the industry.

Demands and Rewards

Hours of work have changed in hotels and restaurants. The 40-hour work week is now in effect throughout much of the industry; the days of extremely long hours and split shifts are history. But work hours may be non-standard or unusual, especially in hotels, which must keep their doors open 24 hours daily. The work may be during the evening and night, and it often includes holidays and weekends. Occasionally, a little extra time may be called for to ensure complete service to the guests. The employee who moves up into the managerial ranks will likely put in some extra hours. Anyone aspiring to management positions cannot be a clock watcher.

While many entry-level jobs in hotels and restaurants pay only minimum wage, advancement may come rapidly. The pay rate for skilled- and managerial-level jobs in lodging and food service is competitive with those in other industries.[3] The U.S. Bureau of Labor Statistics notes that wages for skilled- and managerial-level positions in the hospitality industry vary greatly depending upon the size of the establishment, previous work experience, educational background, and job duties.[4] Labor unions, region of the country, and chain affiliation (if any) may influence wages and benefit programs.

A hotel and restaurant workshift varies dramatically from hour to hour. It has peaks and valleys, changing from quiet to busy in a matter of minutes. Hospitality is never a routine business. Every day brings new problems to be solved and new excitement. Anyone who enjoys a lack of routine will find the business fascinating.

Those who prefer a more orderly routine may find the industry too unpredictable. It is not that hotels and restaurants are disorganized operations; it is simply the nature of the business that it is impossible to harness the ups and downs to produce a crisis-free routine.

Since the advent of mass production in American industry, the opportunities for workers to take pride in what they produce have been greatly reduced. In the personal service field, however, this opportunity still exists. The chef creates his or her own culinary masterpiece and views it with personal pride and satisfaction. The same is true for the baker, the pastry chef, the pantry personnel, and many others. For many hospitality employees, the product—service—is intangible, but the recipient expresses thanks and satisfaction directly, allowing the employee to know that the work is appreciated and to have a feeling of accomplishment.

Hotels and restaurants are sensitive to changes in the national economy. Both types of businesses typically offer stable employment. For those who possess the interest, technical skills, emotional makeup, and motivation, the hospitality industry offers some of the most fascinating, rewarding careers available anywhere.

Endnotes

1. The Council on Hotel, Restaurant and Institutional Education, located at 1200 17th Street, Washington, D.C. 20036-3097, can provide names and addresses of educational institutions with hospitality management programs.

2. Some books which have appeared recently include: *How to Write a Winning Résumé* by Deborah Bloch; *Résumé Writing: A Comprehensive How-to-Do-It Guide* by Burdette Bostwick; *Résumés for Better Jobs* by Lawrence Brennan; *Your Résumé: The Key to a Better Job* by Leonard Corwen; and *The Résumé Handbook: How to Write Outstanding Résumés and Cover Letters* by David Hizer. These or similar books are available in libraries and bookstores.

3. For the latest Bureau of Labor Statistics report on wages and salaries in the hospitality industry, contact the Bureau at the U.S. Department of Labor, Bureau of Labor Statistics, 441 G Street, N.W., Washington, D.C. 20212. The American Hotel & Motel Association and the National Restaurant Association can also provide information on the employment outlook, salaries, and benefits in the lodging and food service industries. The American Hotel & Motel Association is located at 1201 New York Avenue, N.W., Washington, D.C. 20005. The address for the National Restaurant Association is 1200 17th Street, N.W., Washington, D.C. 20036.

4. "Business, Managerial, and Legal Occupations," reprinted from *The Occupational Outlook Handbook, 1988–89* (Washington, D.C.: U.S. Department of Labor, Bureau of Labor Statistics, 1988), pp. 18–19 and 39–41.

Key Terms

contract management company—Businesses that contract their management services to food service operations—often in an institutional setting.

cover letter—In a job-seeking situation, a concise, written message that states what specific job is being sought and relates the applicant's relevant experience for the job.

fast-food service—The single largest segment of the food service industry; composed of commercial establishments that offer drive-through and/or counter service to customers.

institutional food service—Operations that provide meals in non-commercial, closed environments, such as hospitals, schools, or correctional institutions.

management internship—Supervised training that hotel school graduates must have before engaging in actual management; takes place at a job site.

résumé—A formal, written presentation of an individual's work experience, skills, and education. Job applicants use résumés to obtain job interviews.

student internship—On-the-job experience for hospitality students required by most college and university hospitality programs; internships help students gain an understanding of the industry and its job requirements and demands.

Review Questions

1. Why has automation developed relatively slowly in the hospitality industry?
2. What is a management internship?
3. Where can unskilled workers gain skills for skilled-level positions in hotels?
4. What are some of the advantages of starting a hotel career in a small hotel?
5. What are some of the advantages of starting a hotel career in a large hotel?
6. Other than hotels and restaurants, what types of places offer food service employment?
7. What are some pros and cons of a career in the fast-food field?
8. Why is a résumé important for a job candidate?
9. Why is the turnover rate so high among entrants to hospitality management?
10. What are some pros and cons of a career with a food-service management company?

Internet Sites

For more information, visit the following Internet sites. Remember that Internet addresses can change without notice. If the site is no longer there, use a search engine to look for additional sites.

Associations

American Culinary Federation (ACF)
http://www.acfchefs.org

American Hotel & Motel Association (AH&MA)
http://www.ahma.com

Club Managers Association of America (CMAA)
http://www.cmaa.org

Council on Hotel, Restaurant and Institutional Education (CHRIE)
http://www.chrie.org

The Educational Foundation of NRA
http://www.restaurant.org/educate/educate.htm

The Educational Institute of AH&MA
http://www.ei-ahma.org

Hospitality Financial and Technology
Professionals
http://www.hftp.org

Hospitality Sales and Marketing
Association International (HSMAI)
http://www.hsmai.org

International Association of Conference
Centers (IACC)
http://www.iacconline.com

International Association of
Convention and Visitors Bureaus
(IACVB)
http://www.iacvb.org

International Hotel & Restaurant
Association
http://www.ih-ra.com

National Restaurant Association (NRA)
http://www.restaurant.org

University Internship Services
http://www.internsearch.com

Publications—Online and Printed

Bon Appetit
http://food.epicurious.com/
b_ba/b00_home/ba.html

Club Management Magazine
http://www.club-mgmt.com

CuisineNet Cafe
http://www.cuisinenet.com/cafe/
index.html

Electronic Gourmet Guide
http://www.foodwine.com

Food Network: Cyber Kitchen
http://www.foodtv.com

Food Magazine
http://www.penton.com/corp/mags/
fm.html

Foodservice and Hospitality
http://www.foodservice.ca

Internet Food Channel
http://www.foodchannel.com

Lodging Online
http://www.ei-ahma.org/webs/
lodging/index.html

Lodging Hospitality
http://www.penton.com/corp/mags/
lh.html

Nation's Restaurant News Online
http://www.nrn.com http://
smartwine.com

NutritiOnline
http://www.dietetics.com/news

On the Rail-News for Food
Professionals
http://www.ontherail.com

Restaurant Hospitality
http://www.penton.com/corp/mags/
rh.html

Restaurants and Institutions
http://www.rimag.com

Part II

The Lodging Industry

Chapter 3 Outline

The Origins of the European Lodging Industry
       The Grand Tour
       The Professional Hotelier
       Early Hotel Schools
       New Era—New Markets
       Decades of Difficulties
The Early History of Hotels in the United States
       The Colonial Period
       1794–1900
       New Developments
       1900–1930
       The 1930s: The Depression
       The 1940s: World War II and Its Aftermath
       The 1950s and Early '60s
Independents and Chains
       The Growth of Chain Operations
Lodging Industry Developments in the 1960s
       Referral Organizations
American Resorts
       Summer Resorts
       Year-Round Resorts
       Cold Winter Resorts
       Warm Winter Resorts
       Other Developments
International Resorts
The Early History of Caribbean Hotels

3

The Early History of Lodging in Europe and America

A COMPLETE HISTORY of the lodging industry would take us back some 12,000 years; however, from a practical standpoint, innkeeping as we know it today was not possible until the adoption of a standardized medium of exchange. With the establishment of money during the sixth century B.C. came the first real opportunities for people to trade and travel. As travelers' areas of movement widened, their need for lodging became greater. Early inns were nothing more than space within private dwellings. Typically, the inns provided only the basic necessities, paid little attention to service or hospitality, were rarely clean, and, more often than not, were run by disreputable and unprogressive landlords.

In spite of these hardships, travel activity has continued to increase right up to the present. Comparable evolutionary processes for eating and rooming establishments have taken place in many different parts of the world. Many countries have produced their own native form of **hostelry**, such as the riokan in Japan, the paradors in Spain, or the pousadas in Portugal. As much as any others, however, the European hotels have come to impress their particular style and characteristics upon the industry as it is today. Therefore, it is appropriate to focus initially on the history and evolution of European hotels.

The Origins of the European Lodging Industry

Aside from the traditionally nomadic peoples, early Europeans began moving from place to place for very specific utilitarian reasons. Pleasure travel and sightseeing as we know them today were unknown. There were few categories of typical travelers. Mercenaries moved from their homes to their assigned military units and back. Pilgrims and clergymen sought out their places of worship or the seats of their religious orders. A few itinerant merchants provided an early system of distribution for goods and services.

The first innkeepers exercised their hospitality chores on a part-time basis. They were clergymen, mountain guides, coachmen, or farmers who began by taking in short-term boarders. Accommodations were rarely comfortable, but always frugal. In time the pioneer innkeepers began to introduce what they believed to be some of the comforts of home. Design, building materials, the right fabrics, a good down pillow, and wholesome food and drink began playing an increasingly important role.

Innkeepers began transferring their businesses from father to son. A surprising number of the earliest inns and guest houses have remained intact, and continue to be operated as hostelries to this day. Their names evoke the coats of arms of their most illustrious guests: Three Kings, Golden Lion, Cardinal's Hat, Black Eagle, Two Swords, and many more.

From 1750 to 1825, English inns gained the reputation of being the finest in the world. Their early development began in London where innkeepers increased services, maintained standards of cleanliness, and, at least to some extent, catered to guests. As roads improved, new ideas that originated in the metropolitan area were adopted by the countryside inns. The inns of England reached their peak of development from 1780 to 1825.

Voyagers were passing along information to each other about the best places to stay and eat. One of the earliest guidebooks was "The Pilgrim's Guide," dating back to the thirteenth century. Guidebooks at first were not thought of as guidebooks in the usual sense of this term. Rather, they were chance accounts of travel from diaries, letters, or ad hoc remarks intended to inform and offer advice. In the early days they were often written in Latin. Sir Francis Bacon produced an essay entitled "Of Travel," which is probably one of the earliest records of tangible travel advice in the modern sense.

The Grand Tour

In reviewing the great historic travel patterns, mention must be made of the **grand tour**, often referred to as "the golden age of travel," whose heyday occurred in the second half of the eighteenth century, prior to the French Revolution and the advent of the railways. A grand tour of the European continent was an indispensable element in the education of the young offspring of Britain's most powerful and wealthy families. The tours often lasted up to several years. In response to this fast developing demand, inhabitants of the tour destinations in France, Italy, Austria, Switzerland, and Germany began establishing lodging and tourist services. Thus it is clear that European expertise in hotel matters did not develop out of an innate predisposition. Rather, the entrepreneurs of the time evolved their skills in reaction to the requirements of the marketplace.

Increasing expertise brought increasingly elaborate services and accommodations. Hotels such as the Dolder Grand in Zurich, the Imperial in Vienna, the Vier Jahreszeiten in Hamburg, and the Des Bergues in Geneva were the result. Hotels emerged wherever fashion dictated.

The Professional Hotelier

Professional hoteliers began to make their mark in the mid-1800s. The first to become well known on a national level were the scions of pioneering hotel families. Later, personalities such as César Ritz, teaming up with famous chefs (in Ritz's case, Georgés-Auguste Escoffier) became famous beyond their own nation's boundaries. The Ritz hotels in Paris, London, Madrid, and Lisbon constituted the first hotel management chain.

Early Hotel Schools

The first hotel training schools were established at the end of the nineteenth century and early in the twentieth century as a consequence of ever-larger hotels, increased technology, and increasingly complex administrative problems. The traditional methods of on-the-job training supervised by guilds were replaced or complemented by more formal and scientific educational methods. Formal apprentice programs were established. Part of the apprentice's time was spent on the job and part of it in a school-like environment. Those who sought jobs at the managerial level were required to spend more time in school than other hotel students. Being selected for training by one of the great hotels was a noteworthy distinction; it provided a professional reference that often meant more money in terms of future earnings. Work certificates from grand hotels were cherished like some precious scroll. Often, parents of aspiring hotel workers were required to pay the hotel for the privilege of their youngster training there. Apprentices were obligated to work very hard; they received poor treatment and next to no pay. In some instances, these policies prevailed well into the 1950s and 1960s.

New Era—New Markets

As new modes of transportation developed, access to remote but picturesque resorts became possible. **Funiculars** (cable railways) began serving hotels in the mountains. Bürgenstock, Territet-Glion, and Giessbach are a few examples of Swiss hotels that rapidly developed thanks to funicular train service to their areas. Both Alpine and seaside resorts became quite the rage. While many of the transportation lines were established by English companies, the hotels were developed by the local people. With the discovery of winter sports, European royalty began frequenting the winter resorts in Montreux, Switzerland, and other relatively snow-free towns situated in close proximity to higher-lying ski runs.

Three Types of Hotels. The first move toward what today we call **market segmentation** produced three types of hotels: transit, vacation, and grand.

Transit hotels were the descendants of the early inns. (The term "transit" is a European label and does not describe the same property as the "transient" label often used in the United States.) They continued to provide economical, efficient, and clean overnight accommodations at major crossroads. Thus, they were the European equivalent of a much later development in America—the motel.

Transit hotels were geared to rapid turnover, because their guests typically only needed these accommodations for short stays. Services in transit hotels tended to be modest and uniform.

Vacation hotels have been a part of Europe since ancient times when the Romans enjoyed the healthful properties of their mineral springs; these waters—and the resorts and towns located near them—came to be known as **spas** (after Spa, a watering place in eastern Belgium). Gradually the pursuit of health led Europeans to the simultaneous pursuit of pleasure. Spas at Marienbad, Vichy, Wiesbaden, Ragaz, and Loeche-les Bains became centers of social activity. Entertainment, costume balls, concerts, and dancing contributed to the well-being of guests who were "taking the waters." Gambling was added to the attractions and, little by little, the curative side of spas decreased in importance.

The French Riviera resort region was first frequented for health reasons. The region also enjoyed ample sunshine and a mild winter climate. A visit there by Queen Victoria in 1899 was later followed by a multitude of celebrities, members of royal families, statesmen, artists, and financiers, many of whose names became permanently associated with the region. Other vacation hotels were developed at spots of scenic beauty. Zermatt and St. Moritz in the Alps are good examples.

Grand hotels were (and are) establishments which, over the years, afforded their guests an ideal mixture of unique architecture, luxurious interiors, impeccable and truly personal service, a well-trained staff, exquisite food, and style and ambience beyond comparison. Qualification as a grand hotel is earned over a long period of time. It cannot be gained arbitrarily or through luxurious accommodations alone. A very limited number of hotels throughout the world deserve this distinction, and they have to work constantly at preserving it. A true grand hotel enjoys an undisputed international reputation by achieving a delicate balance among luxury, elegance, and good taste.

Decades of Difficulties

The 1930s were rather negative years for hotels across the continent because of the international tensions leading up to World War II.

The 1940s were dominated by World War II, which brought massive destruction and social upheaval to many European countries.

The 1950s could be characterized as years of steady but slow growth. This decade was the first to allow growth and progress unencumbered by the vestiges of a wartime economy. On the other hand, there were still numerous travel complications engendered by prewar bureaucratic methods. Personal and vehicular traffic between countries was complicated. In spite of these drawbacks, modest hotel growth and development did occur, but it was confined to national boundaries.

The European hotel industry became truly international with the advent of jet travel in 1959.

The Early History of Hotels in the United States ─────

The Colonial Period

In the American colonies, inns were located in seaports. Colonial innkeepers patterned their establishments after inns in England, but while English landlords were conservative and slow to change, their American counterparts demonstrated no such inhibitions. American innkeepers were aggressive expansionists who took chances. Within a few years after the American Revolution, inns in the United States were well on their way to offering the finest services available anywhere. Admittedly, by today's standards these services would be totally inadequate, but for their time they were the best. By 1800, it was evident that the United States was assuming world leadership in the development of the lodging industry.

In addition to the pioneering spirit of the American innkeeper, several other factors influenced the rapid rise of the lodging industry in the United States. While European hotels operated on the premise that only the aristocracy was entitled to luxury and comfort, American hotels were run for more universal enjoyment. Anyone with enough money could take advantage of the services of a hotel, and the rates were within the means of almost everyone. In fact, some Americans chose to reside permanently in hotels.

Probably the most important factor in the growth of U.S. innkeeping was that the average American traveled considerably more than typical residents of other countries. In fact, the habit of extensive travel enjoyed by many Americans was—and continues to be—a considerable benefit to the worldwide hospitality industry.

1794–1900

It was in 1794 that the City Hotel—the first building in America erected specifically for hotel purposes—opened in New York City. Until this time, innkeepers had merely converted their own or someone else's home into an inn. The City Hotel was actually an overgrown inn, but with 73 rooms it was generally considered an "immense establishment." It quickly became the social center of New York, which at that time was a booming town of 30,000.

Boston, Baltimore, and Philadelphia, not to be outdone by New York City, quickly opened similar establishments. In Boston it was the Exchange Coffee House, in Baltimore the City Hotel, and in Philadelphia the Mansion House. Each of these landmark hotels became a fashionable meeting place. (It is interesting to note that New York's first skyscraper was the Adelphi Hotel—a building of six stories.) Within 35 years of the opening of New York's City Hotel, the stage was set for a golden age of hotels in the United States.

The Original First-Class Hotel. In 1829, the first-class hotel was born in Boston. The Tremont House richly deserved the title "the Adam and Eve of the modern hotel industry"; it was something absolutely new in the history of hotelkeeping, and it surpassed its contemporaries, both in America and in Europe. With 170 rooms, the Tremont was the largest and costliest building that had ever been erected in America. Its architect, Isaiah Rogers, became the leading authority on hotel construction, and he strongly influenced hotel architecture for the next 50 years. It is generally acknowledged (although some may disagree) that the opening of the Tremont House established America's supremacy in the science of hotel management.

In addition to its size, cost, and luxury, the Tremont offered many innovations that made it a favorite topic of conversation among all who had stayed there. The typical inn of the day consisted of one or two large rooms containing from three to ten beds. The beds were large enough to accommodate several people at one time, and an innkeeper never considered it a profitable night unless each bed was occupied by at least two guests. The Tremont was the first hotel to feature private single and double rooms; for those who valued privacy, this must have seemed like a dream come true. Not only were there private rooms, but each door had a lock. Two other innovations were considered extreme luxuries: every room was equipped with a bowl and a pitcher, and every room was supplied with free soap.

Under the management of the Boyden family, a complete staff was hired, trained, and instructed to treat hotel guests with dignity and respect. French cuisine was offered for the first time in a hotel; the Tremont had the first bellboys; and the an-nunciator—the forerunner of the room telephone—was introduced there.

Ironically, while the Tremont initiated up-to-date hotel development, it soon fell victim to the trend it had started. Other cities took up the challenge of building finer hotels, and within 20 years the Tremont had to close for modernizing. With the fast pace of hotel improvements, the life span of the Tremont was 65 years, but during the last 20 it was a second-class hotel.

A Boom in Hotel Building. Throughout most of the nineteenth century, the contest among hoteliers to build better, larger, and more luxurious hotels continued. Every city in the nation wanted a hotel as good as the Tremont had been, in spite of the fact that often there was insufficient business to warrant such an operation. The theory seemed to be that no city amounted to much if it did not have at least one hotel which could impress upon visitors the greatness and hospitality of the community.

The hotel boom followed the westward movement. The excitement and com-petition of hotel building, which was at its peak between 1830 and 1850 in the East, went on all the way to the Pacific Coast. Chicago had the Grand Pacific, the Palmer House, and the Sherman House; the Planters was the pride of St. Louis; and Omaha extolled the virtues of the Paxton. San Francisco built the Palace, the most ornate and expensive hotel of its day. The original Palace was built in 1875, cost $5 million (a tremendous sum in those days), occupied 2.5 acres in the heart of San Francisco, and had 800 rooms. The Palace never made money, but in appearance, structure, equipment, and lavishness, it was a real triumph.

Near the end of the nineteenth century, the hotel boom slowed; many people believed that every possible convenience, service, and new idea had been incorpo-rated in the country's modern hotels. Little did they realize that within a few years the world's greatest hotelier would be building a hotel so new that it would be called an invention and would set the standards for twentieth-century hotel construction and management.

The intense competition among both cities and hoteliers to build the biggest and best hotel resulted in considerable deviation from the American tradition of hotels designed for everyone. At the close of the nineteenth century, there were many elegant, luxurious establishments, typified by New York's old Waldorf-Astoria, Denver's Brown Palace, and San Francisco's Palace. At the other extreme were the small hotels built close to railroad stations; these were little more than overgrown rooming houses, and, because of their inadequacies, travelers often found them undesirable. Many people of modest means found the luxury hotels too expensive and the small hotels lacking in basic standards of service and clean-liness. Forced to choose one of two extremes, they were seldom content, whatever their choice.

New Developments

At the turn of the century, two new developments in the United States that were to significantly influence the future of the lodging industry appeared. First, as the country's economy expanded, the commercial traveler became increasingly prominent in the business world. As the **commercial travel** group grew in number, there developed an increasing need for suitable lodging accommodations and conveniences to serve this new market. Second, improvements in roads, railroads, and water transportation made travel easier and less expensive. In a society seemingly ever restless and eager to be on the move, such a development immediately led to a tremendous upsurge in the number of travelers. Once the middle class of American society could afford to travel, it became an entirely new and vast population desiring lodging services.

1900–1930

At the very beginning of the twentieth century, the hotel industry was confronted with the challenge of serving a new traveling population. It had to face such questions as: What types of accommodations were needed by the traveling salesperson? Were new services necessary? Would these accommodations and services appeal to the middle-class traveler also, or was an entirely different type of operation necessary to meet these demands? What room rates would attract business and still provide a fair profit? Answers to these questions were not immediately available. Fortunately for the industry, Ellsworth M. Statler had foreseen the development of this situation and was ready to meet the challenge himself; while leaders in the field were discussing the alternatives, he was drawing plans for his first hotel. By 1907, construction was under way in Buffalo on the Statler Hotel.

The First Commercial Hotel. The opening of the Buffalo Statler on January 18, 1908, marked a new age in the American hotel industry; this was the birth of the modern commercial hotel. This "invention" (for as truly as Henry Ford invented the modern automobile, Ellsworth Statler invented the modern hotel) embodied all the known techniques of the day plus a lifetime of Statler's own experiences and ideas, which he had carefully recorded. Many services and conveniences that are taken for granted today were first introduced in this hotel. Fire doors protected the two main stairways. Keyholes for door locks were placed above the knob, so they could be easily located in a dark hall. A light switch just inside the door eliminated groping through the room in the dark. Rooms featured a private bath, a full-length mirror, and circulating ice water. A free morning newspaper was provided for each guest. Besides those specialties designed to increase guest comfort, the hotel contained many new structural and engineering designs, and, because of them, the Statler Hotel became the model for modern hotel construction for the next 40 years. Truly, here was a hotel that provided comfort, service, and cleanliness for the average traveler at an affordable price. The hotel's advertising slogan was, "A Room and a Bath for a Dollar and a Half." Immediate public acclaim ensured the success of the Statler Hotel and promoted the development of the Statler Hotel Company.

Following the excitement generated by the first Statler Hotel, the industry remained relatively inactive; this was caused in part by World War I. But the period from 1910 to 1920 turned out to be only the calm before the storm, for the prosperous Roaring Twenties were a boom period for hotel construction. Just as Wall Street thought there was no limit to the nation's prosperity, hoteliers considered the demand for hotel services and space limitless. During this decade, many of today's most famous hotels were built. New York's Hotel Pennsylvania (now the Penta) was the world's largest when it opened. Only a few years later, Ralph Hitz's Hotel New Yorker surpassed the Pennsylvania as New York's largest hotel. But in 1927 the giant of them all—the Stevens Hotel—opened in Chicago. With its 3,000 rooms, the Stevens (now the 1,600-room Chicago Hilton & Towers) took over the title "The World's Largest Hotel," a distinction it held until the completion in 1967 of the 3,500-room Hotel Rossiya in Moscow. Two luxury hotels that also were opened during this era were the present Waldorf-Astoria and the Pierre, both in New York.

But large cities and name hotels had no monopoly on the building fever of the 1920s. Cities and towns everywhere were acquiring new hotels. Some were financed by communities, some by corporations, and some by private individuals, but the enthusiasm was shared by all.

The 1930s: The Depression

Then, just as bigger and better plans were being readied, the bubble burst, and hotels dropped into the unhappiest period of their history. In 1930, when the country plunged into the Great Depression, hotel rooms emptied, and business sank to an all-time low. Rate wars were commonplace, but even reductions in price did not attract business. So severe were the effects of the Depression that 85 percent of the nation's hotels went either into receivership or through some form of liquidation. Many hotels were purchased for almost nothing by entrepreneurs who would later refurbish them for operation or sell them as part of elaborate real estate deals. Properties worth millions could be bought for a few cents on the dollar. Many financial experts openly expressed the opinion that the hotel industry would never recover. Even later, when the general economy showed definite signs of improvement, investors thought the supply of hotel rooms was too great for any future demand and were unwilling to invest in them. Credit must be given to the hotel operators of this period. Many lost their savings and their businesses, but the majority of them never lost faith and remained to guide the hotel industry through its darkest hour.

The 1940s: World War II and Its Aftermath

By 1940, the industry was slowly stabilizing at a level which, although considerably below that of the 1920s, brought mild optimism about the future to a few hoteliers. However, no one envisioned the tremendous upswing that was to occur only two years later. The outbreak of World War II set into motion the greatest mass movement of people the United States has ever experienced. Millions of Americans went into the armed services. Millions more moved to areas around defense plants. Thousands of others—those coordinating the defense program—also found it necessary to travel. With this activity in full force, the demand for hotel rooms and services reached an all-time peak, and it became common to see people sleeping in hotel lobbies because there just were not enough rooms available. The hotel world had never experienced nor expected such a situation.

Motels offered the casual comfort that the new traveling public wanted. There were no lobby parades, tipping, or parking problems. The rooms were new and featured modern furniture and wall-to-wall carpeting. (Photo courtesy of State Archives of Michigan)

Undoubtedly, the war years presented the greatest single challenge ever faced by the lodging industry. Hotels operated at capacity every day of the week, in spite of the fact that they had often lost half of their trained professional staff to the armed services. Since most hotels were understaffed, managers were forced to employ large numbers of people with no hotel experience. Standards of service necessarily suffered, but the fact that service was even maintained is amazing considering the handicaps under which hotels had to operate. Although the hospitality industry was not classified by the U.S. government as an essential industry as it is today, hoteliers could feel justly proud of their contribution to the nation's war effort.

The 1950s and Early '60s

The prosperity of the war years continued through 1947, with hotel occupancy rates running above 90 percent. In 1948, a downward business trend began which set the scene for hotels for the 1950s.

Unlike the decade following World War I, the 1950s did not give rise to a boom in the building of major hotels. The Los Angeles Statler Hilton, which opened on October 27, 1952, was thought to be a trendsetter in hotel construction. One complete wing of the building was devoted to leasable office space; the theory was that rental income from office leasing would stabilize the hotel's financial structure by carrying fixed costs of operation during the slack periods of the year. While the theory appears valid, few, if any, later hotels followed the pattern.

Noted as a period of many new developments, the 1950s will best be recalled as the period when the motel and the motor hotel really came of age. In retrospect, it is easy to explain the phenomenal growth and success of this segment of the hospitality industry. More and more American families were traveling as a unit, and the prevailing mode of transportation was the automobile. The habits, tastes, and desires of the motoring public had undergone a considerable change. A new note of informality had come into the American way of life. Motels and motor hotels provided a way to eliminate formal dress, lobby parades, tipping, and parking problems. The rooms were new and featured modern furniture, wall-to-wall carpeting, and television; a swimming pool was often an added attraction.

At first, many hoteliers had difficulty deciding just what role motels would play in the industry. To many, they were a novelty that would soon wear out and fade away. To others, they were a new kind of competition and had to be beaten. The more farsighted hoteliers recognized that motels represented progress and quickly adopted the theory, "If you can't beat them, join them." Slowly but surely, established hotel companies moved into the motel business.

Unfortunately, members of the lodging industry spent much time between 1950 and 1960 arguing over the relative merits of hotels and motels. At times, an observer might well have believed that the two proponents were archenemies whose interests were completely incompatible. Slowly, however, the truth of the situation became obvious—motels and motor hotels were not a new and different industry at all. They merely represented a new concept in the art of innkeeping and were very much an integral part of the vast hospitality industry. Some alert individuals had recognized a need and had developed a product to meet it. As more and more professionals in all segments of the industry recognized this fact, suspicion and opposition turned to cooperation and understanding. A significant event occurred in 1962 when the American Hotel Association changed its name to the American Hotel & Motel Association (AH&MA). Today there is a very positive, cooperative atmosphere throughout the Association and the dynamic and exciting industry it represents.

The Motel and Motor Hotel Boom. Once the motel boom got underway, it took off like a rocket. When looking at this segment of the lodging industry today, it is hard to believe that its origin was in the little roadside cabins and motels that were occasional dots on the landscape. From 1939 to 1962, 36,000 new motels were built in the United States. Although the early motels were small and frequently operated by a husband and wife team, a change took place in the 1950s. Motels grew in size (number of units) and in plushness and service. With increased size came many additional duties and managerial responsibilities. Professional management became not only desirable, but, often, essential.

In the early 1950s, a 50-room motel was a real giant; within a few years, it was not even average. That is how rapidly the increase in size occurred. Most new motels built in the late 1950s and early 1960s contained a minimum of 80 rooms; the average was close to 100 rooms. In fact, the size explosion created a problem of terminology or classification. Soon the large motels were being called motor hotels, and it became difficult to differentiate between a motel and a hotel or between either of them and a motor hotel.

Initially, it was said that a motel was single-storied and a hotel multi-storied; furthermore, the hotel offered a much more complete variety of services. Soon motels became multi-storied, and then the larger motels instituted all of the usual hotel services. A new definition had to be sought. In reality, the only difference between the traditional hotel and a motel or motor hotel is that parking is always available at motels and motor hotels. Also, since motel guests more frequently travel by auto than their motor hotel counterparts, the number of parking spaces per room is likely to be greater in a motel. Perhaps the safest conclusion is that motels are becoming more and more like hotels, while hotels are becoming more and more like motels.

A fine example of this trend is the San Francisco Hilton & Towers. The inner core of the building is a parking garage around which the guestrooms are built. Guests arriving by automobile drive into the motor entrance, register from their car seat at the motor desk, and then drive to the floor where their room is located. Having parked their car, they step through a door into the hotel corridor, find their room, and settle down for a pleasant stay. They have reached their room with no lobby parade, no formality, and no tipping; their car is practically outside the door, and every service is as close as the phone in their room. One might well ask, "Is the San Francisco Hilton & Towers a motel, a hotel, or a motor hotel?" It is called a hotel by the owners.

Within any given area, the motor hotels first grew up along the highway outside the city and slowly formed a ring around the city. The outskirts were considered the ideal location, and very few experts believed that motor hotels located in the center of town could succeed. As if to emphasize the rapidly changing nature of the hospitality industry, motor hotels began to appear within many downtown areas. The success of these downtown locations is evidenced by their continued growth. Because of the high cost of land in the city, these downtown motor hotels are usually large, high-rise constructions.

Earlier in this chapter, we noted the decline in hotel occupancy rates throughout the 1950s. This decline occurred in spite of a rapidly increasing amount of travel and number of people needing lodging accommodations. Obviously, these people found rooms, and where they found them, of course, was in motels and motor hotels. Here, then, is the principal reason for the hotelier's concern about the mushrooming motel industry. Rooms business is by far the most profitable aspect of hotel management, and hotels suddenly found this profitable business declining at a rapid rate. Hotels in smaller cities were the first to receive the full brunt of the motel competition, and the attrition rate among them shot up alarmingly. Within a few years, many of these hotels were closed or converted to non-hotel uses. Some disappeared completely and were replaced by parking lots.

Before we bring this history of lodging into the jet age, we must backtrack in our chronology to cover independents and chains, referral organizations, the development of American and international resorts, and the early history of Caribbean hotels.

Independents and Chains

One approach to classifying the lodging industry is to see it as being composed of two basic segments: independents and chains. The term **independent** refers to an

Exhibit 1   The Largest International Chains Based on Number of Properties

Hotel Chain	Properties
1. HFS, Inc.	5,599
2. Best Western International	3,715
3. Choice Hotels International	3,476
4. Holiday Hospitality	2,350
5. Accor	2,205
6. Marriott International	1,381
7. Promus	1,136
8. Societe du Louvre	565
9. Carlson Hospitality	437
10. ITT Sheraton	413

Source: *Hotel & Motel Management,* September 15, 1997, p. 53.

operator owning one or more properties which have no chain relationship. By contrast, a **chain** refers to properties that are affiliated with others. A chain property may be (1) owned by a parent company, (2) a franchise operation, or (3) operated by a management contract company. Many people incorrectly believe that a franchise and a chain operation are the same; they are not. While a franchise property is part of a chain, a chain property is not necessarily a franchise.

The Growth of Chain Operations

Chain operation is not new to the hotel industry. Operation of several hotels by one organization has been a common practice for over 50 years. Initially, the number of hotels under chain control represented only a small part of the total industry.

The tremendous growth of chains started during the last years of World War II and immediately afterward when the three major chains—Statler, Hilton, and Sheraton—began to grow rapidly. The conservative Statler group built the Washington and Los Angeles Statlers and started construction in Dallas and Hartford. Hilton and Sheraton decided a quicker method of growth was to purchase existing hotels. Both groups bought and sold properties so rapidly that a score card was needed to keep up with the transactions. Both Hilton and Sheraton were referred to as real estate brokers rather than hotel operators. Whether the charges were justified or not is now of no consequence, since both groups have long since proved that they are in the business to operate first-class properties.

Today, chains dominate the industry, and the largest of these chains own or operate hundreds of properties around the world, as shown in Exhibits 1, 2, and 3. A quick glance at industry statistics should be enough to convince even the most stubborn independent fan that chain operations overshadow independents in

Exhibit 2 The Largest International Lodging Chains Based on Total Rooms

Hotel Chain	Rooms
1. HFS, Inc.	509,421
2. Holiday Hospitality	395,000
3. Best Western International	298,803
4. Choice Hotels International	283,034
5. Marriott International	283,029
6. Accor	279,145
7. Promus Companies	175,000
8. ITT Sheraton	133,621
9. Hilton Hotels Corporation	102,000
10. Carlson Hospitality Worldwide	98,000

Source: *Hotel & Motel Management*, September 15, 1997, p. 53.

Exhibit 3 Major U.S. Brands

Brand	In U.S.	International	Total
Best Western	1,948	1,514	3,462
Days Inns	1,592	60	1,652
Holiday Inn	1,293	309	1,602
Comfort Inn	1,081	292	1,373
Super 8	1,317	36	1,353
Ramada Inn	804	0	804
Motel 6	759	0	759
Econolodge	626	14	640
Quality Inn	357	207	564
Hampton Inn	522	3	525
Howard Johnson	469	54	523

Source: *Hotels,* July 1997, p. 62.

today's hospitality industry. In 1987, chains owned 62 percent of all the hotel rooms in the United States. Today the figure is 75 percent. Some industry leaders believe this figure could reach 90 percent by the year 2000.

Why are chains growing so quickly? The best one-word answer would be efficiency. When faced with stiff competition from efficient chain operations, an independent hotel operator traditionally has three alternatives. First, he or she might try to compensate for the decline in business by cutting down maintenance expenditures and forcing up room rates. This approach has been popular but is frequently suicidal. Second, if the independent has or can obtain capital, he or she can gamble and invest in improvements, modernization, and promotion. This approach can be sound and has kept many hotels independent. The third recourse is to sell in hopes of making some profit before it is too late; this is the reason that chain operators have been able to expand without engaging in a great deal of new construction.

Some of the advantages of chain operations include:

- Purchasing—Buying anything in bulk reduces costs. Because chains own a number of properties, they can buy everything from room furniture to telephone equipment to catsup in large quantities at lower prices.

- Human resources—By spreading the expense over its properties, chains can hire experts in every area of hotel operations, something few independents can afford to do.

- Promotion—National advertising campaigns in magazines, newspapers, radio, and television cost too much for independent hotels. However, chains can divide advertising costs among their properties so that each receives the benefits of widespread promotion at a small portion of the total expense. A recognized brand name often attracts guests more readily.

- Reservations—Centralized reservations can direct substantial business from one property within the chain to another. A large number of reservations that might otherwise go to other properties are made this way.

- Financing—Groups can raise money more easily than individuals, and thus chains can raise capital for improvement or expansion more efficiently.

- Centralized accounting, research and development, and real estate development—Personnel in these areas can serve all the hotels in a chain at a lower cost per unit than in an independent operation.

Although the world's first hotel chain was created by César Ritz, chain growth and development is most frequently associated with the American hotel industry. However, national hotel chains today are present in many countries of the world. Examples are: Steigenberger (Germany), Oberoi (India), Accor (France), Dusit Thani (Thailand), Mandarin Oriental, New World, Shangri-La (Hong Kong), Ciga (Italy), Othon (Brazil), and Forte Hotels (England). Exhibits 4–8 show the largest chains in major segments of the world.

Because of competitive pressure by chains, the independent operator faces great challenges. However, independent hoteliers can cite many advantages of independent ownership/management which, for some operators, make the competitive efforts worth the time and expense.

Paul Handlery, chairman and CEO of Handlery Hotels, Inc., writes: "Owner/operators must realize that they also have a competitive edge. In most cases, they

Insider Insights

John Norlander
President
Radisson Hotels International
Minneapolis, Minnesota —————————————————————————

Although Radisson is a relative newcomer to the international hospitality market, we have made some dramatic inroads in a very short period of time. We did this by having a vision of where we want to be in the year 2000. This was set down as our mission statement ten years ago. In the mid-'80s, it was easy to see that the results of overbuilding in the United States would put a damper on the growth rates that we had set for ourselves (one new hotel every ten days until the year 2000). So we set our focus on the global market. We determined that we would have to get half our growth from the international market, and the domestic half would have to come from conversions.

We were also aware that we would have to find new ways to handle our international development. Those companies that started their growth following World War II had a different set of opportunities. Every city in Europe needed hotel facilities, and the American was the key target market. That is not the case in the '90s. The globalization of commerce makes the American businessperson/tourist just one of many target markets. And Europe, although not overbuilt, doesn't have the same need for new facilities that it did 40 years ago. On the other hand, Eastern Europe is almost in the same position that Western Europe was in 40 years ago. Perhaps the one difference is that the people of Europe 40 years ago knew that they had years of hard work ahead of them to reach a strong economic and political comfort level. The people of Eastern Europe today don't have that same desire. There is political confusion and economic conditions that are unique in history due to the Communist system that held sway for those 40 years.

Radisson has looked at this set of conditions and decided that Eastern Europe is an excellent bet for the long run. We are very interested in putting our brand on hotels in the key cities in this emerging market. We want to do this now, while the market is still in its development stages. We believe those that come in now will be better positioned when the markets begin to mature.

That is why we set up a joint venture in the USSR with the Intourist organization to manage the 630-room Slavjanskaya Hotel that was already in the construction phase. We created a partnership with an American business center operator to make it a 430-room hotel with 200 business center units, both of which are needed by the western business community trying to establish itself in Moscow.

Of course we expected to have problems on entering this new market. And we have not been disappointed! We got all the problems we anticipated plus the August 1991 aborted coup, and then the disintegration of the USSR and the shaky affiliation of the Commonwealth of Independent States. Our cup runneth over with problems! But, the good news is that our hotel is full! Wouldn't every hotel operator like to have that problem? So we are working every day to keep current with the changes in the banking regulations in the new Russia. These are still

(continued)

Insider Insights *(continued)*

"Byzantine" in comparison to most western countries. And the banking problems are compounded by the uncertainty of the ability of Mr. Yeltsin to make the ruble a convertible currency. All of this is mixed into the stew of the changing (daily) political situation. Russia is experiencing a "war of laws"—new laws are passed almost daily to set the rules for working under a market economy, but the old laws of the managed economy are never voided. This creates an opportunity for every type of problem to arise—from the "Russian Mafia" to the most basic "con" schemes. And all this is occurring in the background of conditions that are somewhere between 40 and 70 years behind the western democracies in everything from transportation to women's rights. If it's nothing else, it's exciting!

And at Radisson, we are jumping in with both feet. Not only are we open and operating in Moscow with the only American-managed hotel, but we are under construction in Poland, Romania, and Latvia (which was the USSR when we started) and under development in Czechoslovakia (or is it Slovakia now?) and Hungary, not to forget East Berlin, which is in a western democracy but operating with many of the leftover problems of Eastern Europe.

We are excited about the prospects for the development of these markets over the next few years. There is tremendous interest from both the business and leisure sectors. Radisson perhaps is the most active American hotel company in the area at this time and we intend to leverage this advantage.

Radisson's plan in the rest of the world is to work with strong local partners in each area. In this regard, we have developed a variety of joint ventures and partnerships in Canada, Mexico, Australia, the United Kingdom, Germany, and Jamaica. In the Eastern Europe arena, there are very few strong partners, so Radisson has set up its own management structure, opening an operations office in Vienna and sales offices in London, Stuttgart, and Vienna.

The training of staff to the level required to service the western clientele's expectations has been a unique challenge. Our "Yes I Can" philosophy of service does not come naturally to those raised under the Communist regimes, but we have had great success in developing excellent service-oriented people. Given a chance to smile (along with some "smile instructions") and an opportunity to receive "incentives" (to help them smile!), the people respond.

are entrepreneurs. This alone should enable them to do a better job of managing and operating a hotel property. Because of their vested interest (not to mention blood, sweat, and tears) they have the upper hand on a paid manager of a chain operation. More important, they can accomplish things more quickly and easily than chain operation managers can. [Independent operators] can do so because they are the decision-makers and have no layers of upper management to go through for approvals. Having permanence in one's property gives stability in, and connection to, the social and business community."[1] Gary Saunders of the Boston Park Plaza put it another way when he said, "Some data say that 74 percent of travelers prefer chain hotels. That means 26 percent don't. I am glad to be fighting along with other independents for one quarter of the market."[2]

Exhibit 4   Africa's Largest Chains

Chain	Headquarters
Protea Hotels and Inns	South Africa
Southern Sun Hotel Holdings	South Africa
Sun Hotels International	South Africa
National Hotels Corporation	Ethiopia
Karos Hotels	South Africa

Source: *Hotels,* July 1997, p. 58.

Exhibit 5   Asia's Largest Chains

Chain	Headquarters
New World Renaissance	Hong Kong
Shangri-La	Hong Kong
Regal Hotels	Hong Kong
Mandarin Oriental	Hong Kong
Prince Hotels	Japan
Tokyu Hotel Group	Japan

Source: *Hotels,* July 1997, p. 58.

Exhibit 6   Mexico and Latin America's Largest Chains

Chain	Headquarters
Grupo Posadas de Mexico	Mexico
Grupo Situr	Mexico
Cubatur	Cuba
Othon Hotels	Brazil

Source: *Hotels,* July 1997, p. 58.

It should be noted that, in contrast to the United States, less than 20 percent of the hotel rooms in Asia, Europe, and Latin America are chain affiliated.

Exhibit 7   Europe's Largest Chains

Chain	Headquarters
Accor	France
Forte Hotels	England
Club Méditerranée	France
Hilton International	England
Sol-Melia	Spain
Intercontinental Hotels	England

Source: *Hotels*, July 1997, p. 58.

Exhibit 8   North America's Largest Chains

Chain	Headquarters
Holiday Hospitality	United States
Hospitality Franchise Systems	United States
Best Western International	United States
Choice Hotels International	United States
Marriott Hotels	United States

Source: *Hotels*, July 1997, p. 60.

Historically, small community hotels faced a double challenge—the efficiency of chain operations and the competition of the motel industry, which had already made heavy inroads into the rooms business. Caught in this cross fire, and with survival directly dependent upon their ability to adjust to this new situation, the independent hoteliers were forced to change their mode of operation. To remain in business, many attempted to increase food and beverage revenue to counteract the decline in room revenue. This strategy worked in some instances, though many independent properties have closed.

The largest first-class independent hotels counterattacked the chains. Jealous of their independence and rightfully proud of their reputation for fine service, they sought various means to gain certain advantages of chain operation without sacrificing autonomy. The Distinguished Hotels group exemplified this attitude. (Today, the industry has Preferred Hotels, an expansion and refinement of the original concept.) The Robert Warner Agency persuaded several famous independent hotels to pool their resources for advertising, promotion, and reservation services.

Working as a group, the hotels were able to match the efficiency of chain operation in these three areas, but they were careful to point out that they were not a chain.

What will happen to the chains in the future? They are likely to expand and to represent an even larger percentage of the hotel room inventory. Not too many years ago, one could point to The Essex House in New York, The Brown Palace in Denver, and The Mark Hopkins and The Fairmont in San Francisco as examples of top-quality independent hotels. Today, however, each of them is a member of a chain operation. The independent fan can still point to a group of real stars—St. Louis's Chase-Park Plaza; The Cloister on Sea Island, Georgia; Grand Hotel on Mackinac Island, Michigan; the Alameda Plaza in Kansas City, Missouri; and the Boston Park Plaza, which, with its 977 rooms, is the largest independently owned and operated hotel in the United States. Around the world, the independent fan can still point with pride to the Vier Jahreszeiten (Four Seasons), Hamburg, Germany; the Ritz in Paris; Claridge's in London; the Dolder of Zurich; the Imperial, Vienna; Raffles Hotel, Singapore; the Hassler in Rome; the Ritz, Madrid; the Bayerischer Hof in Munich; Grand Hotel, Stockholm; the D'Angleterre, Copenhagen; and the Imperial, Tokyo. (This listing is simply representative of the independent hotels of the world; there are many hotels of equal stature around the world.)

Lodging Industry Developments in the 1960s

Referral Organizations

As lodging chains grew, independent operators found themselves in a tough competitive position. Generally, brand names and symbols have attracted American travelers. The chains, of course, had ready-made brand names and symbols that they promoted with great success. A chain operation was easily recognized by its facilities, the rather standardized architectural patterns, sometimes the color and decor, or possibly the road sign or the symbols used in its advertising. Chain properties could and did refer business to one another. They had advance registration and guaranteed reservation plans. In many cases, they enjoyed nationwide advertising and sales promotion campaigns.

In order to service the independent operator, a number of referral organizations grew up in the United States. Several achieved great growth and success. **Referral associations**, which are organized on a non-profit basis, are owned and controlled by the members. Through these organizations (similar to the Distinguished Hotels concept discussed earlier), the independent operator could obtain sales promotion benefits similar to those enjoyed by a chain operation without sacrificing individual control of his or her business. In addition, by belonging to a well-known referral organization, an independent had the brand-name image that could help marketing efforts.

Several of the largest referral associations in the United States were Quality Courts, Best Western, Best Eastern, and Master Hosts. Most of these have now evolved into full-service membership associations that are barely distinguishable from franchise companies.

Today there is a wide spectrum of marketing associations designed to publicize hotels regionally and globally. Both independent hotels and national chains

Exhibit 9   World's Largest Voluntary Associations

Voluntary Association	Headquarters
1. Utell International	England
2. Anasazi Travel Resources	United States
3. Lexington Services Corporation	United States
4. JAL World Hotels	Japan
5. VIP International Corporation	Canada
6. Supranational Hotels	England
7. Keytel	Spain
8. Leading Hotels of the World	United States
9. Hotusa-Eurostars-Familia Hotels	Spain
10. Logis de France	France
11. SRS Hotels Steigenberger	Germany
12. Golden Tulip Worldwide Hotels	Holland
13. Sceptre Hospitality Resources	United States
14. Associated Luxury Hotels	United States
15. Minotel International	Switzerland
16. Top International Hotels	Germany
17. Flag International Hotels	Australia
18. Prima Hotels	United States
19. Robert F. Warner, Inc.	United States
20. Preferred Hotels Worldwide	United States
21. Historic Hotels of America	United States
22. Summit International Hotels	England
23. Ila Chateaux et Hotels de Charme	Belgium
24. Concorde Hotels Group	France
25. Relais et Chateaux	France

Source: *Hotels*, July 1997, p. 72.

join these marketing groups to expand the reach of their name or niche. These organizations are usually classified as voluntary chains/associations.

The 25 largest organizations in this category are shown in Exhibit 9. Today, they represent over 2,000,000 hotel rooms in 17,000 hotels around the world.

Utell, based in London, has some 6,800 member hotels, both chains and independents in 137 countries. The organization has 37 reservation offices and interacts with 75 major airlines.

Supranational has 565 members, many of them chain properties, in 51 countries. Logis de France members are one-, two-, and three-star hotels in France only. Leading Hotels of the World has five-star deluxe hotel members in 60 countries. Deluxe chain members include Okura, Taj, Oberoi, and Regent.

As global competition heats up, the prognosis for voluntary chains/associations is for continued growth.

American Resorts

While hoteliers have always concentrated their heaviest efforts on accommodations for the traveling public, they do not neglect the vacation-minded American. Although there were resorts in colonial America, the real development of the American resort hotel came with the expansion of the railways. The luxury resort developed in the South after the Civil War; The Greenbrier at White Sulphur Springs, West Virginia, and The Homestead at Hot Springs, Virginia, were among the earliest. In this period, the many spas and mineral springs across the country attracted thousands of people every year, so it was only natural that large resort hotels should locate in areas where these were most common—for example, Saratoga, New York, and Warm Springs, Georgia. As transportation systems improved, hotels were opened along the seashore and in the mountains.

Traditionally, the resort hotel was a summer operation, and, in addition to providing comfortable rooms and excellent cuisine, it offered a location with scenic, historical, recreational, or therapeutic advantages. The winter resort—generally a hotel located in an equable year-round climate—did not catch the public's fancy until the beginning of the twentieth century. By then, the automobile was becoming a practical means of travel, and it made balmy areas of the country, where the climate was ideal for wintertime vacationing, more accessible. For example, golf had become a popular American pastime, and the enticement of year-round golf attracted even more people to winter resorts.

Today, it is difficult to classify resorts definitively because of the tremendous variations existing among them. Generally speaking, though, resorts fall into four categories: summer resort, year-round resort, cold winter resort, and warm winter resort.

Summer Resorts

The summer resort opens in late May and operates through Labor Day or, sometimes, early October. The traditional social season is July Fourth to Labor Day. The northeastern section of the United States is probably the largest summer resort area in the country. New England's resorts feature the seashore and mountains. New York is famous for its Adirondack and Catskill Mountain areas. Pennsylvania features the Pocono Mountains. The Atlantic coast from northern New Jersey to North Carolina is dotted with resorts and blessed with many beautiful sandy beaches. Besides the eastern area, Minnesota, Wisconsin, Michigan, Arkansas, and parts of the Rocky Mountains also feature summer resorts.

The resort business in general is very volatile and financially risky, with perhaps the most hazardous of all being summer resort operation. The season is short (usually 10 to 12 weeks) and the operator is at the mercy of the elements. A week of

Spring House, original site of the "healing waters" that first brought fame to The Greenbrier, White Sulphur Springs, West Virginia. (Photo courtesy of The Greenbrier)

rain, cool weather, the threat of a hurricane—any of these factors will start a mass exodus from the resorts. Should this happen during a week in which the resort has a full house, it could easily change a profit into a loss for the year.

In the last few decades, there have been many factors working against summer resorts, often forcing them to close. In the first place, many of the buildings were old, and the accommodations were obsolete in the modern market. Rooms without baths, for example, are rather difficult to sell in today's market. The clientele remained static—the same people were coming back each year—and therefore it got older and smaller. Other things happened, too. The whole concept of a good vacation changed. The winter vacation was becoming ever more popular, and this reduced the amount of summer vacation time. The habits, tastes, and interests of the traveling public were changing rapidly and radically. The American family no longer stayed in one spot for its vacation. Packing the family into a station wagon and roaming over a wide area was much in vogue. These one-night guests slept more often in a motel than in a resort hotel. The formality and tradition of the old-time resort lost much of its appeal.

To make matters even worse, the jet age arrived, putting every American resort in direct competition with Europe and other glamorous areas of the world,

Grand Hotel on Michigan's Mackinac Island—an early summer resort that is still world-famous today. (Photo courtesy of Grand Hotel)

and the southern winter resorts became year-round operations, siphoning off more customers. Still another segment of the public discovered camping. Thus summer resort operators faced the greatest challenge of their careers, and not everyone was able to meet it.

Still, one should not reach the conclusion that all summer resorts are doomed. A number are thriving. To their credit, many owners and operators are battling to stay in business and to meet the demands of the new market.

Year-Round Resorts

For many years, the majority of resort hotels operated seasonally, either in summer or winter. However, year-round resorts began to enjoy success and profit through the 1950s and 1960s. They, too, found their markets changing but somehow managed to stay in step with the times. Most important, they were building a new young clientele to replace the ever-dwindling old-time population.

Today, the trend throughout the entire resort segment is to operate year-round. Many resorts find that the expense of remaining open during the off-season is lower than the cost of closing down, maintaining the property, reopening, and, often, recruiting many new staff members.

Among American year-round resorts, Las Vegas, Nevada, has to be the star of the show. Its growth has been phenomenal. In the early 1990s, when most of the industry was in the doldrums, Las Vegas continued to grow, and is even today growing at a rapid pace. As one consultant put it, "The law of supply and demand simply doesn't work in Las Vegas. You build more hotel rooms and occupancies go up instead of down. It is not predictable."[3] In the past few years, the city has given birth to the Mirage Hotel (3,000 rooms), the Excalibur Hotel (4,032 rooms), the MGM Grand Hotel (5,000 rooms), the Victoria Bay (3,000 rooms), the New York, New York Hotel (2,190 rooms), and the Paris Casino Resort (2,500 rooms), and has others on the drawing board. In 1990, Las Vegas had 73,750 hotel rooms, second only to Orlando, Florida. Today Las Vegas has 103,877 rooms; it enjoys the distinction of being the American city with the largest number of hotel rooms. Although it owes much of its success to gambling, Las Vegas today advertises itself as a "family resort" and lives up to the advertising.

Orlando, Florida, shares star billing with Las Vegas. In 1970, Orlando was a quiet, sleepy city in central Florida with no special claim to fame. Then in the early 1970s came Walt Disney World, and Orlando became a famous year-round resort almost overnight. In addition, SeaWorld, Cypress Gardens, Universal Studios, and a gentle year-round climate all fueled Orlando's growth. Hotels multiplied and multiplied until 1990, when Orlando with its 76,300 hotel rooms displaced New York City as the American city with the most hotel rooms. Although now outranked by Las Vegas, Orlando's number of hotel rooms continues to increase at a rapid pace.

Cold Winter Resorts

As late as the mid-1950s, many hoteliers thought the mania for skiing was limited and had little to offer a resort operator. In those days, the ski enthusiast had little money and was interested primarily in reasonable accommodations, no matter how crowded they might be. Many a wise old financial expert cautioned hoteliers not to invest in ski lodges. There was even a saying, "Unfortunately, bankers don't ski." A few pioneers went right ahead anyway and soon found themselves in possession of a gold mine. The ski craze grew and grew. People with plenty of money took up the sport, and the cold winter resort had a genuine boom on its hands. New ski slopes were building hotels, and older hotels were developing ski slopes. As is true with many sports, just as many people came to watch and to be seen as came to ski. They all needed hospitality services and, to complete the resort operator's joy, they had money to spend and did not seem to be very price conscious.

Warm Winter Resorts

The greatest growth of all came in the warm winter resort area. The lure of the hot sun, golden beaches, and night life is overpowering when someone peers out a window in sub-zero temperatures to see snow driven by gale force winds piling up in the driveway. No wonder the winter vacation grows in popularity each year.

The growth of Miami Beach is one of the success stories of the postwar period. But even Florida can sometimes be cold and cloudy. The winter vacationer wants the sun guaranteed, which it virtually is just a little south of Florida. The hotel growth and development in the Caribbean nearly defies description. Madison Avenue's most flamboyant adjectives are not sufficient. Jamaica, Barbados, Puerto Rico, the Virgin Islands, Nassau, and Trinidad are tropical paradises featuring (in some cases) the world's most modern hotels just a few hours from any metropolitan center in the United States. (A brief account of Caribbean hotel history follows the resort sections.)

Winter is the big season—one need only look at the rates to be convinced—but more and more, the islands are attracting summer business as well. As in Florida, the summer patrons are entirely different socially and economically from the winter patrons. But what the former group may lack in money, it more than makes up for in volume. Not only has jet travel made the trip convenient and reasonable, but the airlines are continually promoting vacations in the sun.

The greatest resort story of the postwar period has to be the development of Hawaii. Blessed with an ideal year-round climate, Hawaii has a 12-month season. Every major U.S. chain has at least one hotel in Hawaii, and several have two or more. Like the Caribbean, Hawaii is deeply indebted to jet travel for much of its popularity and success.

Other Developments

Two other developments have played a major role in the resort business of the recent decades. One is a replay on an old theme, and the other exploits a new one.

As stated earlier, many of the early resorts grew up around natural spas, and health restoration was a primary motive of many of the guests. However, in the postwar years, spas became less and less attractive. A few of the old-timers continued to return each year, but occupancy at spa resorts dwindled. Then, in the early 1960s, the American public suddenly became health-conscious once again. A new emphasis on physical fitness was generated by publicity concerning the number of young people rejected by the draft as physically unfit. Medical discoveries about cholesterol contributed to Americans' increasing diet-consciousness. To a few enterprising hoteliers, these factors pointed out a new opportunity. Health resorts were opened which offered all the usual resort services but also featured special meals, exercise programs under expert guidance, and a small medical staff to provide the guest with a vacation that would increase his or her physical well-being.

In the second development, seasonal resorts—faced with declining occupancy, increased costs of operation, and profits turning to losses—desperately sought sources of new business to augment the income from the regular social season. Attempts to lengthen the social season by opening earlier or closing later met with little success. For one thing, the weather was not good; but more important, the guests would not change their vacation habits. Unable to extend the social season, the resorts sought other business that might occupy these early and late season periods.

Fortunately, resorts discovered conventions, and, for a great many of them, these have been the key to salvation. In many respects, a resort is an ideal location for a convention—especially a working convention. More and more, the emphasis is on serious work, discussion, and education; the good-time social factor is soft-pedaled. The resort offers recreation and relaxation, but is removed from the bright lights and distractions of metropolitan areas. As a result, the number of conventions held at resorts increases each year.

While convention business has been a bonanza to many resorts, it does create some problems. Social guests do not appreciate convention groups, and there are times when the convention season overlaps the social season. If a social guest complains, it may help to point out diplomatically that without the convention business

Las Brisas Hotel, Acapulco, Mexico—a famed year-round resort. (Photo courtesy of Las Brisas)

there would be no resort—and thus no social season to enjoy. If resorts had not discovered and attracted conventions, many a famous vacation spot today would be only a fond memory.

It is clear that the resort atmosphere is more and more sought after by every segment of the lodging market. Even the roadside motel is trying to provide at least a little of the resort flavor. Tennis courts, saunas, heated pools, and even Holiday Inns' Solar Domes are being added to properties that not so long ago would never have thought about promoting a resort atmosphere. Today, resorts are prospering and inspiring other properties to create a touch of resort image and flavor.

International Resorts

The development of long-distance wide-body aircraft in 1968 and the increasing efforts of national air carriers to promote inbound tourism have greatly opened up all areas of the world to vacationing travelers. In response to these phenomena, a number of world-class resorts have opened in recent years.

These resorts appeal to diverse interests of international travelers. Resorts in mountainous regions from the Alps to the Andes and from the Rockies to the Japanese highlands now cater to ski enthusiasts. The powerful lure of remote tropical islands has given rise to luxury resorts on many of the beautiful islands that dot the Pacific and Indian Oceans, in addition to the longer established resorts of the Caribbean and Mediterranean Seas. Companies, most notably Club Méditerranée, have sprung into existence with hedonistic resort villages primarily in remote locales all over the world. These resorts offer guests a seemingly endless variety of recreational and entertainment diversions.

In classifying or categorizing international resorts, one would use the same categories as when categorizing American resorts; that is, summer, year-round, cold winter, and warm winter.

As the economies of the Asian nations continue to grow, the citizens of these countries show an increasing desire to travel overseas. Resort and tour destination operators are catering more and more to these new origin markets which would appear to project a rapid expansion of facilities. Most travel experts agree that the trend toward more international resorts will accelerate rapidly in the first decade of the twenty-first century.

No attempt will be made here to rank or identify the top group of resorts around the world. However, it appears desirable to name a few hotels that are famous and representative of quality international resorts: The Palace Hotel in Gstaad, Switzerland, and the Palace Hotel in St. Moritz, Switzerland, rank among the world's most famous winter resorts. Representative of the year-round category are Las Brisas, Acapulco, Mexico; Hotel Bora-Bora, Tahiti; and Las Hadas, Manazillo, Mexico. Among the world's summer resorts, Hotel du Cap-Eden, Antibes, France; Hotel Puente Romano, Marbella, Spain; Grand Hotel du Cap Ferrat, France; and Fujiya Hotel, Hakone, Japan, all enjoy worldwide fame.

The Early History of Caribbean Hotels

The Caribbean tourism and hotel industries have developed greatly during the past 50 years, but their roots are buried deep in the sands of the Caribbean islands' beaches. The history of travel to the Caribbean dates back to the 1600s, when Europeans colonized the islands. During this period, it was not uncommon for wealthy English, Spanish, French, Dutch, and Danish citizens to make social visits to family members, friends, and business associates living on the various Caribbean islands. Although most of these travelers would not have characterized their visits as vacations in our sense of the word, their primary purpose was recreation. Since no commercial lodging establishments existed on the island colonies, these guests were generally accommodated in their host's main house or guest houses.

During the late nineteenth and early twentieth centuries, adventure tourism created a demand for a Caribbean lodging industry. The first adventure tourists, most of whom were Europeans, were willing to travel in relative discomfort, to destinations about which little was known, and at a pace dictated as much by weather and shipping line schedules as by personal choice. Therefore, their lodging needs were unsophisticated by today's standards. In response to this adventure tourism trend, small commercial lodging establishments on many of the more economically developed islands grew into literal cottage industries.

With the rapid advances in aircraft technology after World War II, the potential for growth in Caribbean tourism and hotel development was never greater than in the late 1940s. A milestone that best symbolized this potential was Pan American Airways' inaugural flight from Key West, Florida, to Havana, Cuba.

Although Cuba was popular with the U.S. market as far back as the 1920s and had been growing since that time, the maiden voyage of the Pan Am Clipper marked a new era of tourism growth and hotel development in the region.

By the late 1940s, the Caribbean tourism industry manifested several elements of fundamental change—internationally competitive hotel operators, the United States' emergence as the dominant feeder market, unique tourism travel patterns, new methods of transportation, and new recreation and accommodation needs on the part of the vacationing public. In 1949 Puerto Rico's Caribe Hilton became the first international chain hotel to open in the Caribbean; this marked the opening shot in the international hotel chains' battle for Caribbean resort market share. Given the availability of regularly scheduled air service between Key West and Havana, this trend was, perhaps, nowhere more pronounced than in the Cuban market where seasonal visits by leisure-class adventurers gave way to the getaway trips of the chic gambling crowd from the eastern seaboard of the United States.

Two significant events affected Caribbean hotel development in the 1950s. First, the overthrow of the Batista government by Fidel Castro's Communist revolutionaries on January 1, 1959, led to the closure of Cuba as an important resort destination. Puerto Rico, the Bahamas, and the U.S. Virgin Islands gleefully geared up to accommodate tourists no longer free to travel to Cuba. Second, the opening of Laurance S. Rockefeller's Dorado Beach Hotel in Puerto Rico in the early 1950s started the trend toward intimate luxury resorts in the Caribbean.

Endnotes

1. Paul Handlery, *Arizona Hospitality Trends*, School of Hotel and Restaurant Management, Northern Arizona University, Spring 1992, p. 3.

2. Gary Saunders, personal conversation, AH&MA conference, late 1996.

3. Michael French, of Coopers & Lybrand, in an interview appearing in *Hotel Business*, April 1997.

Key Terms

chain—Properties that are affiliated with others. A chain property may be (1) owned by a parent company, (2) a franchise operation, or (3) operated by a management contract company. A franchise and a chain operation are *not* the same; while a franchise property is part of a chain, a chain property is not necessarily a franchise.

commercial travel—Travel for business purposes, not for pleasure.

funicular—A cable railway that carried pleasure travelers to remote vacation hotels, such as the Alpine resorts.

grand tour—An extended trip across the European continent that served as part of the education of young British aristocrats; its popularity peaked in the eighteenth century.

hostelry—A lodging operation.

independent—A word referring to an operator who owns one or more properties that have no chain relationship. Contrast with *chain*.

market segmentation—The consideration of sources of business differently according to their purposes and needs. For example, in the lodging industry, business can be divided according to the guests' purposes for visiting: attending conventions, conducting company business, or traveling for pleasure. Hotels can be segmented or grouped according to their level of services also—for example, full-service, limited-service, or all-suite hotels.

referral associations—Associations that provide service to independent hotel owners. They are organized on a non-profit basis and are owned and controlled by the members. Through these organizations, the independent operator can obtain sales promotion benefits similar to those enjoyed by a chain operation without sacrificing individual control of his or her business.

spa—A mineral spring, or a locality or resort hotel near such a spring, to which people resorted for cures (from Spa, a watering place in Eastern Belgium). Today, the word *spa* is used more loosely to refer to any fashionable resort locality or hotel.

Review Questions

1. What types of people took the grand tour?
2. What factors brought about the establishment of early hotel training schools?
3. What types of hotels were produced by the first move toward market segmentation, and what were their distinguishing characteristics?
4. What characteristics defined the Tremont as the first first-class hotel?
5. Why was the Statler Hotel in Buffalo considered an "invention"?
6. What factors influenced the development of motels in the 1950s?
7. What is the primary difference between motels and hotels?
8. How, throughout history, has the hotel industry been affected by the principal mode of transportation of the time?
9. What is the primary difference between chain and independent lodging operations? How have independent operations been affected by the growth of chains?
10. How have referral organizations changed since they were originally formed?
11. What are the four types of resorts and what advantages or disadvantages are associated with each type?
12. What role has convention business played in the recent history of resorts?

Internet Sites

For more information, visit the following Internet sites. Remember that Internet addresses can change without notice. If the site is no longer there, use a search engine to look for additional sites.

Lodging Associations

American Hotel & Motel Association (AH&MA)
http://www.ahma.com

Council on Hotel, Restaurant and Institutional Education (CHRIE)
http://www.chrie.org

The Educational Institute of AH&MA
http://www.ei-ahma.org

Hospitality Financial and Technology Professionals
http://www.hftp.org

Hospitality Sales and Marketing Association International (HSMAI)
http://www.hsmai.org

International Hotel & Restaurant Association
http://www.ih-ra.com

Lodging Publications—Online and Printed

Hospitality Technology News
http://www.hospitalitynet.nl/news/tech.html

Lodging Online
http://www.ei-ahma.org/webs/lodging/index.html

Lodging Hospitality
http://www.penton.com/corp/mags/lh.html

Lodging Companies

Best Western
http://www.bestwestern.com

Choice Hotels International
http://www.hotelchoice.com

Hilton Hotels
http://www.hilton.com

Inter-Continential Hotels
http://www.interconti.com

Opryland Hotel
http://www.opryhotel.com

Ritz Carlton Hotels
http://www.ritzcarlton.com

Walt Disney World Resorts
http://www.disneyworld.com/vacation

Travel and Lodging Search Sites

Business Travel Net
http://www.business-travel-net.com

BizTravel.com—The Internet Company for the Frequent Business Traveler
http://www.biztravel.com

Hotels and Travel on the Net
http://www.hotelstravel.com

HotelsOnline
http://www.HotelsOnline.NET

Internet Travel Network
http://www.itn.net

Meetings Industry Mall
http://www.mim.com

Resorts Online
http://www.resortsonline.com

Travelocity, The SABRE Group, Inc.
http://www.travelocity.com

TravelWeb
http://www.travelweb.com

Chapter 4 Outline

Franchising
Lodging Industry Developments in the 1970s
     Management Contracts
     The Condominium Concept
     Time-Sharing
Lodging in the Volatile 1980s
     Market Segmentation
     Amenities
     Technology
     Gaming and the Hospitality Industry*
     Industry Growth and the Economy
     Consolidation
     Real Estate Investment Trusts
     Conversion
Globalization
A View of the Lodging Industry Around the World
     Europe
     Hawaii**
     Asia and the Pacific Rim
     Mexico: Past and Present***
     The Caribbean
     Central and South America

---

*Portions of this section were contributed by Mr. Michael French, Director, Cooper & Lybrand's Hospitality Industry Consulting Services Group.

**Much of this section was contributed by Ronald K. Watanabe, Director of Management Consulting Services, Coopers & Lybrand, Honolulu, Hawaii.

***The majority of this section was contributed by Mr. Rodolfo Casparius, CHE, Nation's President Emeritus of the Mexican Hotel and Motel Association.

4

The Globalization
of the Lodging Industry

THIS CHAPTER EXAMINES MAJOR ELEMENTS of modern lodging from the 1960s to the present, and traces the beginnings of globalization. The chapter begins with a discussion of franchising, then moves on to 1970s industry developments, including management contracts, the condominium concept, and time-sharing. The chapter then looks at the 1980s, when marketing became especially important because of intense industry competition. 1980s buzzwords included market segmentation, consolidation, real estate investment trusts, conversion, and gaming. Amenities and technological advancements became especially important tools in the 1980s. The chapter closes with a discussion of the lodging industry in various locations around the world, including Europe, Hawaii, Asia and the Pacific Rim, Mexico, the Caribbean, and Central and South America.

Franchising

Starting about 1950, hotel operating companies settled on growth and market penetration as their primary goals. In 1950 there were only three major chains—Hilton, Sheraton, and Statler—whose properties totaled 38,600 rooms, or about 2 percent of the total number of hotel rooms available. Changes occurred rapidly in the 1950s. Hilton acquired Statler, which reduced "the big three" to "the big two." However, Hilton and Sheraton were soon joined by Holiday Inns, Howard Johnson, Ramada, and others, each with the same goal—to increase growth and market penetration nationwide. One way to achieve this goal was to add to the number of company-owned properties by leasing properties from other sources. This kind of renting was quite widespread in the 1950s. Other hotels merged with non-hotel companies having a broader financial base in order to make rapid growth easier. For example, Sheraton merged with ITT, Western International (now Westin) with United Airlines, and Dunfey with Aer Lingus. Most chains, including the three just mentioned, sought to improve their growth by increasing earnings per share. To accomplish this, hotels had to keep their ownership in any new real estate ventures to a minimum, and they did this usually through franchising. The choice of franchising proved to be an excellent one for gaining market penetration, as seen by the figures in Exhibit 1. In fact, the 1960s are often referred to as "the golden age of franchising" in the lodging industry.

Franchising works this way: A development company or individual developer finances and builds a hotel and, rather than operating it as an independent,

Exhibit 1   Chain Operating Companies' Market Penetration

Year	Rooms	Revenue
1963	19%	25%
1970	33%	41%
1975	48%	68%
1986	60%	80%
2000 (estimated)	90%	98%

Source: James J. Eyster, *The Negotiation and Administration of Hotel Management Contracts,* 2d ed. (Ithaca, N.Y.: Cornell University, 1980), p. 101; and AH&MA estimates and statistics.

enters into a **franchise** agreement with a hotel company. The great majority of developers choose the franchise option because of the tremendous advantages it offers. Under the terms of the agreement, the franchisee (developer) pays fees to use the franchisor's (hotel company's) name and agrees to follow the franchisor's business pattern and maintain its standards at the property. In return, the franchisee receives the substantial benefits of chain affiliation, which include:

- The image and reputation of the franchisor

- The chain reservation system

- More easily obtainable financing

- The sales and marketing expertise of the franchisor

- Technical assistance in purchasing, interior design, and architectural planning

- Pre-opening training of staff

Generally, there are four types of fees charged to a franchisee: an initial franchise fee, a royalty fee, an advertising/marketing fee, and a reservation fee. Most of the chains charge an initial fee of $25,000 to $35,000, although the initial fee for some of the new all-suite franchises ranges from $50,000 to $100,000. The other three fees are usually a percentage of room sales.

It is true that franchising might pose risks to a franchisor's name and reputation. After all, the franchisor cannot exercise the same level of control over the operation of its franchises that it does over its own properties. But these risks are offset by a number of benefits. First, as noted earlier, franchises provide an inexpensive way for hotel companies to grow because the developer builds the hotel with his or her own money and is responsible for operation costs as well. Second, franchisors can use franchise properties as booking agents for company-owned hotels. And third, a large hotel company's name is worth money, and franchisees will pay to be affiliated with a reputable company.

It would be difficult to overestimate the tremendous influence of franchising on the lodging industry. Excluding properties under 25 rooms and strictly seasonal inns, 75 percent of all U.S. hotel and motel operations today are franchised. In spite of overbuilding, unfavorable tax law changes, and a slow recovery from a major recession, lodging franchises have grown at a rate of about 8 percent per year in the 1990s. Experts in the field foresee a continuation of this rate to the turn of the century with the greatest growth in the limited service and all-suite segments.

In the mid 1990s, four chains reversed long-standing policies and entered the franchising field. They are Westin, Hyatt, Wyndham, and Motel 6.

International franchisors, even today, are few in number. In fact, Forte Hotels is the only major non-U.S. franchisor of hotels. European reservation and referral systems were quicker to attain international status than were any franchisors. Today, some operators, such as Swiss-based Mövenpick, use a combination formula of franchising, management, and ownership. The French group, Novotel, comes closer to a pure franchising system. Its budget hotels are built and operated by local contractors in accordance with Novotel guidelines under the Novotel concept of a low room rate and minimum food and beverage service. The great majority of international hotel groups have sought to make their mark as reservation-referral systems, management organizations, or a combination of the two. On the whole, international franchising has not gained a worldwide foothold comparable to the U.S. systems.

Lodging Industry Developments in the 1970s

Management Contracts

Obviously, franchising succeeded in getting market penetration for the chains. There was, however, a serious problem that arose with increased franchising: the chain lost much of its ability to regulate both quality and service standards in the franchised operations.

In part to deal with this problem, chain executives developed a new strategy about 1970. Essentially, the strategy was to change from real estate companies to operating companies. Thus, the chains began to minimize ownership in additional real estate ventures and, at the same time, to divest themselves of existing real estate holdings. When the chains sold their properties, they negotiated a **management contract** with the new owners. If the 1960s were the age of franchising, the 1970s and 1980s ushered in the age of the management contract.

Management contract companies are organizations that are hired by a property's owners to manage the hotel for those owners. A chain's use of a management contract achieves many of the same goals achieved by franchising. However, there are some real differences. With a management contract, the chain has complete control over the standards and quality of each property and is responsible for day-to-day operations; franchising does not provide this control. Of course, with franchising the chain does not need a large professional operating staff; with a management contract, it does.

Management contracts are now the principal means by which chain operators expand and gain market penetration. Until the late 1980s, most management contracts strongly favored the operating company. The management contract permitted the chain to increase the number of properties it managed with little or no investment. The negative cash flow usually associated with the first few years of operation was funded by the owner, not the operator. The operator also avoided or at least reduced the hazards of changing markets, overbuilding, recession, and cost overruns. From a strictly financial viewpoint, the management contract permits the chain to improve its earnings per share, a very important statistic for publicly held companies.

A management contract gives full and complete control of the hotel to the operator who is paid a fee for managing the property. The average fee today is 2.9 percent with a range of 1 to 6 percent. Many contracts also contain an incentive fee. In past years, this fee was computed as a percentage of gross operating profit, but today incentive fees are computed as a percentage of net operating income, cash flow, or a specified return on investment. Until recent years, management contracts definitely favored the operator. Today the pendulum has swung to favor the owner.

Competition among management companies to obtain contracts is exceptionally keen and has brought about the changes that shifted considerable risk from the owner to the operator. Operator equity contributions are now the rule, not the exception. These contributions may take the form of working capital, pre-opening expenses, FF&E (furniture, fixtures, and equipment), and even partnership. Most recent contracts also contain an operator performance clause.

In the early 1980s, management contracts averaged 20–25 years in length with renewable options. Between 1985 and 1995, contracts for full-service hotels averaged ten years, while those for limited service averaged six years. Today, contracts are even shorter in length, averaging seven years for full-service and three years for limited-service properties.

Most of the earlier contracts contained cancellation clauses requiring severe penalties if the management contract were canceled. Even today management contracts have cancellation clauses containing penalties, but now also permit cancellation without liquidated damages if the operator fails to achieve the budgeted net operating income.

Not all the management contract activity occurs in major hotel chains. Today, in the United States alone, there are 1,000 companies offering hotel management services. These companies manage independent properties as well as properties affiliated with national chains (franchises). During a recession in the early 1970s, a large number of lenders foreclosed on lodging properties. The lenders needed someone to manage the properties until they could be sold. Independent operating companies were formed to meet this need, thus causing significant growth in the number of independent operating companies.

The world's top ten management companies—in sales, rooms, and properties—are listed in Exhibits 2, 3, and 4, respectively.

Independent management companies are not all organized alike. Some of them are limited to management, others have both ownership and management responsibilities, and a few have even other types of arrangements.

In the major hotel chain category, Hilton, closely followed by Hyatt, pioneered the divestiture of real estate holdings while retaining a management contract. They have since been joined by Westin, Marriott, Accor, Sheraton, Inter-Continental, Canadian Pacific, Radisson, Hilton International, and others.

Exhibit 2   Top Ten Management Companies—Sales

Company	Sales
Interstate Hotels Corporation	$1.3 billion
Carnival Hotels and Resorts	$900 million
Tishman Hotel Corporation	$470 million
Richfield Hospitality Services, Inc.	$424 million
Prime Hospitality	$332 million
Ocean Hospitalities	$305 million
American General Hospitality	$300 million
Winegardner & Hammons	$265 million
Servico	$235 million
CapStar Hotels	$230 million

Source: *Hotel & Motel Management*, March 3, 1997, p. 30.

Exhibit 3   Top Ten Management Companies—Rooms

Company	Number of Rooms
Interstate Hotels Corporation	43,178
Carnival Hotels and Resorts	18,275
Richfield Hospitality Services, Inc.	16,000
Prime Hospitality	15,333
American General Hospitality	12,081
Servico	11,835
Westmont Hospitality Group	11,590
Remington Hotel Corporation	11,400
CapStar Hotels	11,000
Winegardner & Hammons	10,697

Source: *Hotel & Motel Management*, March 3, 1997, p. 30.

Some of these chains both franchise and utilize management contracts, while others engage only in management contracts.

The Condominium Concept

In the hotel industry, as in other business areas, new concepts and new ideas traditionally have been created and developed in this country and then copied by

Exhibit 4   Top Ten Management Companies—Properties

Company	Number of Properties
Interstate Hotels Corporation	212
Journey's End Corporation	108
Prime Hospitality	108
Carnival Hotels and Resorts	78
Amerihost Properties	73
Remington Hotel Corporation	68
Richfield Hospitality Services, Inc.	67
American General Hospitality	66
Beck Summit Management Group	63
Westmont Hospitality Group	62

Source: *Hotel & Motel Management*, March 3, 1997, p. 30.

entrepreneurs abroad a few years later. The condominium concept reverses the usual order of events. Eurotel began developing condominiums back in 1957. **Condominiums** are units of properties sold to individual owners; there are many types. Internationally, the Sol-Melia organization operates apartotels in Spain and Acapulco; Multi-Hotel offers its individual owners time in any of its complexes throughout France, Switzerland, and Germany; and Trans Realty Inc., of Geneva, operates a total of 1,100 rooms in Portugal as well as three hotel properties in Miami Beach. All of these operations are based on the condominium concept.

In the United States, the condominium has enjoyed its greatest growth in Florida, where hundreds of thousands of condominium units have been built and sold. The owners of these condominium apartments tend to be drawn, to a large extent, from the ranks of the traditional hotel-going public. Thus the condominium has become a strong competitor of and threat to the hotel business. Much as it did in the 1950s, when it faced competition from motels and motor hotels, the hotel industry is following the old slogan, "If you can't beat them, join them." Now, faced with this new competition, resort and hotel developers are turning to the condominium concept or a modification of it. The result is a growing number of condominium hotels and condominium resorts.

The condominium in its purest form is found at Sea Pines Plantation, Hilton Head, South Carolina. The site is a landscaped woodland with houses or villas hidden among the trees and sand dunes and offers a complete recreational complex of golf courses, tennis courts, and marinas. Many of the villas are owned and occupied by affluent permanent residents, but a great number are owned by investors who spend only two or three weeks a year at Hilton Head and hope to rent the villas to vacationers during the remainder of the year. The Sea Pines Company's marketing department strives to keep each villa rented at least 40 percent of the year. For this service, Sea Pines collects 20 percent of weekly and monthly rentals and 40 percent of daily rentals. The remaining rental income goes to the investor-owner of the condominium villa. Obviously, the owners hope these charges will cover their mortgage and maintenance costs and provide a tax shelter as well. Hawaii also features a large number of resort rental condominiums among its tourist accommodations. For example, 50 percent of the accommodations on Maui are rental condominiums.

Another rapidly developing trend is the creation of the condominium as a first-class hotel operation. Golf Hosts International is a pioneer in this concept. Innisbrook at Tarpon Springs, Florida, and Tamarron in the Colorado Rockies were its first two operations. Each hotel unit is owned by an individual and placed in a rental pool for use by hotel guests. In addition to all the normal hotel niceties, the complex features complete recreation and health club facilities and a fully equipped conference center to handle any type of business meeting. Management receives 51 percent of the room rentals, while the owner gets 49 percent. Taxes, maintenance, and unit utilities are paid by the owner.

A variation on the condominium theme arises when a hotel company owns an operating hotel and decides to sell the guestrooms and suites to individuals with the provision that the owners place their condominiums in the rental pool. The hotel company continues to operate the hotel as before, but, by selling the rooms and suites, it has recovered its original investment and, very probably, earned a handsome profit. The Marriott Camelback Resort in Arizona is an example of this practice. After purchasing the property from the Stewart family, Marriott operated Camelback for a few years and then sold the guestrooms and suites as condominiums. Today, all the guestrooms and suites are owned by individuals, but are also in the rental pool. When Marriott owned the Essex House in New York City, it sold a number of that hotel's suites as condominiums. A similar example in New York City is the Hotel Pierre, where a portion of the hotel is operated as a cooperative, a kind of ownership similar to condominiums.

Time-Sharing

Time-sharing is, in many ways, a modification of condominium ownership. A developer constructs or purchases a building containing several types of living units. Buyers then purchase periods of one or more weeks per year during which they may live in the unit. For example, John Doe may purchase Unit 301 for the first two weeks in July. Other individuals will purchase Unit 301 for the other 48 weeks of the year. (Most time-share operations work on a 50-week year, leaving two weeks for deep cleaning, maintenance, and refurbishing.) In most cases, each owner will pay pro-rated maintenance and tax fees each year.

Time-sharing is an important element in today's American resort hotel operations. Many resort hotels have been converted wholly to time-sharing, while others allocate a portion of their units to time-sharing. The concept makes good sense, since there are so many similarities between hotel management and time-share management. While some hoteliers have used time-sharing to sell off a single property, other companies view time-sharing as a way to grow.

Like condominium operations, time-share properties originated in Europe, but saw their biggest growth in the United States. Time-share properties began to be popular in the mid-1970s, when many condominium projects went bankrupt as a result of a real estate crash. Developers then used time-sharing to sell off the condominiums. Around the same time, time-sharing was introduced to hotels. However, the time-share industry developed a poor image due to hard-sell, sometimes unethical selling tactics used by a portion of the developers. Fortunately, with the entry of major corporations into the field, the industry has eliminated shady practices and now has a positive image.

Industry growth has been tremendous. In 1980, there were 155,000 owned intervals in 500 resorts. From 1980 to 1995, 4.9 million intervals sold for $36 billion. Since 1995, another 800,000 households have purchased 1.2 million intervals at a cost of $9 billion.

As time-sharing grew, it appeared more and more logical for a hotel company to consider entering the field. In the mid-1980s, Marriott Corporation did so with its Marriott Ownership Resorts, Inc., and is today the largest company in time-sharing. It wasn't long, however, before other hotel companies followed Marriott into the industry. The field today reads like a *Who's Who* of the hotel industry, with Hilton Hotels, Inter-Continental Hotels Corporation, the Disney Company, Ramada, Holiday Inn, Westin Hotels, Embassy Suites, Four Seasons, Sheraton, Outrigger Hotels, Hilton International, Hyatt Hotels, and Colony Hotels and Resorts all involved. At last count there were 4,145 time-share resorts in 75 countries worldwide.

Recently, time-sharing has moved into urban settings. Marriott opened 80 units in a high-rise building in the heart of Boston. The largest mid-town time-share property is the Manhattan Club in New York City. And the owner of the Park Central Hotel has devoted one-half of the hotel to time-share.

One of the major selling points for time-sharing is the possibility of exchanging one's time for a similar time in a different resort each year. Two major exchange organizations, Resort Condominiums International and Interval International, provide these exchanges for their members. They claim to make successful exchanges 85 percent of the time. (It is interesting to note that Hospitality Franchise Systems recently acquired Resort Condominiums International.)

Lodging in the Volatile 1980s

What began on a quiet, positive tone became one of the most volatile decades in the twentieth century. During this period, the nation experienced a real estate boom followed by a bust, a full-scale recession, a threat of terrorism, a full-scale war, and a period of hostage-taking. All of these factors had a significant effect on the hospitality industry. In fact, several of these factors had a global effect. Within the lodging industry, market segmentation, consolidation, conversion, and globalization became popular buzzwords.

Market Segmentation

During the 1960s, hoteliers began using marketing concepts to assess the wants and needs of the consumer and to go after segments whose interests were not being met. However, it was not until the 1970s and 1980s that marketing achieved genuine status as an important function in many hotel organizations. In the 1980s, it achieved star billing because of intense competition in the industry.

Until the 1980s, the industry was categorized basically into four types of properties, each with a rather general market. There were luxury hotels, commercial hotels, resort hotels, and motels/motor hotels. All that changed as competition became a permanent factor in marketing strategies, and segmentation evolved to lure guests with specific lodging packages. Some examples will show how diversified the lodging industry has become.

- Increased airline travel has brought hotels to airport locations. Catering to the business traveler who wants to attend meetings without fighting city traffic, these properties offer convenient locations.

- New emphasis has been placed on the center city. Every major metropolitan area in the United States can boast of new, architecturally splendid hotels aiding in the revitalization of downtown areas. Local businesses, visitors to cultural and tourist attractions, governmental agencies, and local citizens are among the markets for these properties.

- Many properties cater to large group and convention business. They may offer meeting rooms, exhibit areas, or very large special function space, or they may be located close to other properties that offer these facilities. For years, large group meetings were traditionally held in major metropolitan areas. Today, however, more regional meetings are being held to reduce travel costs and attract more attendees. In response, very large meeting facilities are being constructed in relatively small cities—and they are very successful.

- Some travelers enjoy the luxury and ambience of older hotels. Once-grand hotels are being refurbished to attract these guests and offer luxuries of the past with all of today's amenities. Examples include the Westin St. Francis in San Francisco, the Boston Park Plaza Hotel, and the Willard Inter-Continental and the Mayflower in Washington, D.C.

- Other travelers desire budget accommodations. The growing economy segment of the lodging industry offers very clean, new, attractive, and comfortable facilities. Between 1970 and 1991, the economy segment increased by nearly 2,000 percent. Today, it comprises 78 chains—about 620,000 rooms in 6,000-plus properties—or nearly 20 percent of the nation's total room supply. 69 percent of the hotels built since 1991 are in the economy, limited-service segment. Initially providing few amenities (many did not even offer food or beverage service), many of these properties now offer swimming pools, food and beverage service, game rooms, and more. (The differences between economy and other properties are becoming blurred, much as did the distinction between hotels and motels/motor hotels in the 1950s and 1960s.)

- Many travelers like a "home away from home"; others enjoy more space than that offered in most properties. Suite hotels and residence inns offer living areas separate from sleeping rooms, as well as kitchenette facilities. The all-suite sector is second only to the economy group in rate of growth. There are over 1,500 all-suite properties today totaling 250,000 rooms or about 7 percent

Exhibit 5   Market Segment by Chain

Upper Upscale Chains	Marriott, Hyatt, Inter-Continental, Westin, Stouffer, Omni, Four Seasons, Vista, Hilton*, Sheraton**
Lower Upscale Chains	Hilton, Sheraton Inns, Embassy Suites, Radisson, Dunfey, Residence Inn, Americana, Ramada Renaissance, Quality Royale, Crowne Plaza
Upper Mid-Scale Chains	Holiday Inn, Ramada, Howard Johnson, Red Lion, Courtyard, Viscount
Lower Mid-Scale Chains	Best Western, Quality Inn, Rodeway, Travelodge, Masterhost, Red Carpet
Upper Economy Chains	LaQuinta, Days Inns, Comfort Inns, Hampton Inns, Fairfield Inn
Lower Economy Chains	Red Roof, Super 8, Econolodge, Regal 8, Motel 6, Scottish Inns

*These include the high-priced luxury Hilton hotels only
**These include all of Sheraton's "core" hotels. Sheraton Inns are not included.

Source: Smith Travel Research, *Star Report*, Spring 1992.

of the total room supply. Smith Travel, Inc. reports that all-suite hotels maintain occupancies well above average in spite of their rapid growth and expansion. It is interesting to note that the five states of Florida, California, Texas, Hawaii, and Arizona account for over 50 percent of all all-suites.

Today, the industry has the following classifications according to service: full-service, limited-service, and all-suite. The industry may also be segmented by room rate. The three tiers by prices are:

- The upper tier (upscale). This segment includes full-service hotels which typically have concierge floors, secretarial services, and shopping arcades and whose room rates are the highest in the industry.

- The middle tier (mid-scale). This segment includes full-service hotels in the range between the upper and lower tiers.

- The lower tier (budget/economy). These hotels offer limited service with rooms only or with minimum food and beverage service. These hotels rarely have meeting or banquet space.

When Smith Travel Research began reporting statistics for the industry in its *Star Report*, they broke these three tiers into subsets and placed national brands into those subsets as shown in Exhibit 5. Although Smith Travel Research now uses

Exhibit 6   Smith Travel Research Segmentation

I. Luxury Segment (4%)	Hotels with ADR above 85th percentile for their market
II. Upscale Segment (16%)	Hotels with ADR between 70th and 85th percentile for their market
III. Mid-price Segment (26%)	Hotels with ADR between 40th and 70th percentile for their market
IV. Economy Segment (22%)	Hotels with ADR between 20th and 40th percentile for their market
V. Budget Segment (32%)	Hotels with ADR below 20th percentile for their market

Source: Smith Travel Research, *Star Report*, Spring 1992.

Exhibit 7   Room Revenue by Segment

Segment	Percent of Industry Revenue
I. Luxury	24%
II. Upscale	30%
III. Mid-price	24%
IV. Economy	12%
V. Budget	10%

Source: Smith Travel Research, *Star Report*, Spring 1992.

a different method of segmentation, many in the industry prefer and still use the original system. The current Smith Travel Research system uses groupings based on average daily rate (ADR) for their market. Exhibit 6 illustrates the system and shows the percentage of the nation's hotels in each segment. Exhibit 7 illustrates the room revenue share achieved by each segment. Note that, while the combined economy and budget segments account for over half the total properties, they produce less than 25 percent of the industry room revenue.

One other method of segmentation uses the following terms in addition to all-suite: luxury, upscale, mid-price, gaming, extended stay, economy, hard budget.

The influence of market segmentation is visible in the actions and organization of several chains. Holiday Corporation's properties were basically Holiday Inns. Within a short time, however, the corporation moved upscale with Crowne Plaza, into the economy segment with Hampton Inns and Holiday Inn Express, into the all-suite market with Embassy Suites, into gambling with the purchase of Harrahs, and into extended stay with Homewood Suites. Marriott moved down a level with Courtyard Inns, into the economy segment with Fairfield Inns, and up a level with Marriott Marquis. The corporation also developed Marriott All-Suites, purchased Residence Inns, and entered the time-share field—the first major hotel corporation to make the move. Accor has Mercure, Sofitel, Novitel, Ibis-Urbis, Formula One, and Motel 6.

Forte Hotels (now owned by Granada) uses the following six categories: Exclusive Hotels of the World, Grand Hotels, Heritage Hotels, Crest Hotels, Posthouse, and Travelodge and Thriftlodge. Hilton divides into: Conrad Hotels, Hilton Hotels A&B, Garden Inns, Hilton Inns, Hilton All-Suites, Hilton Gaming, and Hilton Grand Vacation (time-share).

Very recently we are seeing segmentation within a segment in at least two chains. Holiday Inns are now either Holiday Inn Select, Holiday Inn, Holiday Inn and Suites, or Holiday Inn Express. Ramada is now Ramada Plaza Hotels and Resorts, Ramada Inns, or Ramada Limited.

Among the major chains, only Hyatt and Westin have resisted the segmentation urge.

Amenities

As competition among lodging companies became more and more intense in the 1980s, hotels sought ways to increase their appeal in order to keep their regular guests and to attract new ones—especially as room rates increased. Here began what some in the field call "the war of the amenities." In his article, "Amenities Then and Now," Tom Lattin recorded the tremendous increase in the number of amenities offered and the percentage of hotels offering them.[1]

Many people equate **amenities** with the personal bathroom items now offered by a great majority of the nation's hotels and motels. The term "amenities," however, encompasses more than these items. A better term might be "guest services." For example, in-room entertainment systems, automatic check-out, free parking, airport transportation, 24-hour service, executive floors, concierge services, and multilingual staff are really all amenities that are designed to bolster the hotel's appeal, enhance guests' stays, and bring them back to the hotel.

Even in the heyday of amenities, they had their critics who were convinced that the "amenity creep" as it became known was an added expense which created little, if any, return. Among them was Curt Strand (then chairman of the board, Hilton International) who referred to amenities as "the TV in the bathroom" syndrome.

As the hotel economic picture turned from gray to black in the early 1990s, the amenity creep became a "negative crawl." Most hotel corporations began to cut back drastically on amenities as one means of reducing costs. Surprisingly, many of the luxury properties led the way. Commenting on the luxury segment in the 1990s, one industry leader said, "Perhaps the most striking change is the elimination of the amenity excesses of the 1980s." In the mid-1990s, the war of the amenities and amenity creep appeared to be approaching obsolescence.

However, as the hotel economy began its move back toward prosperity, amenities, instead of disappearing totally, began a comeback—although in different forms. This time, hotel companies decided to survey guests about which amenities they desired in the guestroom. Topping the list were in-room coffee, newspapers, and ironing boards. Today, most major chains, along with all-suites and extended stay properties, provide these three amenities along with basic toiletry amenities.

The improved economy brought increased business travel, and hotel companies began to focus attention on business travelers and how best to attract their patronage. Surveys were designed to discover which amenities were important to business travelers. One such survey learned that the top five factors were[2]:

A desk with good work space	9.3 on a scale of 10
Ability to adjust guestroom temperature	9.3
A comfortable chair	9.2
Task lighting	9.0
Ability to work comfortably	9.0

When asked what they did in their guestrooms, survey respondents said:

Make phone calls	96%
Spread out and work	85%
Read/Edit	82%
Work on computers	75%

Armed with these results, hotels began to design and introduce "business rooms." Hyatt and Radisson introduced their business rooms in 1994. In 1995, Marriott, in conjunction with AT&T and Steelcase Inc., launched its version titled "The Room That Works." Around the same time, Holiday Hospitality designated Holiday Inn Select as its business room property, and Doubletree introduced The Club Room it describes as equal parts den, office, and cafe. HFS introduced a whole new brand, Wingate Hotels, to attract the business traveler market. Each of these concepts either features or provides access to all types of office equipment and communication channels. The traveling executive is able to perform business functions nearly as efficiently in the hotel as he or she can back in the company office.

Technology

As the final quarter of the twentieth century began in 1975, it was relatively easy to equip a hotel with technology: Order from NCR a Class 42 front office posting machine, some Class 5 cash registers for the bars and restaurants, and a Class 33 bookkeeping machine for back-office accounting. No need to worry about selecting a long-distance carrier since there was only one—AT&T. Choose between black and white televisions or the very expensive color models. Handle security by counting the number of doors and ordering the same number of mechanical locks.

How times have changed! Today, a lodging property has to make dozens of business and technical decisions on the tech-based systems that affect every phase of hotel management, marketing, and operations. Succinctly put, there have been more advances in hotel technology in the past 10 years than in the previous 100 years.

The instigator of these changes is the microcomputer. Microcomputers first reached the lodging industry around 1983. Every year since then, they have been changing most of what we know about data processing's price/performance ratio.

The power of microcomputers continues to increase while their price decreases. Mr. Larry Chervenak, world renowned expert on hotel technology, reports that today a $2,000 personal computer with a Pentium microchip has more power than a $1.32 million IBM Mainframe had in 1975. He predicts that, before the year 2001, personal computers will have 100 times the power of today's models. The result, he says, is that lodging operators will not only have to make correct decisions on what and when to buy, they will have to start finding practical uses for the upcoming power increases.[3]

The Guestroom Phone. As recently as 1980, hotel phone systems were rather simple. Usually there was one phone per room, and that was archaic by modern standards. Improvements came rapidly. Rooms were equipped with two lines and the phones included single-button speed dialing, automatic redial, and call hold.

But the most innovative and most comprehensive addition is the **in-room guest console**, which is a multi-purpose feature phone. In-room guest consoles may include some or all of the following functions:

- Telephone—Two-way speakerphone capability, pre-set dial keys, message light, single-key message retrieval function, and a jack for portable computer use

- Alarm clock—With digital display and quartz oscillator with battery back-up

- Radio—Full AM and FM bands plus automatic mute and telephone operation

- Remote control—Wireless control of heating, ventilating, and air conditioning, television, and room lights

- Energy management

- Built-in theft alarm

- Emergency key

Some consoles allow guests to control the environment without moving a step. When the guest enters the room, for example, the room key card or key tag is inserted in the slot atop the console activating the remote control functions. The air conditioning may be set to desired temperature, the television completely controlled, various room lights turned on or off as desired, phone calls made, or radio tuned to AM or FM.

Then came fax, cellular phones, voice mail messages, automated routing of charges for long-distance calls to guest accounts, and automated wake-up calls.

Property Management Systems. Property management systems were born about 1974 when EECO developed and installed the first real-time property management system. Usage of this new technique was thought to be rather limited in the industry. It was not cost-justifiable to install the property management system in a property of under 300 rooms and the system was not efficient in properties of over 500 rooms. What a difference a few years can make! Today there are property management system versions in use in ten-room bed and breakfasts as well as in the 5,000-room MGM Grand Hotel.

The early versions were limited to reserving rooms, checking guests in and out, and balancing the night audit. During the 1980s, hotels worked to expand the scope of automation by installing supplemental software packages to interface with property management systems.

In the 1990s, a great amount of supplemental software became available to add to the basic property management system. Operational efficiency was improved by all of the following supplemental systems when added to the property management system: group sales and catering, integrated point of sale, F&B management, remote check-in and check-out, credit card authorization/settlement, database marketing, energy management, yield management, and work flow automation.

The technology experts tell us that "since supplemental systems are most effective when integrated or interfaced with the property management system, the role of the property management system as the center of hotel automation will continue to expand."[4]

Central Reservation Systems. In the past few years, the growing power of hotel reservation systems and airline/travel agent global distribution systems has changed the way reservations are made and who gets the business.

What are now global distribution systems started as airline reservation systems on a national basis. Technology then allowed these systems to become global. Airlines placed terminals in travel agency offices to expedite making airline reservations. Next, the THISCO and WizCom switches were created and linked the hotel and central reservation systems to the airline global distribution system, thus allowing the global reservation system to make hotel reservations. The global distribution systems currently account for over 60 percent of hotel bookings, and the number is increasing each year.

The buzzword in hotel circles today is electronic distribution systems (EDS). An EDS is the means by which hotel properties distribute inventory and rates and take reservations without mail carriers, fax machines, or even telephones. Simply stated, the systems work in this way: a consumer shops for hotel accommodations via an EDS that taps directly into each hotel company's central reservation system which is seamlessly connected to each property. The EDS user sees the same rates and availability as the hotel reservationist. The user makes a booking which is received almost instantly at the property. A confirmation or regret is returned to the EDS user within seconds. All along the electronic pathway, that booking is reflected at the moment of confirmation, and inventory and rates adjust accordingly.

Hotel companies are spending millions on new central reservation systems to ensure that they remain competitive in this new age of electronic technology. The goal is to be certain that the central reservation system is flexible enough to adapt quickly to shifting reservation systems.

It is interesting to note that as EDSs gain in influence, the airline global distribution systems are developing approaches that will bypass travel agents and their commissions. Travel agents are exploring ways of bypassing the airline global distribution systems by accessing hotel central reservation systems directly, while hotel organizations are exploring ways to bypass both the airlines and the travel agents.

Hotels and the Internet. As recently as 1994, the Internet was primarily used by universities and the government. Today it appears to have captured the imagination of the world in general and the hotel industry in particular. THISCO (The Hotel

Industry Switch Company) established TravelWeb on the World Wide Web; Hyatt was the first to use it to showcase its properties. Now every major hotel chain and thousands of other travel-related organizations have Internet presence.

Hotel chains are now using the Internet as a source of hotel booking. It is estimated that the Internet reaches 40 million users worldwide. That is 250 times more than all the global distribution systems combined. To date, online bookings have not achieved expected volumes. However, many analysts expect Internet bookings to rival and exceed those of the global distribution systems. They believe that the Internet has the potential to completely alter the way reservations are made. Travel bookings on the World Wide Web currently total $400 million, but are projected to hit $4 billion by the year 2000.

The next question facing hotel ownership is whether or not to provide Internet and E-mail access in the guestroom. Such access would be great for the business traveler, but many question whether the average traveler would know what it was or what to do with it. A few hotels have taken the plunge and installed Internet access in guestrooms. It most certainly is being closely studied by all major players in the industry. The odds appear to favor increased Internet installations in hotel guestrooms.

Interactive TV-based Services. The first attempt to provide interactive TV-based services occurred in the 1980s, when SpectraVision introduced guestroom folio review, check-out, and room service via TV. Then in 1990 came on-demand movies and interactive video games. 1996 introduced interactive guestroom shopping, interactive visitors' guides, fax delivery and voice messaging via TV, interactive guides to hotel facilities and activities, reservations from the guestroom to other hotels within the same organization, and interactive weather reports. These latest additions are attractive to a hotel operator because they provide valid guest services, can improve the bottom line, and can be installed without investment on the hotel's part.

Merging of Technologies. Each of the basic equipment types—personal computer, television, and telephone—is developing the capabilities of the other two. Also under development are techniques of increasing the speed and reliability of data and video transmission while cutting the cost. This merging should hasten the arrival of the long-promised, so-called picture phone.

Automated Check-in, Check-out. A number of hotel chains have been experimenting with automated check-in/check-out for some time. At Choice Hotels International Mainstay Suites, it is a reality and fully operational. When the guest enters the vestibule before the lobby, he or she finds no front desk. Instead, there is a kiosk with a screen that has four moving icons or animations announcing check-in/check-out, other hotel services, and local information. The kiosk screen is designed to guide the guest into the program.

If the system is communicating in a language the guest does not understand, he or she may select another language by pressing one of two other buttons: the three available languages are English, Spanish, and French. Next the guest simply touches the screen. A professional voice takes him or her through the steps. The guest is asked to swipe the credit card used to make the reservation. This tells the system to search the Choice 2001 CRS, retrieve the reservation, and display enough information to corroborate it. The system asks the guest to verify departure date, room type, and room rate. After verification, the guest presses the *Finish* button to confirm the reservation.

Then the machine asks the guest to create a Personal Security Access (PSA) code based on a number that is easy to remember. A calculator image appears on the screen, and the guest types in the PSA code. The guest presses *Finish* again and the machine dispenses a key or keys. The screen also provides a bird's-eye view of the hotel layout so guests know where to go and where to park. Finally, the system prints a check-in receipt that lists the room number, rate, and arrival and departure dates, and directs the guest to the guestroom and parking areas.

At check-out, the guest can either swipe the credit card again or enter the guestroom number. The machine prints the folio and voids the key.

Automated check-in/check-out represents a shift in emphasis from service to efficiency. It probably will work best in the economy and mid-scale markets, but it most certainly will be available at least as an alternative in the upscale and luxury markets.

Guest Security Advances. Today, guest security is a prime concern of all hotel operators but, in the past, it was not always so emphasized. The Connie Francis case in 1975 probably marked the beginning of security emphasis and concern on a major scale. Even in 1986, reports Ray Ellis, former director of Risk Management at the American Hotel & Motel Association, there were more than 500 hotel negligence suits asking for more than $1 million each.[5]

Technological systems that could have minimized risk kept improving but were seldom installed. Today, closed-circuit TV surveillance and access control systems, biometric systems, and electronic locks are widely used and, as a result, security problems have been reduced.

The Telecom Revolution. The telecommunications market is undergoing radical change worldwide. International communications networks are becoming far easier to design and operate. The cost of international data communication is decreasing. Through deregulation or privatization, many government-controlled monopolies are being dissolved. In almost every case, this results in lower prices, more options, and better services for hotels.

The recent passage of the U.S. Communications Law is bringing about the greatest change in U.S. history. The new law has upset the former telecom structure by authorizing:

1. Long-distance carriers to compete in the local-phone call market and to pay local telephone companies reduced fees to complete long-distance calls.

2. Regional Bell companies to manufacture telecom equipment and provide cable television services and long-distance telephone services.

3. Cable companies to compete with the regional Bell operating companies in the local-call market.

Technology has made a major imprint on the hospitality industry to date. Knowledgeable industry experts predict that technology will continue to be a major influence right into the millennium.

Gaming and the Hospitality Industry

Legalized casino gambling got its start in Nevada in 1931. For 47 years, casino operations were confined to that state until the 1978 opening of Resorts International Casino Hotel in Atlantic City, New Jersey. Nevada and New Jersey monopolized the industry until 1986, when Montana authorized the first video lottery machine. The machine resembles a slot machine but does not dispense coin payouts.

The next year, a Supreme Court ruling in a case between the State of California and the Cabazon Band of Mission Indians held that Native Americans could not be prevented from operating various forms of gambling if their particular state did not have a specific public policy against those gambling forms. This ruling, and a subsequent act of Congress that recognized the sovereignty of Indian tribes and their right to operate gaming activities, opened the door for numerous other Native American tribes to structure gaming compacts with their respective state governments. There are currently about 30 legal Indian gaming operations in place with more anticipated in the near future. The most dynamic facility in operation to date is the Foxwoods Casino and High Stakes Bingo, operated by the Mashantucket Pequot Tribe in Ledyard, Connecticut, since February 1992. This full-service casino operation offers all of the most popular table games, including blackjack, roulette, big six, baccarat, and poker. Its success has been phenomenal and has led to the development of hotels and additional recreational amenities in the area. The success of this facility and the Native Americans' sovereign status, which relieves Native Americans of state regulation and taxation, has caught the attention of many state and city officials eager to capitalize on any opportunity to strengthen their tax base.

Riverboat gambling returned to the Mississippi River in 1991 when both Iowa and Illinois launched their first boats. Today, Iowa has five boats in operation and Illinois has ten. Louisiana has launched two riverboats, and has joined New Jersey and Nevada in having opened full land-based casinos and dockside casinos.

Other developments that are having a drastic impact on this rapidly expanding recreational venue include the low-stake ($5 maximum bet) gaming operations that started in Deadwood, South Dakota, in late 1989 and expanded to the Colorado mining towns of Central City, Blackhawk, and Cripple Creek in late 1991.

Next to join the gaming arena was the state of Mississippi, which operates Dockside Riverboat Casinos. These "riverboats" never leave the dock. The state now has 24 dockside riverboat casinos operating in Biloxi, Gulfport, Tunica, and Vicksburg.

Looking back just 20 years, we note that only Nevada permitted commercial casinos and just 13 states had lotteries. Today, 40 states conduct lotteries, and 25 states allow some form of casino gambling. Twenty years ago, Americans wagered about $17 billion on legal gambling. In 1997, this figure was expected to reach $600 billion.

In trying to comprehend why casino gambling is receiving such high visibility and such tremendous growth, two factors predominate. First, there has been a drastic change in public awareness. The evolution in the public's mind has taken gambling from its crudest form to gaming, and from gaming to its most well-received form, entertainment. Rather than as a refuge for less-desirable sorts, gambling has come to be viewed as a means of entertainment for a few hours, a weekend, or an entire vacation. This change in attitude has been augmented by the

Exhibit 8   Mergers and Acquisitions in Gaming Industry

Hilton Corporation and Bally

ITT Sheraton and Caesar's World

Circus Circus and Gold Strike Resorts

Sun International Hotels and Griffin Gaming

Boyd Gaming and Pair A Dice Gaming

William G. Bennett and Sahara Hotel

Hospitality Franchise Systems and National Gaming

Circus Circus and Hacienda Hotels and Casinos

Source: *Hotels*, October 1996, p. 46.

casino mega-resorts that dominate Las Vegas and provide a full gamut of amenities, activities, and theme park attractions. Also critical to the change in perception has been the technological innovations that account for the introduction of video slot, poker, and blackjack machines, which have materially improved the level of entertainment value and the overall gambling experience.

The second factor relates to the need of financially struggling cities and states to find new ways to generate tax revenues and to increase employment opportunities. For example, in 1996 casinos in Mississippi generated $900 million in tax revenues. The state claims that one riverboat casino opening creates 1,000 jobs at that casino alone.

In recent years, hotel companies have shown an increased interest in casinos and gaming. Major players on the gaming scene are Hilton Hotels, Sheraton Hotels, Harrahs, Mirage Resorts, Circus Circus, Sun International Hotels, Caesar's Palace, and Bally. A number of mergers and acquisitions have occurred during the last few years. They are shown in Exhibit 8. Also taking center stage were several alliances: MGM Grand and Primadonna to build the New York, New York Hotel; Circus Circus and Mirage Resorts for an Atlantic City hotel; Players International and Harrahs to operate riverboat gaming; and Circus Circus with Four Seasons Hotels to develop a hotel in Las Vegas.

The question arises as to how popular and how profitable gaming is. In 1996, there were well over 100 million visits to casinos in the United States. About 60 percent of the visits were to the traditional casino destinations and 40 percent to riverboat, dockside, and Indian reservation operations.

Perhaps the best way to illustrate profitability and revenue is with an example. The Empress Riverboat Casino generated $173 million in one year. Now compare the Empress to a 4,000-room hotel at 100 percent occupancy and an ADR of $115 for the year. The hotel neither produces as much revenue nor even comes close to matching the Empress's profitability.

Vital questions arise: What does the future hold? How deep is the national demand for gaming? How many casinos can be supported profitably? Is gaming revenue an added source of income for market areas or a diversion of money from other hospitality businesses? Will the predicted increase in the number of compulsive gamblers cause a public outcry against the gaming industry?

The hotel companies involved are optimistic about the future and have some very good data to support their optimism. The RY&P Yankelovich Partners' *National Travel Monitor* tracks emerging trends in both leisure and business travel. Their most recent survey states, "You can bet on growing interest in recreational gaming. Interest in recreational gaming now surpasses that in golf and tennis, as the availability of gaming has grown to include many new riverboat, dockside and land-based casino alternatives."[6]

Industry Growth and the Economy

Entering the 1980s, the hotel industry was prospering. Business was good and demand for rooms was increasing each year. In fact, a building boom was underway which led to the most frenzied hotel construction since the 1920s.

A number of factors fueled this building boom. First, the federal government passed the Economic Recovery Act of 1981 which encouraged developers to construct hotel properties by allowing them to realize tax benefits much sooner. This tax law encouraged the creation of limited partnerships and syndicates whose members were allowed to recognize depreciation far in excess of their original investment. In some instances, an investor received as much as a $9.00 tax write-off for each $1.00 invested.

Second, there was unprecedented growth in the amount of debt financing available to the industry. Deregulated savings and loans, commercial banks, commercial finance companies, and insurance companies eagerly committed huge amounts of capital to the hospitality industry. Because of this ready availability of debt financing, all the new properties were leveraged to the hilt.

An additional source of financing came from foreign investors who engaged in merger and acquisition activity. Many of these acquisitions were made at inflated prices, thus driving up prices across the board. The Japanese were big investors. By 1991, 206 hotels with 78,000 rooms in 26 states were Japanese owned. The Japanese have a preference for "trophy hotels," which helps explain why they control 7 percent of the luxury hotel rooms in the United States.

Not all the impetus for this feverish building of hotels came from developers and investors. The hotel industry must share a portion of the responsibility or blame. The chains engaged in tremendous market share battles with emphasis, always, on growth and more growth. Some critics insist that market segmentation was really just an excuse to build more hotels rather than an essential marketing tool. Supposedly, any new construction or expansion is carefully evaluated by the finance, development, and operations department of a corporation before approval is given to proceed. There is considerable evidence that such feasibility analysis did not take place or was not too factual, as illustrated by this quote from an (unnamed) executive of a major hotel corporation: "Our executives were dealmakers who could find a way to build a hotel on any street corner in America."

Actually, demand for hotel rooms grew at a very healthy rate throughout the 1980s, but the supply of hotel rooms continuously outpaced the demand and served to add fuel to the heated competition for market share among the chains.

Smith Travel Research succinctly analyzed the situation as follows in its *Star Report*: "Some individual responses to the increased competition compounded the problem in the 1980s. More money was spent on the product, more marble, square footage, the amenities, but without the rate increases needed to pay for them. Deadly rate wars were waged in overbuilt markets, driven by the conviction that lower rates would create more demand. That did not happen either."

The Tax Reform Act of 1986 decreased the attractiveness of investing in new hotel properties by:

- Eliminating investment tax credit

- Lengthening the depreciation period from 19 to 31.5 years

- Restricting deductible passive losses (that is, losses incurred by an investor not actively involved in managing the property)

- Lowering individual tax rates

- Raising taxes on capital gains

Despite the negative aspects of this act, the hospitality industry continued to be perceived by potential equity investors, especially foreign investors, as being very attractive. The country's strong economic performance, the weakness of the U.S. dollar, and the strategic importance of the U.S. market all encouraged investment activity by foreign investors. Unfortunately, the act only slightly slowed the frantic building activity. Over 700,000 rooms were added to the industry inventory from 1985 to 1990. The market share, growth, and rate war competition continued among the chains unabated.

By the late 1980s, the economic environment had changed. The United States and many other countries were experiencing an economic slow-down. Financial institutions suffered a high degree of non-performing loans in their real estate portfolios which led to the savings and loan crisis in the United States. The hotel industry feels any change in the economy almost immediately. With an economic downturn, travel is curtailed by both business and pleasure travelers, who are more cost-conscious when they do travel. The result in the late '80s was a decline in both occupancy and room rates which was magnified by the overbuilt state of the industry. The recession was taking its toll on the industry. In fact, hotels lost money each year between 1985 and 1990.

As 1990 began, the industry was in deep trouble. A headline in the *Wall Street Journal* read, "1,000 Hotel Foreclosures This Year." The industry was not only overbuilt but also badly overfinanced. Three major chains, Prime Motor Inns, Days Inns, and Servico, went into Chapter 11 bankruptcy. Even Hilton Hotels Corporation was up for sale, but was later taken off the market when no satisfactory bids were received. Marriott Corporation stock was at $44.00 in May 1989, fell to $9.87 in November 1990, and struggled back to $16.00 in June 1992.

As though things were not bad enough, the Gulf War and the threat of terrorism further compounded the problem. Most major hotel corporations announced significant lay-offs at every level. At an industry meeting, Hyatt Hotels President Darryl Hartley-Leonard suggested the industry might adopt the slogan, "Stay Alive Until '95."

Exhibit 9   Lodging Industry Profits

1990	($ 5.7 billion)
1991	($ 2.8 billion)
1992	($ 0.0 billion)
1993	$ 2.4 billion
1994	$ 5.5 billion
1995	$ 8.5 billion
1996	$11.2 billion
1997	$13.7 billion

Source: Coopers & Lybrand.

The first quarter of 1991 was the worst in many years for the hotel industry. One industry analyst described the situation in these words: "From the viewpoint of product value, the hospitality industry has, in the last year and a half, experienced as great a decline percentage-wise as it did in the 1930s. The Great Depression was the cause then."[7] The number of both delinquent hotels loans and hotel loans in foreclosure peaked in 1991.

Hotels were not meeting their debt obligations so they were being taken over by savings and loans and other lenders. Many of the savings and loans were in turn taken over by the U.S. government. The Resolution Trust Corporation was formed to sell off the federal government's hotel and real estate assets. During the early 1990s, the Resolution Trust Corporation was probably the single largest "owner" of hotels in the world.

1991–1996 saw the most significant and wide-sweeping ownership changes in the history of the hotel industry:

- There were 42 significant mergers and acquisitions.

- 13 hotel companies went public.

- 12 REITs were formed and, taken together, purchased more than 350 hotels.

- 3,250 individual hotels were sold for a total of $23 billion.

Of particular note was the about-face in Japanese ownership of American hotels and other real estate. From a high of 206 hotels and 7 percent of the luxury hotel rooms in 1991, the Japanese sold off nearly half of their hotels between 1991 and 1996, and continued to offer others for sale in ensuing years. Many of these hotels were in bankruptcy, and losses on the sales totaled several billion dollars.

By 1992 the effects of greatly decreased new construction plus cost-cutting, tight-fisted management began to change the industry profit picture. As shown in Exhibit 9, the industry profit bleeding was under control even though profits were still not realized. Starting in 1992 and continuing through 1996, the increase in room demand exceeded the increase in room supply with resulting increases in

Exhibit 10   New Hotel Brands in the 1990s

Candlewood Hotels	Mainstay Suites
Club Hotels	Platinum Inns/Suites
Comfort Suites	Sierra Suites
Doubletree Guest Suites	Ramada Limited
Executive Residences	Sumner Suites
Extended Stay America	Sundowner Suites
Fairfield Suites	Taj Inns and Suites
Four Points Hotels	Towne Place Suites
Hawthorn Suites	Wingate Inns
Hearthside	Woodfin Suites
Hilton Garden Inn	Woodland Suites
Homegate Studios & Suites	Wyndham Studio Suites
Hampton Inn and Suites	2nd Home-A Suite Hotel
Holiday Inn Express	Asbury Suites and Inns
HoJo Inn	Crossland Economy Studios

both occupancy and ADR. From 1992 to 1996, a total of 2,005 new hotels were built. Of this number, 69 percent were in the limited-service segment. The mid-market, full-service segment grew by 800 hotels. Two brands, Days Inns and Ramada, accounted for 67 percent of that total. There were 153 new hotels added to the first class and luxury segments, but 127 were outside the United States. The fastest growing hotel companies were Hospitality Franchising Services, Choice Hotels International, Holiday Hospitality, Promus, and Marriott International.

The very positive profit picture shown in Exhibit 9 generated glowing optimism and renewed faith in the industry. For example, a generally conservative accounting firm executive said, "Profits in 1995 were 3.7 times the inflation-adjusted profits of 1979, an earlier record year. This is an industry beyond recovery into a period of record profitability and that profitability will continue to increase over the next few years."[8]

By 1996, actual and projected growth figures filled the trade press. Between June 1995 and June 1996, 13 major new brands were announced, bringing the total new brands in a three-year period to 30. A major sample of these new brands is listed in Exhibit 10.

Westin announced plans to open one new hotel per month for the remainder of the decade, while Marriott projected an additional 120,000 rooms by the year 2000. Radisson, with 350 hotels, plans to have 925 by 2000, and Hilton Hotels announced a planned increase of 50,000 rooms. Sheraton, Promus, Choice International, and HFS have all announced plans for significant growth.

In 1996, the industry added 102,400 new rooms, an increase of 20.8 percent over 1995. These figures sounded like a building boom to a number of industry executives who still had vivid memories of the late 1980s and early 1990s oversupply. A question commonly asked was, "Is there room for all the new brands?" One survey showed that industry executives were about evenly divided in their answers.

Words of caution worth quoting came from Tom Lattin, President and COO, Patriot American Hospitality; Barry Sternlicht, Chairman, Starwood Lodging Trust; and David Berins, President, Berins Consulting. Lattin said, "With occupancies at their highest level since 1980, let's not forget the industry's cyclical nature. Although we have a banner year for profits, putting some cash away for a rainy day is a wise strategy. The impact of last year's room starts will lower occupancy figures and, if we have sense enough to assume that ADRs and profits won't rise forever, we will have enough cash in reserve to pay the mortgage and still provide a favorable return on equity. We need to remember that history can repeat itself and often does."[9] Mr. Sternlicht warns, "New flags, new product lines, extended, semi-extended, permanently extended-stay. We're doing it to ourselves again and we will not defy the economic laws. Supply does not create demand. Let's listen to the past, enjoy prosperity and only add capacity that really needs to be built or the gain will be followed by severe pain."[10] Berins states his concern in this way: "Today we're seeing the same overheated, uninformed behavior by the capital markets as we saw in the early 1980s. Developers are taking advantage of this and planning dozens of new projects in most major markets. I keep hearing the click-click-click sound of a roller coaster going uphill—and I predict that in the not-too-distant future, we'll once again be throwing our arms in the air and screaming on the way downhill."[11]

If the industry polices itself properly, there is every reason to believe that the 1990s will be looked upon in history as golden years for the hotel industry.

Consolidation

During the 1980s, newspapers were filled with stories of large corporate mergers, acquisitions, and takeovers, along with a number of insider trading scandals. While no hostile takeovers occurred in the lodging industry, the 1980s can be characterized as a period in which ownership was sometimes like a game of musical chairs. The end result was **consolidation** of hotel brands into fewer owning companies, a trend today in many industries of the world.

Consolidation not only continued into the 1990s but picked up steam both nationally and internationally. To chart the tremendous changes that have taken place is a time-consuming but worthwhile endeavor as this phenomenon certainly is a milestone in the history of the hospitality industry.

As the 1980s opened, the industry comprised a large number of independent chains. Thirty-eight chains are listed in Exhibit 11. Just past the halfway point of the 1990s, only 6 of the 38 had not been sold or merged at least once. The six are Accor; Bass, Plc.; Choice; Hilton; HFS; and Marriott. As one might expect, each of the six added one or more groups to its array of properties. Probably the most active acquirer has been HFS, a company that did not even exist in 1980. Formed by the Blackstone Group, a Wall Street firm, HFS first purchased Howard Johnson Motor Lodges and Ramada Inns from Prime Hospitality. It has since added Days Inns, Super 8 Motels, Knights Inns, Villager Lodge, Travelodge, and Park Inns. Hilton Hotels acquired the Bally Corporation, while Marriott purchased Residence Inn

Exhibit 11   Once-Independent Hotel Chains

Hilton Hotels	Ciga Hotels
Sheraton Hotels	Knights Inns
Inter-Continental Hotels	United Inns
Howard Johnson Motor Lodges	Super 8 Motels
Marriott Hotels	Red Lion Hotels
Western International Hotels	Regent Hotels
Ramada Inns	Microtel
Holiday Inns	Hawthorn Suites
Rodeway Inns	Ritz Carlton Hotels
Doubletree Hotels	Registry Hotels
Guest Quarters Hotels	H.E.I. Hotels
Days Inns	Carefree Resorts
Radisson Hotels	Travelodge
Stouffer Hotels	Kempinski Hotels
Dunfey Hotels	The Bally Company
Omni Hotels	Red Roof Inns
Meridien Hotels	Hospitality Franchise Systems
Forte Hotels	Choice International Hotels
Bass, Plc.	Accor

and the Howard Johnson Company, but then sold the Motor Lodges to Prime Hospitality. In the mid-1990s, Marriott acquired the Ritz Carlton Hotels. Choice purchased Rodeway Inns, Econolodge, and Friendship Inns. Holiday Corporation sold Holiday Inns, national and international, along with Crowne Plaza to Bass, Plc., a large British hotel company. Holiday then changed its name to Promus and kept Hampton Inns, Embassy Suites, Harrah's, and Homewood Suites. Accor purchased the Motel 6 chain in the early 1990s.

Some of the best-known chains have had some interesting journeys through the ownership maze. Inter-Continental Hotels Corp. formed by PanAm was sold to Grand Metropolitan, a British firm, which in turn sold the chain to its present owner, Seibu Saison. Hilton Hotels Corporation built Hilton International into a very successful chain and then sold it to Trans World Airlines. The chain was next sold to United Airlines and then to Ladbroke Limited. Hilton International returned home recently when Hilton Hotels formed an alliance with Ladbroke. Western International Hotels was sold to United Airlines and changed its name to Westin. United sold Westin to the Aoki Corporation, which sold the famous Plaza Hotel in New York to Donald Trump. Later, Aoki sold Westin to Starwood Capital, which sold it to Starwood Lodging in 1997. The Stouffer chain was one of the newer chains in the United States when it was purchased by the Nestle Corporation, the Swiss conglomerate. Nestle, in turn, sold Stouffer to Renaissance Hotels, which at the time was owned by New World Holdings of Hong Kong. Renaissance itself has enjoyed quite a journey. Ramada Inns gave its upscale Ramadas the name

Renaissance. New World Holdings purchased Ramada and sold Ramada Inn franchise rights in the United States to Prime Hospitality, but kept Renaissance. Renaissance has since gone pubic and was renamed the Stouffer Hotels Renaissance. Then in 1997, Marriott International purchased Renaissance for $1 billion. Marriott will operate all of these hotels, but will not reflag them with the Marriott flag. Thus there will continue to be Renaissance Hotels in the United States, Ramada International Hotels in 22 countries, and New World Hotels in the Asia/Pacific area.

Michael Leven formed U.S. Franchise Systems and proceeded to purchase Microtel and Hawthorn Suites. Omni Hotels was acquired by Wharf Holdings (Hong Kong), absorbed Dunfey Hotels, and then was sold to TRT Holdings of Texas. Prince Alwaleed bin Abdulaziz Saud has become a big investor in American hotels. He purchased a large portion of the Fairmont Hotel Chain, then followed up by buying a significant position in Four Seasons Hotels. At a later date, in conjunction with CDL Hotels, he purchased New York's Plaza Hotel from Donald Trump. Doubletree Hotels teamed up with Guest Quarters Hotels and then went public as Doubletree Hotels. The chain then bought Red Lion Hotels. In a major move, Doubletree Hotels merged with Promus Corporation to form Promus Hotel Corporation. The new company became a major player with its 1,136 hotels and 175,000 rooms.

Other activity included the Interstate Hotels purchase of Colony Hotels and Resorts, Wyndham Hotels' purchase of Clubhouse Inns, and Sunstone Investors' acquisition of the Kahler Realty Corporation with its 17 hotels. Prime Hospitality merged with Homegate Hospitality.

There has also been action on the international scene. Forte Hotels purchased Meridien Hotels from Air France but then Forte Hotels was acquired by The Granada Group. Sheraton purchased Italy's Ciga Chain, Four Seasons Hotels bought Regent Hotels, and Dusit Thani (Thailand) acquired the Kempinski chain.

In the 1990s, new players, real estate investment trusts (REITs), entered the consolidation game in the United States. Two of the largest REITs, Starwood Lodging Trust and Patriot American Hospitality, have been very active acquirers. Patriot American acquired Carefree Resorts, the California Jockey Club and Baymeadows Track, Wyndham Hotels, Carnival Hotels and Resorts, Gencom American Hospitality, WHG Resorts and Casinos, Grand Heritage Hotels, and Interstate Hotels Corporation.

Starwood purchased HEI, a small but rapidly developing chain, and the Flatley Hotel Company with its 15 Tara hotels. They followed these with the purchase of Westin Hotels and Resorts. The Trust then won a "bidding war" with Hilton Hotels Corporation to acquire ITT. With the addition of the ITT Sheraton hotels, Starwood grew in size to 650 hotels in 70 countries. (A more complete discussion of REITs follows later in this chapter.)

An offshoot of consolidation has seen some major reorganization in several hotel chains. Marriott split into two companies: Marriott International and Host Marriott. Marriott International is the operating company, while Host Marriott handles the real estate. This maneuver created much controversy when first announced, but it has worked out well and silenced its critics. Hilton Corporation spun off its gaming operations to its stockholders and kept the hotels. Promus also divided the company into Hotels and Casinos. By selling its portfolio of company-owned Holiday Inns to Bristol Hotels while taking a major position in Bristol, Holiday Hospitality has achieved a separation between franchising on the one hand and ownership and operations on the other. Holiday Hospitality will now concentrate on franchising activities while Bristol will own and operate. This purchase, along with its earlier acquisition of United Inns, elevates Bristol Hotel Company into the major leagues of the hotel industry.

Consolidation among independent management companies appears to be long overdue, but, to date, has made only sporadic progress. Hostmark International merged with The Management Group. Economy Lodging Services joined Beck Summit, while Lane Hospitality purchased both Sunbelt Hotels and Victor Hotel Management. The major happening occurred when Regal Hotels bought Aircoa, Motor Hotel Management, and HMS. Regal merged the three companies into one entity it calls Richfield Hospitality Services. Industry experts continue to predict further consolidation and the demise of many small companies that will be unable to meet the competition.

Consolidation has emphatically stamped its imprint on the hospitality industry. It is a trend that many experts believe will continue, although at a slower pace.

Henry Silverman, Chairman of Hospitality Franchise Systems, says consolidation is inevitable. He points out that in the 1950s there were 53 auto companies—now there are a handful. He states that streamlining at the parent company will eliminate overhead and help the name brands keep room rates down and occupancy up.[12]

In a recent interview, Robert C. Hazard, Jr., former chairman and CEO of Choice International Hotels, said: "Consolidation is the only way a company can achieve the resources necessary to compete globally. A mega-chain can spend what's necessary on marketing and technology to help each property increase its market share and profits." He believes that when consolidation has run its course, there will be fewer than ten surviving companies in the field.[13]

Not everyone is a fan of consolidation. Some industry leaders have raised the following questions:

1. Is the industry following in the footsteps of the airline industry where five or six majors will own every name brand?

2. Is consolidation good for the industry, or is it good for chain executives who could make millions from acquisitions and/or mergers?

3. Will individual brands lose integrity and independence under mega-chain control? Do the top executives worry about individual franchisees?

4. Will consolidation put thousands of people out of work?

5. Is big really better?

The anti-consolidation forces have called consolidation an ominous trend. They contend that chains are growing not by satisfying customers and franchisees, but through balance sheet and other manipulations—including taking stocks public, taking them private, and buying and selling interests at a dizzying clip that has little to do with the running of hotels.

Real Estate Investment Trusts

In 1960, Congress passed the Real Estate Investment Trust Act, which created a vehicle designed to enable investors to pool their capital to invest in commercial real estate. The crucial feature of this vehicle is that it is exempt from income taxes at the corporate level as long as it meets a number of specific provisions in the Internal Revenue Code. Thus investors are able to avoid double taxation while also enjoying the benefit of limited liability. In addition, they have a tradable, liquid investment in a pool of assets under professional management that would be impossible for most investors to assemble on their own.

Real Estate Investment Trusts (REITs) can be categorized by the nature of their real estate investments. There are equity REITs, mortgage REITs, and hybrid REITs. Equity REITs own income-producing properties, while mortgage REITs invest in mortgages and mortgage-related securities. Hybrid REITs invest in both commercial properties and mortgages.

Both mortgage and equity REITs are, or have been, involved in the hotel industry. During the boom period of the 1980s, REITs invested in shaky mortgages that fanned the flames of expansion but then helped create the financial disaster experienced by the industry in the late 1980s and early 1990s. Most of these mortgage REITs created losses for their investors.

Once the hotel economy turned the corner and began to rebound, numerous hotel properties and even whole chains were on the market at prices way below replacement cost. Obtaining financing for purchases or development in the industry was a real problem. Traditional lenders (banks, insurance companies, etc.) were avoiding the industry like the plague. It was at this point that equity REITs entered the picture. The equity REITs of the 1990s are self-managed, fully integrated real estate companies with portfolios focused by type of property. The equity REITs of today are far stronger than their predecessors of the 1980s, most of which no longer exist.

Hotel equity REITs own full-service, extended service, or limited-service hotels, or a combination of these categories. Most hotel REITs cannot actively manage hotels since a REITs income must be derived from rents and other qualified sources. Room revenues, F&B revenues, and other hotel income are considered business income and not rent, and thus do not qualify as REIT income. As a result, the REIT owns the hotels which are in turned leased to an operator. The leases are structured with percentage clauses that allow the REIT to realize much of the upside of increasing occupancy and room rental rates.

There are only two exceptions to this lease structure: Patriot American Hospitality and Starwood Lodging Trust. Each of them is set up as a "paired-share" REIT. The paired-share structure allows the investor to own an equal share in the REIT and in the hotel operator/lessee. In other words, both Patriot American and Starwood Lodging Trust can manage the hotels they own.

Industry analysts agree that REITs are playing a lead role during the 1990s and will continue to be major players in the next century. Exhibit 12 lists the major full-service hotel REITs ranked by total market capitalization, as well as the limited-service hotel REITs ranked from highest to lowest.

Exhibit 12 Limited- and Full-Service Hotel REITs

Limited-Service Hotel REITs
Hospitality Properties Trust
RFS Hotel Investors
Innkepers USA Trust
Equity Inns, Inc.
Winston Hotels
Sunstone Hotel Investors
Jameson Inns
Humphrey Hospitality

Full-Service Hotel REITs
Starwood Lodging Trust
Patriot American Hospitality
Felcor Suite Hotels
American General Hospitality
Boykin Lodging Company

Source: Paine Webber, Real Estate Research Report on Patriot American Hospitality, Aug. 14, 1997; also in Deutsche Morgan Grenfell Research Report on Patriot American Hospitality, Sept. 29, 1997, p. 21.

Conversion

A **conversion** takes place when an independent joins a chain, a property changes from one corporate flag to another (for example, a Holiday Inn becomes a Days Inn or a Ramada becomes a Comfort Inn), or a chain property becomes independent.

As the industry entered the 1990s, the flood of new construction was reduced to a mere trickle. The chains, however, were still competing for market share and planning growth. The industry's oversupply of rooms dictated a preference for conversions versus new construction. It was also true that financing for new construction was almost nonexistent.

From 1990 through 1996, conversions from independent hotels to chains averaged 444 per year. Conversions from one chain to another averaged 453 per year, while conversions from chains to independent hotels averaged 299 per year. Hospitality Franchise Systems and Choice International Hotels were the fastest-growing chains during this period. HFS's franchising strategy was about 99 percent conversions, with half the growth coming from independents and half from competitive brands. Choice International growth in the United States was about 90 percent from conversions, while their European growth was nearly 75 percent from conversions. The use of conversions for growth was the rule for most other chains as well.

By the mid-1990s, new construction was taking place with the economy booming and new financing becoming available, so conversions were no longer the only key to growth. However, the number of conversions occurring now and for the foreseeable future will be significant. Independents will continue to be added to chains, and owners will switch flags if circumstances seem to warrant a change. As properties age, they will be downgraded and repositioned. Each year a number of properties are converted to other, non-hotel uses. These are classified as *closures* within the industry.

Globalization

Today, in business circles around the world, the word heard most often is globalization. The end of the Cold War and the demise of communism further enhanced its role in the world economy.

The chief executive officers of two of the world's largest hotel chains place great emphasis on the role of globalization in the hospitality industry. Best Western CEO Ronald Evans and J. Willard Marriott, Jr., Chairman and CEO, Marriott International, have both indicated that the future of the industry rests with globalization. Mr. Marriott described his company's future in one word: "Global."[14]

César Ritz created the first hotel chain. Since the small chain crossed international borders and had a presence in both Europe and Africa, Ritz provided the initial impetus to globalization. Real progress in this trend, however, took place only when Pan American Airways recognized the relationship between air travel and hotel accommodations. Pan Am formed Inter-Continental Hotels Corporation which built hotels along the Pan American air routes. While early growth centered in Central and South America, the chain rapidly expanded around the world with over 100 hotels. Conrad Hilton created Hilton International Hotels to operate internationally. Growth was rapid for Hilton International, which today has over 150 hotels in 52 countries. Within a short period of time, America's other large chain, Sheraton, began its globalization process. Its influence is worldwide and still growing. As these data demonstrate, in the early days, international hotel management was pretty much an American show. It is interesting to note that two of these American pioneers (Inter-Continental Hotels and Hilton International) are now foreign-owned. Exhibit 13 lists the world's most global chains today, while Exhibit 14 lists foreign chains in the United States.

Next, a number of international airlines saw the advantage of establishing hotels in their principal hubs or ports-of-call. The result was a group of hotel chains controlled by Japan Air Lines, All Nippon Airways, Air France, Lufthansa, Swissair, Aer Lingus, Scandinavian Air Systems, United Airlines, and KLM Royal Dutch Airlines. Exhibit 15 lists chains historically owned by airlines.

Throughout the 1980s, national hotel chains on every continent began to expand internationally at a rapid pace. Exhibit 16 lists the major international chains. The number of these chains is little short of amazing when one considers that just 20 years ago 90 percent of them would not have made the list. It should be noted that the chains listed vary tremendously in the number of countries in which they are present. The range goes from 5 to 74 countries. However, most, if not all, of these chains had expansion plans, were in negotiation, and had hotels on the drawing board or already under construction. Most of these chains would agree on a priority listing of world "hubs" or cities where an international hotel chain should have a presence.

Exhibit 13   World's Most Global Chains

Chain	Number of Countries
Accor	70
Best Western International	69
Inter-Continental Hotels Corp.	69
Holiday Inn Worldwide	65
ITT Sheraton	62
Marriott International	51
Forte Hotels	50
Hilton International	49
Carlson Hospitality Worldwide	42
Choice Hotels International	40
Club Méditerranée, S.A.	40
Hyatt Hotels/Hyatt International	37
Grupo Sol Melia	25
Westin Hotels and Resorts	23
Park Plaza International	20

Source: *Hotels*, July 1997, p. 57.

Exhibit 14   Foreign Chains in the United States

Accor	Club Med
Swissôtel	New Otani
Forte Hotels	Penta
Canadian Pacific	Regent
Four Seasons	Delta Hotels
Nikko	CDL Hotels
ANA Hotels	Kempinski

The globalization that prospered in the 1980s really accelerated in the 1990s. Marriott serves as a good example: in 1991, the corporation had 16 international hotels. By 1996, it had 76 and, in mid-1997, 200. Marriott has announced that 60 percent of its future expansion will be abroad.[15]

The globalization occurred in most areas of the world, as can be illustrated by a brief overview of major regions. A visit to Europe would reveal that, while the European economy was very sluggish through the first half of the 1990s, international chains were actively gaining new footholds throughout the continent.

Exhibit 15   Hotel Chains Historically Owned by Airlines

Airline	Hotel Chain
Aer Lingus*	Dunfey Hotels
Air France*	Meridien Hotels
All Nippon Airways	ANA Hotels
Japan Airlines	Nikko Hotels
KLM Royal Dutch Airlines	Golden Tulip Hotels
Lufthansa Airlines	Penta Hotels
Pan American Airways*	Inter-Continental Hotels
SAS Airlines	SAS International Hotels
Swissair	Swissôtel Ltd.
United Airlines*	Westin International Hotels

* No longer owns the hotel chain listed

Exhibit 16   Major International Hotel Chains

Accor	New Otani Hotels
ANA Hotels	New World/Ramada International
Best Western	Nikko Hotels
Canadian Pacific	Oberoi Hotels
Choice International	Othon Hotels
Ciga	Peninsula Hotels
Club Méditerranée	Penta Hotels
Conrad International	Prince Hotels
Dusit Thani	Promus Company
Forte Hotels	Radisson Hotels
Four Seasons	Ramada Hotels
Golden Tulip	Regent Hotels
Hilton International	Sara Hotels
Holiday Inn Worldwide	SAS International Hotels
Hyatt Hotels	Shangri-La Hotels
Inter-Continental Hotels	Sheraton Hotels
Kempinski Hotels	Steigenberger Hotels
Mandarin Oriental	Stouffer Hotels
Marriott Hotels	Swissôtel Ltd.
Sol-Melia Hotels	Taj Hotels
Meridien Hotels	Westin Hotels
Mövenpick Hotels	

Exhibit 17   Major Players in Central and South America

Grupo Posadas	Radisson Hotels
Grupo Situr	Marriott International
Camino Real	Fiesta Americana
Hospitality Franchise Systems	Best Western
Hyatt International	Inter-Continental Hotels
Choice International	Holiday Inn Worldwide
Hilton International	Sheraton Hotels
Conrad Hotels	Westin Hotels
Accor	Sonesta Hotels
Forte Hotels	

Choice International Hotels increased its presence to 300 hotels in 14 countries, and Holiday Inns expanded in the United Kingdom, Spain, and France. Marriott grew substantially, as did Sheraton, Radisson, and Hilton International.

The Eastern European market excited the international chains because the supply of acceptable western-style hotel rooms was drastically limited throughout the area. Occupancy ratios were very high. The greatest need for new properties appeared to be in the three- and four-star segments. With the exception of Berlin and the five eastern states of Germany, successful hotel development can be arduous. There are a number of obstacles to hotel and tourism growth in Eastern Europe, particularly the CIS, the Baltic states, Poland, and Czechoslovakia. Chief among these obstacles are the following:

- A shift to a market economy

- Inflation

- A shortage of staples and raw materials

- An unmotivated work force

- A lack of training and training facilities

- Threats to peaceful change

In spite of these roadblocks, a number of chains are pursuing development there. Poland to date has attracted the most attention, but each of these countries is experiencing development by international chains. Among these chains are Choice, Marriott, Holiday, Sheraton, Inter-Continental, Radisson, Accor, and Hilton International.

In Latin America, only 12 percent of the hotels were affiliated with international chains in the early 1990s, but great changes are about to occur. Both Radisson and Inter-Continental Hotels now have a presence in every capital city of Latin America. Sheraton, Days Inns, and Choice are growing rapidly in South America. Both Days Inns and Accor are flirting with development in Cuba, although myriad political problems must be overcome for such development to take place. Exhibit 17 lists the key players in Latin America.

Exhibit 18   Major Chains in the Middle East

Sheraton Hotels	Marriott International
Holiday Inn Worldwide	Safir Hotels
Inter-Continental Hotels	Radisson Hotels
Hilton International	Hospitality Franchise Systems

Exhibit 19   Key Players in the Asia-Pacific Region

Sheraton Hotels	Shangri-La Hotels
Choice International	Hilton International
Hyatt International	Regal Hotels
Meridien Hotels	CDL Hotels
Westin Hotels	New Otani
Marriott International	Renaissance Hotels
Holiday Inn Worldwide	Hospitality Franchise Systems
Inter-Continental Hotels	Radisson Hotels
Accor Corporation	Nikko Hotels
Prince Hotels	Best Western International
Dusit-Thani Hotels	ANA Hotels International

The Middle East gained 5,000 rooms in 1996 alone; 9,000 additional rooms will be operational by 1999. While both Syria and Israel have their own domestic hotel chains, international chains operate 95 percent of all the hotels in the area. The major chains operating in the Middle East are shown in Exhibit 18.

South Africa has experienced only mild globalization, but Westin, Holiday Hospitality, Days Inns, and Marriott all have a presence there, and each has announced expansion plans. The country also boasts Sun Hotels International, a strong international chain of its own.

In a contest to identify the "hottest" development area of the world today, the Asia-Pacific region would win hands down. So much has happened there, and so quickly, that there is fear of overbuilding in the upscale segment in a few of the market areas. Accor, the large French chain, is number one in the area, and has stated that its principal focus for the future will be the Asia-Pacific region. However, Accor has plenty of competition there, as shown in Exhibit 19.

Globalization can create some problems. In today's world, the flow of investment and management skills has become multilateral. As a result, some countries have defense mechanisms for regulating foreign operators who attempt to establish themselves there. Local hoteliers may accuse international operators of acquiring excessive dominance, of bringing in foreign workers instead of hiring local workers, and of earning prohibitive management fees. In the long run, operators will increasingly be required to assume a share of the investment risk where possible. Other flexible responses will include franchising and marketing agreements.

A View of the Lodging Industry Around the World ——————

Europe

Unfortunately, there is no way to describe the European hotel industry as a whole. The structure of the industry in each country is different, and there is no consistent approach to quantifying or rating the hotels from one country to another. The common denominator is the predominance of independently owned and operated hotels. There are large chains based in each of the countries and often with operations in two or more of the others. The most sophisticated by U.S. criteria is France. It has the most chain-affiliated hotels, the most chains, the most segmentation and branding, and the most hotels affiliated in other European countries. The French hotel industry is dominated by Accor, which has about 40 percent of all chain-affiliated hotels in France. Even so, all chain-affiliated hotels in France account for only about 20 percent of the industry. Chain-affiliated hotels in the United Kingdom account for about 15 percent of the industry. About 10 percent of Germany's hotels are chain-affiliated, and many of them are French and British.

In Europe, generally, the upper economy to mid-market segments are the least organized and least dominated by hotel chains (except in France by Accor). Both the lower budget and the upscale to luxury segments are being increasingly developed or dominated by well-established European chains as well as U.S. chains in the upscale segment.

The United Kingdom, France, Germany, and the Benelux countries (Belgium, the Netherlands, and Luxembourg) are the most advanced economically, have the largest gross national profits (GNPs), and generate and receive the most business travelers. These countries are equivalent to 13 percent of the geographical area of the United States, but contain a population equal to 88 percent of the U.S. figure. The cultures of these countries are still distinct, but they are increasingly integrated economically. The glue bonding this integration is travel, which means an opportunity for Pan-European hotel systems. The region has enjoyed steady growth throughout the 1990s, even during the economic downturn.

European Travel Patterns. Among Europeans traveling within Europe, heavy business/commercial trade tends to move from east to west among the United Kingdom and Benelux countries, France, Germany, and Scandinavia. The United Kingdom is the leading outbound business travel market, and Germany is the major international business travel destination for Europeans. The leisure travel of Europeans tends to move from north to south as people from the more northern and western countries travel to Spain, Portugal, Italy, southern France, and Greece.

Business travelers represent only 15 percent of total European travelers, but that percentage converts to 25 million trips per year. Leisure travelers are very seasonal and generally are very cost-conscious. When they stay at hotels (which many avoid), they tend to stay at inexpensive ones. Business and leisure travel by

Europeans to and from Eastern Europe is not yet significant compared to travel within Western Europe.

Hawaii

Hawaii today is one of the most successful visitor destinations in the world. While its popularity was first conjured up by romantic Hollywood movies of an exotic Polynesian paradise, its enduring popularity is due to its ideal climate, tropical setting, sand and sea, and a unique blend of Polynesian, Asian, and American cultures.

Hawaii experienced an economic and tourism boom in the 1980s. The number of visitors grew from 3.9 million in 1980 to nearly 7 million in 1990 and the tourism industry thrived. Hotel occupancy for the entire state ranged from the mid-70 percent to the low-80 percent levels. Waikiki, the strongest market area, maintained occupancy levels well over 80 percent from 1983 to 1991.

The biggest single impact on the tourism market and the economy of Hawaii began in 1985 when the U.S. dollar was devalued against the Japanese yen and the Japanese government began encouraging travel and investment abroad. (The value of the dollar dropped from 250 yen to 1 dollar to 125 yen to 1 dollar from 1985 to 1988.) That same year saw the beginning of increased tourist activity from Japan and the beginning of the tidal wave of investments in Hawaiian real estate, primarily "trophy" hotels, resorts, golf courses, and commercial buildings.

Since 1987, the largest growth in room supply has been in the outer island luxury hotels. Many of these hotels were built at a cost in excess of $500,000 per room, making it difficult to realize any reasonable rate of return from investment in these luxury properties.

There was a significant drop in tourism in 1991 and 1992 as a result of the Gulf War and the recession in the United States. In 1991, hotel occupancy for the luxury hotels averaged about 55 percent at room rates some $50 to $75 less than budgeted. Visitor counts dropped below 1990 levels, overall tourist spending decreased, stays were shorter, and worldwide competition increased.

1993–1995 showed no improvement. Arrivals were well below 1990 levels as was the occupancy percentage. Tourist officials estimated that the drop in arrivals caused a $750,000 loss per day for the economy. Especially harmful was a significant decrease in the number of Japanese tourists. While a western tourist spent an average of $140 per day, the Japanese tourist spent $344 per day.

The mid-1990s were extremely bad for the luxury hotels located on the outer islands. Many of these hotels were Japanese-owned. As mentioned previously, even in boom times these luxury hotels found it difficult to make ends meet because of their high cost per room. In this period, the demand for expensive deluxe accommodations shrank drastically. At the same time, luxury inventory rose from 4,000 to 14,000 rooms. Many of the Japanese-financed hotels have gone into bankruptcy, and continue to do so. By 1997, Japanese losses in Hawaii totaled over $1 billion, and the end was not yet in sight.

Horror stories abounded. For example, the $180 million Ritz Carlton was sold for $75 million; the $350 million Kahala Hilton brought only $50 million; four hotel properties with a combined value of $129 million sold for $41.1 million; and ANA Hotels closed the doors of their Sheraton Makaha.

Tourism is extremely important to Hawaii, so it is not surprising that the state itself undertook an aggressive marketing campaign to reverse the decline in tourism visitors and income. The campaign appears to be working. 1996 showed a dramatic increase in occupancy over 1995, and 1997 ran well ahead of 1996 both in occupancy and average daily rate.

Asia and the Pacific Rim

The 1980s in Asia were dominated by the buoyant and incredibly aggressive Japanese economy. The Japanese developers, spurred by very favorable credit terms from their lenders, undertook to acquire existing hotels and to build new ones in virtually every corner of Asia.

Paralleling this acquisition and new development was an ever-increasing demand from Japanese travelers to visit overseas. This phenomenon was inspired by the Japanese government strategy to liberalize the lifestyles of workers, encouraging them to take more time away from the job. Major Japanese investment in foreign lands also meant an accelerated pace of foreign business travel.

Japanese-owned (and frequently Japanese-managed) hotels can now be seen along the Western Pacific Basin from Australia and New Zealand to the south all the way to Taiwan and Korea in the north.

Toward the end of the 1980s, a near mirror-image set of developments occurred with Korea, whose foreign travel restrictions were greatly liberalized after the 1984 Seoul Olympics. Korean investment in hotels and resorts is expected to increase well into the twenty-first century.

Some of the key areas that have seen major tourism development in recent years include: Guam and Saipan; Okinawa; Korean Highlands; Cheju Island; Cebu, the Philippines; Phuket, Thailand; Bali, Indonesia; and Queensland, Australia.

As the economies of Asian countries—most notably Taiwan, Hong Kong, Singapore, Thailand, and Malaysia—continue to grow, more investment in tourism both within their borders and internationally can be expected. Their citizens will increasingly demand to partake of the fruits of economic success by enjoying leisure travel. (Exhibit 20 lists the hotel companies with the most rooms under development in the region.)

Hotel companies with extensive Asian experience are enjoying success in securing management contracts on this new wave of Asian resorts and hotels. Obtaining these contracts often involves some investment on the part of the hotel companies. Among the companies most active in the area are: Hilton with its affiliate, Conrad International; Hyatt; Shangri-La; Four Seasons; Regent; Forte Hotels; Swissôtel; and Sheraton. Most recently, Marriott has entered the picture with commitments in Australia, Japan, and Indonesia to supplement its presence in Hong Kong. Hotel franchising is still in a fledgling stage in most areas of Asia.

Development in the second half of the 1990s has moved into four other areas of the region: China, Japan, India, and Vietnam. Mainland China began to show signs of economic liberalization in the early 1990s and consequently attracted a lot of foreign investment. However, the Tiananmen Square incident, along with many confusing signals from the Beijing government, created a sense of wariness on the part of investors. Evidently, the investment community has resolved its uncertainty as

Exhibit 20   Companies with Most Rooms Under Development in Asia-Pacific Area

Company	Rooms	Hotels
Accor Corporation	11,529	62
ITT Sheraton	7,048	21
New World Development Co.	6,603	18
Century International Hotels	5,201	18
Inter-Continental Hotels	3,780	11
Berjaya Hotels & Resorts	3,535	15
Shangri-La Hotels	3,504	07
The Taj Group	3,447	20
Hyatt International	3,304	10

Source: Global Hospitality Resources, Inc., San Diego, July 1997.

development is moving ahead full steam. Omni opened its first hotel in China, Sheraton now has several properties there, and Radisson SAS and Days Inns both have commitments for several hotels. R&R International Group has signed on to develop 50 roadside hotels in the country.

India is both an old and a new development market. Holiday Hospitality, Sheraton, Inter-Continental, and Hyatt have had a presence for a number of years. Each company, however, continues to expand its holdings. These old-timers have now been joined by Marriott, Radisson, Hilton International, Days Inns, and Super 8, all of which are actively developing on a significant scale as the turn of the century approaches.

Japan, like India, has a number of international chains present in its hotel industry. Most recently, two newcomers, Days Inns and Howard Johnson, have inked agreements for multiple properties in Japan.

Vietnam has begun to attract interest and is now enjoying investments in its tourist economy. Accor, Regal Hotels, and Radisson SAS all are operating hotels within the country. International arrivals have increased each of the past two years and are predicted to grow at a modest rate through the year 2000.

Today Hong Kong is a question mark. It passed from British to Chinese rule in mid-1997; it is still too early to predict the effect this will have on Hong Kong's tourist economy. One thing is certain: the whole world watches closely!

Mexico: Past and Present

Long before any European set foot on this continent, there were types of "inns" in the Aztecan empire dedicated to house those who traveled through the extensive domain.

Special buildings existed in Tenochtitlan (now Mexico City) to be used by merchants who came to market their products in Tlaltelolco, an island very close to the artificial island on which Tenochtitlan was built. In the culture of the inhabitants of

Insider Insights

Thomas W. Lattin
President and COO
Patriot American Hospitality
Dallas, Texas _____

Much has been written about the internationalization of the hotel industry and the dominance of the U.S. hotel market by foreigners. It is true that the hotel industry has become more international and that several U.S.-based hotel companies are now owned by foreigners. However, I challenge the idea that foreign chains will dominate, particularly in the United States.

Over the years, service standards in Europe have eroded, prices have gone up, and European ratings have gone down. Also, due to escalating labor costs, Hong Kong hotels (once considered everybody's favorites) are feeling the financial squeeze forcing them to lower their service standards.

Maybe the time is ripe for U.S. hotel chains to be recognized as world leaders in the markets they serve. But before we examine the evidence, let's first define the criteria for success.

To be an industry leader, I believe you must have a successful track record on at least two continents. There are 25 primary hotel chains that do business internationally, 15 of which are American or have American roots.

How have these American chains fared overseas? Well, our record is pretty darn good:

- *Best Western:* The largest lodging group in the world, it is often the international market leader in quality and profitability.

- *Choice Hotels International:* The company is making a name for itself in Europe, Asia, and South America with several of its brands.

- *Hilton International:* Once again aligned with its parent, Hilton Hotels Corporation, its flag flies proudly and profitably in all corners of the globe.

- *Holiday Inn:* "The World's Innkeeper" known on five continents, now speaks with a British accent as well as a southern U.S. one.

- *Hyatt Hotels:* Did you know that one out of every three Hyatts is located outside the United States? The chain has a strong presence in Asia and a growing one in Europe.

- *Inter-Continental Hotels:* Once the polished and profitable jewel of Pan American Airways, it is still an important international player.

- *Marriott Hotels:* The red logo has definitely established itself as a market leader in the capital cities of the world.

- *Radisson Hotels:* The chain continues to raise its flag around the world. Strategically positioned through its affiliations with SAS Hotels and Regent Hotels, Radisson is a bold international risk-taker.

- *Ramada:* Marriott now owns the Ramada rights worldwide as a result of its purchase of Renaissance. The Ramada image and market position internationally are stronger than they are at home.

(continued)

Insider Insights *(continued)*

- *Ritz-Carlton:* Now owned by Marriott, the company has established hotels on several continents and continues to expand around the world.

- *ITT Sheraton:* Did you know that Sheraton has more hotels outside the United States than all foreign-based chains combined have in this country?

- *Westin Hotels:* Once again U.S.-owned, Westin, with its excellent reputation for quality, is accelerating its worldwide expansion.

We should be proud of how American hotel chains have fared around the world. On the other hand, how have foreign hotel chains fared in the United States? Well, let me ask you this: Can you name one foreign hotel chain that has penetrated the U.S. marketplace to such an extent that it has become a market leader in this country?

I didn't think so.

---

the Valley of Anahuac, hospitality was an appreciated tradition. All over the empire, travelers were treated with respect and housed either in private homes or in "inns" built for that purpose.

The Aztecan empire, or its influence, extended all the way to Panama. At the arrival of the Spaniard, Tenochtitlan had an estimated 100,000 households, and there were about 200,000 more in the other cities on the lake's shore.

From 1521 forward, the Spaniards traveled north and south, but mostly between Mexico City and Veracruz, the port from which ships sailed to Cuba and Spain. Inns were built in cities along the roads. One of the best known of these inns was in Perote halfway between Mexico City and Veracruz.

The constant flow of people and merchandise led to the development of roads, housing for travelers, and staging posts where horses could be replaced and cared for. By the end of the eighteenth century, as more roads opened and travel and commerce kept growing, every medium-sized city in the land had inns called "mesones" (from the French word *maison*) or "posadas."

Mexico inherited its hospitality tradition from both the Indians and the Spaniards. It is the foundation for the successful development of today's Mexican hospitality industry.

Small hotels, with better accommodations, appeared all over Mexico at the beginning of the nineteenth century. Their number kept growing and, by the beginning of the twentieth century, there were only a few cities without a hotel. In the Mexican states, the Ancira in Monterey, the Roma in Guadalajara, the Francia in Aguascalientes, and the Inglaterra in Tampico opened to the public. Their success paved the way for further hotel construction.

The railroads built in the last 25 years of the nineteenth century promoted travel and commerce and created additional demand for hotels. Later, between 1918 and 1938, the Reforma, the Regis, and the Ritz opened in Mexico City. The Reforma was the first of the modern hotels in Mexico and operated with most of the advancements of its time.

After World War II, the Hotel del Prado, then the largest hotel in Mexico City, opened with a great Italian staff. This was another major step forward in the Mexican hotel industry. In 1956, the Continental Hilton, operated by Hilton Hotels International, opened with great flourish in Mexico City. It was the first large, modern, and truly international hotel in all of Mexico. Next came the Maria Isabel Sheraton, also in Mexico City. These two were the forerunners of a steady stream of modern properties. Representative of these new hotels were Las Brisas and Las Hadas in Acapulco, the Guadalajara Hilton, the Camino Reals operated by Western International Hotels, and the elaborate El Presidente Chapultepec.

The opening of the skies by the Mexican government had a very important impact on tourist-oriented hotel development in Mexico by making the stopover in Mexico City unnecessary. Acapulco became a mecca for tourists and increased from about 1,000 rooms in 1939 to over 50,000 in 1996. Among its best known hotels are the Princess, the Fiesta Americana, the Pierre Marquez, and Las Brisas. Cancun grew, in 30 years, from nothing to more than 25,000 hotel rooms (1997), and from 180 inhabitants to 400,000. Now, most of the major international hotel companies are represented in its coterie of hotels.

Mexico's beautiful white beaches, clear blue waters, and sunny warm climate have long been favorites of vacationers from the United States, Canada, and Europe. In addition, there is an increasing interest among Europeans for the pre-Columbian archaeological sites, which are attracting more cultural tourists with longer stays. The great sport fishing areas along the Pacific coast of the Baja California Peninsula are enjoying a boom period. Small hotels are being built along the 1,000 miles of beautiful seashore from Tijuana to Cabo San Lucas. Cabo is home to a large number of first-class hotels.

Today, international business is increasing, and so is the number of business travelers. Mexico's large commercial and industrial cities—Mexico City, Queretaro, Guadalajara, Monterrey, and Leon—along with the petroleum areas of Tampico and Tabasco, are welcoming more travelers every day.

Relaxing in Mexico was always easy; doing business in Mexico has historically been difficult. Today, things are changing quickly. Mexico is actively promoting foreign investment. As a result, many activities in the economy are now open to 100 percent foreign ownership. Foreign companies can now own more than 50 percent of Mexican companies and can also own land in Mexico. International hotel companies were among the first to take advantage of this new economic climate. Mexico's largest hotel chain, Grupo Posadas, has been joined by a wide assortment of hotel companies, which are listed in Exhibit 21. Business in Mexico has typically been conducted through strategic alliances and networking. Representatives of these relationships between Mexican entrepreneurs and international chains are:

- Marriott Hotels with Cementos Mexicanos

- Conrad International with Bancomer

- Radisson International Hotels with Banamex

- Westin Hotels with Camino Real

Exhibit 21   Hotel Brands Operating in Mexico

Holiday Inn Worldwide	Hilton Hotels
Radisson Hotels	Ritz Carlton Hotels
Choice International	Melia Hotels
Sheraton Hotels	Krystal Hotels
Renaissance Hotels	Fiesta Americana
Hyatt Hotels	Promus Corporation
Westin Hotels	Club Méditerranée
Howard Johnson	Nikko Hotels
Marriott Hotels	Super 8 Motels
Four Seasons Hotels	Fiesta Inns

- Sheraton Hotels with Banamex

- Renaissance with a group of companies

Mexico uses a star rating system similar to the one used in the United States. However, there are differences that make comparisons with U.S. properties difficult and sometimes misleading. For example, a 5-star hotel in Mexico is equivalent to a 4-star property in the United States. The Mexican government has authorized a study of the rating system with an eye to developing an official government rating system. Currently, the 400,000 hotel rooms in Mexico fall into the following categories:

Unclassified	33.3%
1 Star	10.1%
2 Star	13.5%
3 Star	13.9%
4 Star	13.9%
5 Star	15.4%

The future for the Mexican hotel industry appears promising. While some of the beach resort areas are presently overbuilt, the accelerating tourist flow is well on its way to solving the problem. For the country as a whole, tourism experts predict that, within five years, the economy will face a shortage of hotel rooms.

The Caribbean

The 1960s were years of rapid expansion for tourism in the Caribbean as characterized by improved air access from the various feeder markets and a growing awareness in the minds of the traveling public of the Caribbean as a vacation destination. Of primary importance was the introduction of the wide-bodied intercontinental jet which expanded the base of potential demand to include the United States' Midwest and far-west markets as well as the relatively untapped European markets.

Resorts International opened the Paradise Island Hotel and Casino, and international hotel chains began their expansion into the region. Leading the influx were Canadian Pacific Hotels, Hilton International, Holiday Inns, Inter-Continental Hotels, Sheraton, and Forte Hotels.

The 1970s were marked by strong positive and negative influences on Caribbean tourism and the hotel industry. On the positive side, Gulf + Western developed the Casa de Campo resort in the Dominican Republic. The resort now ranks among the world's elite resorts. SuperClubs introduced Couples in Jamaica. Couples was the first all-inclusive product in the Caribbean. In the States, the Carter Administration deregulated the airline industry, which brought new air carriers and competitive pricing to the market.

On the negative side were oil price hikes in 1973–74 and again in 1979. As oil prices increased, airfare rates increased and hotel occupancy decreased. Perhaps the most damaging to the tourism industry were two events that took place in Jamaica and St. Croix. There was serious rioting in Jamaica, and, on St. Croix, seven tourists were murdered by local citizens.

In the early 1980s, prices of many regionally important commodities (sugar in Jamaica, Barbados, and Dominican Republic; oil in Aruba, Curaçao, and Trinidad; bauxite in Jamaica) became unstable, leading to a greater emphasis on the potentially positive economic benefits of tourism.

Both Eastern Airlines and American Airlines established major hubs at Luis Munoz Marin International Airport in San Juan, which created unprecedented air access to Puerto Rico in particular and to the region in general.

However, the region could not escape some negative situations. The 1982–83 recession in the United States led to a downturn in tourism arrivals, as did the prolonged strike by Eastern Airlines employees and the bankruptcy of a major wholesaler to the region. Hurricane Gilbert hit Jamaica, Cancun, and several islands in 1988, and Hurricane Hugo battered St. Croix and Puerto Rico in 1989.

The 1990s got off to a terrible start. The United States moved into a deep recession, the war in the Gulf along with threats of terrorism greatly reduced travel, and two major airlines (Pan American and Eastern) serving the area completely dissolved operations.

The lodging industry of the Caribbean usually parallels that of the United States. In the 1990s, it has been nearly a mirror image. As American hotel losses began to turn into profits, tourism began to prosper in the Caribbean. By 1995, the lodging economy could be described as strong. Although certain areas were hit by major hurricanes in 1995 and 1996, the overall tourist economy was not significantly damaged. International arrivals reached 13.5 million in 1996, and continue to increase at nearly 6 percent per year. Puerto Rico, the Dominican Republic, and the Bahamas received 47 percent of the international arrivals. However, the fastest-growing areas were Saint Maarten, Barbados, and Cuba.

Cuba is attracting considerable attention in the lodging community as political analysts are hinting at a government change in the country. Even without a change in government, Cuba's international visitors continue to increase. In 1987, 289,000 tourists visited Cuba. By 1995 that number had increased to 700,000, and continues to increase today. Were the U.S. government to lift its ban on American tourism to Cuba, the number of international visitors there would skyrocket.

Even now, Sol Melia, SuperClubs, and Accor are operating and expanding in Cuba. Days Inns will be there soon if they succeed in negotiating permission from the U.S. government.

Central and South America

While Central and South America can hardly be called the new frontier of tourism, a number of countries there could be considered well-kept tourism secrets. Tourism has been gaining strength in each of the past few years. The World Tourism Organization projects Latin American tourism to be strong beyond the year 2000, and thus worthy of attention. The following is a snapshot of each country's tourism industry picture.

Costa Rica. Tourism is now this country's largest source of foreign exchange—ahead of both bananas and coffee. With its tropical rain forests, Costa Rica was one of the first countries to recognize the potential of ecotourism. A number of hotel chains now have a presence in the country.

Colombia. Colombia's hotel sector is predicted to grow 8 to 9 percent annually through the year 2005. International chains are getting a foothold here primarily through the use of franchising. Principal among these chains are Inter-Continental Hotels, Hilton Hotels, Forte Hotels, Holiday Inns, Radisson Hotels, Marriott International, and Days Inns.

Panama. Most of the hotel development activity in Panama centers around its capital city of Bogota. However, the government is targeting ecotourism with its rainforest development near its northern border with Costa Rica. Radisson Hotels, Inter-Continental Hotels, and Marriott International are all active in this market.

Peru. The Peruvian government is actively selling off its hotels and tourist inns through its privatization program. Within the country, Cuzco is the number-one tourist destination, so it is not surprising to find international chains looking for franchise opportunities in that area. Chief among the group are Hilton Hotels, Sheraton Hotels, Hyatt International, Marriott International, and Inter-Continental Hotels. Oro Verde (a small Swiss-run chain) and Cesar Hotels also operate in the area.

Uruguay. The country is gradually shifting from an agriculture-based economy to a service industry-based one with emphasis on tourism and banking. The World Tourism Organization lists Uruguay as the second most popular destination in South America. Punta del Este, the country's most popular resort area, features a Conrad Hotel and Casino. Sheraton recently opened a new 5-star hotel in the city of Montevideo, and both Radisson and Choice have new developments in several parts of the country.

Venezuela. Tourism experts state that Venezuela has the greatest untapped hospitality potential of any South American country. Its features include 1,600 miles of Caribbean coastline, 72 off-shore islands, vast areas of rainforest, the world's highest waterfall, and the world's longest and highest tramway. The country's most popular resort, Margarita Island, features five hotels, the newest of which is the

Hilton International. Also operating in Venezuela are Best Western, Sheraton, and Inter-Continental Hotels.

Argentina. Argentina is the number-one tourist destination in South America. The country features a cosmopolitan city, Buenos Aires; first-class ski resorts; and entire regions of wildlife and waterfalls. Especially attractive are the rainforest areas of Iguazo. Sheraton, Radisson, Marriott, Inter-Continental, and Choice are the principal chains operating in Argentina.

Brazil. Brazil's major attraction is the world-famous city of Rio de Janiero. Although its glamour has been dimmed a bit by its high crime rate, it remains an attractive destination. Fortaleza, Bahia, and Menas Gerais are the chief tourist centers. In fact, Bahia is the fastest-growing tourist area in all of South America. Brazil has attracted development by Choice, Radisson, Hilton International, Best Western, and Inter-Continental Hotels.

Chile. Second only to Argentina in attracting international visitors, Chile is enjoying a tourism boom. The country's stable and growing economy serves as a magnet attracting international chains. Each of the following has one or more properties in operation and is exploring further expansion: Hilton International, Inter-Continental Hotels, Holiday Inn, Howard Johnson, Radisson, Sheraton, and Sonesta.

Endnotes

1. Tom Lattin, "Amenities Then and Now," in *U.S. Lodging Industry—1987* (Philadelphia: Laventhol & Horwath, 1987), pp. 8–10.

2. Crowne Plaza Hotel, unpublished survey.

3. *Lodging Hospitality,* December 1996, p. 70.

4. Tom Lattin, quoting some of the executives at Patriot American Hospitality.

5. Raymond C. Ellis, Jr., and the Security Committee of AH&MA, *Security and Loss Prevention Management* (East Lansing, Mich.: Educational Institution of the American Hotel & Motel Association, 1986).

6. Quoted by Peter Yesawich, at Hotel Conference at the Registry Hotel, Ft. Lauderdale, March 24, 1997. The report is done jointly with Mr. Yesawich's firm, Yesawich, Pepperdine & Brown.

7. Tom Lattin, personal interview.

8. Dr. Bjorn Hanson, speaking at the Registry Conference, Ft. Lauderdale, March 24, 1997.

9. Tom Lattin, Registry Conference, Ft. Lauderdale, March 24, 1997.

10. *Hotel Business Magazine,* June 1996.

11. *Hotel & Motel Management,* April 8, 1996, p. 5.

12. Henry Silverman, personal interview.

13. Robert Hazard, personal interview.

14. Marriott Annual Report, 1996.

15. Marriott Quarterly Report to Shareholders, July 1997.

Key Terms

amenities—A term that encompasses many guest services (such as in-room entertainment systems, automatic check-out, free parking, concierge services, and multilingual staff) in addition to an array of personal bathroom items offered by most hotels and motels. Amenities are designed to bolster a hotel's appeal, enhance guests' stays, and bring guests back to the hotel.

condominium—Units of properties which are sold to individual owners; there are many types.

consolidation—Process by which the number of owning companies of brand hotels decreases due to purchases, mergers, and other ownership transfers.

conversion—The activity that takes place when an independent joins a chain or when a property changes from one corporate flag to another (for example, a Holiday Inn becomes a Days Inn or a Ramada becomes a Comfort Inn) or a chain property becomes independent.

franchise—Refers to (1) the authorization given by one company to another to sell its products and services; or (2) the name of the business format or product being franchised.

in-room guest console—A multi-feature phone that may include such functions as two-way speakerphone capability; a jack for portable computer use; an alarm clock; radio; remote control of heating, ventilating, and air conditioning, television, and room lights; energy management; and a theft alarm.

management contract—A contract that authorizes a chain to exercise complete control over the standards and quality of each property and is responsible for day-to-day operations; franchising does not provide this control. Of course, with franchising the chain does not need a large professional operating staff; with a management contract, it does.

Review Questions

1. What is a franchise operation? Discuss similarities and differences of chain and franchise operations.

2. What are the fundamental differences between franchising and using a management contract?

3. What are independent management companies?

4. How are the condominium concept and time-sharing related?

5. How has market segmentation diversified the lodging industry?

6. How have amenities and advanced technology affected market segmentation efforts?

7. What factors fueled the hotel building boom of the 1980s? What was the situation at the end of the '80s?

8. Why has casino gambling gained such a high level of popularity in the United States?

9. In lodging terms, how does consolidation differ from conversion?

10. How are Real Estate Investment Trusts categorized? Name the various categories and the differences between them.

11. What factors led to globalization? Name ten or more of the major international hotel chains.

12. What factors led to today's high rate of lodging industry development in Asia and the Pacific Rim?

Internet Sites

For more information, visit the following Internet sites. Remember that Internet addresses can change without notice. If the site is no longer there, use a search engine to look for additional sites.

Hotels and Hotel Companies

Best Western
http://www.bestwestern.com

Canadian Pacific Hotels
http://www.cphotels.ca

Hyatt Hotels and Resorts
http://www.hyatt.com

Inter-Continental Hotels
http://www.interconti.com

ITT Sheraton Corporation
http://www.sheraton.com

Marriott Hotels, Resorts, and Suites
http://www.marriott.com/lodging

Radisson Hotels Worldwide
http://www.radisson.com

Ritz Carlton Hotels
http://www.ritzcarlton.com

Smith Travel Research
http://www.str-online.com

Westin Hotels and Resorts
http://www.westin.com

Condominium and Timeshare Organizations

Disney Vacation Club
http://www.disney.com/Disney
VacationClub/index.html

Hilton Grand Vacations Company
http://www.hgvc.com

Hyatt Vacation Club
http://www.hyatt.com/athyatt/
vacation/index.html

Interval International
http://www.interval-intl.com

Marriott Vacation Club
http://www.marriott.com/
vacationclub

Resort Condominiums Internatinal, Inc.
http://www.rci.com/index.html

Timesharing Today
http://www.timesharing-today.com

Timeshare User's Group
http://www.tug2.net

Chapter 5 Outline

Size and Scope of the Industry
American Hotel Classifications
  Commercial Hotels
  Airport Hotels
  Conference Centers
  Economy Properties
  Suite or All-Suite Hotels
  Extended-Stay Hotels
  Convention Hotels
  Residential Hotels
  Casino Hotels
  Resort Hotels
  Bed and Breakfast Hotels
European Hotel Market Segments and Hotel Types
Organization of American Hotels
  The Rooms Division
  The Food and Beverage Division
  The Engineering and Maintenance Division
  The Marketing and Sales Division
  The Accounting Division
  The Human Resources Division
  The Security Division
Organization of European Hotels
The Importance of Cooperation

5

The Organization and Structure of Lodging Operations

THE PROFESSION OF HOTEL MANAGEMENT is one of the most challenging, and, at the same time, least understood, in the American economy. Although most communities have one or more lodging properties, and although the average citizen has had some contact with them, few people realize the diversified knowledge, variety of skills, and creativity demanded of the successful hotel manager.

Size and Scope of the Industry

Hotels are found in every country and city of the world. It is no wonder that hotel-keeping ranks high among the largest worldwide industries. The World Tourism Organization estimates that there were about 11,500,000 hotel rooms worldwide in 1997, with more than 50 percent of the rooms in Europe, and about 33 percent in North America.

In Europe, most hotels are smaller than their overseas counterparts. A hotel with more than 100 rooms is considered large, and one with more than 300 rooms is considered extremely large. Individually owned and managed properties are far more common than chain-operated properties. However, every year more and more hotels become members of chains or associations. This trend will probably gain momentum because of the many advantages of affiliation. Independent hotels will continue to play a significant role for those guests who dislike what they perceive as the uniform quality of chain hotels. Independent hotels may join marketing or referral associations to gain some chain-like benefits without giving up their individuality.

In America, hotelkeeping ranks among the top five service industries, coming only after such giants as public transportation and restaurant management. According to the American Hotel & Motel Association's 1996 statistics, there are approximately 46,000 hotels in the United States with a total of 3.5 million rooms. That year's hotel receipts totaled approximately $72 billion in sales, while the hotels had payroll expenses totaling approximately $19 billion. The lodging industry employs 1.618 million people and creates 120,000 new jobs each year. In 1996, the lodging industry paid $6.8 billion in federal taxes alone.

When we hear or read about a hotel, it is usually a famous hotel in a large city—New York's Plaza or Waldorf-Astoria, Atlanta's Marriott Marquis, the Excalibur in

Exhibit 1 United States Hotels by Type

By Inventory	Property	Rooms
Urban	5.4%	14.3%
Suburban	40.4%	35.1%
Highway	47.7%	33.6%
Airport	2.6%	6.4%
Resort	3.9%	10.6%

Source: American Hotel & Motel Association, 1997 Lodging Industry Profile.

Exhibit 2 United States Hotels by Size

By Size	Property	Rooms
Under 75 Rooms	66.8%	25.2%
75–149 Rooms	21.5%	30.8%
150–299 Rooms	8.6%	22.6%
Over 300 Rooms	3.1%	21.4%

Source: American Hotel & Motel Association, 1997 Lodging Industry Profile.

Exhibit 3 United States Hotels by Rate

By Rate	Property	Rooms
Under $30	26.8%	8.2%
$30–$44.99	28.0%	17.1%
$45–$59.99	16.3%	17.9%
$60–$85	15.1%	22.0%
Over $85	13.0%	34.8%

Source: American Hotel & Motel Association, 1997 Lodging Industry Profile.

Las Vegas, Tokyo's Imperial, or the Orient in Bangkok. However, even though large and famous hotels play an important role in lodging, they are not typical of the lodging industry in the United States or in the world. Less than five percent of all hotels worldwide have over 300 rooms. In the United States, 87 percent of the hotels have 150 or fewer rooms. Exhibit 1 shows a breakdown of United States hotels by type, Exhibit 2 shows United States hotels by size, and Exhibit 3 shows United States hotels by rate.

Traditionally, hotels have been small enough for individuals to own and operate. In recent years, however, skyrocketing costs have resulted in a trend toward

The Willard Inter-Continental in Washington, D.C.

corporate ownership, which has produced a new class of hoteliers—college-trained people who are choosing hotel management as a profession. In addition, absentee ownership has created a maze of sophisticated management, financial, and operating systems whose intricacies and complexities can be understood and handled only by someone with extensive training. Because of this, corporate ownership of hotels has been one of the primary forces in the development of college-level training in the field of hotel management.

American Hotel Classifications

Classifying hotels is not always an easy task. Because of the industry's diversity, many hotels do not fit into one, or only one, well-defined category. Nonetheless, there are several useful general classifications. The following categories are based on location, price, level of service, and amenities.[1]

Commercial Hotels

Commercial hotels, the largest group of lodging properties, cater primarily to business clients. Commercial hotels are often located in downtown or business areas—places convenient for businesspeople. Amenities can range from free newspapers and morning coffee to computer terminals in the guestrooms. The hotel will usually have room service, a coffee shop, and a formal dining room. There may be a cocktail lounge. Laundry/valet service, uniformed service, a ticket office, gift shops, and professional medical and dental services may all be available. Swimming pools, saunas, and health clubs are sometimes provided. Although commercial hotels attract mainly business travelers, many individual tourists, tour groups, and small conference groups use them as well.

Airport Hotels

Located near airports, these hotels derive much of their appeal from their convenience for travelers. Airport hotels may provide any level of service or combination of amenities. Services may include meeting facilities and hotel limousines or courtesy vans that take guests to and from the airport. Markets include business travelers and airline passengers with short layovers or canceled flights.

Conference Centers

Many hotels provide meeting space, but conference centers are designed specifically to handle group meetings and provide all the services and equipment necessary to ensure a meeting's success. Most full-service conference centers offer overnight accommodations as well as meeting facilities.

Economy Properties

Sometimes called limited-service properties, these hotels attract the cost-conscious traveler. They offer clean rooms at low prices and typically meet only the basic needs of guests. Amenities may not be provided. Food service may not be available. The markets for economy properties include vacationing families, government employees, tour groups, businesspeople, and groups of conventioneers.

Suite or All-Suite Hotel

Suite or all-suite hotels are one of the fastest growing segments of the lodging industry. Accommodations feature separate bedrooms and living rooms, or at least clearly defined areas within one room. Hotel suites sometimes also contain a kitchenette, a refrigerator, and a wet bar. These hotels are typically located outside the city center. Businesspeople find suite hotels particularly attractive, since they offer a place to work and entertain separate from the bedroom. Suite hotels may also provide temporary quarters for people who are relocating or for vacationing families.

Insider Insights

Humberto "Burt" Cabañas
President & CEO
Benchmark Hospitality, Inc.
The Woodlands, Texas ————————————————————

Conferences and meetings have been an integral part of companies', corporations', and associations' efforts to maintain internal and external communication. As these organizations have grown in size and complexity, an increasing demand has evolved for facilities to hold their conferences. Typical meeting locations which have been developed to meet this demand range from corporate board rooms to hotels, meeting rooms, resorts, country clubs, and university classrooms.

The characteristics of each of these facilities have often worked against meeting efficiency, and the distractions are many: external noise and congestion; the lure of an active resort; interruption and disruption of important sessions; and the confusion of numerous people at the same facility for different purposes. Furthermore, not all distractions are external. Poorly designed guest and meeting rooms, an insufficient number of meeting and breakout rooms, inadequate lighting, uncomfortable furniture, and a lack of modern meeting aids and trained personnel all add to the inefficiencies and inadequacies of such facilities.

Some corporations and associations have included conference rooms in their headquarters. Such in-house meeting facilities are typically convenient and comfortable. However, subtle considerations often make the corporate conference room less desirable than expected. The frequent intrusions of "important" telephone calls and minor office crises work against the benefit of a controlled environment conducive to learning. Also, the abrupt return to external affairs that occurs when the conferee steps from the meeting room to attend lunch or go home for the evening detracts from information retention and meeting efficiency, and fractures the learning environment. The momentum developed during the session is lost; therefore, the receptive attitude of the conference attendee must then be reestablished, a feat which is often accomplished only after a considerable loss of valuable time.

It is this demand for more appropriate facilities which resulted in the development of the conference center concept. Conference centers avoid the problems which accompany multi-market oriented hospitality facilities and in-house corporate meeting rooms by concentrating full-time on the off-premise small meetings market of typically less than 50 persons per conference.

The primary purpose of conference centers is to satisfy and accommodate conference groups by offering a self-contained learning environment. Maximum results are achieved when a balance among Living, Learning and Leisure™ is achieved.

The conference center concept was originally introduced to the United States in 1950 at Arden House by Dwight D. Eisenhower during his tenure as President of Columbia University. Arden House is the former estate of W. Avrill Harriman and a national historic landmark located in Harriman, New York.

Today, the International Association of Conference Centers classifies conference centers into six categories:

(continued)

Insider Insights *(continued)*

Executive Conference Center
This type of facility is developed primarily to satisfy the requirements of specialized meetings consisting of upper-level management planning and education/training seminars. Groups are typically composed of corporations, associations, and other organizations which emphasize the quality rather than the price of accommodations.

Facilities include sophisticated audio-visual equipment and meeting aids, and the center is staffed with professional conference coordinators. Typically, this center has 100 to 300 lodging rooms for a maximum capacity of about 400 conferees, specially designed meeting rooms, and a large number of smaller "breakout" rooms. The operation is characterized by personalized, friendly service and high-quality food.

Resort Conference Center
Meetings held at a Resort Conference Center are similar to those held at either executive or corporate centers, but there is a greater emphasis on recreation and social activities as an additional incentive for attendees.

The size of meeting facilities varies with the size of the resort, the number of condominiums in any rental program, the commercial amenities, the target market, and the resort's commitment to a conference program. Staff and meeting aids may or may not be developed to the extent that they are in executive or corporate centers, but they nevertheless meet the planner's requirements.

Corporate-Owned (Proprietary) Conference Center
An increasing number of major corporations are designing their own conference center facilities, primarily for in-house use. In some cases, the center is made available to outside users who have the same objectives as users of executive conference centers.

Facilities are professionally staffed and are supplied with sophisticated meeting aids. The size of these facilities varies with the corporation's need for meeting and lodging rooms.

Not-for-Profit/Educational Conference Center
These facilities are generally developed by and associated with a major educational institution or non-profit organization. Meetings held at centers owned by a college or university are held primarily by organizations that are technically oriented or academic or university-related. These groups are typically more price-sensitive than those in the Executive, Corporate, or Resort markets.

These educational facilities range from self-contained, executive-style centers to, in certain cases, on-campus accommodations, and are usually staffed by college or university personnel.

Non-Residential Conference Center
Non-residential centers share many of the attributes of executive, corporate, and resort centers. The major exception is that these facilities do not offer sleeping accommodations. They are designed for "day" meetings in which

(continued)

Insider Insights *(continued)*

attendees do not stay overnight. Since they are usually located in urban areas, lodging is often available at nearby hotels should an overnight stay be necessary.

Ancillary Conference Center
This type of conference center must be connected to or surrounded by the larger entity and managed by that larger entity. For example, a conference wing within a hotel or a conference center facility within a resort complex is considered an ancillary conference center. Like all other conference centers, these facilities must offer a complete package of conference rooms and services.

With the support of the International Association of Conference Centers, several hospitality management companies have been able to capitalize on the specific requirements of the conference market through the design of specialized meeting, lodging, dining, and recreational facilities, the development of specialized services, and the application of a unique blend of proven hospitality industry management and marketing systems with those specifically developed for conference resorts and executive conference centers. Secondarily, this same application has proven to be a successful enhancer at hotels and resorts where the mix of business exceeds 50 percent group meetings.

Extended-Stay Hotels

Extended-stay hotels are lodging facilities that resemble apartment buildings. The guestrooms feature full kitchens, living areas, and bedrooms. They cater to travelers who need to stay in an area for an extended period (usually defined as more than seven days) and thus do not experience the week-end occupancy declines that affect most commercial hotels. These properties also benefit from operating efficiencies resulting from the lower rate of turnover.

Convention Hotels

Convention hotels offer extensive meeting space that attracts the meeting and group market segment. Most convention hotels cater to both commercial and meeting travelers, which limits their dependence on a single segment. These properties require specialized management expertise. The huge cost of developing full-service convention hotels limits new supply growth and thus reduces the risk of overbuilding.

Residential Hotels

No longer as popular as they once were, residential hotels offer principally long-term accommodations, though they may accommodate short-term guests as well. The residential hotel usually offers housekeeping service, a dining room, room meal service, and possibly a cocktail lounge. Rooms may resemble suites in layout and design. The food and beverage division is usually small and exists more as a convenience for the residents than as a true source of income; sometimes outside catering firms provide food service. Residential hotels range from the luxurious, offering full suites for families, to the moderate, offering single rooms for individuals.

Casino Hotels

In casino hotels, the rooms and food and beverage operations may function primarily to support the gambling facilities (though they are expected to contribute their own profit). These hotels may be quite luxurious. They frequently offer top name entertainment, extravagant shows, specialty restaurants, and charter flights for high rollers in order to attract gaming revenues.

Resort Hotels

Unlike some other lodging properties, the resort hotel is the planned destination of guests, usually vacationers. This is because resorts are located in some particularly scenic area, such as the seashore or mountains, or because they offer spa or health club facilities. Generally, resorts are situated away from the clamor of large cities, but can be reached easily by plane, train, or automobile.

Resorts often provide special activities for guests—dancing, golf, tennis, horseback riding, nature hikes, and so forth—and the resort staff may include an activities director or even an entire recreational staff. Because guests expect to be entertained wholly on the premises, the contact between guests and management is much greater than at other hotels.

Although many guests spend from one week to an entire season at a resort, a resort hotel's weekend business often represents the difference between profit and loss for the operator.

There are many types of resorts. Some are classified according to property type, such as condominium resorts. Resorts are also categorized on a seasonal basis, such as summer resorts, year-round resorts, cold winter resorts, and warm winter resorts. In addition, there are other defining characteristics. The following types are especially noteworthy in the Caribbean, but they exist elsewhere as well and often overlap with other classifications. They include:

- Modern resort hotels, which feature a variety of restaurants, extensive meeting and conference space, possibly a casino, pools, golf course(s), a tennis center, retail space, and an ocean beach. They cater to a variety of guests from upscale to economy, depending on their overall level of quality and intended market position. Within this group are the Hyatt Cerromar, Puerto Rico; The Wyndham, Jamaica; Frenchman's Reef, St. Thomas; La Toc Hotel and Suites, St. Lucia.

- Mixed-use destination resorts. These hybrid resorts are typically anchored by a modern resort hotel, but also include a number of real estate units. The residential real estate is composed of attached or detached villas, apartment-style condominiums, interval-ownership units, and building lots. Since these resorts contain hundreds, even thousands, of acres, the open layout of the facilities evokes a greater feeling of freedom and leisure than do the resort hotels themselves. Caribbean examples include Casa de Campo, Dominican Republic; Palmas del Mar, Puerto Rico; and Carambola, St. Croix.

- Urban resorts—typified by the Condado Plaza and the Caribe Hilton, Puerto Rico; the Jaragua, Dominican Republic; and the Caribbean, Curaçao. These hotels are located in or near urban areas proximate to government agencies, business centers, and airports and have relatively outdated designs. They cater more directly to commercial travelers and certain group meeting participants than do the modern resort hotels. Given the nature of the Caribbean market, however, none of these hotels can afford to neglect the leisure traveler.

- Casino resorts. Although many newly constructed hotels have small casinos as part of their entertainment offering, they do not gain a significant portion of their revenues from them. The casino resort depends on gaming operations for a significant percentage of its revenues. Representative are the Paradise Island Resort and Casino and Carnival's Crystal Palace in the Bahamas; the El San Juan Hotel and Casino, Puerto Rico; and the Hyatt Regency, Aruba.

- All-inclusive resorts. Pioneered by SuperClubs in Jamaica, the all-inclusive resort is growing in popularity throughout the Caribbean. The all-inclusive resort offers unlimited use of its product (including unlimited food and beverages, sports equipment and facilities, and entertainment) for a set pre-paid price. Guests need no money unless they wish to participate in off-property excursions and buy gifts. Most all-inclusive packages are sold through wholesale travel agents and usually include airfare and ground transfers. While this type of resort traditionally catered to the cost-conscious guest, upscale all-inclusive properties are now being developed. One example is the Grand Lido in Negril, Jamaica.

- Boutique resorts. These exclusive resorts cater to very wealthy guests by offering the finest accommodations, five-star food and beverage service, an intimate and secluded environment, and the highest level of personal attention. The Cap Juluca and the Maliohuana on Anquilla and the Guanahani on St. Barts exemplify this category.

- Guesthouses and inns. These accommodations are small, provide a relatively high level of personal service, and cater to the individual traveler. Perhaps the best known are the paradors in Puerto Rico.

- Budget hotels, which are often non-chain-affiliated and cater almost exclusively to commercial travelers. They are located in the largest cities of the Caribbean, offer limited amenities and facilities, and maintain a high price-value relationship.

Bed and Breakfast Hotels

Bed and breakfast hotels—or B&Bs—derive their name from the fact that they provide sleeping accommodations and breakfast to guests. These properties come in a variety of forms—sometimes a private home with a few guestrooms, at other times a small building with 20 to 30 rooms. The owner usually lives on the premises and is responsible for serving breakfast to guests. This meal may range from a simple

Insider Insights

Richard L. Erb, CHA
General Manager
Stein Eriksen Lodge
Park City, Utah

One of the latest types of special-purpose hotels is the resort hotel community, or condominium resort. These properties usually emerge through one of two ways: Existing facilities, such as many of the hotels at ski resort areas in Vermont and Colorado, may be sold as condominium hotel investments; or, totally new resort communities may be developed. An example is the Grand Traverse Resort in northern Michigan, where I formerly served as chief operating officer.

Many years ago, I decided to learn about resort development community management, as it appeared that virtually all new resorts would emerge under this umbrella, while most existing ones would be wise to consider real estate projects in conjunction with their resort property. When we opened the Mauna Kea Beach Resort Hotel in Hawaii almost 30 years ago, I saw the value of the barren, lava-covered land around the hotel skyrocket overnight. I've never forgotten that.

At Grand Traverse Resort Village, we built a quality resort to bring guests who would become interested in purchasing a condominium or a second home. The resort development community product is usually a condominium. There are many types of lodging condominiums, from a single room in a hotel to luxurious villas with complete kitchens, bars, fireplaces, and garages.

Resort condominiums may be purchased by individuals and then rented out as hotel or resort rooms by a management firm whenever the owners do not need to use them.

Condominium hotels and resorts often operate within a larger plan for total area development. One common version is the resort development community which offers various real estate and hotel products through a complex marketing plan mix. The market research must identify the potential resort/hotel guest and then go on to qualify the guest as a potential condominium or real estate buyer.

Initially, existing resorts sold home lots around their golf courses or ski slopes to their guests. Now, new resorts exist primarily as a tool for selling the real estate product. They try to attract resort customers who are potential buyers as well—usually those whose incomes exceed $75,000 per year.

AAA has recognized condominium rooms as a subclassification for AAA tour books, beginning with the 1993 editions. This will make full-service condo accommodations available to thousands of AAA travel agents and millions of their members.

Marketing resort condominiums presents a challenge, since the product is still perceived as something other than a hotel room. Now, however, with national affiliations emerging for central reservations and chains showing a sincere interest, the tremendous growth of condominium resorts will continue.

The Stakis Dunkeld House Hotel in Perthshire, Scotland, where traditional standards of warmth and hospitality are observed. (Photo courtesy of Stakis Hotels, East Kilbride, Scotland)

continental breakfast to a full course meal. There are thousands of B&Bs in operation today, popular because of their intimate, personal service.

European Hotel Market Segments and Hotel Types

In some respects, market segmentation in Europe has followed the same patterns as in the United States. In others, Europe has made its own patterns.

Some hotels primarily cater to certain guest segments that are common in Europe. Nationality hotels are organized to serve visitors of a specific nationality. Another prevalent tourist group is the sun worshippers—inhabitants of northern countries who like to vacation near the Mediterranean to prolong their short summers. Sports fans are another large guest segment that hotels may be designed to serve. Cultural events, festivals, exhibitions, and visits to historic sights are favored by cultural tourists. Some hotels do a strong summer business from overseas visitors from Asia, the United States, and Latin America. Ethnic travelers are overseas visitors with European roots making trips to their countries of origin. While not all these groups warrant hotels designed specifically for them, each does represent a significant segment of travelers in Europe.

The typical European classifications—which are fairly self-descriptive—include:

- Grand or deluxe hotels

- Four-star business hotels
- Economy business hotels
- Mountain, sea, lake, and spa resorts
- Airport hotels
- Country inns
- Grand tour operators' hotels

Needless to say, many hotels offer a combination of these characteristics. All-suite hotels are noticeably absent from this list, as they have not found a market in Europe.

Some uniquely European hotel types include:

- Relais et Châteaux, an association of independently owned and operated small inns that offer their guests character, calm, comfort, cuisine, and courtesy. Originally European, the association now comprises about 360 hotels in 35 countries.

- Relais du Silence, an association started in 1968 by a group of French hoteliers. Its member properties focus on peaceful, natural surroundings providing calm and tranquility, comfort, character, authenticity, owner presence, hospitality, and gastronomy.

- Palace hotels, which are large, individualistic, often historic hotels. Most of them date back to the late nineteenth or very early twentieth century, and they enjoy a unique market position. Most of these hotels have remained independent of chain affiliation. Typical palace hotels include Hotel Frankfurter Hof, Frankfurt; Hotel Ritz, Paris; Palace Hotel, St. Moritz; Hotel Imperial, Vienna; and Grand Hotel, Rome.

- Pensions, which are either table d'hôte-type American plan or modified American plan boarding houses, designed for longer average stays. In some respects they resemble American bed and breakfast operations. Some are seasonal and serve as a peak season extension of the rooms business generated by the traditional hotels. For example, Alpine farmers often turn their homes into pensions for the winter season to supplement their incomes.

European restaurants that have a few guestrooms and are famous for their culinary offerings are meccas for gourmets. Owned and operated by famous chefs, they enjoy a local, regional, and even international clientele. They are prominently featured in the guides of Michelin or Gault et Millau. Restaurants with three stars in the Guide Michelin are world-famous; these include establishments operated by Paul Bocuse, Fredy Girardet, and the Troisgros brothers.

Organization of American Hotels

A model or standard organization plan that describes how all hotels *should* be organized does not and cannot exist. The plan for any particular hotel depends on a wide range of variables, such as property location, clientele to be served, services

Exhibit 4   Sample Organization Chart for a Small Property

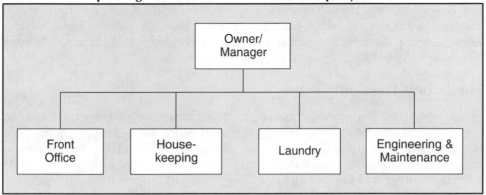

to be offered, structural layout, type of ownership, and the background, personalities, abilities, and training of management staff. For the purposes of discussion, however, we can make some general statements about how hotels are organized.

The use of the terms "department" and "division" is not standardized in the industry. Some properties call their various main functional areas (rooms, food and beverage, accounting, and so forth) departments; the smaller functional areas within departments (for example, catering and room service within the food and beverage department) may then be called subdepartments, functions, or some other term. Other properties (typically larger ones) call their main functional areas divisions; the various units within divisions are then usually called departments. Neither option is better than the other. For consistency, we will call the main functional areas divisions and smaller areas departments.

An **organization chart** is a drawing that shows the relationship between departments or divisions and specific positions within an organization. Exhibit 4 offers an organization chart for a small property. The organization is relatively "flat"—there are only two layers. Nonetheless, small properties still perform the same activities that large properties do. Tasks assigned to specialized positions in large properties are combined into more generalized jobs in small hotels. For example, in a large property, different employees may be assigned to guest registration, reservations, and telephone switchboard duties. In a small property, one employee (the front desk agent) may be responsible for all these duties.

For many years, the terms **front of the house** and **back of the house** have been used to classify the various operational areas within a hotel. Front-of-the-house areas are those in which employees have extensive guest contact. Examples include the food and beverage and rooms divisions (including the front office and reservations departments). Back-of-the-house areas are those in which personnel have very little direct guest contact; examples include the engineering, accounting, and human resources divisions.

Another type of classification is financial. Divisions and sometimes departments within divisions are classified as **revenue centers** or **support centers**. Revenue centers are those areas that directly bring in revenue to the hotel, such as the front office department, the food and beverage division, and any other function that sells goods or services to guests. Support centers do not directly bring in revenue, but are necessary to the functioning of the revenue centers. These include housekeeping, accounting, engineering and maintenance, and human resources. This chapter offers a brief outline of each of these areas.[2]

The Rooms Division

The rooms division comprises those departments most involved in providing hotel services directly to guests. It includes the front office, housekeeping, uniformed service, reservations, and telecommunications departments. (The reservations and telecommunications functions are sometimes part of the front office.) Hotels with garages or other parking facilities often place responsibility for this function with the rooms division. This division, a revenue center, usually earns the most money for the hotel.

The Front Office. The most visible area in a property, with the greatest amount of guest contact, is the front office. The front desk itself is the focal point of activity in the front office because it is where the guest is registered, assigned to a room, and checked out.

The mail and information section of the front office department was once a very prominent section of most properties. In recent years, however, the responsibility for providing guests with information and messages has been divided among the desk agents, PBX (private branch exchange—the term used for the switchboard equipment) operators, and cashiers, so a single full-time person is usually not required for these duties.

Cashiers receive payments and post charges to guest accounts. Point-of-sale terminals (electronic cash registers) help reduce the manual posting of charges. The busiest time for the cashier occurs when guests check out of the property.

Recently, some American hotels have added **concierge** services to their front office functions. Concierge services are special services to hotel guests, such as making theater reservations and obtaining tickets; organizing special functions, such as VIP cocktail parties; and arranging for secretarial and typing services for guests. In a sense, the concierge section is simply an extension of the front office that specializes in guest service. Concierges are often found in European hotels.

Telecommunications. The telecommunications section of the rooms division has a switchboard like that of any large company. Staff may be responsible for receiving calls, placing calls (local and/or long-distance) for guests, tracking and relaying charges, making wake-up calls, monitoring automated systems, and coordinating emergency communication systems.

In hotels using advanced equipment, routing the charges for long-distance calls to guest accounts and making wake-up calls may be done automatically.

Reservations. The reservations section of the rooms division is responsible for receiving, accepting, and making reservations for guests of the hotel. In addition, this department must keep exact records regarding the status of guestrooms and make sure that future dates are not overbooked. Reservations staff members work closely with sales and marketing personnel.

Uniformed Service. Parking attendants, door attendants, porters, limousine drivers, and bell staff make up the uniformed service staff. They meet, greet, and help guests to the front desk and to their rooms. At the end of the stay, they escort guests to the cashier, out the front door, and to their transportation.

Housekeeping. This department's staff cleans vacant rooms to make them ready for occupancy, cleans occupied rooms, and helps the front office keep the status of every room current. An executive housekeeper heads the department and may be assisted by inspectors, room attendants, a laundry manager, housepersons, and, if the department is large enough, an assistant housekeeper. Some large properties may employ people to monitor the housekeeping inventory and people to do sewing repairs.

Housekeepers, also called room attendants, are assigned to specific sections of the hotel. The quota of rooms per attendant may range from 8 to 18 per day, depending on the level of service expected, the room size, the tasks required, and the degree of assistance given to the housekeeper.

Some hotels have their own laundries. In larger properties, the laundry equipment can be quite complicated. It may include folding and ironing machinery in addition to commercial washers and dryers.

The Food and Beverage Division

The food and beverage division is another important revenue center of the hotel. This division is often second only to the rooms division in the amount of revenue it earns.

In properties operating their own food and beverage facilities, a food and beverage director manages the activities of the division. Other positions depend upon the nature of the property's food and beverage operations.

There are many varieties of hotel food and beverage operations—for example, gourmet and specialty restaurants, coffee shops (which may offer 24-hour service), lounges or dining rooms in which live music or shows are performed, room service, and combined banquet and meeting room facilities. Food service in hospitality suites or employee food service may be additional operations. Some chains have attempted to standardize their restaurants so that all the properties within the chain are alike. But, due to the mix of guests, even these operations differ from property to property.

The sale and service of alcoholic beverages is usually a distinct operation, purposely separated from food sales and service. The beverage section has separate storerooms, servers, sales areas, and preparation people (bartenders); its hours of operation may extend well past the hours of the food service operations.

Banquets and catered meals are sometimes handled by food and beverage staff or specially designated personnel. While revenues from banquets are included in the total food and beverage sales, the banquets themselves usually take place in special function rooms or areas of the property. Both banquet and catering services may contribute a significant portion of the revenues earned by the food and beverage division.

The Engineering and Maintenance Division

The engineering and maintenance division maintains the appearance of both the interior and exterior of the property and keeps all equipment operational. A chief engineer or director of property operations directs the division in larger properties. He or she usually reports to the property's general manager.

This division's work can be divided into four main activities—regular maintenance, emergency work, preventive maintenance, and special project assignments. The staff members of this division are often skilled in carpentry, plumbing, and electrical work. Tasks such as painting, minor carpet repairs, furniture refinishing, and preventive equipment maintenance are performed by the maintenance staff. However, major problems or projects may require outside specialists. For example, full-scale refurbishing of public areas and guestrooms is usually contracted to specialists in interior decorating.

Outside, this division handles swimming pool cleaning and sanitation. It also does landscaping, which entails cutting the grass, planting flowers, caring for shrubs and trees, watering plants, and keeping the property's grounds in good condition.

Guest satisfaction depends upon well-maintained rooms. As a result, the engineering and maintenance division must stay in close contact with the front office, handling guest complaints quickly and notifying front office staff when rooms cannot be rented because repairs are necessary.

The Marketing and Sales Division

Although some hotels do not have formal marketing divisions, every hospitality enterprise conducts marketing activities. The primary activities of marketing and sales operations are sales, convention services, advertising, and public relations. The late marketing and sales expert C. DeWitt Coffman once wrote:

> What all this boils down to is that it makes sense to find out, methodically and scientifically, who your best sources of business are, what they want and need, what your competition is doing, what you can do better than your competition; and then plan how, exactly, to get maximum revenue for your operation from those sources.[3]

The size of the marketing and sales division in a hotel can vary from just one person, usually the manager spending only part of his or her time handling this function, up to a staff of 15 or 20 full-time people. Coordination with and knowledge of all other departments and divisions in the hotel is essential for smooth functioning in the marketing and sales division.

The Accounting Division

The accounting division, headed by a controller, handles the financial activities of the operation. A hotel's accounting division must work very closely with the front office's cashiering and guest accounting functions. The number of people on the

Hershey Hotel, Hershey, Pennsylvania.

accounting staff varies, depending partly upon whether most of the accounting is done off the property or on-site.

If the accounting is done off-site, the local property's accounting staff simply collects and sends out the data, without computing the actual operating results. For example, time sheets are forwarded to corporate offices where payroll checks are drawn and mailed back to the properties. Operating figures may be sent out daily, weekly, or at some other regular interval. Income statements are then computed and transmitted from the corporate office to the local property.

If all accounting functions are performed within the hotel, the accounting staff has many more responsibilities and is therefore larger. These responsibilities include paying all bills (accounts payable), sending out statements and receiving payments (accounts receivable), computing payroll information and writing payroll checks, accumulating operating data (income and expenses), and compiling the monthly income statement. In addition, the accounting staff makes bank deposits, secures cash, and performs any other control and monitoring functions required by the hotel's ownership or management.

The Human Resources Division

The human resources division (sometimes called the personnel division) assists other divisions in recruiting and selecting the most qualified job applicants. It also administers insurance and other benefit programs, handles personnel-related complaints, ensures compliance with labor laws, is involved with labor union matters, and administers the property's wage and salary compensation program. In properties that are not large enough to justify the creation of a separate office or position, the general manager may handle the human resources functions.

The scope of the human resources division has changed in recent years. New legislation, the shrinking labor market, and increasing competition among properties have led hotels to place more importance on personnel management. As this division has expanded in size and importance, so have its responsibilities and influence.

The Security Division

Security procedures are generally developed on an individual property basis, because every property has different security needs. National security standards are not feasible for such a varied industry.[4] The security division usually reports directly to the general manager or the manager-on-duty. The staff might be made up of in-house personnel, contract security officers, or personnel with police experience. Some local police departments allow their officers to hold off-duty jobs, and their trained personnel may be hired to work in security at a hotel.

However a hotel's security program is structured, the safety and security of guests, visitors, and employees requires the participation of all staff. For example, front desk staff should issue room keys only to registered guests and make sure all keys are returned at check-out. Housekeeping staff should note any damage to locks, doors, or windows, and the engineering and maintenance division should repair these promptly. All employees should report suspicious activities anywhere on the property to the appropriate security personnel.

The security staff is responsible for helping guests and employees stay safe and secure at the hotel. Specific duties may include patrolling the property or monitoring any television surveillance cameras. The division may also develop and implement procedures for emergencies such as fires, bomb threats, and natural disasters. The security division should maintain a good working relationship with local police and fire departments, since their cooperation and assistance is critical to the security division's effectiveness.

Organization of European Hotels ————————————————

A traditional European hotel at the turn of the century, and into the 1950s or 1960s, was owned and managed by an individual or a family. Under the proprietor or manager were three individuals with near-absolute powers that occasionally even exceeded those of the manager. These three were:

- A *chef de reception,* who had responsibilities similar to today's front office manager

- A *maître d'hôtel,* who had responsibilities similar to today's director of food and beverage division, but had no authority over the chef de cuisine

- A *chef de cuisine,* who had total authority in the kitchen

These three people were present at all hours of the day and were personally known to each guest. They gave special, personal treatment to every guest—they were the current public relations and guest history departments personified.

Exhibit 5   Owner-Managed European Hotel Organization

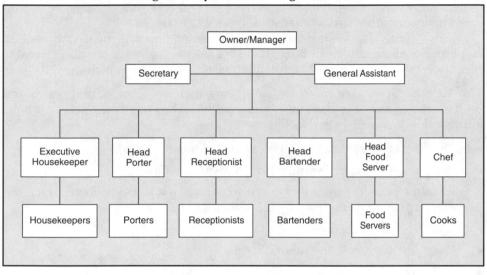

If the hotel was owned by a family, the wife was traditionally responsible for housekeeping, storerooms, and maintenance. She usually carried the title of *gouvernant generale* and acted as the co-manager.

In cases where the manager was a single person, the services of an *aide du patron*, or a boss's helper, were retained. This was usually someone who had just completed studies at a hotel school, but who lacked practical experience. The job did not usually pay well, but it offered excellent opportunities for acquiring practical skills, and it was sometimes a stepping stone to becoming a manager.

Exhibit 5 depicts a typical European hotel organization as it would appear today. As noted previously, European hotels are usually much smaller than their overseas counterparts, which accounts for this rather simple organizational structure in owner-managed properties. The larger and newer European hotels, particularly the chain-operated and big-city ones, are structured more like American hotels.

The Importance of Cooperation

All employees have a role to play in maintaining the property's reputation for value in service and products. Practically every service offered requires the cooperative efforts of two or more departments or divisions. To get an incoming guest from the lobby to a freshly cleaned room involves the front office, uniformed service, and housekeeping. Suppose a hotel sales representative sells a local business manager a special function room for a sales meeting and arranges for a luncheon and an evening banquet in the ballroom. The sales representative makes the arrangements, but the actual setup of the rooms, the preparation and service of the meals, and the general decorative arrangements are handled by departments over which the sales representative has no control. Failure on the part of any one department or any one person in a department can mean unsatisfactory service and a dissatisfied guest. Whether serving a single meal in the coffee shop or handling a large convention, the joint efforts of several departments must be coordinated to ensure successful and satisfactory service to the guest.

Close interaction among the property's owners, management staff, and all employees is necessary. In addition, there are several groups of people external to the property with whom the hotel staff interacts. These groups include:

The Guests. Guests are interested in having their accommodation wants and needs satisfied to the maximum extent possible. The wants and needs of hotel guests are influenced by such factors as:

- The object of the visit (a social occasion or a business trip)

- The guest's concept of value (price relative to quality)

- Absolute price (the price that the customer will not go beyond even if the service or product being purchased is deemed to be of value)

- Social/economic factors

- The guest's age, sex, and marital status

- Ethnic or religious background

Guests choose destinations based in part on the destination's ability to satisfy their needs and wants. The steamship lines, the railroads, and, recently, the airlines have recognized the need for suitable food and lodging along their routes and at their destinations, to better satisfy their guests. As a result, many of the finest hotels and restaurants are owned and operated by transportation companies—for example, Canadian National Railways' and Canadian Pacific Railroads' commercial and resort hotels in Canada.

The Suppliers. Companies that supply products and services to the hotel are another group with special concerns. As business operators, suppliers want to make a profit. Hoteliers should guard against having an "I win—you lose" attitude in negotiations with suppliers. This approach is, at best, shortsighted. Fairness and mutual satisfaction provide the best basis for a relationship between hoteliers and suppliers. Remember that suppliers and their employees may also be prospective guests of the hotel. As residents of the community, suppliers also have numerous opportunities to discuss good and bad aspects of a property with other prospective guests.

The Community. The community is another group that influences the hotel. Since early colonial days, the growth of American hotels has directly paralleled the growth of American cities and towns. In fact, the size and comfort of a city's hotels have long been considered an indicator of a city's prestige.

In recent years, cities have become more keenly aware of the business to be gained from travelers. Large cities often form **convention bureaus**, agencies created to attract regional and national conventions and other large gatherings or meetings. The success of these bureaus depends upon their ability to offer visitors sufficient and comfortable accommodations. Small communities also have recognized the advantages of having a good hotel. In many smaller cities, businesspeople

Insider Insights

Karl-Heinz Hatzfeld
Retired Senior Vice President Operations
Europe and Israel
ITT Sheraton Hotels ————————————————————

When asked "What is the most important factor in determining the success of a hotel?" E. M. Statler's well-known reply was "Location, location, location!" I fully agree with him, especially if someone is planning to build a new site.

However, once the hotel goes into operation, the focus shifts. At that point, my answer to the above question would be service, service, service! Fortunately, most hotel operators have realized this, having seen the success of other service-oriented industries and having created their own service-oriented programs. Good service takes commitment, not just by the guest-contact staff, but by the entire hotel staff, led by the general manager. If the general manager is not committed to quality service, the whole program will fail.

I recently retired after 32 years from the Sheraton Corporation as their director of operations, Europe and Israel. In that position, I supervised as many as 30 hotel general managers at a time. I can tell you from personal experience that those managers who moved about the hotel and were visible and available to guests and to staff always ran a better hotel than those managers who sat in their offices and made guests and staff battle their way past one or two secretaries to get to see them.

This commitment to service must be led by the general manager, and must be seen in every employee. It must be honestly felt, and presented in a cheerful, friendly manner. Therefore, I will rephrase my answer to the opening question. The most important criteria in managing a hotel successfully are commitment to service, honest service, friendly service!

---

conduct fundraising campaigns to finance a community hotel. These people earn much smaller returns than they could receive by investing their money in other areas, but they feel that the presence of a hotel will add prestige to the community and indirectly boost all local business.

Other factors promote the close relationship between a hotel and its community. For example, homes have become smaller, and few people employ servants. This means that large dinner parties, small dances, wedding receptions, and other group gatherings which used to be held in homes are now often held outside the home. Hotels are equipped to handle these functions and to assume all the chores of planning, decorating, and serving. The declining use of domestic help has also contributed to the growing number of people dining out. It is common today to see an entire family enjoying a meal in the local hotel coffee shop or dining room.

Government Agencies. Hotels must also interact with government agencies. These organizations regulate lodging properties, imposing limitations within which hotels must operate, and collect taxes and other fees as required. These agencies have an interest in the success of the hotel because of the tax revenue a viable operation generates. Government agencies sometimes offer tax incentives to encourage hotels to locate in a particular community.

Endnotes

1. Parts of this discussion are taken from Michael L. Kasavana and Richard M. Brooks, *Managing Front Office Operations*, 4th ed. (East Lansing, Mich.: Educational Institute of the American Hotel & Motel Association, 1995), pp. 6–15.

2. This discussion is adapted from Kasavana and Brooks, pp. 38–50.

3. C. DeWitt Coffman, *Hospitality for Sale* (East Lansing, Mich.: Educational Institute of the American Hotel & Motel Association, 1980), p. 16.

4. For further information, see Raymond C. Ellis, Jr., and the Security Committee of AH&MA, *Security and Loss Prevention Management* (East Lansing, Mich.: Educational Institute of the American Hotel & Motel Association, 1986).

Key Terms

back of the house—Areas of a lodging operation in which personnel have very little direct guest contact; examples include the engineering, accounting, and human resources divisions.

concierge—A section of the hotel that provides special services to hotel guests, such as making theater reservations and obtaining tickets; organizing special functions, such as VIP cocktail parties; and arranging for secretarial and typing services for guests. In a sense, the concierge section is simply an extension of the front office that specializes in guest service.

convention bureau—Agencies in large cities created to attract regional and national conventions and other large gatherings or meetings.

front of the house—The areas of a lodging operation in which employees have extensive guest contact. Examples include the food and beverage and rooms divisions (including the front office and reservations departments).

organization chart—A drawing that shows the relationship between departments or divisions and specific positions within an organization.

revenue center—Those areas that directly bring in revenue to the hotel, such as the front office department, the food and beverage division, and any other function that sells goods or services to guests.

support center—Areas of the hotel that do not directly bring in revenue, but are necessary to the functioning of the revenue centers. These include housekeeping, accounting, engineering and maintenance, and human resources.

Review Questions

1. What is the essential difference between front-of-the-house and back-of-the-house employees? Give examples.

2. What is the essential difference between revenue center departments and support center departments? Give examples.

3. What functions does a concierge perform?

4. Hotel food and beverage employees might work in what types of operations?

5. What are three functions of the engineering and maintenance division?

6. The accounting department works most closely with what other department?

7. What three external factors have increased the importance of the human resources department?

8. Hotel staff other than security personnel typically perform what security functions?

9. Which four groups outside a hotel organization play an important role in the hotel's business?

10. In what ways does government become involved in a hotel's business?

Internet Sites

For more information, visit the following Internet sites. Remember that Internet addresses can change without notice. If the site is no longer there, use a search engine to look for additional sites.

Hotels and Hotel Companies

Best Western
http://www.bestwestern.com

Canadian Pacific Hotels
http://www.cphotels.ca

Hyatt Hotels and Resorts
http://www.hyatt.com

Inter-Continental Hotels
http://www.interconti.com

ITT Sheraton Corporation
http://www.sheraton.com

Marriott Hotels, Resorts, and Suites
http://www.marriott.com/lodging

Casino Hotels

Ballys Casinos
http://www.ballys.com

Caesar's Palace
http://www.caesars.com

Casinos
http://www.ct-casinos.com

Harrahs Casino
http://www.harrahs.com

Trump Castle Casino
http://www.trumpcastle.com

Chapter 6 Outline

6

The Rooms Division

THE ROOMS DIVISION is likely to have the largest staff in a hotel. Five departments are often classified as part of the rooms division. These are:

- Front office

- Reservations

- Telephone

- Uniformed service

- Housekeeping

Sometimes the responsibility for parking facilities is also assigned to this division. A sample organization chart for the rooms division of a large hotel is shown in Exhibit 1. Though we will not treat them as such in this chapter, many properties regard reservations, the switchboard, and uniformed service as subdepartments of the front office.

Small lodging operations are not likely to have specialized departments for each of the functions listed in Exhibit 1. In a large property, many staff members may have duties involving only the front office. In a small operation, one or two employees may perform front office duties, provide telephone service, offer guest information, and handle reservations.

The Front Office Department

The importance of the front office cannot be overemphasized. This department represents the single largest profit center for the hotel, which is room sales. The front office is the hotel's nerve center and the liaison between the guest and the property. It is often said that, to the guest, the front office *is* the hotel. During the guest's stay, the front office is the focus of requests for information and services. Check-in and check-out activities are usually the guest's first and last impressions of the property, its staff, and its philosophy of guest service.

First impressions are very important. If a guest begins a visit in a pleasant frame of mind because of front office courtesy and service, chances are good that he or she will view other hotel services favorably as well. However, let the front office err, delay, or be indifferent, and the guest's dissatisfaction may spread to all aspects of his or her stay.

The three main functions of the front office are: (1) to sell rooms, which includes registering guests and assigning rooms; (2) to keep accounts, determine

147

Exhibit 1   Organization Chart for the Rooms Division of a Large Hotel

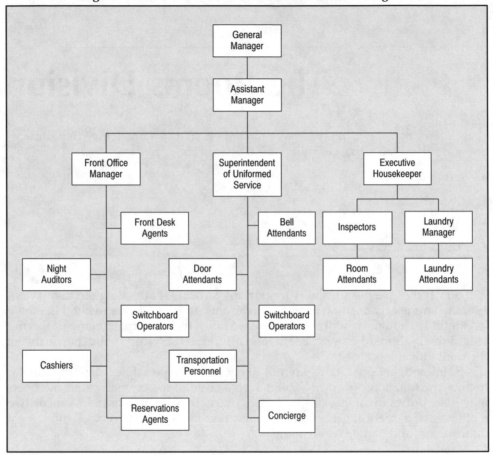

Adapted from Michael L. Kasavana and Richard M. Brooks, *Managing Front Office Operations,* 4th ed. (East Lansing, Mich.: Educational Institute of the American Hotel & Motel Association, 1995), p. 42.

credit, render bills, receive payments, and provide for proper financial and credit accommodations; and (3) to provide services such as handling mail, telegrams, and messages for guests and furnishing information about the hotel, the community, and any special attractions or events.

Although the physical size and layout of front office facilities will differ, every front desk will have three distinct functional spaces, corresponding to the three main functions, and sized to the specific needs of the operation. These three main areas are the rooming section, the cashier section, and the mail and information section. In large hotels, each of these areas may be staffed by a number of clerks in order to handle the numerous transactions involved. In smaller operations, efficient use of space may make it possible for one or two workers to handle all functions in a compact area.

The Rooming Section

Guest registration is the main function of the front office. Here rooms are sold and assigned, and here the guest's registration record is created. A guest's registration record contains information about the guest, including his or her home address and phone number, arrival and expected departure dates, and method of payment. The registration record helps the front office meet special guest needs, forecast room occupancies, and settle guest accounts properly. A guest's registration record may be kept in a guest registration book, on a registration card, or in a computer file.

Although some non-computerized hotels still use registration books, the guest card is more often used in such properties, usually as part of the guest folio (or file) in which a record of all guest charges is kept. The registration card has several advantages over the registration book. It allows several people to register at a time instead of lining up to register in the book. The registration card affords guests more privacy, because it is seen by only themselves and the desk agent before it is filed in the folio. Cards are more easily stored for later use in **guest history files**, a base of information that helps a hotel analyze its clientele and marketing efforts. More and more, hotels of all sizes are streamlining their registration procedures through automation. However, even with computer files, a registration card with guest signature may be required by law in some areas.

Front desk agents use some form of *rooms inventory* system to keep track of the status of all guestrooms. Hotels with computerized rooms divisions include this within the *property management system*, which ties in directly to the housekeeping department to provide up-to-the-minute status of occupied and vacant rooms. Manual properties rely on a **room rack**, located in the rooming or registration area, to get an up-to-date listing of the current and projected status of all rooms. The room rack lists rooms by number and floor and indicates such information as the room rate, the physical facilities of the room, and the view. If the room is occupied, it also includes the names of the occupants, their registration date, and their projected check-out date. Reserved rooms are also noted. The room rack helps the front desk agent control the assignment of rooms for more efficient staff utilization and service. For example, front desk agents try to fill one floor or wing of the hotel at a time to cut down on the amount of traveling a housekeeper or engineer must do to get to his or her assigned rooms.

The Cashier Section

The cashier section of the front office in larger operations is staffed by billing agents and cashiers, and, in smaller facilities, by personnel who provide all the services of front desk agent, information agent, billing agent, and cashier. This section keeps each guest's account up to date, cashes checks for guests (if the hotel offers this service), verifies the outstanding accounts receivable, renders the daily reports to management, and collects payment from the guests.

The primary tool of the cashier is the **guest folio** (see Exhibit 2), a record of the guest's charges associated with the current visit. Because there are so many charges, most larger operations use computers to post these charges to guests' accounts. **Point-of-sale terminals**, which are electronic cash registers that enter a

Exhibit 2   Sample Guest Folio

ROOM	(LAST) NAME (FIRST) (INITIAL)	RATE	FOLIO NUMBER	403131	

STREET ADDRESS	OUT	PHONE READING	OUT	
CITY, STATE & ZIP	IN	FROM FOLIO	IN	
NO. PARTY	CREDIT CARD	CLERK	TO FOLIO	

DATE					REFERENCE	CHARGES	CREDITS	BALANCE	PREVIOUS BALANCE PICKUP
Jul	27	A	RESTR		103	** 14.25		* 14.25	A* 14.25
Jul	27	A	ROOM		103	** 60.00		* 74.25	A* 74.25
Jul	27	A	LDIST		103	** 6.38		* 80.63	A* 80.63
Jul	27	A	MISCCR		103		** 18.38	* 62.25	A* 62.25
Jul	27	A	PAID		103		** 62.25	* .00	

Last
Balance
Amount Due

sales transaction into a hotel-wide computer system, are used in parts of the hotel where items can be charged. For example, charges for a meal at a restaurant in the hotel may be entered into a point-of-sale terminal in the restaurant and instantly transferred to the guest folio at the front desk.

Point-of-sale systems may be found in all areas of the hospitality industry. In hotels, they are in the food and beverage outlets, the gift shops, the barber or beauty shops—just about any location where a guest might make a purchase. In all units of the hospitality industry, point-of-sale systems save tremendous amounts of paperwork and employee time. The systems also provide greater accuracy on guest checks and charges. Compare this system with the traditional method—still used in many small properties—which requires hand-carrying charge slips to the front desk for manual addition to a guest's account. The number of missed breakfast charges at morning check-out is certainly reduced when electronic systems are used.

Properties offering guest credit must have specific policies regarding acceptable guest identification, credit limits, procedures to follow when credit limits are

Exhibit 3   Cash Report

CLASSIFICATION	DATE	TRANS. SYMBOLS	NET TOTALS	CORRECTIONS	MACH. TOTALS	
		CASH REPORT				
PAID						
CLOSING						
OPENING						
CASH RECEIVED						
PAID OUT						
CLOSING						
OPENING						
CASH PAID OUT						
NET CASH						

ON DUTY _____

OFF DUTY _____

CASHIER

_____

N C R   B-6760—114YY

reached, and all other credit-related concerns. Large properties may have credit managers in the cashier's department to administer guest credit services. By contrast, some smaller properties, which offer either limited services or none at all beyond rooming, may ask guests to pay in advance for the rooms upon registration; in this case, no other guest accounting is necessary.

Some small properties still use accounting machines to post charges, update guest accounts, validate vouchers, and so forth. Increasingly, however, hotels of all sizes are switching to electronic machines, which provide detailed guest account information in only a small fraction of the time required by older machines and which also provide far more operating statistics.

The accounting or electronic data machines in the cashier section are used to validate vouchers sent from the charging department, post charges to the guest's account, and calculate up-to-the-minute balances on each guest folio. They maintain daily balances of all transactions posted through them and are used to verify the accuracy of the accounts receivable outstanding balance and the charge-sales records of each operating department.

The accounting machine or electronic register at the front desk maintains a continuous record of cash transactions. Exhibit 3 is an example of a cash report that is usually made at each cashier shift change. *Paid* and *paid out* are keys on the electronic register.

When a cashier begins a shift, he or she subtotals these keys, and machine totals are printed out and recorded on the cash report under the machine totals column. The opening machine totals for paid and paid out must be exactly the same figures that appear on the previous shift's cash report as the closing machine totals for paid and paid out.

At the close of a shift, the cashier subtotals these keys again and records closing figures in the machine totals column. If, during the shift, the cashier accidentally miskeys any transactions, adjustments to the machine totals are made in the corrections column of the cash report and corrected figures are entered in the net totals column. The difference between the closing and opening figures in the net totals column of the paid section should yield the exact amount of cash received during the cashier's shift. Similarly, the difference between the closing and opening figures in the net totals column of the paid out sections should yield the exact amount of cash paid out during that cashier's shift.

The difference between cash received and cash paid out yields the net cash sum for the cashier's shift. Usually, the cashier extracts this sum from the cash drawer and, along with a supervisor, secures the money in the hotel safe until it can be deposited in a bank. Once the net cash has been secured, the cash drawer should contain exactly the same amount it contained when the cashier opened his or her shift. Both the outgoing and incoming cashiers count the contents of the cash drawer and verify the beginning "bank" for the new shift. If cash overages or shortages are discovered, the outgoing cashier must recheck the cash report and search through transaction records for possible miskeyed entries.

With certain exceptions (to be discussed in the next section), transactions that affect the guest's folio must have confirming vouchers to support the posting of charges. The posting of room charges is one exception; this is done by the night auditor. The up-to-date room rack serves as the source document for this posting.

The Night Audit. All accounts are balanced at the end of each day. Because the task is very important and needs to be done after all of the hotel's sales outlets are closed (to be sure that all charges are included), the audit is usually performed during the third shift in the early morning hours. This is called the **night audit**. In larger hotels, there may be more than one night auditor, while in smaller operations the night audit may be undertaken by a staff member serving as a front desk agent or information agent as well.

The first step in the audit is to post any charges that have not yet been included on the guest's account. Then, the totals of all accounts carried in the accounting machines or computer system are compared with the sales reports of the various operating departments to ensure that all charges have been properly accounted for. Any errors or problems must be rectified and resolved by a complete search of folios, vouchers, and departmental sales records.

After the totals are balanced and room occupancy is verified, room and tax charges are posted to each guest account, and a final balance is recorded on each folio. Finally, a report summarizing the up-to-date amounts owed to the hotel in both the guest ledger (the accounts for those currently registered in the hotel) and the city ledger (the accounts of former guests and non-guest accounts) is generated and balanced.

Hotels are increasingly using electronic data-processing equipment to maintain guest accounts, to make the necessary verifications, and to create reports. When a guest registers, guest information is entered into the computer, which prepares a folio automatically. Subsequent charges to the guest are entered into computer terminals and added to the folio. The daily transcript of accounts receivable, completed by the night auditor, is both a verification of departmental totals and a complete printout of each guest's bill. This daily transcript enables cashiers to check out guests early in the morning without calling up their folios for a printout. Display boards are also provided at the cashier's area where guests can review any charges or payments made to their accounts.

Some hotels also offer guests a chance to preview their accounts in their guestrooms through an automated system. Guests can select a designated channel on the room's television and view any charges made to their accounts in the comfort and privacy of their rooms. Any discrepancies or disagreements can be handled before actual check-out time, thus avoiding an annoying delay at the cashier's window when departing.

Sometimes charges are made to guests' accounts without a back-up voucher. For example, guests may use a room key instead of money in vending machines located in guestrooms to purchase liquor, foods, ice, or sundries. The charges for these sales are then recorded in the front office area or directly in the computer for inclusion in folios. Likewise, charges for in-room movies are sometimes automatically tallied and added to the guest folio.

The most often used form of no-voucher charging is the automatic telephone counter. Located in the front office area, this device keeps track of the number of local calls made from any room phone. Differences between registration counts and check-out counts (maintained on folios) tell cashiers how many calls to charge to a guest without having to maintain traffic sheets or to make vouchers for each call through a central switchboard. Long-distance calls may be accounted for on vouchers from the telephone company by means of a direct-dial system keyed to the individual room phone for accounting purposes. Automated telephone systems will be discussed in more detail later in this chapter.

The Mail and Information Section

The mail and information section is the area where services are performed that do not involve registration, check-out, or financial procedures. Services provided in this section may include distributing keys, holding keys while guests are out, handling messages and mail for guests, and answering guest questions about available tours, local points of interest, hours of banking, and the community in general. Front desk agents in this area must know about the services and hours of operation of all in-house departments, such as restaurants, lounges, and room service. In many hotels, front desk agents are fluent in more than one language.

The mail, message, and key rack and the information rack are often important front office equipment. The mail, message, and key rack, often visible to the guest from the desk, provides a pigeonhole for each guestroom in the hotel. It holds keys, mail, and messages for the guests. Some racks have colored message lights to indicate that material is being held for pickup by the guest. The light enables guests to see for themselves whether any messages are waiting. Telephones in the guestrooms of many hotels also have a similar light-coding device that indicates that a message is waiting. This is helpful when the guest goes directly to the room without inquiring about messages at the front desk.

Hotels traditionally have an information rack, which lists all guests alphabetically. This listing is usually compiled from information on the guest's registration record. It shows the name of the guest, the date of arrival, and the room assigned. It is used to help front desk agents process mail and telephone inquiries and handle visitors. Many properties now use computerized systems that reduce or eliminate the need for this manually processed information.

Some hotels assign those guest information duties concerning the local area and entertainment to the bell captain's desk. Other (usually upscale) properties sometimes use concierge services—which may be provided by an individual or an entire staff—to handle these information requests.

While concierge services have long been common in European hotels, they have only recently begun to appear in the United States. The concierge is the information center of the hotel. Even the general manager may rely on the concierge for information about the city, transportation, entertainment, and local news and events. Conveniently located in the lobby, the concierge can provide special attention to the guests and, at the same time, free front desk agents for registration, check-out, and other responsibilities.

Tourist centers and chambers of commerce usually provide printed booklets and brochures that outline an area's major points of interest, the schedule of cultural events, and the hours of operation of major transportation systems, businesses, and governmental centers. Front offices may place these brochures in a convenient place for guests.

The Reservations Department

This department in the rooms division often has the first contact with the guest.[1] To maintain profitability and guest satisfaction, the hotel must have effective procedures and systems in place to handle guest reservations efficiently.

Every property has its own method of processing reservations—taking reservations, filing them, placing them in the racks, assigning rooms, and completing folios. Although the procedures may differ, the purpose is still the same—to satisfy guests, so that the hotel maintains a good reputation and achieves maximum occupancy. The definitions, suggestions, and principles that follow can help achieve this purpose, regardless of the hotel's reservation system.

Methods of Advance Reservation

A little over 70 percent of hotel guests make advance reservations each year. These individuals have a variety of means at their disposal to arrange for hotel accommodations:

- Toll-free telephone lines (800 numbers)—All of the major chain organizations and referral groups and many independent properties maintain one or more 800 numbers. Travelers can call these centralized reservation systems to reserve accommodations at any property within the chain or hotel group. Some chains have special numbers for the exclusive use of travel agents and/or for different areas of the country.

- Direct telephone (excluding toll-free numbers)—Most hotels also receive reservation requests by telephone at the property. Direct lines are frequently used for business generated locally or regionally.

- Hotel representatives—These are usually independent business firms that serve as promotion agents for hotels and act as out-of-town, at-the-market-source sales agents.

- Intersell agencies—These agencies handle all of the clients' reservation needs—hotel room, rental car, and airline ticket.

- Property-to-property reservations—Chain properties can use the company's reservations/communications computer link to make reservations at a different property in the chain. This allows guests to call a local number to make reservations for any chain property. It also allows traveling guests who stay at a property to make reservations for the following night at a chain property near their next day's destination.

- Mail—Postcard and letter requests for reservations are common, particularly for convention hotels. Written requests and convention reservations are sometimes sent by fax machine to the property instead of being mailed.

- Telex, cable, and other—Telex is used most often for overseas transmittals. Other methods of requesting reservations generally account for only a very minor proportion of the total number of occupied rooms.

- The Internet—Advances in computer technology make it increasingly easy for the public to access information and make reservations via personal computers.

Types of Reservations

Guaranteed Reservations. The hotel assures the guest that a room will be held until the guest's arrival or until check-out time the next day—whichever occurs first. In return, the guest guarantees payment for the room, even if it is not used, unless the guest cancels the reservation in accordance with the hotel's required cancellation procedures. A person with a reservation who does not use a room or cancel the reservation is called a **no-show**. Some of the types of guaranteed reservations are:

- Credit card—Major credit card companies have developed systems by which participating properties can be guaranteed payment for reserved rooms that were left empty by no-shows.

- Advance deposit—An advance deposit guarantee (or partial prepayment) requires the guest to remit to the property a specified amount prior to the guest's stay. The prepayment may be for one night's lodging, plus taxes, or for the entire stay.

- Travel agent—Although this type of guarantee was quite common before the 1980s, it is now used less frequently by smaller travel agencies because they prefer to use the credit card or advance deposit guarantee whenever possible. Larger or international travel agencies, on the other hand, often make reservation agreements with chains or very large properties located in major cities.

- Corporate—Under a corporate guarantee, a corporation or business agrees to accept financial responsibility for any no-shows. This procedure is often set up in advance when the corporation signs a contract with the hotel.

- In-house voucher—This method can best be described as a special in-house promotion designed to attract return guests or new business.

Non-Guaranteed Reservations. The hotel agrees to hold a room for the guest until a stated cutoff time. If the guest does not arrive by that time, the hotel may sell the room to a **walk-in** guest (a guest arriving without a reservation) if additional space is not available. Of course, if the guest arrives after the cutoff hour and rooms are still available, the hotel will accommodate the guest.

Confirmed Reservations. The confirmed reservation details the intent of both parties and includes the material points of the agreement—i.e., dates, rate, type of accommodations, number of guests. If it is made early enough, the property may mail the guest a written confirmation, which the guest is expected to produce at registration. An oral confirmation that includes the material points is also a binding agreement between both parties.[2] Confirmed reservations may be either guaranteed or non-guaranteed.

Hotel-Specific Reservations. Hotels may also establish other types of reservations for their own use, based on criteria such as type of guest or source of reservation. Examples include VIP reservations, convention delegate reservations, travel agent reservations, and paid-in-advance reservations.

Special Concerns

A casual observer might think that handling hotel reservations is a rather simple, mechanical, and routine job. However, the job is not as simple as it first appears. The ideal situation, of course, is to have every room booked and every reservation honored. No hotel can hope to have all of its rooms filled every night of the year, but, when the business is available, it is uneconomical to have any rooms vacant. It is often said that there is no commodity more perishable than a hotel room. If the room is not sold on a specific night, that sale is lost forever.

On any given day, when all available rooms are reserved, a hotel is 100 percent booked. Experience tells us, however, that invariably there are last-minute cancellations, no-shows, and early check-outs. How does a hotel protect itself from being left with vacant rooms for which a demand existed? The usual answer is to consider the number of rooms likely to be available for sale based on previous records and reliable estimates. The more accurately a hotel can estimate the

Insider Insights

Richard L. Erb, CHA
General Manager
Stein Eriksen Lodge
Park City, Utah ——————————————————————————

Rating hotels, motels, and resorts is a popular pastime for many travel-oriented magazines today. Those directed at the North American traveler are particularly fond of this practice.

Some travel magazines rate only hotels and resorts. Others rate destinations, golf resorts, new properties, family resorts, bargain vacations, and cruise ships. One major publication even groups airlines, hotels, resorts, cruise ships, and cities together under the listing "Destination and Services" to form their "Top 100."

All hoteliers like to receive awards and good ratings, and, in the past, the traditional rating systems (American Automobile Association and Mobil) seemed to meet our needs. In recent years, however, too many unqualified people have gotten into the rating game, causing grave concerns in the travel industry. What kind of criteria are they applying? Who, exactly, is applying them?

Recently, some traditionally highly graded resorts suffered severe financial damage because of low ratings given by some of these questionable raters. These ratings were given without any warning to the victims; they learned about the ratings after the fact from their local newspapers. In response, the American Hotel & Motel Association (AH&MA) formed the Lodging Industry Ratings Advisory Committee (LIRAC).

LIRAC was formed to assist in the establishment of realistic and equitable systems of lodging industry ratings. LIRAC established the following guidelines to enhance existing rating systems and to assure the traveling public of the highest quality, best value, and most consistent lodging service in the world.

LIRAC respects the public service performed by rating services and acknowledges the difficulties of rating thousands of properties. With that acknowledgment, LIRAC has established the following guidelines.

Lodging industry management has the right to expect:

- Full background information on the rating service

- An explanation of the inspection and rating procedures

- A copy of the guidelines and criteria used in the inspection

- An indication of the inspector/rater's qualifications

- An opportunity for management to assist the inspection by answering questions or offering explanations

- A copy of the inspection report, including the inspector's recommendations

- Private notification of rating prior to publication

- Adequate opportunity to take remedial action

(continued)

Insider Insights *(continued)*

- Rights of appeal
- Consistency in the application of inspection criteria
- The right to choose not to be rated

Inspection systems have the right to expect:

- Cooperation from management to allow an efficient inspection process
- Full access to all areas and services involved in the inspection process
- Background information about developments and changes taking place on the property that would bear on the inspection

Naturally, hotels and resorts are concerned about their ratings. Their business depends heavily on ratings; yet, aside from operating their properties to try to ensure that they are above reproach, they have very little control over ratings. To illustrate the seriousness of the potential problem, the general manager of one well-established five-star and five-diamond resort told LIRAC that his organization had calculated that the loss of a star and a diamond would mean a $10 million negative impact on its business.

We must all maintain our determination to keep ratings meaningful and equitable. More and more, newspapers and magazines are entering the ratings scene with no structure or guidelines, perhaps unaware of the impact their verdicts carry. Many of us are at the mercy of such raters, since we depend so heavily on these scores in our marketing programs and for our ultimate financial success. With this in mind, LIRAC will continue to help refine and temper this all-important ratings game.

---

number of rooms *actually* for sale, the less likely it will be that service problems will occur.

For example, suppose a hotel knows that, on the average, it has about 5 percent no-shows, about 8 percent cancellations, and an overstay rate of about 5 percent (5 percent of current guests will decide to stay longer than the agreed-upon check-out date). During a period of full occupancy, the hotel may choose to accept reservations in excess of actual rooms by 8 percent (5 percent no-shows + 8 percent cancellations − 5 percent overstays).

If these percentages were always accurate, problems would seldom arise. But there are times when things go wrong; no one cancels, or all room reservations are honored, or inclement weather grounds all outgoing planes, greatly increasing the number of overstays. In such a situation, every room may be occupied, and other guests with confirmed reservations may be asking for rooms that simply are not available.

When this occurs, all the front desk agent can do is handle the guest in the most courteous manner and assist him or her in finding accommodations elsewhere. This is called **walking a guest**. Unfortunately, all the guest really understands is that, even with a confirmed reservation, no room was available. These situations can easily lose customers for a hotel.

With increased emphasis on consumer protection, several states have enacted legislation prohibiting the practice of overbooking. Hoteliers who carelessly overbook invite additional restrictive legislation for the hospitality industry. The hotel industry is attempting to develop new solutions to the no-show problem.

The Telecommunications Department

The telecommunications department is a vital part of guest service. Although an operator rarely sees the guest, his or her voice and telephone manner can influence a guest's opinion of the hotel and its service. A switchboard or PBX supervisor (who may or may not occupy a switchboard position) heads this group, which handles in-house, local, and long-distance calls.

Although telephones first appeared in hotels in the early 1900s, it took 40 years before dial phones began to appear in guestrooms, making it possible for guests to place their own calls. Touchtone phones became available in the 1960s, but hotels demonstrated no sense of urgency about installing them to replace the dial phones, though hotels did make use of another 1960s innovation, the message-waiting light.

The 1980s ushered in tremendous progress. Call accounting machines made it possible for guests to place calls directly, without an operator intervening to request the room number. These machines also allow hotels to add surcharges to calls made by guests, thus making the telecommunications department a revenue center. These and other recent technological advances in equipment have decreased the responsibilities and workload of the telecommunications department considerably.

For example, in most new hotels, computers make wake-up calls automatically. In the past, many guest complaints and more than a few lawsuits centered on wake-up calls, or, more accurately, the lateness or absence of a requested wake-up call. With the computer, when the clerk receives the request for a wake-up call, the room number and the time are entered in the system, and the computer makes the call as requested along with any recorded message management chooses. The system has nearly eliminated the missed or late wake-up call.

Telephone systems now frequently include a voicemail option whereby guests can hear actual recordings of callers' messages. This option alleviates a great deal of time for the hotel operator in processing messages and also gives the guest a better level of service and personalization.

The telecommunications department plays a vital role in the hotel's security program. Operators protect guests' privacy by not divulging room numbers, and the department acts as a communications center in the case of accidents and other emergencies.

The Uniformed Service Department

This department is aptly named, since its only product is service. Staff members perform their duties in front of the guest. None of the jobs are complex, but their functions are important, since members of the uniformed service department are often the first and last hotel employees to interact with guests.

Uniformed service includes door attendants, bellpersons, and (in some hotels) elevator operators. Lobby porters may be included in this department, but they are usually assigned to the housekeeping department. In large hotels, a superintendent of service directs the uniformed service staff. In small hotels, the bell captain supervises other staff and is, in turn, directed by the assistant manager or the executive assistant manager.

The door attendant serves as the hotel's greeter. Stationed at the main lobby entrance, he or she meets all arriving guests, helps them unload their luggage, guards the luggage of arriving and departing guests, assists the bellperson in handling baggage, summons taxis for guests, and may supervise the parking of guest automobiles. Door attendants should be well informed on local points of interest because guests will often ask for such information.

The bellperson's principal duty is rooming guests. When a guest has completed registration, the bellperson is called to the desk to receive the room slips and the key. The bellperson checks to see if the guest has any mail or messages, carries the baggage, and escorts the guest to the guestroom. A good bellperson will check the room for orderliness and properly functioning lights, television, and other equipment, and will explain services to the guest, answer any questions, and leave the key and guest rooming slip in the room. (The guest rooming slip includes such information as the guest's name and address, room rate, and check-out time, and may also include information advertising hotel activities and services, such as lounge entertainment, meal specials, and concierge services.) The bellperson's courtesy, tact, and efficiency can solidify the feeling of welcome already generated by the desk agent.

In their frequent trips to all parts of the hotel, bellpersons serve as the eyes and ears of the hotel; it is their duty to report anything out of the ordinary. Other duties include assisting the departing guest with luggage, running errands and handling messages, paging guests, and carrying baggage on room changes. At various times, bellpersons may be called upon to show rooms to patrons or to conduct group tours through the hotel. Because of their direct contact with the guest (who frequently asks for information), bellpersons can be excellent salespeople for the restaurants, lounges, and other services of the hotel.

The Housekeeping Department

The housekeeping department is one of the busiest in the hotel. Housekeeping employees are responsible for the neatness and cleanliness of all the guestrooms and maintenance of most public areas. The housekeeping department is managed by the executive housekeeper. Since the department is a back-of-the-house operation, few guests understand the full scope of housekeeping or see the executive housekeeper unless they have complaints about the department. However, the work of the housekeeping department greatly influences guests' opinions of the hotel.

In a small hotel, the executive housekeeper may be the only supervisor and the housekeepers may be the only staff in this department (housekeepers are also called room attendants in some properties). In larger properties, there are often additional supervisors called room inspectors. These inspectors ensure the proper cleanliness and maintenance of the rooms. Usually there is one inspector for every 80 to 100 rooms. Housepersons maintain the public areas and guestroom corridors and may assist the housekeepers with certain duties. Housepersons are frequently under the supervision of a head houseperson. In many hotels, the head houseperson is also responsible for distributing cleaning and guestroom supplies. Again, depending on the size of the hotel, there may be one or more assistant head housepersons.

The headquarters of the housekeeping department may be the linen room or some other place close to housekeeping supplies. A supervisor coordinates all activities and daily work assignments from these headquarters.

Communication is vital to the functions of the housekeeping department. A telewriter (an electrical communication device similar to the teletype), which connects directly with the engineering division and front office department, may be located in the housekeeping office. The housekeeping department may also be in direct contact with other departments through a property management system, which allows a housekeeper to use a telephone keypad to access the computer; the computer then relays room status reports to the front desk and repair requests to the engineering and maintenance department.

The housekeeping office has direct contact (either by telephone or some sort of electronic status system) with the supply storage closets on each floor and can track the location of any housekeeper with the system. All orders and requests pertaining to housekeeping, mostly from the front office, pass through the housekeeping office. The efficient daily turnover of guestrooms necessitates this close communication.

As soon as a guest checks out of a room, the front desk notifies housekeeping via telewriter or electronic signal. In turn, the housekeeping office notifies the housekeeper by phone or computer of the same information. Once the room is clean and in order, the flow of information is reversed so the front office will know the room's current status.

A double-check of all rooms occurs at least once each day to ensure that the listed room status is correct. This is called *checking the rack* and is a room-by-room comparison of the room status shown at the front desk with that shown on the report made by housekeeping staff. In those hotels with computerized systems, this check occurs automatically. Any discrepancies in the status listed by the two departments must be physically checked by a housekeeper.

The primary responsibility of the day shift in housekeeping (8:00 A.M. to 5:00 P.M.) is to clean all guestrooms. In most hotels, the evening shift (4:00 P.M. to midnight) will be responsible for cleaning any rooms that request late service. Any special VIP service, such as turndown service, will also be done by the evening shift. It is also the responsibility of evening shift personnel to clean offices and public areas.

The housekeeping department frequently maintains the lost and found storage area for the hotel. Typically, all articles found in the hotel by employees or guests are sent directly to housekeeping, where they are labeled, logged, and stored by date. State law may dictate procedures for the storage and eventual disposal of such items.

It takes a large volume of sheets, pillowcases, towels, and table linens to operate a hotel. Large hotels usually operate in-house laundries. There is continuing debate in the industry regarding whether an in-house system is practical and profitable. If a hotel uses a commercial laundry, the housekeeping department is responsible for keeping an accurate inventory of linens. All linen must be checked daily for quality. Most large hotels with in-house laundries have a separate laundry department to perform cleaning and ironing and ongoing quality control checks. They may also have a sewing room where linens are repaired. It is usually the housepersons' responsibility to keep each floor's linen storage closet stocked with the necessary types of linen.

The greatest number of employees in the housekeeping department serve as housekeepers and housepersons. When coming on duty, they report directly to the housekeeping office, sign out keys, and receive the daily report. This report will indicate the status of assigned rooms. Normally, early-service requests and check-out rooms are cleaned first.

The housekeeper's first responsibility upon reaching the assigned floor is to take a "house count" to physically verify the status on the report. Any discrepancies are reported immediately to the housekeeping office, and from there to the front desk. Periodically through the shift, an inspector will visit the rooms and report the progress to the housekeeping office. Before going off duty at the end of the shift, the housekeeper will repack the linen cart and replenish supplies for the following shift. Any rooms that refused service or requested later service are reported to the supervisor of the next shift for the purpose of assigning the task of cleaning those rooms.

The houseperson works in close cooperation with the housekeepers. A typical hotel staffing pattern suggests one houseperson for each five to eight housekeepers. The houseperson regularly cleans all hallway carpets and maintains the general cleanliness of public areas and service corridors. Heavy cleaning jobs within guestrooms may be assigned to the houseperson on a regular schedule. These duties include carpet cleaning with heavy-duty vacuum cleaners and shampooers; cleaning walls, baseboards, and windows; moving furniture for more thorough cleaning; and turning mattresses. Large properties may have personnel with specialized duties who, for example, shampoo carpets on a full-time basis.

The heavy usage and wear in hotel rooms creates a need for frequent maintenance and refurbishing. It is an important responsibility of supervisors and inspectors to keep a close and constant check on the guestrooms for items requiring replacement and repair. Most hotels use a multi-part **work order** form that the housekeeping staff fills out to request specific repairs or maintenance work. One part of the form is sent to the engineering division to indicate requests. These orders are logged and dated. Upon completion of the order, the engineering copy of the form is returned to the housekeeping department and logged accordingly. Requests that are minor and do not require immediate attention may be held by engineering until a slack period of occupancy, at which time they will be completed.

The housekeeping department is also responsible for purchasing all guestroom and cleaning supplies for the hotel. Accurate perpetual inventories of all supplies must be maintained.

Endnotes

1. Parts of this section are drawn from Michael L. Kasavana and Richard M. Brooks, *Managing Front Office Operations,* 4th ed. (East Lansing, Mich.: Educational Institute of the American Hotel & Motel Association, 1995), pp. 113–142.

2. For further information concerning the legal aspects of guest reservations, see Jack P. Jefferies, *Understanding Hospitality Law,* 3d ed. (East Lansing, Mich.: Educational Institute of the American Hotel & Motel Association, 1995), Chapter 2.

Key Terms

guest folio—A file (electronic or paper) containing all of a guest's charges during the guest's stay at a lodging property.

guest history file—Information about lodging guests that is maintained for marketing purposes and for return visits.

night audit—Accounting task in which guest charges are posted and totals of all accounts are compared with sales reports of operating departments; performed after all of a hotel's sales outlets are closed.

no-show—A guest who made a room reservation but did not register or cancel.

point-of-sale terminal—An electronic cash register that transfers a guest's charges from a hotel sales outlet to the guest folio at the front desk.

room rack—A listing of the current and projected status of all rooms.

walk-in guest—A guest who arrives at a hotel without a reservation.

walking a guest—Situation in which a hotel is unable to honor a guest's reservation and helps the guest find accommodations elsewhere.

work order—A document used to initiate requests for maintenance services.

Review Questions

1. What three distinct areas does the front desk in the typical hotel comprise?

2. What information can be found in a hotel's room rack?

3. Where might you find point-of-sale terminals in a typical hotel?

4. How is a guest ledger different from a city ledger?

5. What is a no-voucher guest charge? Provide two or more examples of them.

6. There are several methods by which a hotel might receive a guest reservation. What are they?

7. Why might a hotel oversell on a given night?

8. What technological advance of the 1980s dramatically reduced the workload of the telecommunications department?

9. What department is usually the guest's first and last contact with the hotel?

10. In a typical hotel, what department is responsible for the lost and found function?

Internet Sites

For more information, visit the following Internet sites. Remember that Internet addresses can change without notice. If the site is no longer there, use a search engine to look for additional sites.

Hotel and Hotel Companies

Best Western
http://www.bestwestern.com

Four Seasons Hotels
http://www.fshr.com

Historic Hotels of American
http://www.nthp.org/main/hotels/hotelsmain.htm

Holiday Inn Worldwide
http://www.holiday-inn.com

Hyatt Hotels and Resorts
http://www.hyatt.com

Inter-Continental Hotels
http://www.interconti.com

ITT Sheraton Corporation
http://www.sheraton.com

Loews Hotels
http://loewshotels.com

Marriott Hotels, Resorts, and Suites
http://www.marriott.com/lodging

Preferred Hotels and Resorts Worldwide
http://www.preferredhotels.com

Promus Hotels
http://www.promus-inc.com

Smith Travel Research
http://www.str-online.com

Front Office Technology

Geac Computer Corporation Limited
http://www.geac.com

CCS: Front Office Systems
http://www.csshotelsystems.com

CLS software
heep://www.hospitalitynet.nl/cls

Delphi/Newmarket Software
http://www.newsoft.com

First Resort Software, Inc.
http://www.firstres.com

InfoGenesis
http://www.infogenesis.com

Lodging Touch International
http://www.lodgingtouch.com

Hospitality Industry Technology Exposition and Conference
http://www.hitechshow.org

MICROS Systems, Inc.
http://www.micros.com

Resort Systems Incorporated
http://www.resortsystems.ca

Travel and Lodging Search Sites

Business Travel Net
http://www.business-travel-net.com

BizTravel.com—The Internet Company for the Frequent Business Traveler
http://www.biztravel.com

Hotels and Travel on the Net
http://www.hotelstravel.com

HotelsOnline
http://www.HotelsOnline.NET

Part III

The Food Service Industry

Chapter 7 Outline

Food Service in America
Food Service in Europe
Modern Food Service in America
Modern Food Service in Europe
Franchising Developments in Food Service
    McDonald's: A Case Study in Success
    Consistency Is Important
    Franchise Agreements and Relationships
    Fast-Food Employees
    Franchising Problems
Management Companies in Institutional Food Service
    Major Management Companies
    Management Company Operations

7

The Growth and Development of Food Service

EVIDENCE SUGGESTS that tribes in Denmark cooked food in large kitchens and ate to-gether in large groups as much as 12,000 years ago. The first cabarets (shops selling wines and liquors) were established around 4000 B.C. Cabarets flourished during the Roman and Byzantine empires. Rome also offered thermopoliums, forerunners of the modern restaurant, which provided hot food and drink. Most of these opera-tions were located in cities near temples or government houses. During the Middle Ages, the cities declined, and the feudal manor became the important center of eco-nomic activity. It was in the manors, where kings and lords had to feed courts or households totaling as many as 30,000 people, that cooking first developed a bit of institutional character.

About the year 1200, public cookshops, which offered the customer precooked food to take home, opened in London. Another 200 years passed before refine-ments such as table linen, crystal glasses, and eating instruments that resembled forks and knives as we know them appeared. Instead of merely piling the food on platters, the cooks began to arrange it artistically and in smaller quantities.

When Catherine de Médicis married King Henry II of France in the sixteenth century, she brought with her from Italy the very finest cooks, who added new re-finements to royal cookery and prepared some very artistic banquets. As the years passed, new items were added to the menu. Jacques Coeur, for example, brought turkey to France. Oliver de Serres demonstrated how vegetables could enhance a menu and a diet. He is reputed to be the first Frenchman to praise the potato and strongly influenced culinary practices. Serres took his suggestions to King Louis XIV (1638–1715) and his culinary staff. Many of the suggestions were accepted and influenced the training and development of excellent chefs and expert kitchen masters. Thus was born the French reputation for fine food.

The influence of the royal kitchens eventually filtered down to the inns and taverns that served the travelers of the time. A certain A. Boulanger is credited with originating the restaurant in Paris in the year 1765. A sign on his soup shop invited hungry people to come and be restored. He called his soup *le restaurant divin,* the divine restorative. The French word, derived from *restaurer,* meaning to restore, is the origin of the word restaurant. Boulanger's restaurant was very popu-lar, and many others like it opened in Paris and across Europe.

Food Service in America

The stage had been set for many food service ideas and practices to travel to America. Samuel Cole had opened the first American tavern in 1634. In 1656, Massachusetts

167

passed a law that required every town in the colony to have a tavern or be subject to a fine. The first coffeehouse in Boston was established in 1670.

The American population began to demand more inns and would soon be demanding hotels and restaurants. As inns grew in number, cooks borrowed culinary ideas and recipes from European cooks, slowly modified them, and initiated the first stage of what we know today as American cuisine.

American food service really began its growth and development in the colonial tavern or inn. Located near the center of activity, the tavern provided an informal meeting place, a chance to talk politics with good food and ale to accompany the conversations. The tavern was owned and presided over by a personable innkeeper who was knowledgeable about local events. When there was business in the tavern, he was on the floor with the customers. Saturdays were military training days in the colonies. After marching and drilling, both the officers and men headed for the tavern to relax and sample the innkeeper's food and drink.

About 1740, the first stagecoaches began to roll out of Boston and provided new customers for the inn or tavern. The roadside inn became famous in America and was the birthplace of the American hotel industry. The heyday of the roadside inn lasted until the American Revolution. Until this time, colonists patterned their eating habits after the English, although with a few frontier modifications.

Following the American Revolution, French cuisine became quite popular, particularly in government and society circles, in part because the English were out of favor in America. American and foreign diplomatic corps were served in the French manner. Presidents Washington and Jefferson served French cuisine at social as well as political dinners. Refugees from the French Revolution brought with them both a taste for and culinary expertise in their national dishes, which further promoted American interest in French food.

It was during this period that the roadside inn or tavern began to diminish in importance as the principal gathering place for the people. Even the most famous—The King's Arms and The Blue Anchor Tavern—felt the competition from the next European import to American food service, the restaurant. Historians disagree over which establishment deserves to be designated the first American restaurant—the Sans Souci, Niblo's Garden, or Delmonico's. All three opened in the 1820s in New York and soon became the most fashionable eating places in the city. The Sans Souci and Niblo's Garden both served French cuisine while Delmonico's brought the Swiss influence into American food service.

Delmonico's deserves special recognition because it was more than a famous restaurant; it became a symbol of American fine dining. The Delmonico brothers opened the first of many eating establishments in 1827, a cake and wine shop on William Street in New York City. In 1832, the brothers opened another Delmonico's operation on Broad Street. The year 1832 is important in American restaurant history because in that year the Delmonico brothers brought their 19-year-old nephew Lorenzo from Switzerland to the United States. It was Lorenzo, the world-famous Delmonico, who, for over 50 years, cultivated the excellent taste in food, decor, and clientele that was so important in New York society circles. Delmonico's closed in 1923, a victim of Prohibition.

A number of significant events occurred during the 1800s that directly affected the growth and refinement of American food service. Harvey Parker of Boston offered the first à la carte menu in his restaurant. The first ice refrigerator went into use in 1803, and 1825 marks the first recorded use of a gas stove. In 1815, Robert Owen established a large eating room for workers and their families, and industrial food service began in America. The Bowery Savings Bank of New York instituted an employee food service program in 1834 that is still operational today, making it the oldest in the nation. In the 1860s, the dishwashing machine was invented, the first martini was made in San Francisco's Occidental Hotel, George M. Pullman developed railroad dining cars, and H.J. Heinz opened his food business. Late in the century, Antoine Feuchtwanger introduced America to the hot dog in St. Louis, Missouri. He sold hot "franks" along with cotton gloves to hold the hot sausage. Harry M. Stevens really popularized these franks when he sold them at New York's Polo Grounds as "Red Hots."

Following the birth of the American restaurant, the next important milestone in commercial food service was the development of the cafeteria. Credit for developing the cafeteria belongs to John Krueger. Inspired by the **smorgasbord** that he had seen served in Sweden, Krueger designed a similar commercial food service system. The cafeteria made its first appearance in California during the famous Gold Rush days. On the east coast, the cafeteria arrived around 1890 when the Exchange Buffet opened near the Stock Exchange in New York City. The cafeteria has also found great popularity in Europe.

Although its birth goes back to 1815, employee food service did not really begin to grow extensively until around the turn of the century. In 1902, Illinois Bell began a form of in-plant food service. By 1906, when Sears Roebuck opened the Seroco Restaurant to provide food service for its employees in Chicago, employee food service became big business. Yet, as impressive as the Seroco Restaurant was (it prepared as many as 12,500 meals daily), employee food service was only in its infancy and would grow and develop even more, particularly after World War II.

Two other aspects of American food service that have their roots in Europe include school food service and hospital food service. School lunch programs go back to 1849 when canteens for school children first appeared in France. Writer and social commentator Victor Hugo started school food service in England in 1865 by providing warm meals in his home for children from a nearby school. In the United States, the first food service in a school was provided by The Children's Aid Society of New York in 1853. By 1910, "penny lunch programs" had become quite widespread in elementary schools.

While hospital food service can be traced back several centuries in one form or another, it was rather primitive until Florence Nightingale made her contribution. It was in 1854 that Nightingale, reformer of the nursing profession and the first hospital dietitian, assumed charge of the nurses in the English Military Hospital at Scutari, Turkey, during the Crimean War. From her emphasis on the role of a proper diet in a patient's recovery came the development of a more scientific approach to patient care and food service.

Food Service in Europe

Food and food service as we know them today have always played an important role in Europe. Perhaps it was through the advent of the celebrated gourmets and

Virtually every nation's cooking has been influenced by the French.
(Photo courtesy of Le Palais Restaurant, Resorts International Casino Hotel)

party hosts, such as Jean-Jacques de Cambacérès, arch chancellor under Napoleon, Anthelme Brillat-Savarin, frequent dinner guest of Foreign Minister Charles-Maurice de Talleyrand-Perigord and author of the legendary *La Physiologie du Gout*, that French cuisine gained its reputation as the cradle of culinary art. Or perhaps it was only through the legendary chefs, Marie-Antoine Carême, Prosper Montagne, Curnonsky, and Auguste Escoffier, that the world at large became aware of the overwhelming influence the French have had on modern cooking. While all countries of the world have manifold culinary traditions, it is also true that every nation's cooking has been influenced by one or both of two cultures of gastronomy: the French and the Chinese.

Along with the culinary art, the service of food and beverage was also raised from simple delivery to a highly ritualistic and artful ballet. The basic score for this ballet has always been the bill of fare or menu. There have always been two basic types of menu:

- The **à la carte menu**, a complete list of all food items served

- The **table d'hôte** or **prix fixe menu**, a complete breakfast, lunch, or dinner menu sold at a fixed price

Exhibit 1   Pre-1900 Formal Banquet Menu Structure

Hors d'oeuvre froid	Cold appetizer
Potage	Soup
Hors d'oeuvre chaud	Hot appetizer
Poisson	Fish
Pièce de résistance	Main dish
Entrée chaude	Hot entrée
Entrée froide	Cold entrée
Sorbet	Sherbet
Rôti, salade	Roast, salad
Légume	Vegetable
Entremet de douceur chaude	Hot sweet
Entremet de douceur froide	Cold sweet
Dessert	Dessert
Fromage	Cheese

Until the end of the nineteenth century, the classical menu structure of at least 12 courses was followed for the service of formal banquets. Exhibit 1 shows this classical structure. At the beginning of the twentieth century, these menus were greatly reduced. A menu of six to eight courses became the standard. Today, a menu of three or four dishes is the rule rather than the exception.

Food and beverage service also reflects the trend toward greater simplicity and informality. Just as menu structures were very formal, so too were special service styles. When Ueli Prager, founder of Mövenpick Restaurants, replaced tablecloths in his restaurants with American-style place mats, it was considered a very courageous innovation. Today, place mats and informal plate service constitute the rule.

Modern Food Service in America

Although American food service history goes back hundreds of years, it is during the twentieth century that growth, development, change, and innovation have accelerated to an almost unbelievable pace. Several noteworthy events occurred in the early part of the century. The hamburger was served for the first time in 1904 at the St. Louis World's Fair. In 1919, the National Restaurant Association was founded, and Roy Allen and Frank Wright opened a root beer stand—the first of what would become over 2,500 A&W Root Beer units. Most of these properties were franchised, so Allen and Wright became the men who pioneered the franchise concept in the food service industry. While franchising has played a part in the growth of the food industry since the 1920s, the amazing growth of franchise operations was still to occur 50 years in the future.

In 1920, Prohibition came upon the American scene and wrought major changes in the food service industry. Suddenly, neither hotels nor restaurants could serve liquor. The American food service operation found it difficult to change the patrons' habit of having wine and liquor with a fine meal. Those patrons soon learned that wine and liquor were available, although illegally, at local **speakeasies**. To the hotel and restaurant owners' dismay, speakeasy owners soon learned that customers liked food with their drinks. Starting with sandwiches, the speakeasy was soon serving full meals to its customers. Both hotel dining rooms and regular restaurants were forced to close for lack of business. On the other hand, after the repeal of Prohibition in 1933, many speakeasies developed into successful restaurants, among them the famous Club 21, Lindy's, and El Morocco. Many guests who had formerly eaten in hotel dining rooms never returned. Rather, they continued to eat in the speakeasies-turned-restaurants. In fact, Prohibition affected the restaurant industry more positively than negatively in its competition with hotels for dining patrons.

The 1920s are often referred to as the Roaring Twenties because of great economic growth in many industries and the atmosphere of optimism and enthusiasm. However, this decade did not have the great positive effect on restaurant growth that it had on many other industries, including hotels. When the nation started to sink into the depths of the Great Depression in 1929, the food service industry was severely hurt. During the 1930s, more than the usual number of restaurants went out of business, and both gross sales and gross profits suffered severe blows in those properties that remained open.

During the Depression, the school lunch program grew dramatically. Massive government aid was channeled into the program at this time, and significant subsidies were granted under the Federal School Lunch Program and related programs established in the 1940s.

The 1930s were not, however, an entirely dismal period for the food service industry. In 1932, the National Restaurant Association selected Chicago as its permanent headquarters. Prohibition was repealed in 1933. Attendance at the NRA convention exceeded 10,000 in 1937, establishing a record to that time. (That record would be broken many times in the future—well over 100,000 people attend the convention today.)

In 1941, the United States entered World War II. Wartime restrictions were placed on travel, but the war accelerated the demand for restaurant meals. The demand went from the pre-war level of 20 million meals a day to more than 60 million meals after war was declared. Restaurant operators found rationing, price controls, labor shortages, and the incredible burden of reports and government red tape extremely frustrating. However, they survived and actually prospered. The close of World War II brought on a period of great prosperity for the nation, and the food service industry shared in this prosperity. By 1951, the industry became the third largest in the United States. Growth was the order of the day throughout the 1950s, and, by 1960, the American food service industry accounted for yearly sales of $18 billion.

The 1960s were eventful times for the food service industry. In 1964, a U.S. Supreme Court ruling strengthened the prohibition against racial discrimination in hotels and restaurants. Katherine Manchester introduced computer programming to military food services. The first minimum wage law was passed and applied to hotels and restaurants grossing $500,000 or more in annual sales. In 1969, the minimum wage law was applied to hotels and restaurants grossing $250,000 or more in annual sales. While all this was transpiring, food service sales continued to grow. During this 10-year period, yearly sales grew from $18 billion to $45 billion.

The 1960s could very properly be labeled the Era of Convenience Foods. Predictions of a diminishing supply of trained culinarians led to the development of methods that would spread the talents of chefs, cooks, and bakers over a much wider area. The efforts of university personnel and the research and development departments of supply companies were enlisted. Their goal: to develop prepackaged food that could be prepared quickly by relatively unskilled workers and still offer quality to diners.

An approach that appeared to have merit was to develop manufacturing centers where food could be produced and then transported to retail outlets for final preparation and service. A number of companies had **commissary** operations where this process had been used to a limited degree. After preparation and with proper presentation, food could be transported to various locations or inventoried in a single large operation. Once the food arrived at the individual property, it needed only to be prepared for serving.

As early as 1925, Clarence Birdseye had developed a method of freezing certain foods that would preserve them for long periods and then permit thawing and cooking without quality deterioration. Many scientists worked to develop ways to freeze entrées and other menu items while maintaining the same quality achieved in conventional food preparation.

By the 1950s, a number of large companies entered the frozen food business. Stouffer's and Armour were two of the largest manufacturers to produce complete lines of frozen entrées. Kaiser Hospitals in California began to use frozen meals, which were simply transported to the hospital and stored there. At mealtime, personnel reconstituted the platters and served them to the patients. Kaiser Hospitals received tremendous publicity for their "kitchenless kitchens." During the same period, Philip Parrott introduced a similar idea with his "kitchenless kitchen" at Continental Airlines. Frozen entrées were reconstituted by either the boil-in-the-bag method on a range top or in microwave ovens. Either system could be handled by flight attendants with limited culinary skills. In spite of the tremendous amount of research and attention given to convenience foods, industry experts never felt that convenience food quality quite measured up to freshly prepared quality.

As the country moved through the 1960s, young Americans began to develop keen interest in the culinary arts as a profession. The Culinary Institute of America in New York had more applicants than it could handle. Other fine professional cooking schools developed around the country and began to produce qualified graduates. Suddenly, the predicted shortage of culinarians was less of a problem. This fact, along with general skepticism about the quality of reconstituted convenience foods, blunted much of the interest in and development of convenience foods in the food service industry. Nonetheless, convenience food technology has had great applications in items that are sold in supermarkets for home consumption.

As the industry entered the 1970s, a great sense of optimism was evident. Public interest in food and wine was reaching new highs, sales were accelerating, and the industry was on a firm financial footing. Most important, franchising and chain operations climbed to new sales records. In spite of two recessionary periods, yearly food service sales grew from $45 billion in 1970 to $118 billion in 1980.

During this period individual entrepreneurs began to sell out to chains, and whole chains were acquired by conglomerates. Space does not permit the detailing of all these events, but one example will demonstrate the trend: Kentucky Fried Chicken was acquired by Heublein, a major distilling company. Del Monte acquired Service Systems Corporation (a food management company) and other operations. Then R.J. Reynolds (now RJR Nabisco) acquired both the Heublein and Del Monte companies.

The largest fast-food franchising chains—McDonald's, Wendy's, Burger King, Jerrico Inc. (owner of Long John Silver's), Kentucky Fried Chicken, and others— had their greatest growth period, both in sales and unit expansion, during the 1970s. It was only toward the close of the decade that sales began to slow down.

An important factor influencing this phenomenal growth was the American public's greatly increased interest in food, wine, and cooking. Many television stations regularly featured gourmet cooks who taught the novice how to prepare even ordinary foods in more interesting ways. Thousands enrolled in private cooking schools operated by chefs or cooking experts. Even the very young now view cooking as a recreational outlet and a highly interesting and worthwhile way to spend some time.

The creation of the so-called *nouvelle* (new) *cuisine* in France led to a great deal of journalistic comment. The new cuisine recognized that Americans and Europeans alike need to eat smaller amounts of lighter foods and more fresh fruits and vegetables. Indeed, the eating habits of the American public have changed dramatically in the last 20 years. The American restaurant patron is eating simpler foods and is staying away from sauces, fatty foods, and fancy cookery. Dessert consumption has decreased, and the typical diner is selecting fewer items. There is no question that the interest in dieting and weight control has had a lot to do with this. Less complicated foods are being consumed at home, and guests also desire such foods when they go out to eat.

Another recent development has been the growth of food festivals. During the last 15 years or so, festivals held in major cities around the United States have drawn millions of people. Many of these festivals are now annual affairs, and the number continues to grow every year. Guests gain exposure to an area's restaurants and hotel food and beverage operations, and to many new food items as well. Also, many culinary arts shows are being held annually in cities in just about every state. Through such events, the industry advertises and promotes its products and services and, in doing so, builds business.

Appreciation for American wine is a phenomenal development. Just 30 years ago, few Americans drank wine with their meals, and those who did rarely considered a domestic product. Today, however, all of this has changed. Europe's fine wines are very expensive, and wine connoisseurs in the United States now speak glowingly of many domestic wines, particularly those from California and New York. As a matter of fact, even Europeans admit that the best American wines compare favorably with their European counterparts. Young adults in particular have learned to enjoy wine with their meals, and, consequently, wine sales have exploded as never before. Today, even supermarkets carry a large assortment of wines.

Dollar sales in the food service industry continued to increase in the 1980s, but real growth slowed considerably, usually fluctuating between 2.5 and 3 percent annually. However, compared with other industries, the food service field did well. In fact, certain areas of the industry enjoyed excellent prosperity. Hamburger and pizza chains did well, as did Mexican and down-home properties such as Grandy's. However, because of federal budget cutbacks, the school food service program declined significantly.

In the mid-1980s, upscale restaurant chains showed greater growth than the fast-food element. This was especially true in operations like Chi-Chi's, Bennigan's, and TGI Friday's. Many of these units did a volume of $2 million yearly due to large-volume alcoholic beverage sales and a high check average. However, in the late 1980s, sales for this segment leveled off quickly. A principal reason was the strong public campaign to de-emphasize alcoholic consumption led by Mothers Against Drunk Driving (MADD) and other organizations.

The acquisition and divestiture activity that marked the 1970s continued through the 1980s and into the 1990s at a rapid pace. Marriott acquired Host, Saga, and Howard Johnson and made an unsuccessful run at Denny's. More recently, Marriott sold Roy Rogers to Hardee's, spun off the Marriott Inflight division to a management-led leveraged buyout, and completed the divestiture of its remaining restaurants. Weinerwald sold both IHOP and Lum's, while the Quaker Oats company sold Magic Pan. Carson Pirie Scott acquired Dobbs Houses, Inc., but, after less than ten years, sold the airline catering division to Viad Corporation and the food service management segment to Morrison's. RJR Nabisco acquired KFC only to turn around and sell it to PepsiCo. TW Services purchased Denny's, and then sold it and its other restaurant concepts to Flagstar Companies, Inc. TPI bought Shoney's South. American Airlines sold Sky Chefs.

International companies continued to invest in the American food service industry. Kyotaru, a Japanese restaurant company, purchased Restaurant Associates (recently, however, Nick Valenti, president of Restaurant Associates, orchestrated a management-led buyout of it from Kyotaru). Another Japanese chain, Skylark, bought Red Robin. Allied Domecq, a British firm, acquired Baskin-Robbins, Dunkin' Donuts, and Mr. Donut. Grand Metropolitan, also British, purchased the Pillsbury Company and sold off Steak & Ale and Bennigan's, but kept Burger King. At home, Grand Metropolitan added Wimpy's, Pizzaland, and Perfect Pizza to its holdings.

In the United States, Foodmaker, Inc., bought both Chi-Chi's and Jack in the Box, only to be acquired itself by Gibbons Green. Chi-Chi's was then sold to Family Restaurants, Inc. Mr. John Kluge, chairman of Metromedia, Inc., built a small restaurant empire by acquiring control of Ponderosa, Bonanza, Steak & Ale, and USA Cafes. In the seafood segment, National Pizza bought Skipper's and Castle Harlan acquired Jerrico, parent of Long John Silver's. Both Perkins Family Restaurants and Friendly Ice Cream Stores became units of The Restaurant Company.

The mid-1990s were relatively calm in the merge, sale, and acquisition arena. However, consolidation activity accelerated as the new century approached. CKE Restaurants, Inc., parent of Carl's Jr., was a major player. It acquired Hardee's from Imasco and now has a chain of over 3,800 restaurants carrying the combined logos of Hardee's and Carl's Jr. Next, the company acquired or took a major interest in Rally's, Checkers, GB Foods, Taco Bueno, and Star Buffet, Inc.

Darden Restaurants acquired both Red Lobster and Olive Garden. Flagstar Companies, Inc. purchased Coco's and Carrow's. DenAmerica became the owner of The Black-Eyed Pea, and Enterprise, Inc. gobbled up Chesapeake Bagel. Ground Round Restaurants were sold to GRC Holdings, and The American Restaurant Group sold its Black Angus chain to a Florida-based consortium. Applebee's South, the largest Applebee's franchisee, expanded aggressively with its purchase of the Canyon Cafe, Hops Grill and Bar, and McCormick & Schmick's chains.

In late 1997, PepsiCo took center stage. First, the company sold off its smaller restaurant brands: East Side Mario's, Hot 'N Now, Chevy's Mexican Restaurant, California Pizza Kitchen, and D'Angelo's Sandwich Shops. Then it spun off its three major chains (Pizza Hut, KFC, and Taco Bell) into a new company, Tricon Global Restaurants, Inc.

Modern Food Service in Europe

The food service industry in Europe is very diversified, as it is in the United States. Virtually any category of food service is represented in various dimensions and volumes. There are notable differences between the industry in the United States and that in Europe due to cultural, historical, and socioeconomic factors.

The differences start with guest behavior and expectations. Traditionally, Europeans are accustomed to more involved, varied cooking at home. Especially in the southern regions, the traditional role of the homemaker has changed little over the centuries, and cooking and its related activities play a major role in the homemaker's life. Dining at home is also more formal than it is in the United States. A dining table is set with a variety of dishes and the entire family is expected to be present every day at a set time for the main meal. The type and time of this meal varies from country to country. In northern Europe, lunch tends to consist of a cold sandwich or similar fare, and dinner, taken around 6:00 P.M., is a full hot supper. British working classes actually call this meal "tea," but it is very similar to an American dinner. Further to the south in Europe, the lunch becomes more extensive and lasts longer, and in the Mediterranean countries is often followed by a siesta. The dinner time varies from 8:00 P.M. in northern France to 10:00 P.M. or later in southern Italy and Spain.

The result of these cultural differences is quite evident in the food service industry. In those countries where the noon meal is more elaborate, many companies offer rather extensive dining facilities where the employees take a full hour for a three- or four-course meal, some even accompanied by a glass of wine or beer. Institutional catering is a vast industry, particularly in France, which has some of the largest companies in this field worldwide. Employers may subsidize up to 50 percent of the total cost of the meal, or may require employees to pay for the food products at cost while the employer covers the fixed and operating expenses. Also very popular in these countries is a restaurant luncheon voucher offered by small employers that do not have an employee dining facility. In other countries people often take their lunch to work, though more and more companies have restaurants that are operated by outside catering companies, a rapidly growing segment of the industry.

Due to the high quality and variety of home-cooked meals, guest expectations of dining out are much higher. Restaurant meals are more involved and extensive. Because of this and the higher social emphasis on eating, guests tend to spend much more time eating dinner in a restaurant. Two hours is the norm, but dinner can be an all-night affair lasting up to four hours, especially in larger groups. Full-service restaurants generally do not expect to turn their tables and must be satisfied with a one-seating evening.

There are exceptions, however. The brasseries in Paris are notorious for their lively environment with servers running large platters from the kitchen to the tightly spaced tables filled with guests from 7:00 P.M. to 1:00 A.M. daily. Three to four table turns are common in these restaurants.

Two major factors affecting guest behavior are a generally lower discretionary income and relatively higher restaurant prices. The result is a dining-out frequency that is a mere one-tenth of that found in the United States. Businesses entertain less frequently due to more restrictive and lower deductibility rules in many European countries. Thus, dining out becomes a much more special occasion. It is safe to say that the European restaurateur has to live up to much higher guest expectations than does his or her American colleague.

On the other hand, younger people tend to visit a restaurant more often and eat more rapidly, but they frequent lower-priced restaurants. In Holland, the "choose-your-own" menu is more popular than a fixed, rather low-priced menu.

The food service industry work force in Europe is also significantly different from the food service work force in the United States. Some of these differences are based on culture and history; others are influenced from the outside due to government regulations and union contracts.

Technical qualifications are required both in the front and the back of the house. Traditionally, an apprentice system is used in both service and kitchen areas, with boys and girls starting as young as 14 to 16 years of age, working several days a week and being schooled in mostly technical aspects on the remaining days. A strict system of different levels of qualifications, each with clearly defined tasks, must be mastered one step at a time. A good example is the French restaurant hierarchy, which has as many as seven levels from assistant busperson to maître d'. The emphasis on technical qualifications contrasts with the emphasis on friendliness found in the United States. European visitors never cease to comment on the outgoing, accommodating demeanor of the American restaurant service employees, and find that it more than overcomes any lack of technical qualifications.

Whereas in the United States many restaurant workers are students or others who view their jobs as only temporary, in Europe, many service workers view their careers as lifelong ones. But as the number of restaurants in Europe rises and younger people increasingly live on their own, more and more part-time students work in the food service industry for just a few years.

Remuneration is also quite different. In most European countries, the gratuity is included with the meal and then either distributed in a trunk system to the servers or kept by the operation, which pays the staff a fixed salary. The concept of tip

Insider Insights

Jonathan Silver
UK Foodservice Business
CFO, Banquets Group
Oxford, England

These observations are more idiosyncratic than comprehensive, but may give a feel for recent developments in the United Kingdom.

For many years, we have run a medium-sized foodservice business primarily in the leisure or "quick service" sectors. We've seen it medium good and medium bad, but never quite like this. There are more restaurants on the market today than I've had hot dinners. Or put another way, if all the unused till rolls in that drawer below the till were laid end to end, you could wrap all the take-away fish and chip sales here for a week—and that is going some.

In truth, though, these generalizations hide a wide range of experience. In the quick service restaurant sector, all the major players are involved in a wild-West-style promotional shootout, designed to offer the customer ever greater "value lines" in a depressed market. This has been great for families who eat out only on Mondays between 5 and 7 P.M.—they get the best deals—but not so good for the operators who take a more self-interested view.

Grapeshot is also high on the menu. McDonald's sells pizzas; Burger King sells chicken; and KFC sells burgers. "If the other guy has it, let's give it a go," is the motto. Strangely, this logic extends to location also, with all the major operators vying for the same sites at ever-increasing location costs. Only now are the juggernauts of the business looking at lower-cost entry into trading.

Location of McDonald's has become a favorite preoccupation of journalists in recent time. McDonald's has succeeded, amazingly, in locating at London's famous Tower Bridge. It has been less successful against the effete leaders of Hampstead who have been fighting against the arrival of the golden arches in the streets of the famous North London suburb. If it is any consolation to McDonald's, these same worthies banned baseball from Hampstead Heath—thank goodness the objection must be purely cultural and not targeted at any particular business!

Pizza is still the hot number. The roads of most major towns are made uniquely hazardous by the high-speed scurrying of motorcyclists balancing pizzas somewhere between their bodies and machines en route to their home delivery destinations.

Probably the greatest threat to the pizza home delivery business is the growth in range and quality of convenience food products offered by the major supermarkets, which are found on most UK High Streets. These supermarkets have already captured a major part of the lunchtime snack business and are becoming more and more adventurous in their offers to the customer.

Pubs and bars have had a welcome boost recently with the relaxation of licensing laws. Pubs can now remain open all afternoon, which has allowed Brits the pleasures of day-long European café-style brasseries. The breweries, however, have had a nasty jolt from the government, which is now requiring the largest ones to sell off parts of their public house estates, in the interest of opening up the

(continued)

Insider Insights *(continued)*

market and offering a greater choice of beers. The short-term effect of this move has been merely to reduce the number of pubs, though beer aficionados have welcomed the improvement in the range of beers generally available.

Back on Main Streets, or, more accurately, just off them, the 1980s saw the development of a rash of new enclosed shopping malls. Each of these has its own food court, designed by some spiky-haired youngster who's never set foot inside a kitchen and located in the least-accessible part of the shopping mecca. Many of these have fallen on hard times, though there are now moves to pump new life into them from all sorts of angles. Airports and rail terminals have also benefitted from the government-led drive to privatize all operations that it reasonably can. The range of food service offered has dramatically improved as private operators compete to offer customers a wide range of experience.

The government has also been forced to respond to problems within the food supply chain. Recently, British beef, offered in a humanitarian gesture to the impoverished Russian people, was initially rejected at its destination amidst fears that "mad cow disease" would be unwittingly exported by the food relief agencies, a very big embarrassment all 'round. The newspapers are never slow to whip up a scare on this subject, and no one really believes the problem has been solved, despite draconian controls on the operation of the beef industry. Listeria in eggs has also been a good topic of dinner party conversation since a government minister was sacked for suggesting that this may be a problem.

What other country can boast one government official as minister for agriculture, fisheries and food? With the newspapers clamoring for action, something had to happen. So we now have a new Food Act, which came into force this year. This requires all operators selling food to register with their local government authority and then demonstrate that they can handle food within the framework of the new legislation. This legislation covers food-holding temperature controls and general hygiene procedures and diligence. Thermometer manufacturers have had a boom time, but the poor caterer trying to offer, say, a hot four-course meal in a tent to 200 regatta guests would have a particularly difficult problem. It is early days on the legislation, but it has had a profound impact on every aspect of the business, increasing operating costs considerably. We are all waiting for the first few "celebrity" prosecutions as the next stage in this highly public excursion.

There are many outstanding new restaurants in the gourmet dining sector, making imaginative use of space, materials, and marketing. Many have been helped by the increasing space given in newspapers and magazines to a new phenomenon of restaurant critic as celebrity. Here the critic's refined taste buds pass precious judgment on some poor chef's soul (or sole!).

The ubiquitous push to link us to Europe has influence here. A range of menu items, unheard of a short while ago, became essential accoutrements to any aspiring provincial city menu. Mange tout, courgettes, radicchio—all are items now generally available nationwide. Ersatz French cafés and restaurants are flourishing under British management, as are a new wave of Belgian, Swiss, and Eastern European restaurants, along with the surreptitious entry of Australian

(continued)

Insider Insights *(continued)*

cuisine to the field. All this is good for the business and the customer, but there is a darker side to current conditions.

The top end of our business has been hammered by the current economic woes. Some years ago, tax authorities disallowed (with a few rare exceptions) entertaining as a tax-deductible expense. This move, plus the general tightening of company belts, has resulted in very difficult trading conditions for many of our most famous restaurants. Regrettably, the exceptionally high real estate costs that plague the business have not decreased, and many excellent operators are throwing in the towel; or, more correctly, many banks are now forcing operators to shut up shop. Even the royal caterers at Buckingham Palace went out of business.

Ultimately, though, the ever-improving standards, expectations, and skills are what keep the British scene so exciting and ultimately resilient. As a team of British master chefs travel to France to prepare a menu of traditional English fare for French gastronomes, Popeye's Pizza has just arrived from the U.S. This must be the dough that foreign exchange dealers earn!

---

credit is non-existent, and labor costs make up a significantly larger portion of the profit and loss statement. While labor costs in a typical U.S. restaurant run about 30 percent, these expenses reach up to 50 percent of sales in Europe. A portion of this difference is caused by the social charges and benefits, which are much higher in Europe. Tips are given and, though highly appreciated by the servers, are not an official part of the salary. The usual tip amounts to about 5 percent of the total bill.

In most European countries, industries are subject to a series of strict government regulations and union rules. Employees tend to have contracts specifying their exact positions and the number of hours worked per week. Interestingly enough, much of this regulation and its restrictive effects are avoided in many of the small-scale food service environments. In many European countries, beating the system has become a national sport.

From a culinary standpoint, the variety found in Europe is vast. Distinctive regional cuisines are abundant. The major metropolitan areas boast a bountiful selection of restaurants from Europe and around the world. Smaller towns have at least one Chinese restaurant and an Italian pizzeria. The United States has also contributed a vast array of hamburger chains, fried chicken, and American-style bistros like TGI Friday's. International hotel chains many times offer an American-style restaurant and European restaurateurs are discovering "California cuisine."

Some typical differences exist. In addition to their stateside menu, the popular American hamburger chains offer some items not offered in the United States. For example, mayonnaise is served with french fries more often than catsup is. The portion size and plate composition differ in that the meat portions are considerably smaller and the vegetable selections more extensive. Also, the dinner salad offered as a starter or separate course in an American restaurant is virtually nonexistent. Luncheon salads are common, but, at dinnertime, salad is offered only as an accompaniment with some dishes and, rarely, as a course after the main course in a French restaurant.

Physically, European restaurants differ little from their American counterparts. Anything can be found from a "hole in the wall" to large-capacity restaurants. The use of place mats rather than tablecloths is more limited, and Europeans tend to offer a wider variety of cutlery with specific implements for different food products, such as the use of fish cutlery and up to three different sizes of regular cutlery. The spacing of tables is generally tighter, with the French leaving barely an inch between adjacent tables. Outdoor terraces are popular and abundant even in northern countries, and are used for afternoon coffees, drinks, and light meals. In the south with late dining in warm climates, many restaurants offer strictly outdoor seating.

Due to the higher labor costs, low table turnover, and sometimes extensive preparations, restaurant prices are considerably higher than in the United States. In addition, most of Europe has embraced the value added tax (VAT) system with a tax on restaurant meals of about 18 percent. Next, a 12 percent to 15 percent service charge is included in the menu price, resulting in prices almost double those in the United States.

With an understanding of the differences and similarities between the industries on these two continents, a restaurateur can succeed in either. This understanding also helps in catering to the needs and expectations of the European visitor.

Well-known American chains are finding their way in Europe, but are learning that success may vary from country to country. For example, McDonald's is successful in the Netherlands, but Burger King and KFC were not. TGI Friday's is a success in England but not on the continent.

In 1993, the European Community became a fact. The following years led to increased interchange among the European countries, people, and cultures. People became more used to foreign differences and more open to other habits, trends, and tastes. Both chain and individually owned restaurants have benefitted from this interchange.

Franchising Developments in Food Service

Perhaps more than any other force, franchising has shaped the development of the food service industry. A few recent statistics from the International Franchising Association will demonstrate the role of franchise restaurants within the food service industry, both nationally and internationally:[1]

- There are 131,170 franchised restaurants in the United States. Of this total, 39,351 are company-owned and 91,819 are franchisee-owned.

- In 1996, franchise restaurant sales totaled $100 billion, an increase of nearly 8 percent over the previous year.

- More than 3.2 million persons are employed by franchised restaurants in the United States.

- Internationally, there are more than 13,500 units of U.S.-franchised restaurants.

- In the restaurant franchise segment outside the United States in number of units, Canada is the leader, followed by Japan, the United Kingdom, Australia, the Caribbean region, and Mexico.

Franchising in the food service industry has developed along two traditional lines. Early in this century, product franchising was undertaken by A&W Root Beer of Los Angeles. Later, the Coca-Cola Company of Atlanta, Georgia, built its business by franchising its products through independent bottlers. After this initial phase, no great strides were made in franchising in the food service business until the early 1950s, when business operations rather than products began to be franchised.

In 1954, James McLamore and David Edgerton franchised their first Burger King restaurants. They were just barely under way when supersalesman Ray Kroc received permission from the McDonald brothers of California to franchise the now well-known Golden Arches. Few people remember that Beverly Osborne of Oklahoma City preceded both of these pioneer organizations with his chicken-in-a-basket operation. Today the annual sales of the McDonald's franchise organization worldwide have passed the $30 billion mark. Burger King's sales are $8.4 billion, followed by Wendy's at $4.5 billion and Hardee's at $3.4 billion.[2] At least 20 others have passed the $1 billion mark.

All of these organizations operate under what is called a *business format* franchise. This kind of franchise seeks to establish a fully integrated relationship that includes product, operating and service standards, trademarks, marketing and strategic planning, quality control, and a communication system that assists in the flow of information through the organization.

In the 1980s, American food chains began expanding internationally. That expansion continues in the 1990s at an accelerated pace. Today, American chains operate on every continent except Antarctica.

KFC has 40 percent of its restaurants outside the United States, while McDonald's operates 3,500 units overseas. Domino's units are located throughout Europe, while Pizza Hut has an even broader international market including two stores in Moscow. About 90 percent of all major chains are represented in both Canada and Mexico.

One of the most interesting events in recent years was the opening of McDonald's in Moscow. It is by far the largest McDonald's in the world. It was a smash hit from the day it opened. One reporter wrote that the new McDonald's had replaced Lenin's Tomb as Moscow's number-one tourist attraction. During the first year of operation, the unit served 40,000–50,000 customers per day, 15 million for the year. More than 4 million Big Macs and 5 million soft drinks were purchased by customers who regularly waited in line 20–90 minutes.

The newest market is eastern Europe, and many American chains are already there. A number of them, including both McDonald's and Burger King, operated with mobile units until they could establish permanent stores.

As is the case with hotels, franchisors typically operate some company-owned stores in addition to offering franchises. (Exhibit 2 shows the ratio of company-owned to franchised units in some of the major franchise companies.) This approach enables multi-unit chains to expand quickly. Given this expansion, the need to operate under strict franchise agreement terms becomes obvious; all units—

**Exhibit 2 Ratio of Company-Owned and Franchised Units in
Major Food Service Companies**

	Percent of Total Units	
Chain	**Company-Owned**	**Franchised**
McDonald's	16%	84%
Subway	0%	100%
Burger King	7%	93%
Denny's	61%	39%
Wendy's	28%	72%
Pizza Hut	59%	41%
KFC	40%	60%
Bob Evans Farms	100%	0%
Hardee's	21%	79%
Olive Garden	100%	0%
Dairy Queen	0%	100%
Dunkin' Donuts	1%	99%

Source: *Nation's Restaurant News*, April 1996.

company stores and franchises—must offer a consistent product and level of service to attract and retain customers (who will not know whether they are eating at company-operated or franchised units).

For a number of years, the principal growth of franchise restaurants came from the addition of new units to the chain. Gradually, prime locations became fewer in number and, to at least some extent, expansion in the number of new units slowed; the average sales per unit also flattened (remained the same) or decreased.

Eager to maintain or even exceed the yearly growth figures they had achieved, companies began to look for other ways to increase sales. During the past several years, their approach has focused on building unit sales. Companies have spent large sums on advertising, hoping to boost their share of the market. During the late 1970s and early 1980s, these organizations concentrated on expanding their menus. Some augmented their menus by introducing breakfasts or by adding new breakfast items. Still others experimented with salad bars or introduced new sandwich accompaniments or dessert items. These efforts have increased unit sales dramatically for many properties. Today, there are many franchised units with sales greater than $1 million annually.

During the past several years, sales in franchised units have been built primarily on four or five best-selling items. Hamburgers are the largest-selling products in franchised operations. Hamburgers, steak, pizza, chicken, pancakes, and waffles account for 75 percent or more of food service sales in franchised restaurants. Today, there is a trend toward increased sales of Mexican food, seafood, and various specialty sandwiches such as those made with croissants. The future of ethnic foods, particularly Mexican and Chinese foods, looks excellent. The sale of seafood has been growing at a steady, sometimes spectacular rate.

Some organizations seem to be increasing their popularity (and sales) at a consistent rate. Hardee's and Shoney's are among these. The three dominant operations in the pizza field are Pizza Hut, Domino's, and Little Caesar's Enterprises, each of which has a special niche. Pizza Hut ranks first in dine-in sales. Domino's is the leader in delivery service, and Little Caesar's leads the way in take-out. In the early 1990s, competition heated up in the delivery segment when Pizza Hut challenged Domino's. To implement delivery service, Pizza Hut bought 265 Winchell's Donut Shops, which were converted to home-delivery Pizza Hut units. The delivery competition reached such an intensity in radio, TV, and newspaper ads that court action was threatened. To date, Domino's maintains the number-one delivery organization, but the gap has narrowed.

A new twist in the franchising field was introduced by Marriott, which developed fast-food complexes at Travel Plazas on tollways and at its Host airport terminal operations. Marriott has become a franchisee of Sbarro, Nathan's, Dunkin' Donuts, Roy Rogers, Popeye's, Mrs. Field's Cookies, Bob's Big Boy, TCBY, and Burger King, and operates several of these franchises at each complex.

McDonald's: A Case Study in Success

While the listing of successful franchised operations could continue, one such operation draws particular attention to itself. In many respects, the McDonald's story is almost a fairy tale, an unbelievable success story of a franchise organization that continues to improve its performance year after year. Over the last 40 years this organization, built around a concept originally put together by the McDonald brothers in California, has grown from a single roadside restaurant located in Des Plaines, Illinois, to more than 15,000 units located throughout the world.

In some respects, the McDonald's organization can be compared to Du Pont or General Motors. Like these two industrial giants, it has not only produced leadership for itself but also for a score of other companies. Unprecedented growth and constant change are among its special accomplishments. During a recent year, McDonald's spent more than $1 billion on advertising and promotion ($3 million per day). The average McDonald's franchise unit now produces $1.6 million in sales annually. The company's closest competitor, Burger King with 7,027 units, averages $1.23 million in sales per unit. McDonald's officials readily admit that each of its competitors has certain strengths and that occasionally the competition effectively anticipates certain trends. But for more than 40 years, no competitor has matched this corporation's unerring instinct to anticipate the mood of the American public and to exploit consumer moods in the right way and at the right time.

McDonald's has changed in appearance as well as in management tactics. Architectural changes show how this organization stays in tune with the times. Just a few years ago, every McDonald's franchise was stamped out of the same mold. Today, in response to changing demographics and urban pressures, a refreshing new atmosphere is being created at new McDonald's locations. The company now offers its franchisees a wide selection of exterior designs. Some new buildings house a small red barn in which seats are constructed to resemble saddles, and chairs and tables look like rustic barn wood. Children everywhere are excited by the chance to sit in Old McDonald's Farm. In these special areas, reservations for parties can be made, and employees help serve food and drinks.

The new franchised McDonald's restaurant is larger, more sophisticated, better landscaped, and operated quite differently from yesterday's units. Company executives and franchise owners alike agree on the value of decor as a drawing card for the unit. As a result, the company encourages annual landscaping and decor award programs to reward innovation and new ideas among its franchisees. All this, of course, is merely the outward manifestation of the kind of spirit that has made the organization respond to the ever-changing mood of its customers.

Perhaps less immediately apparent to the casual observer is McDonald's concern with efficient energy management. As further evidence of its versatility, this company maintains a very effective research and development program, which has developed much of the equipment used in the McDonald's system. For several years, McDonald's engineering personnel have been preparing for a severe energy shortage and, at the proper time, may well unveil even more industry-leading innovations in equipment technology.

Occasionally, McDonald's has been called a real estate concern that is in the food business. At one time, there was real justification for this statement. When the company started, about one-half of its corporate revenue came from rentals. But all of this has changed. Currently about 80 percent of corporate revenue comes from the sale of food and beverage products.

From the very beginning, McDonald's has experimented with various menu offerings. As a result, today's menu contains 30 or more items. But quarter-pound hamburgers, fish fillets, french fries, scrambled eggs, sausage, hot cakes, English muffins, and so forth did not become menu items accidentally. Rather, extensive research and field testing in selected units preceded their introduction system-wide. Having successfully conquered the breakfast area, McDonald's is now putting considerable emphasis on, and many advertising dollars into, promoting dinner business.

Consistency Is Important

Franchising's first great strength was (and is) its consistency. Consumers quickly learned to expect similar products and services at every store in the chain. Standardization was the hidden persuader that caused people to return again and again. Achieving such operational consistency has traditionally been one of the most difficult goals for fast-food franchisors to accomplish. Inattention to the small details often accounts for restaurant failures. All successful franchises have certain things in common:

- Quality—Franchises consistently produce a good, standard product.

- Service—Franchises consistently provide fast service.

- Cleanliness—Franchise units are consistently cleaner than most of their independent competitors.

- Value—Franchises consistently offer good quality products for the consumer's money.

Much of the success of fast-food franchises lies in the fact that unit buildings are engineered and built with ease of maintenance and constant cleanliness in mind. In addition to these concerns, the design of the units emphasizes ease of construction, flexibility for future expansion, and economical use of labor.

The interiors of most franchised operations are masterpieces of planning that make it possible for each unit to consistently deliver its type of food service to thousands of customers with maximum efficiency. In this respect, fast-food franchisors are far ahead of most of their counterparts in the restaurant field. They deliberately build for high volume and fast service. High sales per square foot and greater levels of productivity per employee are keys to the kind of profitability that fast-food franchising can deliver.

Franchise Agreements and Relationships

As in every other kind of business organization, relationships between a parent company and its franchisees are important. There are sometimes stresses and strains between partners, which may intensify as the nature of food franchising continues to be redefined or as franchise contracts move closer to their expiration date. As a result of the inevitable disagreements between franchisors and franchisees, just about every successful company has a franchise council, sometimes operated at arm's length between the two organizations.

Franchisees are concerned about the terms of the renewal of their franchise contract. The major franchising organizations know that their basic ideas and programs have made millionaires out of their franchisees. In addition, franchisors know that one poorly run, dirty unit with ineffective employees can affect the reputation of many other operations in an entire area. Therefore, they insist on checking the prescribed standards imposed by the contracts. To further protect themselves, they include in their contracts the right to cancel a license with a franchisee when there is good cause.

A standard contract usually requires the franchisee to use the franchisor's trademarks, company insignia, and standard packaging. At one time, many franchisors insisted that franchisees also purchase all or many of their supplies from a central source controlled by the franchisor. In the past, McDonald's franchisees even operated on leased land and in company-owned buildings. In recent years, the courts have generally ruled that franchisors may not require such tie-ins as a part of their contract with the franchisee. Nonetheless, many franchisees believe that franchisors are primarily interested in satisfying their own stockholders or the company that owns them. They say that franchisors often violate their own agreements and "invade" territory that has been set aside for the exclusive development of franchisees. Says one franchisee, "It is unfortunate that some franchisors refuse to accept their franchisees as their business partners." Some franchisees complain that franchisors continually underestimate the intelligence and the ability of their franchisees and fail to acknowledge and use their expertise.

Under the best of circumstances, the franchisor-franchisee arrangement results in imprecise definitions and differing perceptions of the nature of the relationship. There is simply no way that everything that might occur can be covered in a contract. It is not like the relationship of an employer and employee. Franchisors refer to their franchisees as independent businesspeople. However, many franchisees feel that the control exercised by the franchisor and the latter's ability to terminate contracts keep them feeling quite dependent on the franchisors.

But even with a long history of strained relationships, difficulty in agreeing on business methods, and other problems that arise from the peculiar compact between unequal partners, the necessity for maintaining standards and uniformity in operating procedures is proven again and again by the success stories of huge organizations that even operate internationally. There can be no denying the power and strength that reside in the franchising concept. Nor can anyone who knows the history of the great weakness of the small independent restaurant business deny that franchising has been the one vehicle that has made this small business a strong and viable force in the American business system.

Fast-Food Employees

Franchised fast-food units employ thousands of people. The fast-food industry offers employment opportunities with good salaries and benefits to those who have the education and experience to move up to the corporate level. The majority of these employees come to the company without any previous background or training in food service. It has, therefore, been necessary to develop complete training and development programs for all franchisees. Training and human resource development is a necessary part of corporate and regional planning and development. Some franchisors such as McDonald's, Burger King, Long John Silver's, Shoney's, and others operate their own training schools, using classroom instruction, audiovisual aids, and participatory situations. They also offer programs in advanced restaurant operations, multi-unit management, regional general management, local marketing, and small business management. In addition, they develop and coordinate training programs at regional centers located throughout the country. Instructors in the training programs have all had experience in running a fast-food restaurant and thus are well equipped to answer questions.

All franchises have difficulty motivating hourly workers who must do repetitive tasks. These hourly workers have, until recently, been drawn almost entirely from high school students and others who have had little interest in staying on the job long and therefore little commitment to an operation. But the work force in fast food is slowly changing as more and more mature individuals apply for positions in fast-food restaurants. The typical assistant manager is in his or her middle or late twenties. Today there are many more mature people who want part-time employment in these restaurants. Unlike high school students, these people want to know why things are done, how they fit into the company's plans, and where the company is heading.

Franchising Problems

Franchising as a system has not only proven its basic strengths but has also proven to be the most effective way to expand the food service industry using a standard formula. However, franchising has potential problems. There have been notable failures along with successes.

A classic case was the demise of Sambo's. While there were a number of factors that led to Sambo's failure, one of the most significant began when the United States government ordered the company to end a fringe benefit plan the company called "a piece of the action." This plan allowed each manager to buy a minority interest in his or her own restaurant as well as others being built. This program was so successful that the Sambo's chain grew quickly during the early 1970s. Over 800 units were built all across the country. When the federal government ordered Sambo's officials to end their unique program, the company offered a less lucrative substitute program to its managers without many of the benefits of the original package. The result was management resignations on a wholesale basis; the organization that had been built with a liberal benefits program collapsed as a "piece of the action" ended.

Lum's of Miami is another franchising organization that had a history of financial problems. Even ownership by Friedrich Jahn, one of Europe's most successful restaurateurs, failed to solve Lum's problems, and the company went into bankruptcy. Minnie Pearl Country Dairy Stores, designed especially for small towns, hardly got off the ground before it, too, was in serious trouble. Hardly a trace remains of the original organization, and the few units that do remain are independent restaurants. Famous names (including Joe Namath, Al Hirt, and Mickey Mantle) were not enough to save a number of other franchises, either.

Even these well-publicized failures or near-failures often do not discourage people in the industry from trying to build a successful new concept. Nonetheless, all of these examples of instability and failure point out that franchising has not always proven to be a cure-all for every promoter or restaurateur who thinks his or her ideas are good enough to sell.

Management Companies in Institutional Food Service ——

Just as franchising has greatly affected the development of commercial food service, management companies have affected the development of institutional food service.

Major Management Companies

Exhibit 3 lists the leading management companies based on worldwide sales. Two of the companies have headquarters outside the United States, but, through purchases of or mergers with U.S. companies, now have a significant presence in this country. Using only North American sales figures, Compass ($5.0 billion) takes second place before Aramark ($3.5 billion), with Sodexho Marriott Management, Inc. ($6.4 billion) taking first place.

Management companies in Europe operate in areas similar to their American counterparts. Companies active internationally in the institutional, airline, and shipboard food service fields include Belgavia (Belgium), Servair, Eurest and Wagon Lits (France), SAS Service Partners (Scandinavia), LSG Lufthansa Services (Germany), Forte and Cunard (England), Holland America Line and Cuisinair

Exhibit 3   Leading Management Companies

Company	Sales	Accounts
Sodexho Marriott Management	$ 6.4 billion	15,166
Compass Group (England)	$ 5.0 billion	8,600
Aramark	$ 3.5 billion	2,400
Service America	$715 million	7,030
SHRM Group (France)	$700 million	1,139
Restaura	$370 million	395
The Wood Company	$335 million	312
Daka Restaurants	$322 million	396
Morrison Health Care	$220 million	300

Source: *Restaurants and Institutions*, July 15, 1997, and *Nation's Restaurant News*, October 13, 1997.

(Holland), International Catering Services (Switzerland), Saudi Catering (Saudi Arabia), Abela Corporation (France), and Cara (Canada).

Management Company Operations

Management companies operate in the food service segments of recreational food service, employee food service, health care food service, and educational food service.[3]

Recreational Food Service. Unlike health care, educational food service, and, to some extent, employee food service, recreational food service is primarily a for-profit segment of the industry. The trend is for increased participation by management companies, especially in recreation and sports centers. Currently, management companies account for nearly 50 percent of the $6 billion in annual sales generated at these centers.

Employee Food Service. For years, manufacturing plants and other business organizations operated their own employee cafeterias. Today, the majority of employee food service operations are run by management companies. Employee food service is a major segment of the industry, with annual sales over $5.3 billion. Many changes have occurred in this segment. Gone is the institutional image of old—unimaginative fare such as meat loaf and gravy served up on stainless steel and plastic serviceware. The management companies call this segment *business and industry food management* and run it virtually like a commercial restaurant enterprise. Operations range far beyond cafeteria service into executive dining rooms, catering operations, and semipublic restaurants.

With more and more business organizations viewing employee food service as a key tool for improving employee productivity, management companies, according to ARA Services' Michael Cronk, are becoming more commercial, especially in the sense that they have the same sales and marketing and merchandising drive as a restaurant. Operations are designed to be more efficient and cost effective with fully computerized food production, inventory, and accounting systems.

Health Care Food Service. The health care segment of the industry involves the three principal markets of (a) acute care hospitals, (b) long-term care facilities, and (c) retirement communities. Many industry experts state that this segment has the greatest short- and long-term growth potential in the food service industry. With current sales of over $16 billion, it is readily understandable why nearly every major contract management company, along with many smaller, specialized firms, is involved in the health care field.

Health care facilities have traditionally operated—and still do operate—their own food service departments to emphasize health and nutrition rather than financial considerations. However, reduced income and pressures for cost containment are creating a need for managers to run health food service operations as professional businesses. Consequently, a growing number of health care facilities are turning to management companies.

Those in favor of management companies in the health care setting cite the following advantages:

- Organizational resources of large nationwide companies can focus on solving specific problems in the individual units with expertise, automation, and savings brought about by effective negotiations with food suppliers.

- Contract management companies can often operate dietary programs at a lower cost than their self-operated counterparts.

- Reduced internal direction by staff administrators may be another plus. Facility administrators, trained in areas other than food service operations, can delegate responsibilities for making decisions to professional food service managers.

Opponents of management companies cite the following disadvantages:

- Loss of internal control means that management companies may have too much discretion in matters that affect the institution's public image, long-range operating plans, and other important issues.

- Questions about the propriety of involving a profit-making business in a health care food service program are often raised.

- Miscellaneous operational problems include concerns that the company will decrease quality or take other contractual shortcuts.

- The health care food service operation may depend too much on the management company. What will the operation do if the management company wants to discontinue the contract? How long will it take the operation to implement its own program or find another management company?

- Higher operating costs are also possible when management companies are used. How is it possible to use a management company to *reduce* costs when now we are suggesting that operating costs might *increase*?

The answer to whether management contract companies belong in health care food service depends on the specific management company and on the food service operation. Minimizing costs while retaining quality is at the heart of the food management company controversy.

In spite of management company inroads into the health care market, many institutions continue to run their own food service operations. Significant among them are Baptist Memorial Hospital, Memphis; Beth Israel Medical Center, New York City; Massachusetts General Hospital, Boston; The New York Hospital, New York City; NYU Medical Center, New York City; Carolinas Medical Center, Charlotte, North Carolina.

Educational Food Service. This segment includes food service at primary and secondary schools, colleges, and universities. As is the case with health care facilities, the majority of educational institutions operate their own food service. However, the trend is toward increased management company participation. Currently, management companies account for approximately 49 percent of the sales at colleges and universities and 40 percent of the sales at primary and secondary schools. The advantages and disadvantages of management companies for health care facilities also apply to educational food service.

As in the health care category, a number of well-known universities continue to operate their own food service facilities. Prominent among them are Pennsylvania State University; Brigham Young University; Michigan State University; Harvard University; University of California, Los Angeles; University of Wisconsin; Cornell University; and Notre Dame University.

Endnotes

1. International Franchising Association, 1997; via correspondence with IFA personnel.

2. *Restaurants and Institutions,* July 15, 1997.

3. This section is adapted from Jack Ninemeier, *Management of Food and Beverage Operations,* 2d ed. (East Lansing, Mich.: Educational Institute of the American Hotel & Motel Association, 1990), pp. 16–17.

Key Terms

à la carte menu—A menu in which food and beverages are listed and priced separately.

commissary—A central food production area from which food is transported to individual outlets for final preparation and service.

prix fixe menu—A menu that offers a specific meal consisting of several courses at a fixed price; also called a *table d'hote* menu.

smorgasbord—A variety of foods presented in a buffet-type arrangement.

speakeasy—During Prohibition, a type of establishment serving alcoholic beverages illegally. Starting with sandwiches, the speakeasy was soon serving full meals to its customers. Both hotel dining rooms and regular restaurants were forced to close for lack of business. After the repeal of Prohibition in 1933, many speakeasies developed into successful restaurants.

table d'hôte menu—A menu that offers a specific meal consisting of several courses at a fixed price; also called a *prix fixe* menu.

Review Questions

1. What establishments began offering food service in colonial America?

2. What important developments or inventions of the 1800s led to the growth of food service in America?

3. What two events contributed to the deep decline in restaurant sales during the 1920s? How did they affect sales?

4. What challenges did World War II create for the food service industry?

5. What does the term "kitchenless kitchen" mean?

6. Why does nouvelle cuisine appeal to restaurant patrons?

7. How did franchising begin in the food service industry? Describe and discuss franchising's early days and the pioneers in the field.

8. What phases or steps does a food service franchise company go through as it seeks annual growth in sales?

9. Why would a franchisor create its own training center?

10. What are the pros and cons of management companies operating in the health care setting?

Internet Sites

For more information, visit the following Internet sites. Remember that Internet addresses can change without notice. If the site is no longer there, use a search engine to look for additional sites.

Food Service and Related Associations

American Dietetic Association
http://www.eatright.org

American Culinary Federation (ACF)
http://www.acfchefs.org

American School Food Service
Association (ASFSA)
http://www.asfsa.org

Dietary Managers Association
http://www.dmaonline.org

The Educational Foundation of NRA
http://www.restaurant.org/educate/educate.htm

The Educational Institute of AH&MA
http://www.ei-ahma.org

Hospitality Financial and Technology
Professionals
http://www.hftp.org

Hospitality Information Technology
Association
http://www.hita.co.uk

International Association of Culinary
Professionals
http://www.iacp-online.org

International Food Service Executives
Association
http://ifsea.org

International Franchise Association
http://www.franchise.org

International Hotel & Restaurant
Association
http://www.ih-ra.com

National Association of College and
University Food Services
http://www.nacufs.org

National Restaurant Association (NRA)
http://www.restaurant.org

Society for Foodservice Management
http://www.sfm-online.org

Restaurants and Restaurant Companies

AFC Enterprises (formerly America's
Favorite Chicken Company)
http://www.afc-online.com

Bittersweet Bistro
http://www.bittersweetbistro.com

Burger King Restaurants
http://www.burgerking.com

Dive Restaurant
http://www.dive-subs.com

Hard Rock Cafe
http://www.hardrock.com

Hemispheres
http://www.hemispheres.com:80

KFC Corporation
http://www.kfc.com

Macayo Mexican Restaurants
http://www.macayo.com

McDonalds Restaurants
http://www.mcdonalds.com

Perkins Family Restaurants
http://www.perkinsrestaurants.com

Pizza Hut
http://www.pizzahut.com

Taco Bell
http://www.tacobell.com

Food Service Search Sites

CuisineNet-Menus Online
http://www.cuisinenet.com

Dine Out Chicago
http://dine.package.com

DineFind
http://www.dinefind.com

DineSite U.S.A.
http://www.dinesite.com

eaTneT
http://www.eatnet.com

Interactive Gourmet
htttp://www.cusine.com

World Wide Waiter
http://www.waiter.com

Chapter 8 Outline

Composition and Size of the Food Service Industry
    Eating and Drinking Places
    Hotel Operations
    Food Services for the Transportation Market
    Food Services for the Leisure Market
    Retail Food Services
    Business/Industrial Food Services
    Student Food Services
    Health Care Food Services
    Club Food Services
    Segmentation by Menu
    Other Food Services
    Giants in Food Service
The Organization of Hotel and Restaurant Food Service
    Hotel Food and Beverage Divisions
    The Organizational Structure of Restaurants

The Organization and Structure of the Food Service Industry

THIS CHAPTER WILL EXAMINE the segments of the food service industry and illustrate that food service operations are not at all limited to fast-food restaurants, conventional restaurants, or hotel dining rooms.

Composition and Size of the Food Service Industry

The food service industry may be classified in many different ways. One way is to categorize it according to various markets. These major categories are shown in Exhibit 1 and will provide the basis for most of the discussion in this chapter.

Food service operations may also be classified according to the economic objectives of the operation. There are three main categories of food service operations under this type of classification: commercial, institutional, and military. Exhibit 2 lists these main categories and their subcategories.

Commercial, institutional, and military food services each have different economic objectives. Commercial food service operations, for example, exist primarily to make a profit on the sale of food and/or beverage products. These operations attempt to maximize or at least to emphasize profits. In institutional food service operations, the main economic objective is to minimize expenses. The military's main objective is to stay within the budget allotted by Congress. Food and beverage operations in restaurants and lodging properties are typical examples of commercial food and beverage programs. Food services operated by schools and health care facilities are examples of institutional programs (although some institutional food service programs are now operated by for-profit management companies and might be classified as commercial operations).

Exhibits 3 and 4 show the approximate share of sales and purchases each of these categories commands in the total food service industry. The value of purchases is probably a more realistic way to gauge the relative size of commercial, institutional, and military categories of the industry because operations in each of these categories sell food at different prices to meet their different economic objectives. For example, a commercial restaurant will sell food at prices needed to make a profit, while institutional food services typically charge only enough to meet expenses.

Exhibit 1   Major Classifications of Food Service Markets

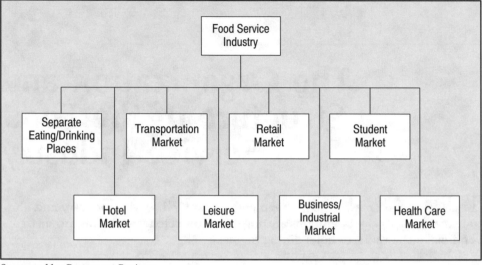

Suggested by *Restaurant Business.*

Whether the food service industry is classified by markets or by economic objectives, a few statistics will detail the size and illustrate the importance of this major industry:[1]

- Today, total industry sales are over $320 billion. Commercial food service accounts for the vast majority (90.2 percent) of all sales. (Exhibit 5 shows the growth in food service sales, 1970–1997.)

- Eating and drinking places generate about 70 percent of industry sales and about 60 percent of total food and beverage purchases.

- Food and beverage purchases total $116 billion with commercial food service responsible for a little over 76 percent of all purchases.

- The industry has 787,000 units and employs 9.5 million people.

- Just over two of every three supervisors are women and 20 percent of all supervisors are either African-American or Hispanic.

- More than 12,000 eating and drinking places are owned by African-Americans or Hispanics.

While the food service industry is growing, there is a difference between dollar volume (or *nominal*) growth and what the industry designates as *real* growth. Real growth comes from selling more food and from increasing customer counts. Nominal growth may result merely from raising food prices. In a period of high inflation, it is quite possible to have increased dollar sales growth (because of increases in selling price) and negative real growth (because of decreased customer counts).

A general description of some of the major market segments composing the food service industry points out the industry's diversity.[2] The chapter will also

Exhibit 2   Food Service Classifications by Economic Objectives

Group 1 Commercial Food Service
    Eating and Drinking Places
        Restaurants and lunchrooms
        Limited-menu restaurants and refreshment places
        Commercial cafeterias
        Social caterers
        Ice cream, frozen custard, and frozen yogurt stands
        Bars and taverns
    Food Contractors
        Manufacturing and industrial plants
        Commercial and office buildings
        Hospitals and nursing homes
        Colleges and universities
        Primary and secondary schools
        In-transit food service (e.g., airlines)
        Recreation and sports centers
    Lodging Places
        Hotel restaurants
        Motor hotel restaurants
    Other
        Retail host restaurants
        Recreation and sports
        Mobile caterers
        Vending and non-store retailers

Group 2 Institutional Food Service—Business, Educational, and Government
Organizations Operating Their Own Food Service
    Employee food service
    Elementary and secondary schools
    Colleges and universities
    Transportation
    Hospitals
    Nursing homes
    Clubs, sporting, and recreational camps
    Community centers

Group 3 Military Food Service
    Officers and non-commissioned officers clubs (open mess)
    Food service—military exchanges

Adapted from *Restaurants USA*, National Restaurant Association, December 1996.

examine more detailed statistics about the two largest commercial markets: eating and drinking places and hotels.

Eating and Drinking Places

This market can be divided into six categories. Each of the categories could include single- or multi-unit companies.

- Full-menu restaurants and lunchrooms offer a wide variety of menu items and table service. They may serve only one meal or stay open 24 hours a day.

Exhibit 3   Food Service Industry Sales

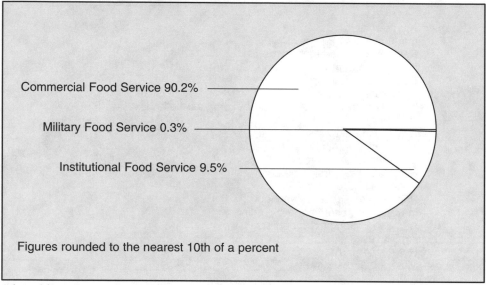

Adapted from *1997 Foodservice Industry Pocket Factbook* (Washington, D.C.: National Restaurant Association, 1997).

Exhibit 4   Food Service Industry Purchases

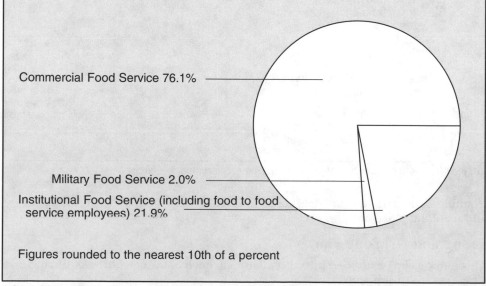

Adapted from *1997 Foodservice Industry Pocket Factbook* (Washington, D.C.: National Restaurant Association, 1997).

Exhibit 5   Growth of Food Service Sales

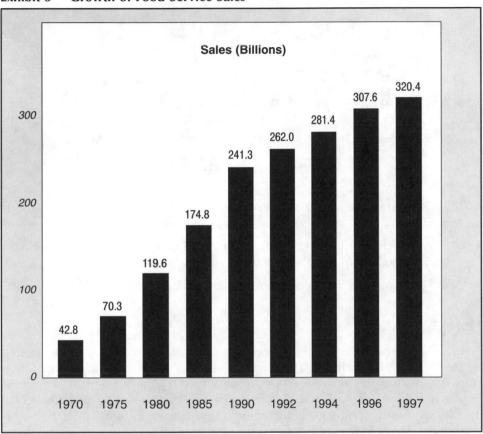

Adapted from *1997 Foodservice Industry Pocket Factbook* (Washington, D.C.: National Restaurant Association, 1997).

Some offer a California-style menu on which items that are usually served for breakfast, lunch, or dinner are offered at all times. Full-menu restaurants and lunchrooms generally have indoor seating and may serve alcoholic beverages.

- Limited-menu restaurants offer only a few items (for example, only or primarily pizza or hamburgers). Typically, the customer walks to a service counter or drives up to a service window and orders food. Then the customer carries the food to a table, if there is inside seating, or consumes the food off the premises. Some limited-menu properties offer table service.

- Public cafeterias are often similar to full-menu restaurants and lunchrooms because they offer a wide variety of menu items, but table service is usually limited. Their markets include families and, as the check average increases, businesspeople and adults without children.

Exhibit 6   Leading Providers for the Transportation Market

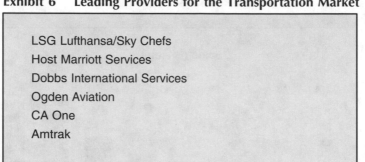

LSG Lufthansa/Sky Chefs

Host Marriott Services

Dobbs International Services

Ogden Aviation

CA One

Amtrak

Source: *Restaurants and Institutions*, August 1, 1996, p. 76.

- Social caterers prepare meals for large or small banquets and may provide food service in off-site locations.

- Ice cream, frozen yogurt, and frozen custard stands offer primarily frozen dairy and related products, sometimes with indoor seating.

- Bars and taverns serve alcoholic beverages and offer only limited food service.

Hotel Operations

Food and beverage sales generate about 31 percent of the total sales dollars earned by the U.S. lodging industry. These figures suggest that food and beverage divisions are much more than casual operations offered for the convenience of guests. In fact, many hoteliers and management personnel realize that food and beverage operations usually cannot generate required profits from in-house sales alone; extensive patronage by the community is necessary for food and beverage operations to realize their economic goals.

Food Services for the Transportation Market

Food services offered on planes, trains, in terminals, on interstate highways, and aboard passenger and cargo ships are included in this segment. These services may be provided by a for-profit management company, or they may be operated by the transportation company itself. Services can range from vending operations to sandwich and short-order preparation to extravagant, expensive food service. As the American public travels more, this market segment will expand. (Exhibit 6 lists leading food service providers for the transportation market.)

Food Services for the Leisure Market

This segment comprises food service in theme parks and for sporting events in arenas, stadiums, and racing tracks. Also included are food service operations in drive-in movie theaters, bowling lanes, summer camps, and hunting facilities. These programs may be self-operated or operated by management contract companies. An

Exhibit 7   Leading Providers for the Leisure Market

The Walt Disney Company	Mirage Resorts
Carnival Cruise Lines	Royal Caribbean Cruise Lines
Ogden Entertainment	Delaware North Corporation
Club Corporation America	Circus Circus Enterprises

Source: *Restaurants and Institutions,* August 1, 1996, p. 78.

increase in the public's leisure time will increase sales in this market segment. (Exhibit 7 lists leading food service providers for the leisure market.)

Retail Food Services

Retail food service may range from simple lunch counter or cafeteria service to formal, high-check-average table service. Examples include:

- Department stores that have employee and public dining facilities.

- Variety and general merchandise stores that have food service operations for employees—even if only vended services are provided.

- Drug and proprietary stores that have public dining outlets and/or vended services for employees.

- Convenience food stores that offer sandwiches, snacks, and beverages. Some stores even have booths and tables for in-store consumption.

- Other specialized retail stores—grocery stores, gasoline stations, and a variety of other properties—that sell food items for on- or off-premises consumption.

Business/Industrial Food Services

Business and industrial food services include the following categories:

- Contract food service—Outside, for-profit companies provide food service in plants and business offices.

- Internal food service—Plants and business offices provide self-operated food service. (Exhibit 8 lists some major companies that provide their own food service operations.)

- Food service to waterborne employees—This category includes food service to employees on ships, oil rigs, and so forth.

- Mobile on-street catering—"Meals on wheels" programs involve **canteen** operations that visit construction sites and factories, and street vendors who sell a variety of products.

- Food vending machines—Foods from snacks to complete meals are offered for customers and/or employees.

Exhibit 8   Major Companies with Self-Operated Food Service

Motorola Company	Procter & Gamble Company
Aetna Life & Casualty Co.	The 3M Company
Ford Motor Company	The EDS Corporation
J.P. Morgan & Company	Hallmark Cards

Source: *Restaurants and Institutions,* August 1, 1996, p. 80.

- Food service to military personnel—Meals consumed by members of the armed forces make up this category.

- Food furnished to food service employees—One way of again stressing the immense size of the food service industry is to note that the cost of food purchased merely to feed food service employees runs over $4.7 billion per year, nearly 6 percent of the total purchases for commercial and institutional food services.

Student Food Services

Food service in the student market includes self-operated and management company-operated programs in public and parochial elementary and secondary schools, and in colleges and universities. Elementary and secondary schools may participate in the federally subsidized National School Lunch Program and related Child Nutrition Program. Some programs, such as those in large cities, may serve hundreds of thousands of meals daily. School food service programs may include breakfast, milk, supplemental foods, and senior citizen meals in addition to traditional lunches.

The college and university food service market is tremendous. There are more than 3,000 accredited post-secondary schools in the United States. There are another 3,000 or more trade schools which, while they do not offer extensive food service operations, may have vending machines or snack bars. Perhaps 1,500 of the post-secondary schools arrange for food service through a for-profit management company. Of the remaining schools, an estimated 500 offer only vending machines or buffet food services; 1,000 schools are large enough to have extensive food service programs for boarding students and others attending classes.

Health Care Food Services

Hospitals and nursing homes of all types make up a primary segment of the health care food service market. Some of these facilities are privately owned; others are run by the government. Besides traditional acute-care hospitals and nursing homes that provide permanent residences for patients, there are also homes for orphans and mentally and physically handicapped people. Programs that are self-operated and managed by for-profit companies are included in this category.

As is true with many types of institutional food service operations, nutrition is emphasized. In many operations, the patients and residents receive all their food at

Insider Insights

Phil Parrot
Founder
Inflight Food Service Association
Former Vice President of Food Service
Continental Airlines

Few people understand what an important role airline food service plays in the psychology of the airline passenger or how much a well-planned, well-prepared, and well-executed food program can affect an airline's overall reputation.

Why is airline food service so important? The primary reason for providing food in flight is not to nurture the body. It is to provide a needed diversion to help passengers forget—or at least not dwell on the fact—that they are airborne.

Most people are afraid to fly or are apprehensive about it. As we have become more sophisticated and blasé about air travel, we tend to deny this fact (although recent increases in hijackings and other terrorist activities have added a new dimension of fear that most fliers will admit). If you doubt this, visit a few airline terminal bars and watch otherwise brave people fortifying themselves for a flight. Or take an early flight and watch people drinking Bloody Marys and screwdrivers as if before-breakfast libations are the norm.

No, fear of flying is real. So, to make people comfortable in flight, we must provide a maximum diversion that will permit them to forget where they are. Liquor will provide this distraction for some. Movies will divert others. But food is the only diversion that has universal appeal. Quality food, tastefully prepared and attentively served, can help dispel passenger anxiety. And when passengers feel confident about flight, they will leave the plane feeling good about the airline.

So where does the airline food service manager's role begin? It begins with the design of the galleys and the food service equipment. Aircraft galleys are expensive pieces of equipment, some going at roughly half a million dollars per fully equipped unit—and usually several units are needed for each aircraft. The food service manager must justify these costs to the accountants.

Equally critical is the space the galleys require. The sales department, a profit center, argues that more revenue could be generated if galley space could be converted to seating space.

In general, less galley space means that serviceware must be smaller and cheaper, and that it will provide a less gracious presentation. Why is presentation important? Louis Vaudable, owner of the famous Maxim's restaurant in Paris, answered this question when complimented on a particular wine: "You like that wine? It's not only the wine! It's the linen, the silverware, the fine crystal, the music! Do you think for a moment that the wine would taste the same out of a paper cup?"

Dishware should be of a color and style that are pleasing to the eye and easy to eat from in cramped quarters. For example, must the entrée plate be shaped like a dog dish? Or can it be of the shape we associate with fine food to help us forget where we are? Cost-cutters can prove that every pound not carried by reducing size and weight of dining equipment saves so many cents per revenue mile in fuel.

(continued)

Insider Insights *(continued)*

Unfortunately, it is not as easy for the food service manager to put a dollar value on what a satisfied customer means to the airline's future revenues. But there is real value there, and managers would do well to remember this.

Presenting food to the passenger requires careful and complete cooperation between the food service staff and cabin attendants. For this reason, it is generally accepted throughout the industry that the food service personnel and the cabin attendants be under the same supervision. This ensures complete understanding of goals, eliminates petty conflicts among departments, and permits food service expertise to be a part of cabin attendant training.

The role of the airline food service manager is to understand the psychology of fear and how best to cope with it in flight; to be willing to take the unpopular view with the accountants by insisting on at least the minimum requirements for food service to reach the airline's financial goal within his or her area of expertise; to be inventive, ingenious, and innovative in designing galleys and equipment that suit that goal; and to participate in the training and motivation of the cabin attendants who, without supervision and having no professional food service training, are responsible for the proper in-flight presentation of the product.

---

the sites, so nutrition plays an important role in protecting their health and well-being. In other facilities, nutrition is important because of its recuperative effects. Dietitians are often retained on a full-time or consulting basis, and, in some cases, might actually manage the food service operation. In other cases, they provide specialized assistance to managers in areas involving clinical and therapeutic dietetics.

Club Food Services

Although clubs are not mentioned in Exhibit 1, they form an important segment of the hospitality industry. The service of food and beverages is one of the prime functions of most clubs.

Clubs existed in ancient Greece and the Roman Empire, but clubs as we know them today in the United States are generally little more than one hundred years old. The Olympic Club in San Francisco and the Union League Club in Philadelphia were both founded during the 1860s. The Country Club in Brookline, Massachusetts, founded in 1882, is considered the oldest country club in the United States.

There are many different types of clubs and even subtypes within types. The principal kinds are country, city, yacht, fraternal, military, development, and specialty clubs.

- *Country clubs* have a clubhouse with lounges, food and beverage facilities, and recreational outlets. Country club activities usually center on the golf course(s), but swimming and tennis are also very common. The larger clubs may offer a much wider variety of athletic accommodations. There are about 4,900 private country clubs in the United States.

- *City clubs* serve the needs of individuals working in the city. In addition to the food and beverage function, this type of club may offer athletic facilities, a library or reading room, and overnight accommodations. There are approximately 2,000 city clubs in the United States.

- *Yacht clubs* are similar to country clubs except for location and the fact that activities center on boating rather than golf.

- *Fraternal clubs* are social organizations like the Elks, Knights of Columbus, Eagles, or American Legion. Typically, a restaurant, bar, lounge, billiard room, and card room are found in these clubs.

- *Military clubs* were developed to provide recreation areas for the officers and enlisted personnel. These clubs resemble country clubs without golf courses and may provide swimming facilities. Each branch of the armed services operates its own clubs, which are divided into officers clubs, non-commissioned officers clubs, and enlisted clubs.

- *Development clubs* are really country clubs built as integral parts of real estate development projects. The existence of a club is often an incentive for a customer to purchase or rent property in the development.

- *Specialty clubs* center on one particular activity (for example, tennis, swimming, racquetball) and usually do not have a clubhouse but do need a manager. Snack bar food service is often available.

Clubs are either member-owned or proprietary. Most of the older private clubs are owned by the members and governed by a board of directors elected by the members. The members are considered shareholders, and normally each member has one vote. Member-owned clubs may be tax exempt, but must meet certain criteria established by the Internal Revenue Service.

An outside individual or a corporation owns a proprietary club. The members have no equity interest in the club and, in many cases, little effective control over its policies or operation. Development clubs are the prime example of this type of ownership. The club is a for-profit operation and subject to corporate income taxes.

Whether member-owned or proprietary, a club needs management. An individual is hired to manage the club and reports to either the board of directors or the owner. Country clubs and development clubs have the most extensive organizational hierarchy because of their diversification. There will be a clubhouse manager whose responsibilities cover every aspect of operations within the building. Primary among these responsibilities is the food and beverage function; clubs are noted for providing the very finest in food and service for the members. The clubhouse manager usually has no authority over most of the recreational activities. The golf pro manages the golf course, the tennis pro runs the tennis facility, and the greenskeeper maintains the golf course. Each of these individuals reports to a committee of members. Recently, some clubs have employed general managers. The general manager is in charge of the total club operation, and those in each of the positions previously mentioned report to the general manager.

In most of the other types of clubs, the top executive who controls all phases of the operation is the manager. The word *control* may be misleading when one is speaking

Exhibit 9   Restaurant Segments and Their Sales Leaders

Segments		Leaders
Burgers	33.2%	McDonald's, Burger King, Wendy's, Hardee's
Pizza	10.1%	Pizza Hut, Domino's, Little Caesar's
Lodging	7.8%	Sheraton, Holiday Inn, Hilton, Marriott
Family	7.6%	Denny's, Shoney's, Big Boy
Chicken	6.8%	KFC, Church's, Popeye's
Dinner House	5.3%	Applebee's, Chili's, TGIF
Sandwich	5.0%	Subway, Arby's, Roy Rogers
Sweets/Snacks	4.8%	Dairy Queen, Dunkin' Donuts, Baskin Robbins
Mexican	4.7%	Taco Bell, Chi-Chi's, El Torito
Steak	4.5%	Outback, Sizzler, Ponderosa
Seafood	2.5%	Red Lobster, Long John Silvers, Captain D's
Italian	1.9%	Olive Garden, Sbarro, Pizzeria Uno

Source: *Restaurants and Institutions,* June 15, 1997, p. 82.

of a member-owned club because various member committees exercise most of the control. The manager coordinates activities as directed by the committees.

For many years, the person who operated the club was called the steward and really was more of a glorified maître d'hôtel than a manager. Then, in 1927, the Club Managers Association of America was formed. This fine organization has been most successful and effective in increasing the level of expertise of its members and in enhancing the role and image of the club manager. Today, the position carries the same professional status as hotel or restaurant manager. The great majority of club managers are college graduates, and courses in club management are taught in the major hospitality schools of the country.

Segmentation by Menu

Another way to describe the restaurant portion of the industry is to classify by type of menu. *Restaurants and Institutions* uses 12 segments and publishes data on them yearly. The segments are shown in Exhibit 9 along with the top sales producers in each segment.

Other Food Services

Other food service operations include programs operated by correctional institutions, religious seminaries and convents, and government-sponsored programs. Communities may have athletic facilities, libraries, and reading rooms that provide some form of food service.

One point should be clear by now: The food service industry is enormous. It includes any type of operation that prepares meals for people away from home—and sometimes even at home, in the case of caterers.

**Exhibit 10   Leading Food Service Companies by Number
of Units (over 4,000)**

McDonald's	21,022
Subway Sandwich & Salads	12,516
Pizza Hut	12,335
KFC	9,863
Burger King	8,700
Taco Bell	6,867
International Dairy Queen	5,717
Domino's Pizza	5,500
Holiday Inn Worldwide	5,136
Wendy's International	4,933
Little Caesar's	4,740
Dunkin' Donuts	4,446
Baskin Robbins	4,244

Adapted from *Restaurants and Institutions*, July 15, 1997.

Giants in Food Service

Exhibits 10, 11, and 12 list some of the largest food service companies ranked by number of units (Exhibit 10), U.S. system-wide sales (Exhibit 11), and system-wide world sales (Exhibit 12). International operations are of major importance to McDonald's, KFC, and Pizza Hut. As a study of Exhibits 11 and 12 reveals, McDonald's earns nearly $16 billion, KFC earns $4.5 billion, and Pizza Hut earns nearly $2.1 billion from their overseas operations.

Exhibit 13 lists the 20 overall top-ranking companies. There may be some surprises on the list shown in Exhibit 13. For example, few people may realize that Tricon Global Restaurants is the second-largest food service company with its three principal operations (Pizza Hut, KFC, and Taco Bell). Tricon Global has the largest number of units worldwide. Grand Metropolitan, a British company, owns Burger King as a result of having purchased Pillsbury, Burger King's previous parent. Imasco USA (owner and operator of Roy Rogers) is not well known by its organizational name, but it plays a major role in the industry. Few individuals outside the industry realize that Flagstar Companies, Inc. is a major player in the food service field with Denny's, Hardee's, Quincy's, and El Pollo Loco; Flagstar owns all of these except Hardee's, which it franchises. Darden Restaurants, Inc. owns Red Lobster and Olive Garden, two of the fastest-growing concepts.

Exhibit 14 lists the top 15 parent food service companies by both sales and number of units. Exhibit 15 ranks food service companies by the number of international units they hold.

Exhibit 11   Top 20 Restaurant Chains Ranked by U.S. System-Wide Sales

Restaurant Chain	U.S. Sales (in millions)
McDonald's	$15,905
Burger King	8,400
Pizza Hut	5,440
Taco Bell	4,600
Wendy's	4,150
KFC	3,700
Hardee's	3,325
Marriott Management Services	3,100
Aramark	2,782
Subway	2,600
Domino's Pizza	2,100
Little Caesar's	2,050
Red Lobster	1,838
Arby's	1,817
Denny's	1,790
Dunkin' Donuts	1,437
Marriott Hotels & Resorts	1,282
Shoney's	1,260
Applebee's	1,242
Olive Garden	1,228

Source: *Nation's Restaurant News,* June 23, 1997, p. 96.

The Organization of Hotel and Restaurant Food Service

Since hotel food service in particular has changed greatly in the last half of this century, our discussion of hotel food and beverage divisions will begin by placing current developments in their historical context.

Hotel Food and Beverage Divisions

Through most of the first half of the twentieth century, food and beverage service occupied a position of minor importance in the minds of many hotel operators. In some cases, it was treated as a necessary evil—a service available strictly for the guest's convenience. From an economic standpoint, it was important to break even or to lose as little as possible, a feat made more difficult by the fact that the food and service offered were often of very high quality. Room sales, where the

Exhibit 12   Leading Food Service Chains by World-Wide Sales

Company	Sales in Millions
McDonald's	$31,812.00
Burger King	9,010.00
KFC	8,200.00
Pizza Hut	7,481.00
Wendy's International	4,700.00
Taco Bell	4,416.80
Hardee's	4,085.00
Subway Sandwiches & Salads	3,200.00
Domino's Pizza	2,800.00
International Dairy Queen	2,508.00
Little Caesar's	2,000.00
Arby's	1,979.10
Denny's	1,933.00

Adapted from *Restaurants and Institutions,* July 15, 1997.

profit was to be made, were expected to make up the difference. As long as one could fill the guestrooms, the profit or loss figures on food and beverages were relatively unimportant.

During the 1950s, this whole concept changed radically. Perhaps the most important factor was the growth and expansion of motels and motor hotels. As motel occupancy rates grew, hotel occupancies declined, and income decreased. At the same time, operating costs increased. The financial pinch was on. Managers had to seriously re-evaluate the entire operation. They could no longer afford to operate the food and beverage division at break-even or loss levels. Small hotel operators were in the most serious position because of their competition with motels. Much of their rooms business was gone. If they were to continue operation, it would be necessary to develop other sources of sales and profit.

Clearly, there were profits to be made in food and beverage sales. After all, restaurants had made money for years. But hotels clearly needed a change of image. The average citizen considered hotel dining too expensive and too formal.

Hotels have worked hard to change this image and, fortunately, have succeeded. They recognized that the traditional formal hotel dining room was largely obsolete, or at least insufficient in itself. Guests demand a variety of dining alternatives: a rapid-service coffee shop, a snack bar, a cocktail lounge with a distinctive atmosphere, a specialty theme restaurant. Today, the coffee shop is standard in hotels, and **specialty restaurants** are thriving. Specialty steak houses and even key clubs are common in hotels today.

Exhibit 13   Twenty Overall Top-Ranked Companies and Their Franchises and/or Operations

> **McDonald's**
> **Tricon Global Restaurants**
>> Pizza Hut, Taco Bell, KFC
>
> **Wendy's**
> **Imasco USA**
>> Roy Rogers
>
> **Marriott International**
>> Marriott Hotels & Resorts, Marriott Management Services
>
> **Darden Restaurants**
>> Red Lobster, Olive Garden, Bahama Breeze
>
> **Aramark Corporation**
>> Aramark Global Food Services, Aramark Leisure Services
>
> **Flagstar Companies, Inc.**
>> Denny's, Quincy's, El Pollo Loco, Hardee's
>
> **Compass Group**
>> Eurest, Bateman, Canteen, Flik International
>
> **Brinker International**
>> Chili's Grill & Bar, Ramano's Macaroni Grill, Cozymels
>
> **Family Restaurants, Inc.**
>> El Torito, Chi-Chi's, Coco's, Carrow's, Reubens, Casa Gallardo, Charley Brown's, jojo's
>
> **Dial Corporation**
>> Dobbs International Services, Restaura, Inc.
>
> **Little Caesar's**
> **Metromedia**
>> Ponderosa, Bonanza, Steak & Ale, Bennigan's, Rising Star Grill, Montana Steak Company
>
> **Host Marriott Services Corporation**
>> Host, Burger King, Taco Bell, Sbarro, Cinnabon, Starbucks
>
> **Grand Metropolitan**
>> Burger King, Häagen-Dazs
>
> **The Restaurant Company**
>> Perkins Family Restaurants, Friendly Ice Cream Corp.
>
> **Shoney's Inc.**
>> Shoney's, Captain D's, Fifth Quarter, Pargo's
>
> **Foodmaker, Inc.**
>> Jack in the Box
>
> **Cracker Barrell Old Country Store**

Adapted from *Nation's Restaurant News,* June 23, 1997, pp. 96–97.

It is interesting to note that almost every hotel restaurant has a street entrance. In many cases, the guest may not even realize that the restaurant is part of the hotel.

Exhibit 14   Parent Food Service Companies by Sales and Units

Company	Sales (millions)	Units
McDonald's	$31,812	21,022
Tricon Global Restaurants	20,630	29,539
Grand Metropolitan PLC	9,097	8,970
Flagstar Companies, Inc.	3,345.1	2,661
Darden Restaurants	3,200	1,206
Allied Domecq PLC	2,648.1	8,690
International Dairy Queen	2,582	6,138
Carlson Hospitality	2,558.2	1,078
ITT Corporation	1,990	1,350
Marriott Corporation	1,832	900
Shoney's	1,717.7	1,461
Applebee's	1,606.7	849
Brinker International	1,459.3	649
Metromedia Restaurant Group	1,427	1,092
America's Favorite Chicken	1,442.8	2,307

Source: *Restaurants and Institutions*, July 15, 1997, p. 67.

Exhibit 15   Food Service Companies by International Units

Company	Units
McDonald's	8,928
KFC	4,784
Baskin Robbins	1,700
Burger King	1,700
Domino's Pizza	1,200
Dunkin' Donuts	1,198
Subway	1,168
Wendy's	564
Church's Chicken	292
Coco's	278
Sbarro	204

Source: *Restaurants and Institutions*, July 15, 1997, p. 68.

Insider Insights

Ueli Prager
Founder of Mövenpick
Retired
Zurich, Switzerland

Ueli Prager is the creative and organizational spirit behind the worldwide success of the Mövenpick Restaurants, Mövenpick Hotels, and Mövenpick Quality Food Products. This insight reveals the thoughts that were on his mind when he started his first Mövenpick Restaurant in Zurich in the late forties.

At the outset, the Mövenpick idea sprang from eight driving forces and ground rules:

1. I wanted to do something on my own that reflected my way of thinking, and for which I would be responsible to no one but myself.

2. My father taught me the virtues of tolerance, a happy life-style, a yen for perfection in products (foods and beverages), and an understanding of things artistic (architecture, writing, painting).

3. A three-year stint at the Swiss Hotel Association's Fiduciary Company gave me a sense of the importance of economic obligations and an understanding of entrepreneurial freedom. Furthermore, I learned to attend to the importance of numbers. Many encounters with hoteliers of every quality showed me what a person can achieve by responding to market forces rather than to tradition.

4. After becoming aware that the problems of businesses depended on seasonal fluctuations, I opted for an establishment that could operate 18 hours a day, 7 days a week, and 52 weeks a year with as little business fluctuation as possible. From the beginning, it was clear that I could achieve such results only by offering a product that catered to everyday needs. I wanted to provide pleasure and enjoyment while fulfilling these needs, and do so at affordable prices.

5. If I wanted a 365-day, 18-hour-a-day business, four basic principles had to apply:
    -   The selection of only high- or highest-quality products (the same as those used by the best, most elegant restaurants) for the plate as well as for the glass. No compromise in quality, even for the simplest, most unassuming items offered.
    -   An absence of formality and conformity, offering small and large servings. The guest wishing to merely sample a salad plate was just as welcome as the guest with more expensive desires. This was often likely to be the same individual—under different circumstances and at different times.
    -   Variety in the dishes offered—expensive delicacies and home cooking, along with both unusual and more routine items.

(continued)

Insider Insights *(continued)*

- This variety combined with a very flexible price mix to encourage guests to "board" with us during the workweek and return on weekends with their families to show where they were served with *joie de vivre*, three times a day throughout the workweek.

6. I was striving always to offer at particularly reasonable prices the items that even guests knew to be particularly expensive, and now and then to offer these same items at especially advantageous prices. I had no doubt that this concept would attract the right type of clientele: young urban sophisticates. Today we would probably call them yuppies.

7. Since I regarded myself as a young urban sophisticate then, too, everything that we did had to please me personally—while I played the part of the consumer. I was not interested in market research or advice. My deep-rooted conviction that as a guest (not as a restaurateur) I wanted a certain product or service to be *just so* served as my research, my security. If—as a guest—it pleased me, it would very likely please 2 percent of the population of Zurich. At the time, that equaled at least 10,000 patrons—quite enough to fill 75 seats.

8. Not only was the Mövenpick Restaurant to be completely different from any other establishment, but the message it conveyed publicly was to be totally unprecedented. Its style would allow no general welcoming messages, no meaningless advertisements. Instead, we would feature sales texts that expressed opinions, took positions, and were occasionally just a little controversial. For the first five years, every day I personally wrote the ad that appeared on the bottom left of the theater page in the *Neue Zürcher Zeitung*. Now—38 years later—we advertise in the same spot, day in and day out, except that others are writing the text in my stead.

These eight ground rules sound very systematic. They appear to reflect an orderly mind having set itself some clear goals, and having pursued them in the most precise manner possible.

That is not the way it was. If anything, I would rather characterize myself as chaotic than as systematic. This may sound contradictory when one writes about corporate leadership—but isn't life full of contradictions?

These eight axioms are stored in my mind and soul. I have applied them in the strictest fashion, without ever deviating from them. However, it took ten years to become aware of their existence and to set them down in writing.

Perhaps I also share another quality with many other pioneers: I have never sought or followed advice, since all it does is confuse me. Rather, I have always done things in a certain fashion out of a deep conviction that it was right. Perhaps my underlying motive might also have been a certain innate stubbornness.

The beginning was undoubtedly an act of will. To this day I readily subscribe to the beliefs I had at the beginning. This constant red thread has been sustained throughout all my subsequent actions.

The street entrance symbolizes the hotel restaurant's growing importance as a revenue center in its own right. No longer is the food and beverage business simply a necessary evil; it is promoted, merchandised, and sold through creative planning.

Hotels have made tremendous strides in increasing food and beverage sales, though they would be the first to admit there is still room for improvement. For example, most analyses of hotel guest eating habits reveal that a majority of the guests eat breakfast in the hotel, fewer have lunch there, and the smallest number eat dinner in the property. Hotels would like to reverse these figures because dinner frequently offers the greatest **contribution margin** (income minus direct costs) and breakfast the smallest contribution margin (although breakfast buffets and champagne brunches have been very successful for many properties).

Changing the image of hotels and attracting new business was a start in making hotel food service more profitable. However, if food service suffered a loss, increasing the number of patrons merely increased the loss. Food and beverage divisions had to be put on a profit-making basis, and this meant a major revision of standards and procedures in many lodging operations. The chain properties were the pioneers. Every aspect of an operation was analyzed; every procedure was scrutinized. Most important, new ideas and methods were instituted. Purchasing and receiving standards and specifications were developed, sophisticated pre-cost and pre-control systems were adopted, yield tests were conducted, forecasting became a management tool, and staffing guides were created and followed. The result has been an increase in food and beverage profits.

Any manager will acknowledge that making a profit on food is difficult and requires modern operating procedures and experience that is not acquired quickly or easily. Today, there is a tremendous demand for qualified food and beverage managers. Salaries are excellent. In addition, the path to top-level hotel management is wide open for executives with a sound food and beverage background.

Though national figures still show room sales as the number-one source of revenue, many hotels produce more food and beverage revenue than rooms revenue. The importance of the food and beverage division to the overall success of the lodging property is clear.

The five primary departments in large hotel food and beverage divisions are:

- Catering—responsible for banquets and special functions
- Culinary operations—responsible for food production
- Stewarding—responsible for warewashing, clean-up, and (in some operations) purchasing
- Beverage—responsible for production and service of alcoholic beverages
- Restaurant operations—responsible for food service in all outlets, including room service

The Organizational Structure of Restaurants

For the most part, restaurants have not faced the type of problems hotels have had to face in the last 50 years. Still, it is true that, like hotels, restaurants have had to

Exhibit 16   Sample Organization Chart for a Large Restaurant

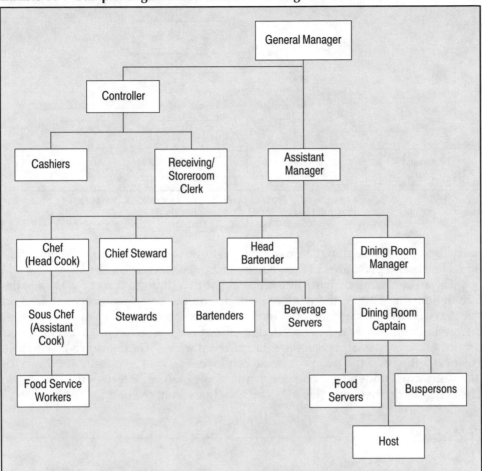

Source: Jack D. Ninemeier, *Management of Food and Beverage Operations,* 2d ed. (East Lansing, Mich.: Educational Institute of the American Hotel & Motel Association, 1990), p. 34.

face a tightening budget and have therefore had to improve their methods of planning and control.

Exhibits 16 and 17 provide sample organizational structures of large and small restaurants. In the larger organization, the restaurant manager immediately supervises two positions: the controller (who is responsible for cashiers and a clerk) and the assistant manager (who is responsible for four department heads). The department head positions involve food production (chef/head cook), purchasing and sanitation (chief steward), beverage production (head bartender), and the front of the house (dining room manager). Each of these department heads also supervises employees. In some cases, fourth-level personnel (**sous chef**/assistant cook) supervise food service workers. Again, while each of the functions

Exhibit 17   Sample Organization Chart for a Small Restaurant

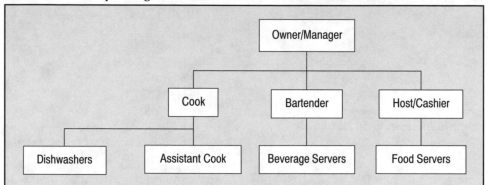

Source: Jack D. Ninemeier, *Management of Food and Beverage Operations,* 2d ed. (East Lansing, Mich.: Educational Institute of the American Hotel & Motel Association, 1990), p. 33.

must also be performed in the smaller property, the number of required organizational levels and personnel in each position can be reduced.

These organization charts illustrate at least two important facts: (1) While the terminology may differ, the work to be done and the basic positions required do not vary significantly among operations of different sizes; and (2) a great deal of interaction and cooperation is needed to make things work in food service. Food service managers at all levels have heard the phrase, "Food service is a people business." It is, and the people include employees as well as guests. Food service managers must understand and constantly apply skills in interpersonal relations. The ability to do this separates the good managers from the bad.

Endnotes

1. *1997 Foodservice Industry Pocket Factbook* (Washington, D.C.: National Restaurant Association, 1997).

2. This discussion is adapted from Jack D. Ninemeier, *Management of Food and Beverage Operations,* 2d ed. (East Lansing, Mich.: Educational Institute of the American Hotel & Motel Association, 1990), pp. 17–19.

Key Terms

canteen—Portable or mobile food service operations.

contribution margin—A food or beverage item's selling price minus direct costs of preparing the item.

sous chef—An assistant chef or cook.

specialty restaurant—A theme restaurant that features certain types of food.

Review Questions

1. What three markets does the food service industry serve? How does each of these markets compare to the others?

2. What is the difference between nominal growth and real growth?

3. What are the differences between a member-owned club and a proprietary club?

4. In the 1950s, hotels placed greatly increased importance on the food and beverage department. What caused this change in emphasis?

5. Briefly discuss the several categories or types of clubs.

6. The chain properties were the pioneers in putting hotel food and beverage divisions on a profit-making basis. How did they do so?

Internet Sites

For more information, visit the following Internet sites. Remember that Internet addresses can change without notice. If the site is no longer there, use a search engine to look for additional sites.

Food Service and Related Associations

American Dietetic Association
http://www.eatright.org

American Culinary Federation (ACF)
http://www.acfchefs.org

American School Food Service Association (ASFSA)
http://www.asfsa.org

Dietary Managers Association
http://www.dmaonline.org

The Educational Foundation of NRA
http://www.restaurant.org/educate/educate.htm

The Educational Institute of AH&MA
http://www.ei-ahma.org

Hospitality Financial and Technology Professionals
http://www.hftp.org

Hospitality Information Technology Association
http://www.hita.co.uk

International Association of Culinary Professionals
http://www.iacp-online.org

International Food Service Executives Association
http://ifsea.org

International Franchise Association
http://www.franchise.org

International Hotel & Restaurant Association
http://www.ih-ra.com

National Association of College and University Food Services
http://www.nacufs.org

National Restaurant Association (NRA)
http://www.restaurant.org

Society for Foodservice Management
http://www.sfm-online.org

Chapter 9 Outline

The Role of the Hotel Food and Beverage Division
Some Misconceptions About Food Service
A Recipe for Success in Food Service
      Excellent Environment
      Excellent Service
      Excellent Food and Beverage Products
      Excellent Value
      Excellent Management Controls
Food Service Subsystems
      Menu Planning
      Purchasing
      Receiving
      Storing and Issuing
      Food Production (Cooking and Holding)
      Serving
The Beverage Department
      Beverage Sales and Promotions
Food and Beverage Control
      Production Forecasting
      Calculating Food and Beverage Costs
      Payroll Costs and Controls

9

The Management and Operation of Food Services

ANY COMMUNITY BENEFITS from a good food and beverage establishment, whether in a restaurant or in a hotel, since a good (and therefore busy) operation provides employment for more people. In the end, the good operation returns a better investment to the owner, and this, of course, is what the free enterprise system is all about.

Effective food service operations are vital to the financial goals of restaurants, many hotels, and a wide range of institutional facilities. Unfortunately, various factors (many of which cannot be controlled by management) cause food and beverage profits to fluctuate tremendously—often going from a profit to a severe loss from month to month or from one season to another. Food costs can be affected by weather, a turn of political events, labor unrest, crop failure, or any number of occurrences. While the volume of business can vary unexpectedly from day to day, many expenses are fixed and will not fluctuate with sales levels.

This chapter will focus on restaurant and hotel food service, but many of the points made in the discussion apply to food service operations in any setting. Although this chapter will treat hotel and restaurant operations together, any significant differences will be noted.

The Role of the Hotel Food and Beverage Division

The food and beverage division occupies an important and unique position in the lodging industry. For example, about 31 percent of the revenue in an average hotel comes from food and beverage sales. However, because of the division's complex operation, it contributes only 18 percent to 20 percent of the property's actual profit.

A food and beverage operation in a hotel performs an important threefold mission: (1) to produce an adequate profit; (2) to provide suitable food and beverage service within the hotel; and (3) to help support the role of the hotel in the community.

The importance of the hotel food and beverage operation may be illustrated by the history of two hotels in New York City. For years, the Plaza Hotel has had one of the leading food and beverage divisions in the city. Today, it is considered one of the finest and most profitable hotels in the world. It enjoys a high room rate and a very high occupancy level, and does a very large food and beverage business. As a result, it continues to operate at a substantial profit.

Twenty years after the Plaza Hotel began operating, the Savoy Plaza Hotel was built. Just across from its competitor, the Savoy Plaza was a modern and, in some ways, far better hotel. Unfortunately, over the years, the Savoy Plaza's food and beverage division did not produce its proportionate share of profits. One problem

219

was a very limited catering facility. As a result, the Savoy Plaza was torn down and an office building put in its place.

A good food and beverage operation does more than help establish the quality of the hotel in the eyes of the traveling public. Such an operation may become a very valuable profit maker, may give the hotel a distinct competitive advantage over other operations, may help justify an increase in the average room rates, and may help to keep occupancy levels high.

Some Misconceptions About Food Service

Over the years, some misconceptions about the food and beverage business have evolved. One example is the old saying, "Hire good chefs and leave it to them." This is probably one of the quickest ways to failure. While a good food and beverage operation is almost impossible without a good chef, the entire food service operation must work as a team. The chef is an important member, but there are other equally important players. A complete team is necessary for a successful food and beverage operation. A chef who is capable of running an operation can be promoted to food and beverage manager and coordinate all the division's functions. However, as food and beverage manager, the former chef will still need a good chef to handle food production.

Another misconception: Successful food and beverage managers are "born." This is simply not true. A review of the hospitality industry's past 50 years reveals that all successful operators have one thing in common: the desire to get ahead. There is an old axiom that states, "We do best the things we enjoy." It follows that people who are interested in food and beverage operations and who like to meet people are likely to succeed if they are committed to the job. Perhaps the observations of some successful hoteliers will make the point. Conrad Hilton said many times that he never saw a successful hotelier who did not have much curiosity. Ernest Henderson, founder of the Sheraton Hotels, said that all the successful people that he ever met, regardless of what business they were in, wanted to be the best. Other industry leaders have said that the success of a food and beverage operation corresponds directly to the time and effort the manager gives to it.

One sometimes hears of hotels that "the food and beverage division is a necessary evil," and that "it can't make any money anyhow—so just keep the losses down and forget about it." In fact, however, the leading accounting firms in the country indicate that practically every well-run food and beverage division in a hotel, regardless of size, does make a profit; the better the operation, the greater the profit and contribution to the overall operation.

Some people also believe that a hotel's food and beverage division has to be a loss-leader to attract rooms business. In truth, experience shows that a poorly run food and beverage division actually detracts from overall business. Any manager who would run a food and beverage division at a loss generally does not have the skill to run the rooms division at a profit either.

A Recipe for Success in Food Service

For every ten restaurants that open, only one will be open and making a profit after five years. This is a very high mortality rate. Of course, hotel restaurants do not go out of business with such frequency, since the property has the profit from the rooms to rely on; in many instances, the convenience of a restaurant to hotel guests keeps it going. However, in general, the operating profits of restaurants in hotels are actually less than the profits of independent restaurants.

There is an old saying that there are no secrets in any business. To find out how to be successful in the hotel and restaurant business, discover what successful operators do, and learn what causes other operators to fail. Comparing their activities can help unlock the "secrets" of hotel and restaurant business success.

Much of what is necessary for a successful food and beverage operation can be summarized in five distinct elements, the five Es. Although not all-encompassing, these factors are vital; no operation will be successful without all five of them. They are:

- Excellent environment
- Excellent service
- Excellent food and beverage products
- Excellent value
- Excellent management controls

Excellent Environment

Excellent environment starts with a good location. Some of the most successful operators say an easily accessible location accounts for half an operation's success. A restaurant has to be located in or near a community or near important intersections.

Studies consistently show that guests are very concerned about the restaurant building and grounds, especially its cleanliness, restrooms, and outside environs. Attention to these areas helps create repeat business for food and beverage operations in restaurants and hotels.

Environment also refers to the restaurant's theme. Many successful operators believe that the theme should create a mood that enhances guests' dining pleasure. The theme is created by coordinating the decorations, the menus and menu covers, food server uniforms, silver, china, glassware, linens, and the type of food and service offered.

Excellent Service

Wanting to go back to a restaurant because you feel welcome is about the best illustration of excellent service there is. Excellent service is primarily a matter of attitude and begins with that of management. If the manager is dedicated to giving friendly service and is courteous to employees and guests, this encourages the employees to be friendly and to make guests feel welcome.

Very few people can continually smile and be friendly to everybody they meet unless they are trained and encouraged to do so. One of management's most important jobs is to have a continuing training program for servers. Today, there are many training aids available from various sources so that even the smallest and most remote food operation can have an excellent training program.

Food service operations range from the classical French restaurant to the snack bar, each with different requirements for excellent service. A primary factor in all excellent service is that employees must be trained to recognize the importance of guests. They must realize that their livelihood depends on being courteous and friendly. The manager of any restaurant should understand that guests like to be recognized. When practical, the manager should learn guests' names and stop by their tables for polite conversation. If a problem arises, a little personal attention from the manager can often resolve it, and the guest will leave happy.

Excellent Food and Beverage Products

Many successful restaurant operators have said that excellent food is food that tastes better to the guest than the same food that the guest had somewhere else. Excellent food is basically a comparative matter, and as long as the food that is being served tastes better, looks better, and receives favorable comments from guests, it is excellent food. The same principle applies to beverages. The formula is simply to purchase excellent products, store them properly, prepare the food and beverages according to proper standard recipes, control costs, package the food and beverages attractively, and satisfy guests with quality service provided by friendly employees.

Excellent Value

The way to measure whether a restaurant offers excellent value is to talk to guests and find out if they think that they got their money's worth. Repeat business is vital to a successful food service operation. Having many repeat guests proves that the restaurant is giving excellent value. Some restaurants are very expensive but generate repeat business. On the other hand, a low-check-average restaurant can lose guests if they feel that the food and service they get are not worth the price, no matter how low. Excellent value is in the mind of the guest.

Value may also relate to the size and cleanliness of the parking lot, the restrooms, the general appearance of the restaurant, the dishes on which food is served, the friendliness of the servers, the price of the food and beverages, and other factors. Sometimes, value is just a matter of the manager wishing guests a pleasant good evening and stopping to chat with them for a moment.

Excellent Management Controls

An operation can have the first four Es of this group, but, if the manager does not practice excellent supervision and accounting control, the operation is likely to be another casualty in the food service business. No operation can be successful unless the manager gives the necessary personal supervision and ensures that the operation meets desired standards.

Management controls can be briefly summarized as the controls necessary to yield competitive prices; to ensure that what is purchased is received, and that what is received is properly stored and issued; and to ensure that the products are prepared and served properly, that all income is collected, that all money is deposited in the bank, and that all bills are paid. The internal control system also should ensure that there is a budget for the operation and that incurred costs do not become excessive. If the costs exceed the budget, the manager should find out why and take corrective action quickly.

Food Service Subsystems

There are many distinct but closely related subsystems or control points that must be managed if a food service operation is to meet its goals. These control points include menu planning, purchasing, receiving, storing, issuing, producing, and serving. The following discussion illustrates the interrelationships among these elements in a food service management system.[1]

Menu Planning

Food service management begins with the menu. Exhibit 1 shows some of the factors menu planners must consider. The menu dictates what resources are needed and how they must be expended. It is also the property's most powerful marketing device. Menu planning is probably one of the most important but least understood phases of the food and beverage business today. Many people can write a menu for a specific meal consisting of an appetizer, soup, entrée with potato, vegetable, salad, dessert, and coffee. However, it is much more difficult to develop an entire marketable and profitable menu for a particular restaurant. The menu planners (usually food and beverage directors and chefs) must determine who the guests are, how large the market is, and where potential guests are located. The next step is to define the types of food, beverage, and service these guests want. Planners must also consider the location of the property, transportation and parking facilities, the special concerns of the operator, and the competition.

Large chain organizations typically have marketing personnel who know what to consider when planning menus. The individual restaurant or hotel operator seldom has this specialized capability. There are, however, consultants who, for a fee, can create menus for restaurants and hotels. These specialists can work with the staff in developing a customer survey, creating the menu, and getting it designed and printed. They can also work with the chef and others in standardizing recipes and in training the staff in the proper preparation and service of the food and beverage products.

Menu planners emphasize marketing concerns and the guest while recognizing the operation's budget constraints. The menu planning task takes on complexities imposed by the operation itself. When deciding whether to offer a wide or narrow range of items, menu planners must keep in mind that, as the number of items to be offered increases, a wider variety of them must be purchased, received, stored, issued, and otherwise managed. Compare, for example, the demands a daily changing gourmet menu in a high-check-average property would place on operations with the demands of a fixed (seldom changed) menu in a fast-food establishment.

The menu affects a large number of resources, and these impose constraints that should be recognized as the menu is planned. Among these are:

- Labor—An adequate number of qualified employees with the appropriate skills are required to produce all menu items.

Exhibit 1   Priority Concerns of the Menu Planner

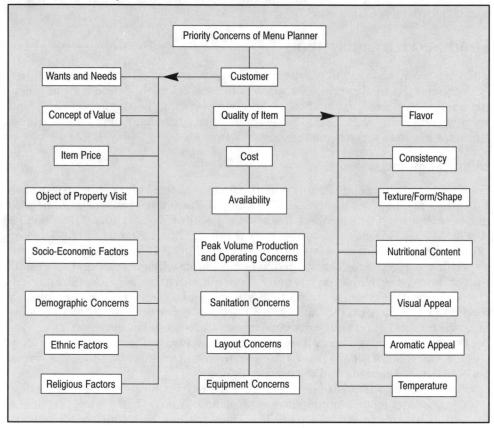

- Equipment—Equipment must be available to produce all items required by the menu.

- Space—Adequate square footage is required for all equipment and for receiving, storing, serving, clean-up, and other needs.

- Layout and design—The menu affects space and equipment necessary for efficient production.

- Ingredients—Recipes, which specify necessary ingredients, are important. All ingredients should be readily available at costs that support anticipated product selling prices.

- Time—The menu will affect timing of food production and service.

- Cost implications—Equipment, space, personnel, and time concerns, mentioned previously, can all be translated into costs. Other expenses, such as utilities and supplies, will also be affected by the menu. Since a menu item's

Insider Insights

Lou Tremonti
Associate Professor
Hotel and Restaurant Management
State University of New York—Delhi _____

The ability to maximize profits through proper menu pricing is an essential skill for success in the food service industry. Finding a market niche and developing a menu pricing strategy requires a thorough knowledge of the individual operation and the competition. Price is the most visible part of a marketing program.

The *formula method* is commonly used to set and adjust menu selling prices. The menu selling price equals the cost of the food divided by the desired food cost percentage. For example, if the cost of the food (cost per cooked portion plus the cost of the accompanying items) is $1.70, and the desired food cost percentage is 40%, the menu selling price, according to the formula method, would be $4.25 ($1.70 divided by .40).

For the formula method to be useful, managers must determine the food cost percentage that maximizes profits. Generally speaking, as the menu selling price is reduced, the food cost percentage increases—assuming, of course, that the cost of food remains the same. For example, reducing the menu selling price to $3.40 would raise the food cost percentage to 50% ($3.40 divided by $1.70 = 50%). Conversely, as the menu selling price is increased, the food cost percentage is reduced: $5.67 = $1.70 ÷ .30.

The food service establishment's operating strategy, combined with careful analysis of the competition, will help determine the desired food cost percentage. A restaurant I visited recently provides a good example of how strategy can affect menu selling price. This restaurant serves large portions of food with low menu prices. Management's desired food cost percentage is 50%. The more-than-reasonable food prices are very attractive to the local market. The restaurant does not take reservations. All guests wait about 20 minutes in a very attractive cocktail lounge before they are seated. The service in the lounge is superb. Two drinks per customer is the general rule. Beverage costs run 19% with almost a one-to-one ratio between food and beverage sales. The high food cost (low menu price) draws customers, and the low beverage cost provides a healthy profit and works well for this operation.

A reasonable profit objective can be determined by financial investment and risk. A well-planned budget can aid in guiding proper menu selling price by establishing reasonable cost and profit percentages. The Texas Restaurant Association advocates the *planned profit method* for arriving at desired food cost percentages. Some examples:

Operating Cost Percentage   = 38%
(Operating Cost divided by Total Sales)

Labor Cost Percentage   = 19%
(Labor Cost divided by Total Sales)

(continued)

Insider Insights *(continued)*

Planned Profit Percentage   = 13%
(Profit divided by Total Sales)

Desired Food Cost Percentage   = 30%
(Total Sales − Operating Cost Percentage
− Labor Cost Percentage − Planned
Profit Percentage = 30%

OR

100% − 38% − 19% − 13% = 30%)

Profit and price objectives may vary, depending on the type of operation. Subsidized institutional food service operations, for example, may desire low menu selling prices as a fringe benefit to employees. Maximizing profits is not the objective in this case. The result is a higher than desired food cost percentage, but one that is acceptable because of the operation's economic objectives.

Once the desired food cost percentage is determined, the formula method becomes useful as a guide for determining individual menu selling prices and as a target for overall food and beverage control. All menu items may not have the same food cost percentage on a given menu. Each menu item should be analyzed for popularity and profitability. Most menu consultants, however, recommend no more than a 10% to 20% differential between the lowest and highest items on a menu. Menu analysis may show that to maintain a realistic price spread between items in a particular food category, a higher desired food cost percentage on certain items may be necessary.

Careful analysis will show that a menu item with a high menu selling price and a higher-than-desired food cost percentage may deserve more attention on the menu than an item with a low food cost percentage.

Many factors contribute to a sales mix achieving an overall desired food cost percentage. Recognizing that the formula method creates profits by controlling costs, and that profit can also be increased by improved revenues, is important. Good managers will control costs and build a customer base and sales volume with menu selling prices that make "cents."

selling price will be influenced by its costs, at least in part, the menu planner must constantly guard against incorporating additional, unsupported costs into the operation by making unwise menu planning decisions.

Purchasing

Food and beverage items may be purchased by a food and beverage manager or by a purchasing agent in a special purchasing division or department. Whoever does the food and beverage purchasing must bear in mind that no amount of skill in food preparation can make up for food that is of poor quality to begin with; excellent food, to a large extent, depends on excellent purchasing judgment. Moreover, the control of food costs begins at the time of purchase. Profits lost through poor purchasing judgment or dishonesty cannot be recalled.

A good food and beverage purchaser cannot judge food items by price alone, or quality will suffer. By the same token, price must be an important purchasing consideration if the property is to remain financially viable. To make wise purchasing decisions, purchasers must understand:

- What the property's financial goals are and how purchasing decisions will affect them

- How much food is needed to prevent both **stock-outs** and overstocking

- How food and beverage items will be prepared and presented

- What guests expect from the food and beverage service operations

Receiving

After products are purchased, they must be received. The receiving clerk in large properties is a member of the accounting division, independent of the food and beverage division; he or she is responsible only to the controller. This arrangement allows the clerk to receive and control any merchandise that comes into the hotel without being influenced by anyone else and provides one of the best means of reducing dishonesty in the purchasing system.

Even in small operations, food, beverages, and other supplies should not be received by the same person who does the purchasing. In some operations, however, receiving clerks still report directly to the food and beverage manager. Such a system may work in practice, but it certainly provides opportunities for dishonesty. Most food and beverage experts agree that hiring an independent receiving clerk who reports to the controller will pay dividends in any operation, regardless of its size.

Unfortunately, receiving functions in the past have often been neglected. Food service operations have suffered substantial losses because of the lack of trained receiving personnel and the use of ineffective receiving practices. Because a receiving clerk can be responsible for several million dollars' worth of merchandise in a year, the property obviously needs a well-paid and well-trained person in this sensitive position.

The receiving area should be located conveniently between the receiving dock of the property and the storeroom so that the receiving clerk can see everything that goes in or out of the building. It should be equipped with an adequate floor scale and a small table scale. A complete set of purchase specifications should be developed to help in checking incoming merchandise. The proper tools should be available to open boxes and to check crates.

Everything that is received should be written up on a receiving clerk's daily report (see Exhibit 2). This report itemizes invoices that accompany the merchandise and indicates whether it is charged to that day's account for immediate use (listed under "food direct") or to the food storeroom (listed under "food stores"). This report should be completed each day, totaled, attached to the invoices that should accompany all incoming merchandise, and sent to the food and beverage

Exhibit 2   Receiving Clerk's Daily Report

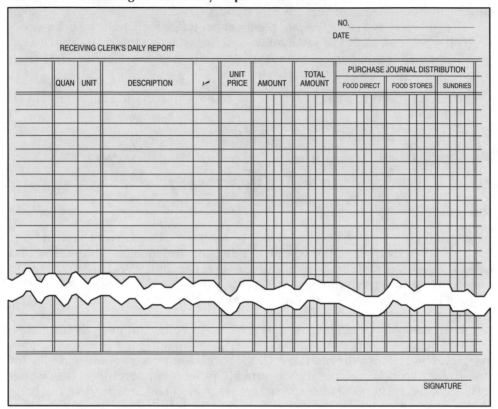

controller for auditing. In turn, the report should go to the general manager, where each invoice should be initialed and sent on to the accounting division for payment.

The receiving clerk's office should also be equipped with a **credit memorandum** form and a form that can be used for recording merchandise received without invoice. By using these forms, the receiving clerk will help ensure that the property pays only for items actually received. It is important that all incoming items be weighed, counted, or measured to ensure the orders are complete. This careful analysis of incoming items should be undertaken *before* the delivery invoice is signed.

The receiving clerk should quickly move all items to their proper storage areas. This practice helps to reduce theft, as well as losses in product quality. The clerk should never permit delivery people to move products into inventory. It is important to limit access to storage areas to only those relatively few people who need to enter them.

Storing and Issuing

The next control points in the food service system are storing and issuing food and beverage products. In some properties, the storeroom is under the direction of the

Regularly scheduled inventories of food and beverage items discourage theft and ensure that needed products are always on hand.

purchasing agent. In other, smaller operations, the storeroom is under the direction of the steward (who may also act as purchasing agent). In all properties, the controller should be responsible for the internal control system and for accounting for products that go into and out of the storeroom.

Food and beverage storage facilities, including refrigerated areas, can occupy a large portion of the food and beverage storage area. The entire storage area should be protected with locks. There should be only one entrance. Unauthorized personnel should be kept out of the storeroom at all times. Only one person should have the key to the liquor storage area (which should be separate from the food storage area) so as to be accountable for all the merchandise in that area. The area should be clean and properly lighted. Merchandise should be stored off the floor. Unpacked merchandise on shelves should be kept to a minimum, and regular storeroom hours should be adhered to. The food and beverage storeroom should be inspected every day by the food and beverage manager, the chef, or the general manager.

A properly authorized requisition should be required before merchandise is issued from the storeroom. To increase the accuracy of issuing control, every item in the storeroom should be priced with a marking pencil. This process is necessary for inventory purposes. Month-end inventories are the responsibility of the accounting division. Even though perpetual inventories are not kept on all storeroom items, they should be used for expensive and theft-prone items. **Perpetual inventories** provide a running balance of the quantity of items in stock. As items are received, the balance is increased; as products are issued, the balance is decreased. At the end of the month, the accounting division checks the perpetual inventory balance against the actual stock on hand; a list of overages and shortages should be

---

The Executive Chef

A property's executive chef is far more than a glorified cook. The executive chef may be responsible for all food production in the hotel or restaurant. He or she may also oversee the entire kitchen operation and manage the food production and clean-up staff as well. These responsibilities include preparing menus, working with the catering manager on banquet menus, and determining how much food is necessary to meet the forecast of business. The chef must make sure staff purchase and issue the proper quality of food. The chef must keep payroll costs in line and maintain contact with other department heads. The chef must be ready to correct any breakdown in food preparation.

A good executive chef who can produce good food at the right cost is getting to be a rarity. We do have some excellent chefs' training courses in schools in the United States, but our former source of chefs, the European apprentice system, has all but disappeared.

Today, a good chef is well paid. In many instances, the salary may be similar to or higher than the general manager's. Many chefs receive more money than the food and beverage manager. Good chefs command a high salary and a bonus for performance. Their responsibilities are tremendous, the pressures are great, and the hours are long. The chef is a business executive and a valuable business associate. The chef's profession today is one that is highly respected.

---

prepared for management. A list of dead stock (items stored for more than a specified time) should be circulated monthly to the chef and food and beverage manager so that they can make plans to use these items.

Storeroom keys must be tightly controlled. Many properties use a log book that indicates to whom keys have been issued and for how long. When people with access to storeroom keys leave the organization, keys and locks should be changed.

Food Production (Cooking and Holding)

Excellent food is one of the five basic requirements for a successful food operation. Experience has proven that no restaurant or hotel food operation can continue to operate unless the food served is as good as or better than all nearby competing food service operations. Although we cannot provide details of food production in this chapter, we will point out certain basics about food production and kitchen operation that are always found in well-run food departments producing and serving excellent food at a reasonable profit.[2]

The first basic requirement is the proper management attitude. Managers must want to serve excellent food. This means that the general manager of the restaurant or hotel has to be interested in food (although he or she does not necessarily have to know how to cook). A manager with the desire to offer quality food will motivate production personnel to prepare excellent food.

The hotel general manager typically has some involvement in the day-to-day operations of the food and beverage division, but most of the responsibility for this area falls to the food and beverage manager and/or the chef. In the past, the chef was often an excellent cook but less effective as a manager. Times have changed; today's top chefs are better kitchen managers, know how to control costs and merchandise foods, and have learned to work as a team with department heads and others with whom they come in contact.

Excellent food requires quality ingredients. To get the best results from quality ingredients, the food should be produced as close as possible to the time of service. One of the problems confronting the chef in a large hotel is that he or she may have four or five restaurant outlets plus as many as 20 different banquets going on in one day. It can be very difficult to produce all this food just prior to the time of service. Consequently, some food must be prepared in advance. Unfortunately, some chefs regularly "cook for the refrigerator." They cook food ahead of time, place it in refrigerated storage, and then withdraw foods on an as-needed basis. This approach may keep payroll costs down, but it certainly does not yield excellent food.

The use of convenience foods also has quality implications. It is difficult to keep the flavor and taste of convenience foods comparable to the same foods cooked from scratch. Many synthetic ingredients are used in convenience foods to keep costs down and to maintain long shelf-life. Moreover, some synthetic foods may actually pose a health threat to people who are allergic to them. A good chef will be very wary of using any synthetic flavoring or convenience foods and will ensure that the property's quality and cost requirements can be met if they are used.

Proper cooking methods must be followed as food is produced. If a stew is to be simmered for two to three hours, it should be simmered and not boiled violently. If the standard recipe for lamb stew calls for cooking the lamb with fresh potatoes, onions, carrots, and celery, the various ingredients should not be cooked separately, and canned potatoes and carrots and dehydrated onion and celery flakes should not be used.

Another basic requirement is that food should be properly cared for after it is prepared and before it is served. Keeping food on the steam table too long reduces its quality; sanitation problems can result as well. Food must be kept hot or cold for the shortest possible time before service. Quality foods are typically those that are prepared in small batches on an as-needed basis.

Excellent food cannot be produced unless production staff have the proper tools and equipment with which to work. Employees cannot operate successfully using ranges that will not heat, refrigerators that will not cool, stock pots that will not boil, freezers that will not keep foods frozen, or warming cabinets that will not keep banquet foods hot. Likewise, measuring containers and other small equipment required by standard recipes must be available and in good working order.

A complete kitchen in a large hotel may consist of a range section (which includes the stock kettles, ranges, broilers, grills, steamers, fry kettles, and roasting ovens); the garde-manger (cold food) sections; the pantry (salad) area; the butcher shop; the pastry shop and sometimes a bake shop; the scullery (dish and pot washing) areas; an employees' cafeteria kitchen; the banquet kitchen(s); and the room service kitchen. In smaller operations, it is not uncommon to find the garde-manger and pantry areas in one section. The butcher shop is often eliminated if pre-portioned meat is purchased, and the pastry and bake shops are often combined or eliminated.

In a large hotel, each one of the kitchen production departments may be under the supervision of a department head, who works a shift and reports to the chef, either directly or through a sous (assistant) chef. Today, kitchen personnel are often well-paid, and each year a more highly educated group is entering the kitchen. Chefs and cooks are producing better food in less time, and, in spite of problems with low productivity and high turnover, the cooking profession is becoming more respected than ever before.

Serving

In all types of food service operations, management must establish and enforce minimum quality standards for employees in front-of-the-house areas.[3] Managers cannot rely on the employees' common sense to tell them to do the right thing at the right time. Planning is necessary to identify required tasks and to develop procedures for effectively performing them. Carefully consider the guest. The type of service provided should be that which is best from the guest's perspective. What does the guest desire, and how can the operation best provide for these wants and needs?

This question must be answered by each operation. While it is not possible to develop specific practices that apply to all properties, there are many general principles that can be used to develop consistent procedures for all front-of-the-house employees. Supervision is necessary to ensure that shortcuts that violate standard operating procedures are not used. Asking questions such as, "If I were a guest, what things would I like or dislike about the serving procedures?" offers ideas about which procedures should or should not be used. The answers to these questions also govern the development of standard operating procedures. They indicate where and even how training programs to teach required activities should be conducted.

Each property must strive to develop service that pleases guests. Dining room managers must inspect the facilities to ensure that they are clean and safe, assign food server stations so that guests are served efficiently, properly communicate with and train service staff, and make sure that server stations contain the necessary products and supplies. They must develop sales income control procedures to protect the property and guests from dishonest employees, and schedule and ensure that sidework (clean-up) duties are performed correctly.

The Beverage Department

An exceptionally well-run food department can produce a departmental profit of 15 percent to 18 percent of sales. By contrast, a well-run beverage department can and often does produce a profit of as high as 50 percent of sales. The beverage operation is, then, an integral part of the property's financial and organizational structure. In fact, because of the many complex problems of food service, beverages alone often account for the entire profit of the operation.

Historically, the general supervision of the beverage department was the responsibility of a wine steward (sommelier), perhaps assisted by a head bartender.

Today, the position has been renamed beverage manager or, in some cases, director of beverage operations. This official is responsible for the day-to-day operation of the bars, and reports to the food and beverage manager. In small hotels where there is no need for a food and beverage manager, the beverage manager normally reports to the general manager. In other small operations, a food and beverage manager may operate the beverage department.

In properties with union contracts, the head bartender (who assists the beverage manager) actually works at the bars, sets up the banquet bars, and, in many instances, relieves bartenders when necessary. The beverage manager cannot, by union rules, act as a bartender except in case of an emergency; but in non-union houses, especially in small operations, it is common practice for the beverage manager to relieve bartenders for meals and other occasions.

Beverage purchasing responsibilities are typically assigned to the purchasing agent. With the beverage industry so closely regulated by the government and with all bottles of liquor and wine required to have a full disclosure of contents, the purchasing of this merchandise has been simplified. It does not require the high degree of skill it did in the past. In fact, beverages are typically purchased by brand name from a supplier with exclusive distribution rights or from a state-operated store; there are relatively few decisions to make after brands are chosen.

Certain basic ground rules must be followed to achieve good beverage department operation. First, the decision concerning which brands to offer must be based on what the guest actually desires. Any attempt to force a lower-than-desired quality of liquors or wines on guests will merely drive away business. The profit in beverage sales is so great that it is often unwise to use anything other than high quality merchandise. Using well-known brand names will give the customer confidence in the bar and its operations.

On the other hand, certain highly advertised brand names are often much more expensive than less advertised brand names. Management might want to consider making taste tests and experimenting with some of these lesser known names to measure acceptance by the customer. In some states, it is possible to purchase private label merchandise, often of superior quality.

Some properties buy too many different brands of liquors and end up with funds tied up in a large inventory, which is an expensive practice. Ideally, inventory should turn over completely about once a month, depending on discounts offered for volume purchases. This is best accomplished when the property management approves a list of acceptable brands with a maximum and minimum quantity established for each.

The receiving of beverages, like the receiving of food supplies, should be done by the receiving clerk of the property under the control of the accounting division. The receiving clerk should be given a list of the merchandise expected to arrive each day and should check it off as it arrives. Beverage receipts may be written on a special receiving sheet or on the same form used for food supplies. These receiving sheets should be written in duplicate and totaled each day. The original should be attached to the approved invoices and routed through management, purchasing, and accounting channels in the same way that food purchases are. The food and beverage controller should use the duplicate of the receiving sheet for establishing perpetual inventory controls. In large operations, it is also wise to use bin cards, which show receipts and issues and help keep a running balance of the merchandise. This information serves as a basis for submitting a purchase request for additional supplies.

Supplies of liquor and wine should be stored in areas separate from food supplies and should be issued only upon the receipt of a signed requisition in accordance with the instructions set up by the food and beverage control department. Par stocks (**par** is the number of bottles management has determined must be behind the bar at the beginning of a shift in order to avoid run-outs) should be maintained on all the bars; the empty bottles should be returned to the storeroom as a basis for bottle-for-bottle exchange when the bars are restocked. The keys to the liquor and wine storage area should be in the hands of one person who is held responsible for the security of all the merchandise in the storeroom. The accounting division should keep a perpetual inventory on these products and should take a physical inventory at the end of each month with the person responsible for the keys to the area.

In any property doing a substantial amount of banquet business, a banquet beverage storeroom should be set up. All issues to banquets should be made to this area from which merchandise can be issued to the various banquet bars and to which any liquor remaining from a banquet bar can be returned and recorded. With such a setup, a banquet bar can operate with a par stock, and a daily banquet cost can be determined if required by management.

It is just as important for a restaurant or hotel to be known for having a good bar as it is for serving good food. Smart managers insist that standard drink recipes be followed and that proper measuring tools, such as jiggers and shot glasses, be used by the bartender. The head bartender must train and supervise the bartenders to ensure that no shortcuts are taken, that drinks are the correct size, and that, whenever possible, fresh juices and ingredients are used in the preparation of drinks.

One of the best ways to obtain consistent quality of drinks is to prepare a bar operation manual. The manual should be prepared specifically for the operation by the beverage manager and/or the head bartender and should include all the standard recipes of the operation plus instructions about service, the glasses to be used, and how to merchandise certain drinks, as well as a complete wine list, instructions on banquet bar setups, and an outline of the internal control system of the property as it applies to bar operations. The control system outline covers such things as accountability of bar checks and the collection of money, accountability for cash and charges, register readings, and security measures.

Beverage Sales and Promotions

There are some proven ways of increasing beverage sales and merchandising beverages and wines. The first step is to provide a training program for all bartenders and servers. The more these employees know about products and merchandising, the greater the sales and profits will be.

Today, the great and legitimate concern about drunken driving is changing the promotion of alcoholic beverages. Many properties and some states have halted certain types of promotions—for example, happy hours featuring two drinks for the price of one. Promotions must recognize the responsible and safe use of alcoholic beverages. Alcohol awareness programs (for guests and employees), designated driver programs (in which one member of a group does not consume alcohol), and merchandising no- or low-alcohol drinks all stem from today's concern about alcohol abuse.

Many books have been written on how to sell wine, but the writers usually fail to discuss pricing. New pricing strategies have unquestionably contributed to the rapid increase of wine sales. In-house marketing of house wines and even the sale of more expensive premium wines by the glass (made possible by new dispensing equipment that injects nitrogen into opened bottles, enabling high quality wines to be kept for very long time periods) have yielded increased revenues for many properties. One of the best ways to sell wine is to package a bottle or a carafe of wine with banquet meals or with dining room meals where state laws permit. Another good strategy is not simply asking the guests if they would like wine with their dinners, but actually suggesting the type of wine that would go well with an entrée.

Every bar operation should have at least one or two specialty drinks. Such drinks are often just a variation of some of the old standbys served in a specialty glass or container and in a manner designed to attract attention. These drinks (which do not need to be alcoholic) can be attractively packaged with unique glassware and garnish and can be merchandised by the menu, tent cards, suggestive selling, or in any other appropriate manner.

To help promote beverages, a short but interesting list of cocktails, beers, and wines can be available for guests. Some properties use long wine lists, but it is hard to maintain complete stocks. Moreover, long lists may overwhelm guests and discourage them from ordering wine at all. Useful for elegant, classical restaurants, these wine lists should be replaced in more casual properties by an abbreviated list or wine card that offers a limited variety at prices designed to encourage the customer to buy.

Food and Beverage Control

Food and beverage control systems have been used widely since Prohibition (1920). Before that time, most of the better hotels and restaurants had no trouble making money in the food and beverage operation, primarily because of the large profits made on beverages. During Prohibition, the profits in the beverage department disappeared overnight. Restaurant and hotel operators realized that to stay in business they had to get control of operating costs in the food department.

Hotel and restaurant accountants in the early 1920s did not have food control systems as such, but some of the more progressive hotel and restaurant accounting firms quickly devised food control systems to meet the needs of the hotel and restaurant industry. After Prohibition was repealed in 1933, the hotel and restaurant industry found that it had to continue with a good food control system. It also had to create a good beverage control system so food and beverage operations could make a profit.

Most operators agree that one control system is needed by large operations, and a smaller, less expensive system is needed by smaller operations. Many operators

Duties of the Food and Beverage Controller

The food and beverage controller is a member of the accounting division. He or she must:

- Help the property's accountant prepare the annual budget, monthly forecasts, and related financial information applicable to the food and beverage division.

- Keep a daily review of the manner in which the receiving clerk carries out his or her duties and observe daily the quality of merchandise coming into the property through the receiving department.

- Check daily food and beverage requisitions and production tests and confirm that a daily sales analysis is being made on entrée sales.

- Review purchase records for price comparisons, for trends in seasonal foods, and for cost figures in order to correctly cost out menus.

- Prepare daily food cost reports and weekly beverage potential cost reports.

- Keep perpetual inventories on beverage storerooms and on the frozen and expensive dry ingredients.

- Assist in or take month-end inventories of both food and beverage.

- Prepare food and beverage reconciliations of costs for the accounting division.

- Attend weekly food and beverage meetings and provide cost information to management or the food and beverage manager for operational decisions.

- Work closely with top management, the food and beverage manager, chef, and purchasing agent in the testing program designed to set up standard purchase specifications and to provide a continuous check on portion costs.

- Help the food and beverage manager and the chef prepare and maintain standard portion size lists posted in the appropriate operating departments.

- Assist management in the preparation, maintenance, and continuous use of the standard recipe files.

are now working to computerize systems that will be more efficient and less costly in labor hours. A computerized standard beverage control system is now available from a number of companies. In addition, various phases of the food control system, such as inventory, sales income, and menu engineering, have been computerized.

Sometimes food and beverage control personnel become involved in the management of operations and the development of policy. This naturally causes trouble. When there is trouble between the operating staff and the controller, it is often due to a lack of understanding of what a controller does. In fact, the controller is in a staff (advisory) position. He or she reports facts and makes suggestions to managers, but it is the managers who must make policy and operating decisions.

Production Forecasting

One of the most important questions in regard to food and beverage control is: how many meals/guests will we serve in the future? The right answer helps ensure acceptable food and payroll costs. The food controller tries to provide the right answer by forecasting. In hotels, for example, the forecaster considers facts and figures for a given period of time which then determine the number of guests served based upon the number of guests in the hotel.

Assume, for example, that a hotel food controller uses a factor of 40 percent for breakfast guests in the coffee shop (that is, 40 percent of hotel guests without group banquet meal commitments eat breakfast in the coffee shop). The house count is 1,400, and the banquet office indicates that 200 people staying in the hotel will have breakfast in a banquet room. From this information, a preliminary forecast can be made as follows:

House count	1,400	
Less banquet	200	
	1,200	guests without banquet commitments
	$\times 40\%$	breakfast factor
	480	guests estimated for coffee shop breakfasts

(While any hotel can use this method for forecasting, each must determine its own factors.)

One forecast is typically made a week in advance. Such a forecast could, of course, become obsolete, but this is just a preliminary forecast. Every day, the food controller adjusts a three-day forecast as well. Factors are developed from the previous year's record of guests served and house count, and are constantly checked to maintain accuracy.

Other considerations when determining the number of people to be served are the weather and the day of the week. For example, Friday evening meal counts may be small in food service operations catering to travelers. On Sundays, a hotel's lunch business may be low if most lodgers eat a late breakfast, skip lunch, and then have an early dinner. There are other considerations, and each restaurant and hotel will have its own explanation for the rise and fall of guests.

A forecast has various uses. First, it determines staffing. For example, the dining room manager uses the forecast of meals to be served to decide how many food servers and buspersons will be required. The chef then determines the number of cooks and pantry people required. It is essential that the correct number of people be scheduled—enough to get the job done well, but not more than are actually needed.

The chef also uses the forecast to ascertain how much food should be prepared. Therefore, the forecast helps maintain low food costs, since overproduction often increases costs more than any other factor. The purchaser uses the forecast to purchase, as accurately as possible, the amount of food needed for a given period. The food and beverage manager can use the information provided by the forecast for planning other purchases. By knowing the approximate income to expect, he or

Exhibit 3 Daily Food Report

DAILY FOOD REPORT

Hotel_____   Day and Date _____

| EXPLANATION | TODAY | | TO DATE | | Last Year to Date |
	Amount	%	Amount	%	%
Sales—Restaurants					
—Banquets					
—Total					
GROSS PROFIT OF FOOD CONSUMED					
Less: Employee Meal Credits					
Net Cost of Food Sold					
PAR NET COST—Restaurants					
—Banquets					
—Total					
DIFFERENCE					

Remarks

_____
Food Controller

she can determine expenses and arrive at a profit figure that will help clarify how much money can be spent.

Calculating Food and Beverage Costs

Actual food and beverage costs are calculated and indicated as *cost of goods sold* on monthly income statements. However, food and beverage management personnel need food cost information more frequently in order to make timely control decisions. One of the chief duties of the food and beverage controller is to prepare and distribute the daily food cost report. All food and beverage department heads receive this report, which indicates whether food costs are running higher than the budgeted standard cost set up by management.

Daily food cost information is also frequently tabulated for the general manager's daily food report. This rather simple report (see Exhibit 3) keeps managers informed about the food costs for the day and to date and how these food costs relate to the same period of the previous year. Properties with several food outlets may best record food costs separately for each restaurant. If the costs run higher than they should, managers and the food and beverage controller analyze the operation to find out why food costs are high.

Fortunately, beverage costs do not fluctuate greatly from day to day, and it is not necessary for the controller to publish a daily beverage cost report. Experience has shown that excellent results can be obtained by the use of the analysis of beverage sales and costs report (see Exhibit 4). This report—which can be prepared on a

Exhibit 4   Analysis of Beverage Sales and Costs Report

November 19—	ANALYSIS OF BEVERAGE SALES AND COSTS			
	Combined Operations	GREEN ROOM BAR	BANQUET BAR	LOUNGE
SALES				
Drink	62,039.80	51,339.40	7,364.95	3,335.45
Bottle	18,687.25	5,725.50	12,961.75	
Total Sales	80,727.05	57,064.90	20,326.70	3,335.45
Potential	81,198.75	57,578.10	20,223.55	3,397.10
Bar Difference (over or short)	471.70	513.20	103.15	61.65
Percent of Difference	.6	.9	.5	1.8
COST OF SALES				
Drink	19,229.88	16,052.02	2,147.54	1,030.32
Bottle	8,642.04	2,711.87	5,930.17	
Total	27,871.92	18,763.89	8,077.71	1,030.32
PERCENTAGE COST				
Drink	30.9	31.3	29.2	30.9
Bottle	46.2	47.4	45.7	
Actual	34.5	32.9	39.7	30.9
Potential	34.3	32.6	39.9	30.3
Difference	.2	.3	.2	.6

weekly, semi-monthly, or monthly basis—shows what the sales actually were, what the costs were, and what the sales should have been (potential sales) for each individual bar based on the sales price per drink, the current cost of liquors, and the standard size drink being served at the various bars. The report also shows sales and costs for full bottles (wines, beers, mineral waters, and full-bottle liquor sales) separate from the sales and costs of mixed drinks. From this information, management can readily locate possible losses in the bar operation and take steps to correct this.

Payroll Costs and Controls

Wages and salaries paid to managers and employees make up a large percentage of the operating expenses incurred by a food and beverage operation. *Prime cost* is a concept managers use in all types of food and beverage operations. To explain, Prime Cost = Food Cost + Labor Cost, each expressed as a percentage of sales. The general rule of thumb says that prime cost should not exceed 65 percent if the operation is to be profitable. The reader should note that two very dissimilar operations—one with a high food cost but a low labor cost and the other with a low food cost but high labor cost—can have identical prime costs and be profitable.

The increase in payroll costs is not due only to increased payroll rates (although rates have gone up substantially in the past 15 years). One of the biggest factors in increased payroll costs has been the cost of benefits. These include vacation pay, pensions, medical and dental benefits, life insurance, unemployment benefits, workers' compensation, personal holidays, and sick leave. In 1950, the cost of benefits in a food and beverage operation, including employee meals, was about 5 percent of the payroll. Today it is around 36 percent.

Increasing labor and benefits costs will unquestionably force a change in the facilities and service offered to the commercial food service customer. Some restaurants have begun eliminating a great deal of service and moving toward self-service bars featuring pre-prepared food. In hotels, banquet service is sometimes offered as buffet service. Even many high-check-average restaurants are now offering buffet service at noon, and salad bars, soup bars, and dessert bars for dinner. There are even restaurants offering guests the opportunity to do their own cooking. Innovation seems to be the key in hotel and restaurant operators' attempts to offset high payroll costs.

Excessive Payroll Costs. While average payroll costs are about 40 percent of sales, a great many operations incur much greater payroll costs. Such a situation requires concentrated efforts to find out why high payroll costs are occurring and what can be done about it. Excessive payroll costs generally stem from poor management.

Some situations occur in which the location, the physical setup, or the need to offer a service makes it impossible to reduce payroll costs. Fortunately, these situations are relatively rare. Excessive payroll costs are generally caused by any one or more of the following reasons:

- No basic staffing guides
- Poor or no budgeting and forecasting
- No work schedules
- No control of overtime
- No control over variable staffing for banquet service
- Poor payroll cost reporting
- Union job restrictions
- Poor communication between managers and employees (further complicated by poor communication between management and unions)

To control payroll costs, managers must first recognize the problem and then make a commitment to resolve it. Top-level managers must coordinate the efforts of the various people involved. It is their job to follow up and ensure that plans are carried out. The actual program for controlling payroll costs should be developed by someone with the time and ability to do the job. It does not matter whether this is the human resources manager, an operations analyst, the controller, or an assistant manager. The individual must be familiar with the operation as a whole, read and analyze operating statements, be methodical, and have empathy for the employees.

Many hotels and restaurants have a bargaining agreement with one or more employee unions, and consequently some payroll control procedures may require changes to abide by the union contract. The person who is in charge of payroll control must know the conditions of the union contract and must know how to work with union representatives to protect the best interests of the hospitality operation.

The following is a step-by-step program for controlling costs.

1. An annual operating budget (compiled from monthly operating budgets) for the food and beverage operation should be prepared under the supervision of management.

2. A staffing guide which incorporates required performance standards should be developed. Allowable labor hours permitted by the staffing guide should be in harmony with the operating budget standards.

3. A revised budget or forecast should be prepared by the 25th of each month for the coming month by the food and beverage manager with the help of department heads; it should then be approved by upper management. This labor budget should reflect the forecast of expected business volume.

4. Personnel in all positions should be scheduled on a weekly (or another regular) basis, according to the business forecast and to staffing guide requirements.

5. There should be a regular monthly comparison of the actual results of the operation with the annual and revised budget as soon as management receives the monthly operating statement. A comparison of actual hours worked with the scheduled hours should also be made.

6. Each department within the food and beverage operation should have a current organization chart and a basic staffing guide that shows the number of employees and hours allowed in the basic staff, day by day, for the week.

In addition to the basic staffing guide that shows the regular salaried employees, there should be standards set up for variable staff such as dishwashers, extra banquet help, extra food servers, housepersons, buspersons, and other help that are hired on an hourly basis as the workload requires. These standards are, in many cases, specified in the union contract. However, in other instances they are subject to negotiation; this is where goodwill on the part of everyone can pay off for both sides.

Overtime becomes extremely costly unless it is strictly controlled. There should be a procedure for pre-approval of overtime by the food and beverage manager or other official. There should be a policy of no built-in overtime for anyone. This policy should be diligently followed by the general manager.

Most operations make use of a weekly report of the payroll showing regular time, extra time, and overtime, and a comparison between the actual and the allowable time and cost in these categories. This report should be discussed in the weekly food and beverage meeting.

Endnotes

1. Readers desiring more detailed information about the management of a food service operation are referred to Jack D. Ninemeier, *Management of Food and Beverage Operations*, 2d ed. (East Lansing, Mich.: The Educational Institute of the American Hotel & Motel Association, 1990).

2. The Educational Institute has developed an entire course dealing with food production. Contact the Institute (P.O. Box 1240, East Lansing, MI 48826) for details.

3. The remainder of this section is adapted from Ninemeier, pp. 200–203.

Key Terms

credit memorandum—A form that is to be completed by the purchaser when merchandise received from a supplier does not match the specifications of the purchase order.

par—The standard number of a particular inventory item that must be on hand to support daily operations.

perpetual inventory—An ongoing tally of the quantity of items in stock.

stock-outs—Depletion of an inventory item.

Review Questions

1. What factors can cause food and beverage profits to fluctuate tremendously?

2. What factors enter into creating a restaurant's environment?

3. What five elements must be present if a food and beverage operation is to succeed? Briefly discuss them.

4. What are the factors involved in planning a menu?

5. Why does the receiving clerk in larger properties work in the accounting department rather than the food and beverage department?

6. What precautions should food and beverage operations take when storing and issuing supplies?

7. What is a perpetual inventory?

8. How does the chapter treat the subject of convenience foods in hotel kitchens?

9. Why is forecasting of sales so important to food and beverage operations?

10. What are some of the basic ground rules that must be followed to ensure that the beverage department operates smoothly?

Internet Sites

For more information, visit the following Internet sites. Remember that Internet addresses can change without notice. If the site is no longer there, use a browser to look for additional sites.

Food Service and Related Associations

American Dietetic Association
http://www.eatright.org

American Culinary Federation (ACF)
http://www.acfchefs.org

American School Food Service
Association (ASFSA)
http://www.asfsa.org

Dietary Managers Association
http://www.dmaonline.org

The Educational Foundation of NRA
http://www.restaurant.org/educate/
educate.htm

The Educational Institute of AH&MA
http://www.ei-ahma.org

Part IV

Functional Areas in Hospitality Operations

Chapter 10 Outline

The Changing Nature of Engineering
       The Engineering Division as a Savings Center
       The Need for Effective Management
The Work of the Engineering Division
       Electrical Systems
       Plumbing Systems
       HVAC Systems
       Refrigeration Systems
       Life Safety Systems
       General Maintenance and Repair
       Preventive Maintenance
       Renovation
       Water Management
Energy Management
       Energy Problems
       Energy Management Programs
The Green Movement

10

The Engineering and Maintenance Division

WERE ONE TO DESIGNATE an unsung hero in hotels and restaurants, the engineering division would win the competition hands down. Until very recently, engineering has been undervalued, underappreciated, and underrecognized by both owners and managers. A hotel or restaurant requires a huge investment in land, building, and equipment. The building and the equipment both have a projected life span that must be achieved if profit and return on investment projections are to be realized. Every division uses the building and the equipment, but only one—engineering—has the responsibility for keeping them in efficient working order. When it comes to overall importance, the engineering division takes a backseat to no one.

A property of any size must have a chief engineer who can meet the management and technical needs of this division. The chief engineer directs the activities of the division and supervises a staff of skilled technicians. The exact titles of engineering positions and the degree of specialization each position requires depends on the size of the operation and whether or not the division is unionized.

The engineering divisions of hotels are typically larger and more elaborate than those of restaurants. Therefore, this chapter will focus on those of hotels. Large hotels have electricians, carpenters, formative repair specialists, and many others on staff. Smaller properties must rely more on general maintenance and repair crews. As staff specialization decreases, outside help may be required to help maintain the building and equipment, especially as properties use more sophisticated computerized equipment.

Although some people use the terms *engineering* and *maintenance* almost interchangeably, in the hospitality industry (and in this chapter), engineering technically involves the operation of the systems and equipment necessary to provide the building support services. Maintenance is the servicing of equipment and systems.

The Changing Nature of Engineering

Traditionally, engineering's main goal was to minimize equipment maintenance and repair expenses. While this task was never easy, equipment was less complex than it is today, so the overall cost of operating this division was not high. Guests also expected less. Only since the 1950s, for example, have guests demanded air-conditioned guestrooms. Now-common Jacuzzis, saunas, and other amenities did not appear before the early 1970s. As customer demands for higher levels of comfort

---

Insider Insights

William L. Smith, CEOE
General Manager
The Chicago Hilton & Towers
Chicago, Illinois_____

In my years with Hilton, I have been involved with many building/renovation projects. I oversaw the building of the Hilton Inn in Tarrytown, New York, and the New York Hilton in New York City in the 1960s. My next project was the renovation of the Fountainebleau in Miami Beach, Florida (1978–1980), followed by the remodeling of The Washington Hilton in Washington, D.C. (1980–1984). I was also in charge of the renovation of the former Conrad Hilton Hotel in Chicago, now called the Chicago Hilton & Towers.

The major reward of working in engineering is the hands-on experience. It is exhilarating to be creative and to have the opportunity to handle something from start to finish. The greatest reward of working in the hospitality industry in general is the lack of limitations. It is such a large industry with so many facets that there are any number of rewards. Some days may have been better than others, but there has never been one that I did not enjoy in our profession.

People who join the hospitality industry through an entry-level job in the engineering department are fortunate indeed. Few departments offer better opportunities to learn the inner workings of the operation as a whole. If you want to develop your career in the hospitality industry, you will need to learn to expand your knowledge. You must develop your skills to suit your needs and the needs of others, while keeping an eye on your future goal and the skills you will need to attain this goal. Given the changing nature of the industry and the world in general, you will need to be flexible in your attitudes and unafraid of constructive change.

For a long time, there was very little change in engineering operations. Most plants basically replaced their equipment with the same makes or models. The energy crisis forced us to change this replacement method and become more conscious of the need for energy-efficient equipment and buildings. We have done this by seeking new building designs and using computer technology to control and monitor energy use. There will continue to be a need for energy efficiency in the hospitality industry and this will be a major concern of the engineering department.

---

and service have increased, the knowledge, skills, and abilities of the engineering staff have had to increase accordingly.

The job of the engineering division can no longer be taken for granted. The systems and equipment which it operates are expensive to purchase and to maintain. Energy costs also are affected by the way the division is operated. And the division has a direct impact on how guests react to the lodging and dining facilities.

The engineering division is an important part of the entire property and participates in all property management functions with full knowledge of the operation and its goals. Engineering should be thought of as a staff division: a specialized and technical advisory team providing managers with useful advice and assistance in areas such as energy management, equipment operation and repair, and guest comfort.

The Engineering Division as a Savings Center

The engineering division has traditionally been seen as a cost center. That is, instead of generating revenues as the rooms or the food and beverage divisions do, engineering merely costs money. It is really more appropriate to see the division as a cost savings center. Efficient management principles and energy management procedures in this division can save money and increase the property's profit.

Consequently, the chief engineer should understand basic management principles. The average hotel incurs operating, maintenance, and energy costs equal to about 40 percent of its **undistributed operating expenses**. Managers can reduce approximately 15 percent to 30 percent of this cost with good management procedures. Top-level managers in the property need to recognize the important role that the engineering division plays in attaining the property's economic goals and other objectives. Suggesting that the division merely keeps the equipment going and delays the need for capital expenditures ignores this division's ability to increase profit significantly.

While top management needs to recognize that the engineering division can help save money, the engineering division should try to demonstrate this ability whenever possible. For example, when the engineering division proposes improvements that cost money, the most effective way to approach management is not to focus on how much the equipment costs, but on how much the equipment will save. This approach concentrates on profit and puts the proposal in the same terms as those from revenue centers such as the rooms or food and beverage divisions.

The Need for Effective Management

It is easy to argue that the chief engineer must be a technical specialist, considering the extensive knowledge needed to understand refrigeration, heating, ventilation, electrical, and mechanical control systems. In many areas, engineers who work with the equipment and systems must be licensed. Licensing requires training, experience, and completion of a battery of tests covering the highly technical information that the engineer must possess.

As noted previously, however, the chief engineer must be a good manager. In addition to possessing highly specialized technical skills, he or she must also know how to manage available resources—people, money, time, and so forth. Many top managers in the hospitality industry agree that chief engineers generally have better technical than managerial skills. Engineers who have problems on the job more often need help mastering general management techniques than specialized technical knowledge. Some of these techniques include developing budgets, keeping records, or effectively selecting, orienting, training, supervising, and managing personnel.

General managers often assume that the engineer who can effectively repair and maintain equipment and make decisions about new high-technology systems can also manage people, time, money, and procedures. Knowledge of basic management principles is not, however, inherited. These techniques must be learned. In many instances, the engineer's shortcomings stem from top management's failure to provide relevant operating information to him or her.

A good chief engineer can effectively perform all required job tasks. Exhibit 1, a sample job description for a chief engineer, provides examples of commonly required tasks.

The Work of the Engineering Division

The engineering division performs work in several areas: electrical; plumbing; heating, ventilation, and air conditioning (HVAC); refrigeration; general maintenance and repair; preventive maintenance; renovation; and water management. The property's own engineering staff concerns itself primarily with maintenance in each of these areas. Local building codes and/or lack of time or personnel in the engineering division may dictate that outside contractors must handle large installations, changeovers, or new construction. The use of contractors is often dictated by applicable codes and by the fact that the engineering staff frequently has insufficient time and personnel to handle such work while attending to regular repair and maintenance.

Electrical Systems

Hospitality operations use a tremendous amount of electrical equipment, and electrical repair takes the engineering division to every corner of the building. An elaborate electrical system with its many circuits requires hundreds of fuses, and every blown fuse must be replaced. Should a fuse continue to burn out, the short circuit must be located and repaired. All electrical fixtures, outlets, and switches must be kept in good working order. Maintaining and servicing a *modern* electrical system is very complicated, but consider the woes of an engineer whose property may be 50 to 100 years old who must contend with obsolete equipment and wiring. Engineering personnel also handle display lighting, spotlights, movie projectors, and appliances for sales meetings or conventions.

Today, most properties buy electrical power from public utilities. However, many properties have an emergency generator ready in case the regular source fails. A few hotels still generate their own power, but this requires added staff and equipment and usually costs more than power from a public utility.

Plumbing Systems

Maintaining a plumbing system, especially that of a hotel or institution, is no small job. With a bathroom in every guestroom and elaborate restaurant kitchen equipment, a good-size hotel often has a larger plumbing system than many American communities. In addition to the circulating hot water system, hotels have a separate and complete cold water system. A guest without either hot or cold water wastes no time making this fact known, and engineers must remedy the situation

Exhibit 1   Job Description for a Chief Engineer

Job Title ___Chief Engineer___   Date _____

Basic Function:

Performs, manages, or supervises maintenance operations for exterior and interior facilities including electrical, refrigeration, plumbing, heating, cooling, structural, groundcare, parking areas, and other maintenance work necessary to maintain the property in an optimum and efficient condition. Also, ensures the safety and comfort of the guests and employees.

Responsibilities:

1. Maintain all distribution systems for electricity, water, steam, gas, etc.
2. Maintain and operate air conditioning, heating, ventilation, and refrigeration systems.
3. Maintain buildings and grounds.
4. Monitor and coordinate the services performed by outside contractors in accordance to all contracts, leases, service agreements, and warranties.
5. Keep all records pertaining to heat, light and power, and costs of the facility.
6. Ensure timely response to requests for services by guests, employees, and management to include repair or replacement of all interior fixtures and furnishings.
7. Schedule all work to be done on a daily basis at a minimum of inconvenience to guests and employees.
8. Plan, implement, and administer an effective preventive maintenance program in accordance with good engineering practices.
9. Plan, implement, and administer an energy management program.
   - Maintain appropriate equipment operating logs
   - Maintain utility consumption records
   - Educate other operating departments in energy management
   - Establish annual energy reduction objectives
   - Analyze and modify operation of the physical plant to conserve energy
10. Assist in the preparation of capital expenditures and maintenance budgets.
    - Select vendors and contractors that meet quality standards and pricing specifications
    - Initiate purchase orders
    - Approve invoices
    - Maintain adequate inventory of parts, tools, and supplies
    - Maintain purchasing records
11. Train and supervise subordinates and assist in safety and emergency training for other employees.
12. Conduct continuing inspection of buildings and grounds to ensure compliance with OSHA, fire and safety laws.
13. Recommend and/or take action to ensure compliance.
14. Maintain a clean and orderly work area free of hazards.
15. Perform other duties as assigned.

Supervision Exercised:

Assistant chief engineer, carpenters, electricians, grounds maintenance, lock and key, maintenance, painters, plumbers, refrigeration mechanics, and sound technicians.

Supervision Received:

- Supervisor:
  General Manager

(continued)

Exhibit 1   *(continued)*

Minimum Requirements:
- Education: high school or equivalent.
- Mechanical or equivalent training in the following: refrigeration, boilers, plumbing, air conditioning, power or building construction. Higher education or experience of such kind and amount as to provide a comparable background required.

Experience:

Five years in any combination of mechanical trades with hotels/motels, hospitals, high-rise apartments, or similar duties with the armed services. Must have license where required or qualifications to become licensed. Knowledge of carpentry and painting required.

Other:
1. Applicant should possess the following traits:
   - Effective communication skills
   - Administrative abilities
   - Good personal relations skills
   - Self-motivation
   - Mechanical aptitude
2. Applicant must be willing to relocate when and where directed.

---

immediately. Faucet washers are bound to wear out, and many hours are spent replacing them. Drains can become stopped in the course of everyday use, or guests may discard objects that plug up sinks or bathtubs. On upper floors, plugged drains may cause flooding. Even minor flooding can cause extensive damage.

The engineering division also frequently receives calls about toilets. Basic tools can generally be used to resolve problems, but, in serious cases, the toilet may have to be removed to let the plumber locate the source of difficulty. Water-closet valves must be frequently checked and kept in good working order to avoid noises.

Some plumbing work can be rather messy. One example is cleaning the kitchen grease traps and the basement grease line. Chemicals can help keep these lines open, but, occasionally, cleaning must still be done manually. An additional problem for hotel engineers is the fact that the original plumbing in most hotels probably was not intended for all the use it now gets. Properties can modernize systems gradually, but few properties can undertake such a job in a short period of time.

HVAC Systems

In many parts of the world, the engineering staff must keep the property heated for a good part of the year. In the winter, this means simply maintaining a comfortable, even temperature. During spring and fall, however, it is desirable to take off the chill without overheating the building—no small task if the heat is manually controlled.

Hot water heating systems are still used in some properties, but steam systems are more common. While many properties purchase their steam from public utilities, others operate their own boilers. Coal-stoked boilers are dirty. Gas or oil burners are clean, but they require additional employees. Buying steam reduces the number of employees needed to maintain the boilers. But even hotels that buy steam usually maintain standby boilers, so the engineering crew must have the technical knowledge and skill to handle them. Both the kitchen and the valet service require high-pressure steam, which is usually provided by a separate boiler.

Maintaining a heating plant may appear to be simple routine work, but, in reality, it requires highly technical knowledge. Burners must be maintained and repaired, thermostats must be kept in good working order, radiators and valves need attention. New types of controls are being developed that will bring heating closer to an automatic operation, but the automated repair and maintenance engineer just does not exist and probably never will.

Another responsibility of the engineering division is the ventilation and air conditioning system. Regular changes of air are required, and it takes machinery to provide this. The public today demands air conditioning in all first-class hospitality operations. A central system provides a central point for maintenance and repair. Air conditioners in each guestroom greatly increase work.

Refrigeration Systems

Every food service operation requires refrigeration equipment. Large **walk-ins**, reach-ins, and other types of refrigerators and freezers must operate 24 hours a day. The failure of a reach-in refrigerator may not be too serious if detected reasonably soon, since the unit's contents can be transferred. Even if the contents of a reach-in were to spoil, it would not involve a major sum of money. The failure of a well-stocked walk-in, however, would be a different story, since spoilage here would mean a major loss. Preventing such failures requires continual maintenance by the engineering division.

Life Safety Systems

Guest and employee safety is a major concern of all hospitality businesses. Fire and building codes are very stringent and have led to complex and complete life safety systems. These systems include sprinkler systems, smoke detectors, general fire alarms, an annunciator communication system, special systems for the kitchen area, pull alarms, and individual fire extinguishers. (This listing is representative only.) Modern systems have a centrally located map board of the property that immediately reveals the location of the fire when an alarm is triggered. The hotel alarm system is usually linked to the local fire station, which can save precious minutes in the answering of an alarm.

These systems must be maintained, kept in perfect working order, and tested on a regular basis. Most of this responsibility rests on the shoulders of the engineering division.

General Maintenance and Repair

When it becomes necessary to break through walls in order to make plumbing or electrical repairs, engineers make the subsequent repairs. The engineers also handle small welding jobs and maintain door hinges and locks. Engineering staff may also be involved in a wide range of miscellaneous tasks such as window replacement, painting, carpet installation, and so forth. An outside firm is usually contracted for the maintenance, repair, and inspection of major equipment such as elevators.

Preventive Maintenance

A quick look at the history of the hospitality industry reveals that thousands of restaurants and hotels have died unnecessarily because of deferred maintenance. Whenever the budget got a little tight, management deferred equipment maintenance for a year or so. Unfortunately, maintenance was deferred so often that sales, occupancy, and profits diminished, and then there was not sufficient money to bring the building and equipment back to a satisfactory state. Deferred maintenance had taken its toll. The old saying, "Never put off until tomorrow what should be done today," certainly applies to the engineering division. Progressive ownership and management stress **preventive maintenance**, which is the perfect antidote to the poisonous deferred maintenance.

A preventive maintenance program offers a systematized approach to equipment operation. Every item of equipment receives scheduled attention to make sure it is operating efficiently and to reduce downtime for emergency repairs or service.

Most hotels buy equipment with warranties, which cover most or all of the equipment's expected lifetime. Unfortunately, some properties treat the warranty as sufficient insurance against equipment breakdowns. The property simply installs the equipment, puts it into operation, and forgets about it. This is a poor management practice. Even when equipment continues to operate, there is constant deterioration and decline in its efficiency resulting from normal wear and tear, age, and accumulation of dirt and debris. This eventually causes costly service calls—usually emergencies—and a loss of revenue.

A good preventive maintenance program provides many benefits to a property. Not only will the equipment last longer (bringing a better return on investment), but it will use less energy. Service calls and their costs will diminish, and inventory levels for spare parts will be reduced. Furthermore, overall property operation will be enhanced, since service breakdowns can be largely eliminated. Equipment that is beginning to fail (as all equipment will do eventually) can be repaired or replaced before breakdowns interrupt the normal operation of the property.

Procedures. A preventive maintenance program is really a catalog of manufacturer's recommendations regarding the maintenance of all the property's equipment and systems. The engineering division develops a program by first identifying all property equipment requiring periodic checking and/or maintenance. Once this equipment has been identified, a schedule of routine inspections and maintenance activities can be established based on the equipment manufacturer's recommendations for proper maintenance. The inspection schedule will also list activities to be performed during the inspection. Exhibit 2 illustrates a **preventive maintenance schedule** that can help schedule inspections. These schedules can be simple or detailed, depending upon the property and equipment.

Supervision. The maintenance program must be supervised by responsible individuals. All staff must be familiar with the inspection and maintenance activities schedule and know who is responsible for the duties it requires. Maintenance

Exhibit 2   Preventive Maintenance Schedule

PREVENTIVE MAINTENANCE SCHEDULE

Description of Work	No. Items	Month																							
		Week	1	2	3	4	1	2	3	4	1	2	3	4	1	2	3	4	1	2	3	4		

Section/Person Responsible: _____   Signature (When Completed): _____

Source: *Energy Maintenance Manual: Volume II* (San Antonio, Texas: Technical Services Center and The Hospitality, Lodging & Travel Research Foundation, Inc., undated), p. A5.

shifts, for example, can be responsible for checking certain areas of the property. It is also possible to divide the property into areas or sectors for which individual engineering personnel are responsible. Under this system, personnel in any given department are responsible for checking their own equipment and reporting any problems to the engineering staff. This procedure keeps the established in-house engineering staff at a minimum number. But it also adds to the responsibility of various department and division heads.

How does management control the activities of assigned engineering personnel? The answer to this question provides the key to a successful maintenance program. Managers need to ensure that activities are taking place when required. In addition, checks must ensure that repairs have been performed. **Work orders** (see Exhibit 3) received by the engineering staff from other departments can be an excellent control mechanism if they are filed after the required work has been completed. A review of completed work orders will reveal what was required for various units of equipment, what was performed, and when it was completed.

Another valuable checking aid is a file containing an information card for each piece of equipment. Completed inspections, maintenance activities, and repairs can be noted on the cards and signed and dated by the person performing them.

Exhibit 3 Work Order

WORK ORDER   No. _____

Requested Service:_____
_____

Person Requesting:_____

Nature of Problem: _____
_____
_____
_____
_____

Work Performed: _____
_____
_____
_____

Person Completing Work: _____

Date Performed: _____

Maint. Supervisor Signature: _____

Source: *Energy Maintenance Manual: Volume II* (San Antonio, Texas: Technical Service Center and The Hospitality, Lodging & Travel Research Foundation, Inc., undated), p. A7.

Other variations of this system could be developed. The system should remain as simple as possible while retaining data required for future reference.

Renovation

A restaurant changes its theme or modernizes its food production equipment and space more frequently than a hotel. This is because it costs far less to overhaul a restaurant than to renovate an entire hotel, especially a luxury property.

While there has always been some **renovation** of older properties, it was only in the 1980s that hotel renovation really escalated. Owners and operators found themselves with once-successful properties that were now showing their age both in the front and back of the house. The locations of these properties, however, were still excellent, and, after careful analysis, it was determined that these properties could be renovated more cheaply than demolishing the hotels and constructing new ones.

Obviously, the hotel's engineering division cannot perform all phases of a renovation, but it is directly involved with both corporate and outside architects, engineers, planners, and contractors. This involvement is vital to the success of the project.

Renovation activity is occurring everywhere in the lodging industry at mind-boggling expense. Two examples in the resort segment are the Breakers Hotel in Palm Beach, Florida, and the Boca Raton Hotel & Club in Boca Raton, Florida. In 1988, the Breakers lost a star in the Mobil Travel Guide, going from a five-star (highest rating) to a four-star rating. Owners and managers reacted immediately and authorized a $16 million renovation program. Between 1983 and 1988, the Boca Raton Hotel & Club spent $34 million in capital improvements to make sure the hotel maintained its five-star rating. It did. As Michael Glennie, president of the Boca Raton Hotel & Club, stated, "In addition to keeping everything first class, you have to deal with the fact that the standard of first class is also rising."

The most vivid illustration of renovation was Hilton Hotel Corporation's $1.2 billion facelift of its 12 finest properties, completed in 1988. It has been called the most aggressive project of its kind in the history of the hospitality industry. Barron Hilton, chairman and president of Hilton Hotels Corporation, described the project as "polishing our Picassos." He explained:

> Several years ago, we determined there was work to be done in terms of restoring our great classics to their original luster and making them fully contemporary. Building such classic hotels from the ground up today would be almost impossible. Together with our investment partners we have been able to capitalize on some of the best locations in America and create a whole new economic life for these hotels.[1]

The Chicago Hilton & Towers provides a good example of the scope of this renovation program. The property opened in 1927 as the Stevens Hotel with 3,000 rooms, making it the world's largest hotel. Conrad Hilton purchased the hotel after World War II, renamed it the Conrad Hilton, and reduced the number of rooms to 2,200. The latest face-lift reduces the number of rooms even further, to 1,620, all of which are completely renovated and have new ceilings and walls. In addition, the project restored the hotel's historic design elements, and added an adjacent seven-story building with parking space, 30,000 square feet of exhibit space, and a complete health club. The hotel certainly deserves its new nickname, "The Miracle on Michigan Avenue." Exhibit 4 shows the 12 properties that were involved in the Hilton renovation program and their cost.

The renovation trend has picked up again in the 1990s. In 1992, Sheraton Hotels, owned by ITT, spent $1 billion on renovation and new construction, with by far the greatest portion spent on renovation. The corporation completely refurbished hotels in Anaheim, Los Angeles, Miami Beach, New York City, San Francisco, and Toronto.

Special attention was given to three of what Sheraton calls its "Trophy Hotels." Sheraton spent $143 million in completely refurbishing its St. Regis luxury hotel in New York City. The St. Regis now holds the distinction of being one of the most expensive refurbishing projects in the history of the hotel industry. Both the Sheraton Manhattan and the Toronto Sheraton were renovated at a cost of $47 million each.

During the recession years of the 1990s, the majority of hotels engaged in cost-cutting across the board. As a result, even normal refurbishing did not occur. Now

Exhibit 4   Hilton Renovation Program Properties

Property	Renovation Price
The Beverly Hilton	$30 million
The Las Vegas Hilton	$35.8 million
The Chicago Hilton & Towers	$180 million
The Hilton Hawaiian Village	$90 million
The Fontainebleau Hilton	$23.5 million
The San Francisco Hilton & Towers	$180 million
The Capital Hilton	$52 million
The Flamingo Hilton	$64 million
The Los Angeles Hilton & Towers	$60 million
The Palmer House & Towers	$118 million
The New York Hilton & Towers	$60 million
The Waldorf-Astoria & Towers	$110 million

Source: Tony Lima, "The Best of Hilton's Best," *Lodging Hospitality,* August 1988, p. 79.

that the industry is enjoying an economic upturn, much-too-long-neglected refurbishing and renovating is taking place. During 1991–1996, 3,250 individual hotels changed hands. At least 95 percent of these hotels were scheduled for extensive renovation and refurbishing by their new owners. Millions of dollars have gone into these renovations, but the new owners knew that the purchase price plus the renovation cost equaled a figure well below replacement cost for these hotels.

Water Management

Hotels and restaurants cannot operate without a clean, plentiful supply of water. Water is used in all types of restaurants, hotels, and institutions for drinking, cleaning, sanitizing, cooking, cooling, and fire sprinkling systems. In hotels, water is also needed for bathing and often for swimming.[2]

Hotels and restaurants need two kinds of water systems: a **potable water** system, which brings water into the property, and a sewer system, which channels wastewater away from the property. Purchasing and installing water and wastewater systems constitute 5 percent to 12 percent of the total building costs of a new hotel. Water and wastewater systems account for 5 percent to 15 percent of total energy expenses once the hotel is built.

Most properties purchase potable water from a local utility, but occasionally a hotel has its own water supply. Properties that provide their own water must carefully treat it to maintain state and federally mandated drinking water standards. But even properties that buy water from local utilities may need to treat water further.

The cleanliness, quantity, and appearance of a property's water supply not only affects guest satisfaction, but the staff's ability to perform their duties. The engineering department must evaluate water for:

- Hardness—Guests may complain about hard water that prevents soap from lathering. Moreover, hard water will make cleaning duties for housekeeping and kitchen staff more difficult. Hard water can be softened with chemicals that are safe to drink.

- Taste/odor—Water that smells or tastes bad may be completely safe to drink, but it may be difficult to convince guests of that fact. Such water can also affect the taste of coffee and tea. Properties can treat their water supply to eliminate undesirable odors and tastes.

- Color—Minerals in the water can stain linens and porcelain. Again, water can be treated to eliminate these problems.

- Turbidity—Turbid water appears cloudy because it contains a large number of solid particles. Such water may not only look unappetizing to guests, it may also clog pipes and machinery. Water filters can correct this problem.

- Corrosion—Water with high acidity can corrode pipes and other equipment. Corrosion leads to extra maintenance and repair. Water treatment can help reduce acidity that causes corrosion.

Water pressure also concerns the engineering department. Generally, a water main will provide enough pressure for a four- to six-story building. However, high-rise properties often need pumps to provide additional water pressure.

Until recently, water shortages appeared only to be a phenomenon of drought in most areas of the United States. The availability and cost of water were not major concerns in hospitality operations except in very remote areas. However, this is changing as the production of clean water becomes more difficult and expensive both at home and abroad. On the island of Aruba, for example, where fresh water is produced through desalination plants, the cost of water for hotels equals that of energy. By the year 2000, this could occur in many areas of the United States.

As the hospitality industry enters the twenty-first century, certain concerns about water will become more and more important to engineers and managers. These concerns include water potability, rising costs and shortages of water, and hot water use.

Potability. Pollutants such as herbicides, insecticides, fertilizers, household wastes, industrial wastes, and urban runoff (rubber, salt, gas, and oil deposits washed from city roads) pose threats to the **potability** of the water supply. Hotels and restaurants must be vigilant about protecting their water supplies. Moreover, state and federal regulations designed to curb pollution may dictate how and in what amounts hotels and restaurants can dispose of certain kinds of wastes.

Rising Water Costs and Shortages. Potable water costs between 50 cents and $4.50 per 1,000 gallons. However, costs may rise to as much as $28 per 1,000 gallons where desalination is used. Sewer rates vary between 20 cents and $1.20 per 1,000 gallons. While the average property uses about 218 gallons of water per occupied guestroom per day, actual use varies considerably from property to property. A recent American Hotel & Motel Association study showed that water use is lower at smaller properties without food service and higher at large convention and resort properties with pools and restaurant operations.

Whatever its use level, however, virtually every property wastes a certain portion of its water supply. Preventive maintenance and other conservation measures can eliminate much water waste, saving the property more and more money as water and sewer rates increase. For example, a one-sixteenth-inch leak in a toilet wastes enough water in one month to supply a single-occupancy guestroom for 220 nights. Water can be conserved in kitchen areas by cutting the amount of water used for washing, thawing, and cooling. Tunnel washers in laundries can recycle water from some rinse cycles. Showerheads that restrict water flow prevent guests from wasting hot water. Irrigation—watering lawns and shrubs—consumes 25 percent to 30 percent of a hotel's water supply. This amount can be reduced by watering plants every two or three days instead of every day, a schedule that not only saves water but promotes better plant growth. Other properties are using **gray water** (treated sewer and laundry rinse water, for example) for irrigation or other non-drinking purposes.

Hot Water Use. Wasted hot water not only depletes water resources, but the energy used to heat the water as well. In many U.S. properties, heating water consumes more energy than any other function. The cost of heating the water may be 4 to 20 times more than the water itself.

Some properties are using the latest conservation technology to save on water heating costs. Heat rejected by refrigerators and freezers, for example, can be captured and used to help heat water. Some washers can use hot waste water from one laundry cycle to heat the water for the next cycle. And some hotels have turned to solar technology to help heat water.

Energy Management

Energy management is a fairly new responsibility of the engineering division and deserves some detailed attention here. In the past, energy in the United States was readily available and relatively inexpensive. The United States has 6 percent of the world's population. However, before 1973, it consumed approximately 36 percent of the world's energy resources. The hospitality industry, of course, was not immune to the false sense of security created by a seemingly endless supply of energy resources. In 1977, the average energy consumption of hotels in the United States was 29 percent greater than it was in 1982.[3] The dramatic reduction in consumption illustrates how energy-wasteful the operating and management philosophies were for many properties. Although many operations have made great strides in energy management, energy use has leveled off since 1982. Many of the easy steps have been accomplished, and further gains must be achieved through more difficult processes.

Energy Problems

Energy problems in the hospitality industry are many-faceted, but the causes essentially break down into the following categories:

- Lack of awareness
- Inadequate maintenance or personnel
- Poor design
- Little or no tracking of energy consumption
- Attitude problems

Lack of Awareness. There are numerous properties where energy-saving measures have been implemented to no avail. The problem is that managers do not understand how a property consumes energy. Wise professionals perform energy audits to determine how a property really uses energy and, thus, how to conserve it.

Inadequate Maintenance or Personnel. Preventive maintenance programs in the hospitality industry were almost unheard of in the early 1970s. Since the energy crisis, they have proliferated, but many managers still do not recognize them as tools for savings. Consequently, not enough staff is hired to carry out preventive maintenance programs.

In many cases, unqualified personnel in the engineering divisions of the hospitality industry have been both the cause and the result of many of the problems in management. In many properties, janitors perform maintenance functions—even though it is hard to believe that several million dollars would be invested in the construction of a property and people would be hired at minimum wage to maintain it. The obvious result is inadequate maintenance, inoperative equipment, disconnected controls, and numerous leaks.

Poor Design. In the past, property designers were basically unconcerned with energy consumption because it was not a big factor in operations. Today, many people feel that energy consumption is still not a high priority in the development of a property, so poor design frequently continues. There is a common belief that an energy-efficient building must cost more to build. This is a myth. Companies today such as Hilton Hotels make energy evaluations on new construction and major renovations. This has resulted in reduced energy consumption of at least 25 percent for new properties.

Little or No Tracking of Consumption. In the past, properties often did a poor job tracking energy costs—and still do today in some cases. These costs merely appear on the monthly financial statement as a group of bills that were paid that month with little correlation to the property's operation. If energy is managed properly, consumption is accurately tracked and identified. Property managers must realize that utility bills do not necessarily cover the same operating periods and that some effort must be made to match energy use and cost.

Attitude Problems. Several or perhaps most of the factors which have contributed to energy problems in the hospitality industry can be traced to attitude problems. Consider, for example, personnel who are not concerned about energy management problems and do not want to develop operating, maintenance, and design systems to reduce energy usage. Or how about the manager who believes that energy consumption cannot be reduced and is relatively unimportant anyway, since the costs are passed on to guests? Some management staff express concern, but place a relatively low priority on energy management in the belief that "we'll get around to it someday." As a final example, consider the often-expressed thought that only pennies can be saved unless major capital investments are made. In fact, this is usually not true, but a bad attitude can make it seem true.

Energy Management Programs

The hospitality industry has made great progress in developing comprehensive programs to help reduce energy consumption. It understands the following benefits of good energy management practices:

- Education—Local utility companies can offer information to pass along to employees and guests about ways to conserve energy and water.

- Reduced consumption—Effective maintenance, a prerequisite of a good energy management program, can reduce energy consumption by as much as 20 percent.

- Improved equipment performance—The equipment and the systems last longer and perform better.

- Increased guest satisfaction—Management goals that emphasize reducing energy costs through adequate maintenance by trained personnel will lead to increased guest satisfaction. The guest's comfort need not be sacrificed to save energy. On the contrary, an efficient, adequately maintained system is a better guarantee of guest comfort and satisfaction. How much revenue is lost, for example, when guests never return because a poorly maintained air conditioning system cannot meet their demands?

- More accurate forecasting—Energy management allows more accurate forecasting of costs of energy and maintenance and minimizes emergency expenditures for unforeseen repairs.

Organizing an Energy Management Program. In order to coordinate and monitor the development of an ongoing energy management program, several basic steps must be followed. They are:

- Obtain top management commitment

- Establish an energy coordinating committee

- Establish an ongoing energy consumption tracking program

- Summarize the current consumption data

- Survey/audit the property

- Determine energy management opportunities

- Establish measurable goals

- Establish operating procedures and policies for no- or low-cost energy management improvements

- Consider building modifications and equipment needs programs

- Implement high-cost energy management improvements (but only after no- or low-cost improvements have been made)

- Modify and revise goals as necessary

- Evaluate and continually monitor/improve the energy management program

- Evaluate and install an appropriate energy management system (EMS)

Inter-Continental Hotels Corporation's program serves as a good example of what can be accomplished when reduced energy comsumption practices are established. Clear targets are set each year both locally and globally. Energy costs are allocated to all energy-consuming departments—kitchens, food and beverage, rooms, laundry, and health club. Meters are installed in the departments. Regular audits of performance are conducted to measure the efficiency of each hotel, department, and staff member.

The program is working. From 1988 to 1995, energy costs were reduced by 27 percent. In 1996 alone, the corporation achieved $5 million in energy savings. One hotel, the Yokahoma Grand Inter-Continental, reduced its energy bill by $2.3 million (24 percent) over a three-year period despite an occupancy increase from 56 to 71 percent.

Energy Management Systems. Computer and other electronic devices called **energy management systems** (EMS) have been developed to control peak power demand; regulate the heating, ventilating, and air conditioning throughout the building as needed; use photoelectric sensing to control lighting intensity; and, generally, control every aspect of energy usage in the operation.

A good example is guestroom HVAC control. Sensors located in guestrooms detect whether a room is occupied and adjust temperatures accordingly. Management can program default temperature settings—both minimum and maximum—to kick in while the guest is away from the room. When the guest returns, the temperature he or she had chosen is restored. Statistics indicate that a rented room is unoccupied 60 percent of the time, and an unsold room nearly all the time, so most energy is wasted heating and cooling an empty room. It is also a fact that a property's HVAC cost is second only to its payroll expense. Payback time to install this system runs from two to three years.

These systems are all technically very complex and require a knowledgeable and experienced staff to operate and maintain them. One seasoned hotel manager with no previous experience with an EMS said of the system after a few weeks: "It's great, I guess. The only problem I see is that I am convinced one needs a Ph.D. in physics to understand and operate it!" The point, of course, is that the EMS is only as good as the staff's ability to operate it, and managers should do some research and comparison shopping to make sure the system they choose is right for their staff. The complexity of energy management systems also underscores the need for better training and education of the engineering staff.

It should be understood that the EMS is a subsystem of the property management system. Leaders in the design and development of property management systems are HIS, Lodgistix, Encore, CLS, and Compusolv. Energy control systems are designed and manufactured by IBM, Johnson Controls, Honeywell, and others.

The Green Movement

Any doubt about humanity's concern for the environment should have been dispelled by the attendance and agenda at the United Nations Conference on Environment and Development held in June, 1992. This concern directly involves the hospitality industry and its practices. As one industry leader put it, "Ecology is the trend of the 1990s in the quick service restaurant field." On the hotel side, the theme of the International Hotel Association Annual Congress was "Fit for the Future," which focused on the industry's response to environmental issues.

As discussed earlier in this chapter, the industry has made excellent progress in both water and energy conservation. The latest efforts relate to solid waste reduction, hazardous waste disposal, and environmental health. Today, the quality of the environment has become a determining element in attracting hotel visitors.

Industry environmental concerns are worldwide even though hotels are not known to be major polluters. In fact, in Mexico, hotels are sometimes referred to as "la Industria sin chimeneas," or "the industry without smokestacks." While it is true that the hotel industry does not pollute the air, it is also true that hotel expansion raises environmental concerns. The industry's detrimental effects are more subtle and thus less readily perceived. In most areas of the world today, it is virtually impossible to develop hotel projects without regard for their impact on the neighborhood because of environmental awareness on the part of local officials. The principal concerns that accompany the planning of any new hotel project in Europe are:

- Visual compatibility with the neighborhood and the region, which must, however, be coupled with market positioning criteria

- Energy efficiency and conservation without an accompanying decrease in comfort

- Controlled waste disposal

- Optimum pollutant emission standards

- Permanent controls and supervision of the preservation of standards

Any hotel in the planning stages in Europe today must anticipate compliance with present and future European Community standards, which are among the world's most stringent. Right now, with land prices in desirable locations at all-time highs, compliance with environmental standards almost certainly will escalate skyrocketing hotel investment costs. Because of these costs, future hotel projects are likely to be fewer in number and more carefully planned and executed. The resulting decrease in the number of additional hotel rooms has to be welcomed by an industry badly overbuilt in many areas of the world.

Endnotes

1. Tony Lima, "The Best of Hilton's Best," *Lodging Hospitality,* August 1988, p. 79.

2. Much of the information in this and the following sections is adapted from Robert E. Aulbach, *Energy and Water Resource Management,* 2d ed. (East Lansing, Mich.: Educational Institute of the American Hotel & Motel Association, 1988) and Michael H. Redlin and David M. Stipanuk, *Managing Hospitality Engineering Systems* (East Lansing, Mich.: Educational Institute of the American Hotel & Motel Association, 1987).

3. Technical Services Center, "Annual Energy Use Surveys: 1977–1982" (San Antonio, Texas: American Hotel & Motel Association Technical Services Center and The Hospitality, Lodging & Travel Research Foundation, Inc., 1982), p. ii.

Key Terms

energy management system—A device, usually computer or microprocessor based, that is designed to be programmed on-site to control energy-consuming equipment and to reduce overall energy consumption.

gray water—Relatively clean wastewater, such as that produced from certain laundry cycles and effluent from wastewater treatment systems, that can be used to supply needs for landscape water and other non-potable uses.

potability—Suitability for drinking.

potable water—Water that is suitable for drinking.

preventive maintenance—Maintenance stressing inspections, lubrication, minor repairs or adjustments, and work order initiation. Generally performed using manufacturers' information as a guideline.

preventive maintenance schedule—A schedule for maintaining elements of the building that are critical to guest satisfaction, overall property image and marketing, safety and security, and the performance of other departments' duties.

renovation—The process of renewing and updating a hospitality property to offset the ravages of use and modify spaces to meet the needs of changing markets.

undistributed operating expenses—Costs a property incurs as a whole; they are not assigned to any particular division or department.

walk-in—A large refriderator or freezer used in high-volume kitchens for storage of perishable items.

work order—A document used to initiate requests for maintenance services.

Review Questions

1. In what ways does the engineering and maintenance division deserve the title of unsung hero in hotels and restaurants?

2. How does the engineering department operate as a cost savings center?

3. What are the effects of deferred maintenance? What are the effects of preventive maintenance?

4. What are the possible reasons for the tremendous amount of renovation of hotels occurring in the 1980s and early 1990s?

5. What usual evaluations of water must the engineering division conduct?

6. What approaches could a hotel take to reduce water waste and realize savings in the process?

7. What are some of the advantages of an energy management program?

8. What leads to energy problems in the hospitality industry?

9. What are the basic steps in a preventive maintenance program?

10. What four major areas of work is the engineering department involved in? Describe them.

Internet Sites

For more information, visit the following Internet sites. Remember that Internet addresses can change without notice. If the site is no longer there, use a browser to look for additional sites.

Associations

American Culinary Federation (ACF)
http://www.acfchefs.org

American Hotel & Motel Association (AH&MA)
http://www.ahma.com

Commercial Food Equipment Service Association
http://www.cfesa.com

Club Managers Association of America (CMAA)
http://www.cmaa.org

The Educational Foundation of NRA
http://www.restaurant.org/educate/educate.htm

The Educational Institute of AH&MA
http://www.ei-ahma.org

Hospitality Financial and Technology Professionals
http://www.hftp.org

Publications—Online and Printed

Club Management Magazine
http://www.club-mgmt.com

Foodservice and Hospitality
http://www.foodservice.ca

Internet Food Channel
http://www.foodchannel.com

Lodging Online
http://www.ei-ahma.org/webs/lodging/index.html

Lodging Hospitality
http://www.penton.com/corp/mags/lh.html

Nation's Restaurant News Online
http://www.nrn.com http://smart-wine.com

Chapter 11 Outline

The Modern Marketing Emphasis
Product and Service Marketing: The Sale of Hospitality
Planning for Guest Needs
     The Feasibility Study
     Situation Analysis
The Marketing Planning Process
     Five Elements
The Organization of the Marketing and Sales Division
     Interdepartmental Relationships
     Bringing Business to the Property
Hotels and Airlines: Birds of a Feather
The Business of Selling
     Rooms Business
     Public Space
     Food and Beverage Business
     Internal Selling
     Personal Selling
Star and Other Rating Systems
Advertising, Special Promotions, and Public Relations
     Advertising
     Special Promotions
     Public Relations

11

The Marketing and Sales Division

PEOPLE OFTEN THINK OF MARKETING as selling or advertising and public relations. But marketing involves many more activities than these. Marketing strives to produce the maximum profit through sales, advertising, public relations, promotions, merchandising, and pricing activities. Marketing brings buyers and sellers together. Put another way, marketing matches product with customers. A hotel must accurately determine what types of customers are most logically attracted to the hotel's location and features. The job of marketing should begin well before a hotel opens; in fact, it should begin even before the hotel is designed. This phase will be discussed in more detail later in this chapter.

Marketing also helps identify groups of current or potential guests by (1) geographic location, (2) industry, (3) economic status, or (4) behavioral characteristics. Marketers call these groups **markets**. Marketing also helps identify groups with common buying traits called **market segments**. Marketing activities can help reveal a property's **market mix**—that is, the various market segments it hopes to attract. And marketing indicates the approaches and tools—the **marketing strategy**—that can be used to attract the market mix.

Marketing helps managers see operations from the guest's perspective. For example, marketers may conduct feasibility studies and situation analyses to help them determine what guests want and need and how to provide it. Or they may make pricing decisions and develop competition strategies, activities critical to the success of today's hospitality operation.

The Modern Marketing Emphasis

Until the 1930s, companies in the United States marketed goods and services in mass quantities hoping to persuade consumers to buy them. Mass production allowed the companies to make products cheaply so that the average consumer could buy them. Consumers purchased these products as fast as companies could produce them. The job of marketing was simply to sell products.

During the hard times of the Depression, consumers could no longer afford to buy all the goods and services that companies produced. Companies were forced to produce only goods that consumers really wanted. As a result, marketing strategies became more consumer-oriented.

Today, most producers of goods and services use consumer-oriented marketing. Marketing activities determine what consumers want, and marketers then

Insider Insights

James E. Lattin
General Manager
Park Ridge Hotel and Conference Center
Philadelphia, Pennsylvania

Marketing a hotel or resort located outside the United States is dramatically different from marketing a property located in the United States. One noticeable difference is that properties outside the United States often rely heavily on third-party travel wholesalers for their marketing.

A primary reason is that properties located outside the United States often get very little business from their country of location, receiving most of their business from a variety of other countries. This dependence on international travelers requires a different marketing approach.

A local selling organization and an easy means to make reservations are keys to marketing a property in another country. However, many independent properties and small chains find that their size precludes establishing their own marketing and sales organizations in each target market. For these properties, travel companies that package tours to specific destinations for residents of their countries are an important resource.

These travel wholesalers may be responsible for the largest portion of business for overseas properties. The more remote a destination is and the less business it generates from domestic sources, the more travel wholesalers will dominate its marketing. Hotels and resorts on tropical islands in the Pacific may depend exclusively on travel wholesalers for their marketing.

Sales and marketing personnel in overseas hotels must carefully research wholesalers in each market they choose to develop. One-on-one meetings with the wholesaler principals, either in their offices or at one of the growing number of travel trade shows (for example, ITB Berlin, World Travel Mart, London, PATA Travel Mart), are vital to negotiating favorable contract terms.

The greatest advantage to working with origin-market wholesalers is that a property can spread its promotion and distribution widely at minimal expense. The greatest disadvantage is that the property loses direct control of how it is priced and positioned, since these functions are delegated to the wholesaler. Thus, it is important that a property's manager carefully determine the room prices given to the wholesaler, who is, in all likelihood, also marketing the property's competitors. The property manager must ensure that the wholesaler describes the property favorably and has attractive photos in the brochure it uses to promote the property to travel agents and the general public.

The hotelier working outside the United States must understand the role of the wholesaler and the nuances of the wholesaler business to a much higher degree than the hotelier working in the United States.

inform production so that goods and services meet those wants. Marketing also informs consumers—through selling, advertising, and promotion—that the goods and services are available.

Product and Service Marketing: The Sale of Hospitality —

A hotel or restaurant sells products (rooms, food, and beverages) and services (hospitality). There are significant differences between marketing services and marketing products. A product can be demonstrated or shown, and thus guests can assess its value rather easily. Marketing service is more difficult because it is less tangible than a product. Every service provided must meet the expectations of the guests the property hopes to attract and satisfy. Otherwise, the guests will be either disappointed or overwhelmed. For example, a room escort might surprise or even embarrass guests in an economy hotel. On the other hand, guests visiting a deluxe hotel might feel cheated if a nightly turn-down service were omitted.

When a property is marketed well, its image and position relative to the competition are so clear that the specifics of its service become an instantly recognizable permanent signature. For example, what frequenter of resort hotels has not heard of the impeccable service of The Greenbrier? Similarly, who can think of the Waldorf-Astoria and not think of the highest standards of service and the highest quality of food and drink? And among convention-goers, what hotels conjure up more positive images as convention headquarters than the Sheraton Waikiki in Honolulu and the Opryland Hotel in Nashville?

Hospitality, then, is not something a property presents to a guest on a plate or in a glass. It includes every aspect of the guest's stay and must meet or exceed the guest's expectations. Hospitality can be thought of as the property's personality. Developing that personality begins with the attitude of owners and managers and includes the way all employees provide hospitable service to guests.

Planning for Guest Needs —

How does the marketing and sales division tackle the difficult job of selling hospitality to potential guests? The task begins with proper planning and continues through the delivery of products and services to guests. It also must consider how to draw potential markets to the property.

The Feasibility Study

The goods and services that potential guests want must be determined even before a property is built or purchased. A **feasibility study** analyzes a proposed site to determine what type of property has the best chance for success. The feasibility study ultimately determines whether investors should construct or purchase an operation. It concentrates on four areas: location, guest demographics, the competition, and financial analysis.

Location. Location is the most important element in the success of any property. An operation may have great food and service, beautiful decor, a wonderful atmosphere, the newest guestrooms, and low prices. However, it can fail if it is poorly located. Likewise, a poor-quality property may succeed *in the short run* if it is in a good location. Some of the criteria that determine whether or not a proposed site is in a good location include:

- Population of the surrounding area

- Number of people living or working in the immediate area

- Number of people within easy driving distance

- Types of business in the immediate area

- Availability and convenience of parking

- Traffic flow patterns

- Distance from exits off main highways

- Location of air transportation

The type of property envisioned must also be considered. Most hotel properties fit into one of three basic categories, with some overlap. These basic types are commercial hotels, convention hotels, and resort hotels. Each of these types must consider location to determine its appropriateness for the kinds of customers it hopes to attract. For example, a commercial hotel must know how many companies are located in reasonable proximity and determine how much business can be generated. A convention-oriented hotel must have easy access to a convention or trade center. Distance from a major airport is critical for a resort hotel.

Guest Demographics. Demographic studies identify such statistical characteristics as average age, sex, marital status, average number of children, average family income, and occupation of potential guests. Surveys can identify preferences of potential guests: what kind of dining do they like? what do they want in a guestroom? how much are they willing to pay for certain goods and services? will they be using banquet/catering facilities? Marketers can conduct surveys via personal interviews, telephone interviews, or direct mail questionnaires.

After marketers obtain guest demographic and preference information, they decide what level of service and prices, type of food and beverage service, decor, and so forth best match potential guests.

Competition Analysis. To determine whether their own property will succeed, marketers must know how financially successful the competition is and how well it meets the needs of its guests. This analysis should uncover the strengths and weaknesses of each competitor, how long each competitor has operated at its current location, how busy each competitor is on various days of the week, and how current guests feel about each competitor.

After analyzing the competition, the investors can reasonably estimate the number of guests the new property can expect to attract. This estimate comes from adding the number of potential guests not currently satisfied by the competition and the number of potential guests that would patronize the new operation instead of competing facilities. The estimated number of expected guests becomes the basis for the financial analysis of the feasibility study.

Financial Analysis. Unless the property can make a profit, it should not be constructed or purchased. If the other parts of the feasibility study have been conducted properly, they will offer reliable data to help investors estimate expected revenues and expenses.

Situation Analysis

After a property opens, a **situation analysis** determines what guests like and dislike about the operation.[1]

Situation analysis gathers information about a property's current market position and promotion opportunities. Situation analysis does not rely on hunches, intuition, or lucky guesses. It requires thorough, careful research and analysis of five basic components: the product, the market, the competition, guest segmentation, and evaluation.

The Product. The product is the goods and services the property sells. Analysis of the product considers both physical and psychological factors. These may include the strengths and weaknesses of the property, the number of guestrooms, the property's image, and the atmosphere created by its furnishings. Current marketing efforts should be evaluated. These include the marketing objectives and how well the property accomplishes its goals.

The Market. The marketing and sales division should identify and analyze past and current guests to determine group and individual markets. Market analysis yields a picture of "what guests look like" and "what they think and do." Market analysis should be completed for the whole property and for each of its separate facilities.

The Competition. A property should also conduct product and market analyses of all competitors in the local area and in other cities and locations. What are the competitors' strengths and weaknesses? How does the competition differ from the property under study? How is it similar? Which of the differences will be significant to which markets?

Guest Segmentation. This portion of the situation analysis matches property needs with guest needs. First, marketers identify revenue centers that need to generate additional sales. The analysis should note guest preferences for physical facilities (for example, meeting rooms) and their desired level of luxury, convenience, security, and so forth. Once property and guest needs are determined, marketers can classify market segments and choose target markets to fulfill property needs. For example, if the hotel has a cocktail lounge, which guest segments will increase its early evening sales? Developing a position and a mission statement will define the property's place in the market and its marketing objectives.

Evaluation. Situation analysis is not a one-time activity but an ongoing process that monitors the property's success in the marketplace. Updating the market plan allows staff to compare objectives with actual results so that new strategies can be developed. Research should constantly monitor changes in the market and the environment and develop plans to help the property maintain a competitive edge.

Guest surveys and comment cards help managers understand what guests want and need. In turn, this helps the operation maintain long-term profitability.

Easily recognizable signs and architectural designs, such as those of the LaQuinta Motor Inns, help brand-loyal guests find their accommodations of choice.

Individuals and groups can be surveyed at the time of room check-out, after they have eaten meals, or after they have attended banquets or other functions. These surveys attempt to find out how guests liked the food, service, cleanliness, price, and atmosphere. Guest comment cards are very similar to guest surveys. The property places these tent-shaped cards on dining room tables or in guestrooms. Guests can then rate various aspects of the property. The back of guest checks in a restaurant or lounge can also be used for guest comments.

The Marketing Planning Process

The completed situation analysis tells the marketing and sales division what it sells, what business it currently attracts, and who its competitors are. Its target markets have been defined. The situation analysis thus paves the way for the market plan.

The market plan indicates both short- and long-term approaches to attracting and retaining guests.

Marketing planning is not just for large properties with marketing and sales divisions. In fact, it is even more vital for a small property to have a written market plan. Jobs are often more generalized in smaller properties. It is therefore easy for employees to overlook marketing activities in favor of other duties. In small properties, managers can get distracted from sales goals and spend far less time on marketing and sales than they intended. However, a written market plan helps prevent staff from neglecting marketing functions.

Regardless of the size of a property, its market plan should be easy for owners and senior managers to understand. Key people in every department or outlet of the property should contribute to the plan. This builds team spirit, especially important if unpredicted major setbacks occur.

Five Elements

A good market plan helps marketing and sales division staff sell the right products and services to the right markets at the right time. The marketing planning process includes five basic elements:

1. A mission statement—The mission statement should clearly state what the property is and what markets it intends to serve.

2. A situation analysis

3. Comparative statistics—Actual business volume during the current year should be compared with projections for each month of the next year. Such comparisons help properties plan business activities for the future. Hotels, for example, need statistics on occupancy rate, rooms volume, food and beverage volume, marketing overhead expenses, and, if possible, **gross operating profit**. The hotel should project its individual and group business for upcoming years. Managers can determine the status of bookings by comparing the amount of future business already on hand for a given date with the amount of business booked on the same date a year earlier.

4. Action plans—The property needs to produce a monthly plan for each market segment—group, social/recreational, business traveler, and the like. Each plan should include: assignment of accountability (assigning individual managers specific parts of the plan for which to be responsible), sales activities, target dates, and standards of measurements (criteria by which the success of the plan will be measured). Media for advertising can then be considered, and a marketing budget to guide expenses can be planned. A **key account** list can be compiled along with an action plan for attracting these key accounts during the upcoming year. Using this information, management can develop sales quotas for the year.

5. A calendar of promotional events—Managers should compile a calendar of the property's promotional events. The objectives of the promotion, the advertising media to be used, and any creative managerial recommendations should be noted for each event.

Exhibit 1   Sample Organization Chart of a Marketing and Sales Division in a Large Hotel

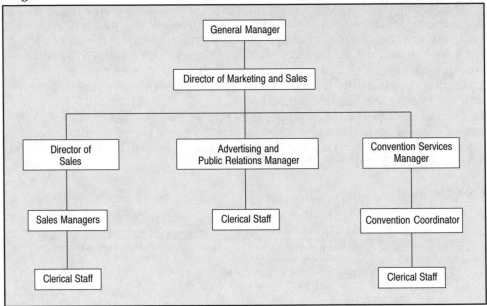

The Organization of the Marketing and Sales Division ——

The organization of the marketing and sales division depends on the property's needs and size. For example, independent restaurants need someone to handle marketing and sales activities. But, unlike restaurant chains and many hotels, they seldom have a separate marketing and sales division. This chapter will focus on hotel marketing and sales functions, which are often more detailed than those in restaurants. However, many of the concepts presented here apply to all types of hospitality operations.

Exhibit 1 illustrates one possible organization of a marketing and sales division in a large hotel. As this exhibit shows, the director of the marketing and sales division reports to the general manager. The division director supervises three separate departments headed by these managers:

- Director of Sales—The director of sales heads the sales department. He or she supervises sales managers (increasingly called account executives) and clerical staff. This department generates group business from conventions and meetings of associations and corporations and from tour/travel companies. After the sales department books group business, the convention services department generally handles further contact with the group. This includes making arrangements for food and beverage services or guestrooms. When groups do not require food and beverage services or meeting rooms, the director of sales must work with other divisions, such as the front office, to coordinate service to the groups.

- Advertising and Public Relations Manager—This manager oversees the advertising and public relations department(s). He or she develops the advertising budget, determines which media offer the most effective outlets for the property's advertising efforts, and develops advertising messages or works with the hotel's advertising agency. This manager also develops and carries out short- and long-range plans so that guests and the general public receive a positive and consistent image of the property through brochures and fliers. Increasingly, these functions are handled by the director of marketing, frequently in liaison with outside agencies specializing in advertising or public relations.

- Convention Services Manager—This manager, head of the convention services department, coordinates meeting rooms needed for group business sold by the sales department. Frequently, this department handles all contacts with the new account after the sale. Sometimes the convention services director handles only the setup for the meeting. When the meeting requires food and beverage service, this department must work closely with the food and beverage division.

Interdepartmental Relationships

The marketing and sales division's primary mission is to sell the property's products and services. As a result, staff must work closely with many other departments and divisions within the operation. The following examples help illustrate the close working relationship between the marketing and sales division and other divisions.

- Suppose the sales staff sells a group meeting that requires food and beverage services. In a large property, the sales department may turn over final arrangements for the group to the convention services department. Convention services would then coordinate the group's arrangements with catering and other departments.

- The sales department may sell a group meeting that requires guestrooms. In this instance, sales staff would work closely with the front office or reservations manager to make sure enough rooms would be available.

- Suppose the catering sales manager sells food and beverage events to a group that does not require any other property services. (This may be for a wedding reception, social party, anniversary party, or the like.) While some out-of-town guests may stay at the property overnight, the food and beverage division generates the primary sales revenue. Before the catered event can be booked, marketing and sales must check with the individual in charge of scheduling meeting rooms. If a specific room has already been scheduled, it obviously will not be free for catered functions.

Exhibit 2   Bringing the Traveler to the Hotel

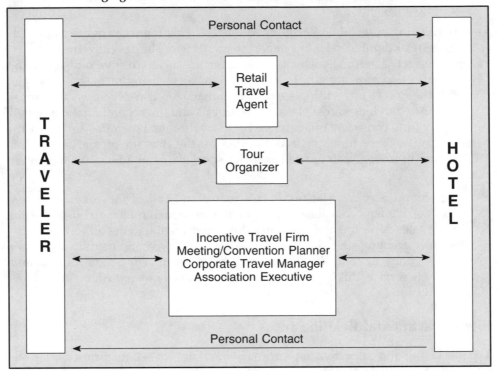

In the end, making a guest's special event truly special depends on planning. And good planning happens only if the marketing and sales division effectively communicates the guest's needs to other departments.

Bringing Business to the Property

Besides working closely with divisions within the property, marketing and sales staff must maintain close ties with outside businesses that can bring guests to the property.

In addition, there are a number of methods by which guests can be brought to the hotel. The marketing and sales division plays an important role, directly or indirectly, in these methods. Some ways guests can be brought to the hotel are outlined in Exhibit 2 and discussed in the following sections. Exhibit 3 shows how a sample of businesspeople rated 16 possible sources of information in deciding where to stay when they traveled for business.

Personal Contact. Guests may come to the hotel through direct personal contact. Perhaps the guest wants to stay at a certain chain-affiliated property. He or she can make reservations by calling a toll-free reservation service. Guests can also make reservations by calling a local affiliated property. Reservations staff there will then reserve a room at any other property in the same chain. In either case, the marketing and sales division will play an important part in promoting these reservation services.

Exhibit 3 Information Sources Affecting Lodging Selection

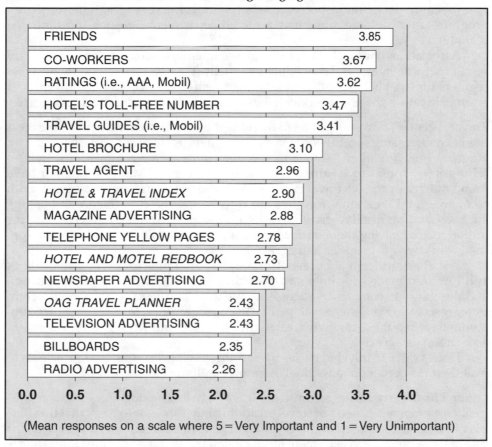

Source	Mean
FRIENDS	3.85
CO-WORKERS	3.67
RATINGS (i.e., AAA, Mobil)	3.62
HOTEL'S TOLL-FREE NUMBER	3.47
TRAVEL GUIDES (i.e., Mobil)	3.41
HOTEL BROCHURE	3.10
TRAVEL AGENT	2.96
HOTEL & TRAVEL INDEX	2.90
MAGAZINE ADVERTISING	2.88
TELEPHONE YELLOW PAGES	2.78
HOTEL AND MOTEL REDBOOK	2.73
NEWSPAPER ADVERTISING	2.70
OAG TRAVEL PLANNER	2.43
TELEVISION ADVERTISING	2.43
BILLBOARDS	2.35
RADIO ADVERTISING	2.26

(Mean responses on a scale where 5 = Very Important and 1 = Very Unimportant)

Source: Ken W. McCleary and Pamela A. Weaver, "Simple & Safe," *Hotel & Motel Management*, July 6, 1992, p. 23.

The guest may also stop by chance at the property or make a reservation there on the recommendation of a friend or business associate. Word-of-mouth recommendations show that the hotel's marketing and sales division has done a good job promoting the property's image and that employees are aware of their own role in good public relations.

Advertisements on billboards, in airline magazines, and on radio and television may all influence a guest to check into a particular property. These advertisements are developed by the marketing and sales division, who choose the media most likely to reach the target markets.

Companies and Associations. In developing accounts for their hotels, sales and marketing managers concentrate most of their attention on companies and professional or trade associations that have or may have occasion to book groups into their properties.

Sales managers carefully research the ranks of companies to determine which employee or department books hotels for individual reservations or group programs. In some large companies, a special department is responsible for travel planning.

Associations on a local, state, regional, and international level plan thousands of seminars, trade shows, and conventions annually. This is a very important business segment for most hotels, so their sales departments expend considerable time and effort cultivating good relations with these associations' travel staff and executives.

Travel Agents. The role of the retail travel agency in the booking of hotel business has been increasing steadily for many years. Travel agents have seen that they can augment their traditional source of revenue (from airline commissions) by also selling hotel rooms to leisure and business customers. Many businesses have found that they can save travel expenses by booking through travel agencies. Both companies and individual travelers are discovering the convenience of booking air, hotel, and car rental reservations through one agency. Hotels now recognize the importance of having their sales departments solicit business and negotiate contracts directly with agencies and agency groups.

Travel agents learn about hotels through special directories that list facilities and rate information for hotels worldwide. Increasingly, this same information and the ability to book reservations is now available to agencies through the computer reservation systems developed by the major airlines. Many large hotel companies have modified or newly created their own computer reservation systems to accommodate agencies.

Hotels cater to travel agencies by encouraging agency staff and principals to visit their properties on individual or group familiarization tours.

Other Third-Party Business Sources. Travel wholesale companies package destinations and many aspects of travel, including hotel stays, into tours that they display in brochures and sell to the general public through retail travel agencies. The role of the wholesaler is extremely influential in travel outside of the United States and to vacation destinations.

Companies offer travel as an incentive to encourage their sales staff to make more sales. Travel wholesalers who specialize in incentive travel have emerged. They sell tailor-made travel programs to companies with large sales forces.

Both wholesalers and incentive travel companies are actively solicited by hotel sales managers.

Finally, the hotel may contact guests through sales blitzes, outside sales agents, and other types of personal selling coordinated by the marketing and sales division. In today's competitive economy, the use of outside sales calls is increasing, especially in areas where the number of hotels exceeds guest demands. The hotel that can persuade local businesses to encourage clients to stay at the hotel will improve its occupancy rates significantly.

Hotels and Airlines: Birds of a Feather

Were one to study the various components of the hospitality industry, he or she would surely note the many similarities between the hotel and airline segments.

Both offer products that are among the most fragile to be found anywhere. An unfilled seat on any flight, or an unoccupied hotel room on any night, can never be recovered. They are gone forever because airline seats and guestrooms cannot be inventoried.

The business traveler is a key market for the hotel and airline industries and the target of many marketing campaigns. Both industries have experienced the full brunt of the consolidation steamroller through acquisitions and mergers.

In the mid-1980s, several major U.S. airline carriers initiated frequent traveler programs designed to increase customer loyalty and attract new customers by offering rewards for a certain number of miles flown. The more miles flown, the richer the reward. Within two years, several major hotel companies introduced frequent traveler programs. Holiday Inns and Marriott created their own programs, while other companies joined existing airline programs. By 1988, most lodging firms had adopted some kind of frequent traveler program. Now, in the 1990s, both the airline and hotel segments have many of these programs.

Next, the airline marketers devised the advance purchase discount practice in which the customer gets a significant discount on the regular fare by reserving and paying for the ticket at least 14 days in advance. The ticket usually is non-refundable and flights cannot be changed. Advance purchase discounts worked for the airlines, and hotels quickly took a notice of this success. As a result, hotel companies have experimented with some pricing strategies adpoted from the airline procedures. At one point, there was high expectation that discounted, non-refundable advance purchase room rates would become commonplace in hotels as similar pricing strategies are with the airlines. This has not occurred to any major degree except in some limited occasions with leisure travelers.

A strategy borrowed from the airlines that has become much more prevalent in hotels is the concept of yield management. In simplified terms, this concept means that rates and room availability are controlled to allow the best rate and occupancy for each night. When demand justifies, discounts will be eliminated, certain dates may be closed to arrival, and multiple night stays may be required. Likewise, when demand is low, yield management will ensure that discounts will be readily available to generate maximum occupancy. Computerized reservation systems are now in use in many hotels to facilitate effective yield management activity.

The Business of Selling

To many young people interested in hospitality employment, sales appears glamorous and fun, and, to an extent, it is. But it also requires hard work. A successful operation focuses group sales effort on guest segments most likely to use the property. Staff responsible for obtaining business from these segments make up the core of the sales department. Each day they meet the potential guest face-to-face.

It is important to sell all products and services, but the most profitable must take precedence. By far the most profitable is rooms.

Rooms Business

Room sales are focused in two distinct directions: group business and individual business, each of which can be divided into pleasure and business segments.

A good sales department staff must maintain balance in the amount of group business booked for guestrooms and space. This requires staying abreast of past and current booking trends. A hotel cannot overcommit space to groups and conventions at the expense of turning away individual business. At the same time, a hotel must attract groups that will book a good mix of guestrooms and function space.

Maintaining these balances in the **business mix** requires good interdepartmental coordination. Thorough knowledge of the property's booking trends helps marketers place limits on group rooms committed by season and night of the week. A salesperson must get approval from an appointed executive committee member to exceed a limit. Likewise, catering staff need guidelines for booking advance times and the amount of space assigned. If caterers must exceed time and space guidelines, they should obtain permission from the director of sales first. Following these guidelines helps the property draw the best mix of business for the hotel overall.

Booking conventions requires considerable planning and skillful execution. Senior sales staff in smaller properties and specialized departments in large hotels usually perform these jobs.

Conventions. About 25,000 professional, trade, and fraternal organizations provide big business each year for hospitality operations and cities. Major conventions bring enormous amounts of money into properties and the community, so the competition for this market segment is intense. Hotels and convention centers try hard to book major groups during slack times.

Associations holding conventions and meetings vary widely in size and scope. They may be international or local and include fewer than 100 or more than 100,000 people. Such a wide range allows many properties and cities to find their niche in the market.

Booking conventions into hotels that do not depend primarily on this business can be risky. Conventions may lower the availability of rooms for repeat individual guests and, worse yet, may create noise and partying, which could lose these guests altogether. These risks are even greater for resorts where the individual guest stays to "get away from it all."

In recent years, resort properties have begun searching for convention business to fill shoulder (pre- and post-season periods) and off-season periods. Even major destination resorts have now begun to compete for conventions. They offer good meeting facilities with many recreational amenities that appeal to convention delegates.

Contract Rooms. A company that continuously needs hotel space may contract for a number of rooms every day on a yearly basis. Airline companies, for example, will choose a hotel for their flight crews and negotiate a contract with the hotel for the rooms needed. The company usually receives a discount for the rooms.

Company Business Meetings. Corporate travel (individuals and groups) is the biggest segment of rooms sales in most hotels and many resort properties. Hotel sales departments expend considerable effort attracting company meetings and special events. Except for hotels in popular destinations, many hotel sales departments count on local companies to use their facilities. Company needs include sales meetings, human resources and training programs, executive sessions, and reward programs. Resort sales departments look primarily for gatherings requiring attractive locations with extensive recreational facilities or tourist attractions.

Tour Groups. The travel industry books more and more hotels and resorts each year for individuals, groups, and business travelers. As noted earlier in this chapter, travel wholesalers create individual or group packages and market them through retail travel agencies. Retail travel agents directly handle individual bookings for business and pleasure purposes. Travel agents and special incentive travel companies book company meetings and special event groups. Hoteliers know that, to remain competitive, their sales departments must have one or more managers skilled in dealing with the travel industry.

Individual Business. Competition for individual business has increased as much as it has for group business. Marketers use a wide range of advertising methods to attract individual business. Business travelers are extremely important to most hotels, since they represent a continuing source of business.

Public Space

Besides promoting guestroom sales, the sales department must sell ballrooms and other meeting rooms. Local and out-of-town groups use this **public space** for meetings. Many larger operations have a separate sales team devoted to booking local functions. In smaller properties, this is an additional function of the sales department. While hotels need local business and promote their facilities to local groups, guestroom sales remain the biggest source of income. As a result, the sales department's first priority will be to accommodate out-of-town groups who will book both meeting facilities and guestrooms.

Often conventions select hotels based on the availability of public space. Sales staff must know about booking trends, lead time for bookings, and public room layouts and capacities. Cooperation between sales and the department that handles banquet and local meeting sales helps ensure the most profitable use of public space and guestrooms. Likewise, the sales department must work with the front office to develop group room plans for specific seasons or nights of the week.

Food and Beverage Business

In many hotels, food and beverage sales generate 30 percent or more of total revenues. Complaints from group meeting attendees often involve food and beverage services. Properties serving quality food and beverages make the job of the marketing and sales division easier. Group business planners are most interested in properties with a good reputation for food and beverages. Staff in "problem" food and beverage operations must work harder to assure prospective clients that food and beverage needs can be met.

Besides catering services for large groups, many operations offer one or more restaurants or lounges that cater to small groups and individuals. In today's competitive marketplace, free-standing restaurants of all types compete with hotel food and beverage operations. Therefore, marketing food and beverage services in the hotel is challenging and difficult.

Properties need a great deal of space and equipment to make food and beverages available. Many properties use prime space, such as hotel lobbies, for food and beverage service areas. Some have outside entrances to food and beverage facilities. Few hotels can afford to rely on overnight guests alone to make their food and beverage operations successful. Community business fills seats in restaurants and lounges, and marketers therefore conduct aggressive advertising campaigns to attract local residents.

The property's marketing and sales staff help food and beverage operations by conducting a situation analysis and by developing market plans. Typically, food and beverage operations receive attention when these marketing tools are developed for other aspects of the property. Likewise, selecting advertising media, developing advertisements, and maintaining a food and beverage public relations program involve the marketing and sales staff.

Internal Selling

Internal selling is a marketing technique for increasing sales and profits. Internal selling occurs when front desk agents sell more expensive rooms first and when servers use suggestive selling techniques to move high-profit items, such as orange juice, appetizers, cocktails, glasses of wine, and desserts. Internal selling also refers to in-house signs and displays that promote the sale of the operation's products and services. Examples include signs in the entrance listing daily food and beverage specials, menu clip-on cards promoting specialties of the house, and tent cards with promotional messages in guestrooms.

Personal Selling

Personal selling (outside selling) is a marketing technique that is used in the lodging industry but rarely in food service. Personal selling requires salespeople who are employed specifically to generate sales for the operation. Manufacturers, wholesalers, and retailers of products use salespeople extensively. Lodging operations with large banquet or restaurant facilities may need salespeople to generate profitable bookings for these facilities.

Marketing and sales division staff may send out brochures, banquet menus, or packages to prospective groups and follow up these mailings with personal sales calls. They also handle all group inquiries and personally discuss the details involved with putting on special meetings. Salespeople work with other management people in designing packages or package plans. Then they sell these packages to help increase the total revenue of the entire operation. The difference between personal selling and internal selling is that personal selling uses salespeople to sell groups. Internal selling uses service employees to suggestively sell to individual guests.

Star and Other Rating Systems

All hotel owners and executives are very conscious of the various rating systems that judge their hotels and publish the results in terms of star, diamond, or other ratings. Perhaps most directly concerned are marketing executives who are responsible for building room, food, and beverage sales at the property.

Hotels throughout the world are classified by one or more of these rating systems. In a number of countries, the government controls the classification of hotels. Greece, Spain, and Jamaica are examples. The classification is based on published standards of design and service for each category. In Switzerland, the system is set up by the National Hotel Association although it is essentially voluntary and based on the hotel's self-assessment. In the United States, the Mobil Star Guide and the American Automobile Association Diamond Rating are by far the best known. The highest are five-star and five-diamond ratings.

There is no truly international star rating system applicable throughout the world. One country's four-star rating may be another's five-star designation. France and Spain both have a maximum of four stars but also feature a Four Star Deluxe category for which very few hotels qualify. In all of Spain, only nine hotels are ranked in this category. Because of the different rating systems with their varied standards, to equate hotels by their star or diamond ratings provides, at best, only a partial measure of their comparative quality levels.

However, these rating systems strongly affect customer selection of lodging accommodations. The loss of a single star or diamond can have a devastating effect on a hotel's sales and profit picture and has, on occasion, resulted in the release of a top-level executive.

Advertising, Special Promotions, and Public Relations

Advertising

Advertising is a major part of marketing and uses several communications media to reach target markets. Each medium's advantages and disadvantages are discussed here.

Newspapers. The only print medium that regularly goes to many family homes is the local newspaper. It is not surprising, then, that many hospitality operations advertise in newspapers often. Newspaper ads have a well-defined circulation, reach many people, offer intensive coverage of the local market, and have targeted readership, immediacy, and flexibility.

Newspapers, however, have a short life. Readers typically skim papers and throw them away. Reproduction quality is often poor. And there is a limited opportunity to reach market segments. For example, a luxurious property advertising expensive food service in a local newspaper will reach many readers who cannot afford such service.

Magazines. Magazine advertisements have many advantages over newspapers. These include high-quality reproduction, color availability, prestige, audience selectivity, and a long life. Advertisers can take advantage of high-quality paper, excellent reproduction, and life-like color in magazine advertisements to show off their operation's appetizing food items, attractive guestrooms, recreational facilities, and so forth.

Magazine advertisements, however, usually take longer to prepare than newspaper ads, sometimes weeks or months. They also cost more and reduce an advertiser's ability to repeat ads.

Radio. Almost 99 percent of U.S. households have at least one radio. Local radio stations reach people within a convenient driving distance of a property. Radio advertisements can saturate an entire local area.

In addition, advertisers can reach specific target markets by matching the radio station's format or time the ad is aired with the property's target market. For example, if an operation features jazz in its lounge, advertising on a jazz station or during a jazz program will reach the target market directly. If businesspeople are a target market, advertising on an "easy listening" station during rush-hour would make sense. Unless repeated, however, radio messages have a short life span and offer only audio messages.

Television. Television's main advantage over radio is that it combines sight with sound. No other medium can combine these elements to make such an attractive presentation to its audience. Television commercials can show friendly front desk agents greeting guests or chefs preparing magnificent food. Television also commands a high attention level in its audience, so viewers retain many advertising messages.

Another advantage is saturation. That is, commercials can run many times daily and reach many households. Also, advertisers can reach specific audiences by selecting shows they prefer.

Disadvantages include high costs and extensive lead times necessary to produce commercials.

Outdoor Advertising. Outdoor advertising is widely used by the hospitality industry. Billboards along highways are vital to hospitality establishments. Billboards are also used in and around large cities to promote local facilities. Almost all managers use exterior signs to attract guests and to advertise the establishment's name and features. Outdoor advertising is basically a reminder that tries to attract the attention of potential guests who pass by the billboards or signs. Outdoor advertising must be bold, dynamic, and graphic so that passersby can get the message at a glance. Advantages of outdoor advertising include large circulation, broad reach, and low cost. A primary disadvantage is the limited message length.

Direct Mail. Direct mail simply involves the mailing of the advertising message in brochures, coupons, or other formats. Direct mail advertising is used by many managers, especially in clubs and other establishments with private memberships. Direct mail advertising allows audience selectivity and specific target marketing. Only those people who fit the operation's target market receive advertising material. Another advantage of direct mail advertising is that it can be personalized. It is also flexible, and the markets it reaches can be easily measured.

A primary disadvantage of direct mail is the high cost of developing and mailing a high-quality professional brochure or information packet. The cost per unit of circulation for direct mail advertising is generally greater than that for any other advertising method.

Special Promotions

Special promotions are widely used in almost all hospitality operations. They are limited only by one's imagination. Examples include couponing, product sampling, contests, packages, premiums, gift certificates, discounting, and bonus offers.

Couponing. Coupons attract potential guests with a special offer, such as a free night's lodging after a special number of credits. Coupons can be given out personally, included in direct mail advertising, or printed in newspapers and magazines. The property may also increase slack-time business by using coupons with other special promotions, such as bonus offers or discounting.

Product Sampling. Product sampling acquaints guests with new food items. Samples help determine whether guests like a new product and also encourage them to order the item if they do.

Contests. Contests organized by the marketing and sales division can increase sales. A contest should be cost-effective; that is, increased sales should offset the cost of contest promotion and prizes.

Packages. Properties can offer products or services in packages at a discount price to attract new guests and to increase sales. One example is a weekend package complete with lodging, champagne, meals, and tickets for a local attraction. The package would cost considerably less than each item paid for separately.

Premiums. Premiums are given to guests who pay the regular prices for certain products or services. For example, an upgraded room might be provided or free movie tickets might be given to each adult eating dinner on Wednesday night, the slowest night of the week for most restaurants.

Gift Certificates. Gift certificates are used most often by chains or exclusive properties to increase sales. They are handled the same way as gift certificates sold in retail stores.

Discounting. Many properties discount prices to attract more guests and increase total sales. For example, one dinner on the menu might be reduced by 50 percent. Offering discounts through coupons allows the property to track how many guests use the offer.

Bonus Offers. This promotional technique, very similar to discounting, is also widely used in the food industry. In a bonus offer, the guest buys a product or service at the regular price and then receives a bonus. For example, guests receive three dinners at the regular price and a fourth dinner free. Bonus offers can be used with coupons. These can be very effective in attracting new guests and increasing food and beverage revenue.

Public Relations

Marketing and sales staff will probably spend a significant amount of time on various public relations activities. Public relations, as the term indicates, fosters a good relationship between the operation and the public. It also maintains good relations with the media, competitors, chambers of commerce, convention bureaus, trade and visitors' bureaus, business groups, trade associations, government groups, employees, and, especially, current and future guests.

Publicity and the Media. Public relations departments work most often with television, radio, newspapers, and magazines. One of the challenges facing the marketing and sales staff is getting **publicity** in the media. Publicity refers to editorial coverage as opposed to advertising.

Publicity is important because it helps create a public image for the property. While the property has less control over publicity than advertising, publicity is often more credible. That is, the public generally believes what the media say more than it believes paid advertising.

Some people think publicity is free. Though the property does not pay the media directly for publicity, it spends a good deal of money to generate it. Merely hiring someone at the property to generate publicity requires money. The property may also spend money on a variety of events or activities that will generate publicity.

To get publicity, the property must make news in some way. The public relations department anticipates newsworthy events involving the property and informs the media about them. Staff hope the media will cover these events and create a favorable impression of the property. Newsworthy events might include the grand opening of an operation, the opening of a new wing or remodeled section, the opening of the facility under new ownership or new management, or the celebration of a significant anniversary of the property. Often, managers host a party along with these events and invite members of the media.

Public relations staff often ask media travel writers, restaurant reviewers, or free-lance writers eager for a good story to visit the operation. Staff hope these reviews will be positive and generate sales as a result.

Even handling emergencies and accidents effectively can create a favorable public impression of the operation and improve its chances for long-term survival.

Public Relations and the Community. Hospitality operations of all sizes may participate in charity work. They collect donations from employee paychecks, sponsor fund-raising activities, support telethons, and contribute company funds. Other examples of community public relations activities include sponsoring Little League teams, bowling teams, Boy Scout and Girl Scout troops, and other local organizations.

The Employee's Role in Public Relations. Meeting and exceeding guest expectations contributes to good public relations and to the success of the operation. Hospitality managers keep employees well-informed of special programs and important groups meeting in the facility. A well-informed employee can greatly aid the property's selling efforts. Actually, sales and marketing is the only division with an overall view of the operation. The division is therefore in the best position to help managers deliver the best products for guests.

Endnotes

1. This discussion of situation analysis is drawn from Julia Crystler, *Situation Analysis Workbook* (East Lansing, Mich.: Educational Institute of the American Hotel & Motel Association, and Hotel Sales and Marketing Association International, Washington, D.C., 1983), pp. 1–3.

Key Terms

business mix—A hotel's desired blend of business from various segments such as business transient, corporate group, leisure, and convention.

feasibility study—A study that analyzes a proposed site to determine what type of property has the best chance for success. It ultimately determines whether investors should construct or purchase an operation. It concentrates on four areas: location, guest demographics, the competition, and financial analysis.

gross operating profit—Departmental profits minus other overheads.

key account—A prospective guest that the property especially wants to attract.

market—A group of current or potential guests identified by geographic location, industry, economic status, or behavioral characteristics.

market mix—The various market segments a property hopes to attract.

market segment—A group of consumers with similar needs, wants, backgrounds, incomes, buying habits, and so on.

marketing strategy—The marketing approaches and tools used to attract a property's market mix.

publicity—Editorial coverage as opposed to advertising.

public space—Areas of a hotel that can be privately reserved by groups.

situation analysis—Survey commonly performed by a marketing department using customer input and feedback to analyze a marketing strategy.

Review Questions

1. In what three ways can markets be divided and tracked? Describe them.
2. What major effect did the Great Depression have on marketing?
3. What are the basic responsibilities of a convention services department?
4. In what ways have hotels imitated marketing practices used by airlines?
5. What role does marketing play in a hotel's feasibility study?
6. What location-related criteria are used in feasibility studies?

7. Do guest comment cards serve any useful purpose to a hotel?

8. What are the pros and cons of convention business for hotels of different types?

9. What is internal selling? Cite examples of it.

10. What are the differences between publicity and advertising?

Internet Sites

For more information, visit the following Internet sites. Remember that Internet addresses can change without notice. If the site is no longer there, use a browser to look for additional sites.

Associations

American Hotel & Motel Association (AH&MA)
http://www.ahma.com

Association of Corporate Travel Executives
http://www.acte.org

The Educational Foundation of NRA
http://www.restaurant.org/educate/educate.htm

The Educational Institute of AH&MA
http://www.ei–ahma.org

Hospitality Sales and Marketing Association International (HSMAI)
http://www.hsmai.org

International Association for Exposition Management (IAEM)
http://www.iaem.org

International Hotel & Restaurant Association
http://www.ih–ra.com

International Association of Convention and Visitors Bureaus (IACVB)
http://www.iacvb.org

International Society of Meeting Planners
http://www.iami.org/ismp.html

Meeting Professionals International (MPI)
http://www.mpiweb.org

National Restaurant Association (NRA)
http://www.restaurant.org

Publication—Online and Printed

Convene
http://www.pcma.org/pub_convene.htm

Event Solutions
http://www.successmtgs.com

Meeting News
http://www.meetingnews.com

Meetings and Travel Online
http://www.mtonline.com

The Meeting Professional
http://www.mpiweb.org/tmp.htm

Meetings and Conventions
http://www.traveler.net/m+c/index.html

Publications—Online and Printed *(continued)*

Meetings in the West
http://www.meetingsweb.com

Successful Meetings
http://www.successmtgs.com

Trade Show Central
http://www.tscentral.com

Trade Show News Network
http://www.tsnn.com

Tradeshow Week
http://www.tradeshowweek.com

Chapter 12 Outline

What Is Accounting?
    Who Manages the Accounting System?
    Who Uses Financial Information?
Accounting Principles and Practices
    Generally Accepted Accounting Principles (GAAP)
    Uniform System of Accounts
Accounting Tools
    Operating Budgets
    Income Statements
    Balance Sheets
    Ratio Analysis Techniques
Managerial Accounting
    Internal Controls
    Other Managerial Accounting Techniques
Routine Activities of the Accounting Division
    Revenue Accounting
    Expense Accounting
    Salary and Wage Accounting
Purchasing
    Objectives of Effective Purchasing
    Purchasing Equipment, Supplies, and Services
    Food Purchasing
    Ethics and Supplier Relationships

12

The Accounting Division

IN THE HIGHLY COMPETITIVE FIELD of hospitality, successful careers often depend on the ability of managers to make daily operating decisions based on their analyses of financial information. The primary responsibility of the accounting division is to supply management with the financial information needed to make these decisions. In order to achieve satisfactory profit objectives for their areas of responsibility, managers must thoroughly understand how the accounting division accumulates and processes financial information. Moreover, the results of operating decisions are reflected in the information gathered by the accounting division, and managers themselves are evaluated, in part, by assessing whether their decisions improved the profitability of the business.

What Is Accounting?

Accounting can be thought of as the "language of business," a language with its own vocabulary, rules, and procedures that turn financial data into useful reports. Basic accounting activities include recording, classifying, and summarizing financial information. *Recording business transactions* refers to the procedure of entering the results of transactions in an accounting document called a **journal**. *Classifying* refers to the process of assembling the numerous business transactions into related categories. *Summarizing* refers to the preparation of financial information according to the formats of specific reports or *financial statements*.

Simply put, accounting is a language that "translates" ideas, decisions, and actions into dollars and cents. For example, a manager may have very creative ideas for new menus or for innovative guest services, but, before these become reality, the ideas must be reduced to numbers—the symbols of accounting. Accounting systems provide a framework for evaluating the potential worth of ideas, and, once concepts are implemented, these systems help to assess how successful those ideas have been in reality.

Those new to the field of hospitality sometimes think that accounting can be understood only by specialists who thrive on "number crunching." However, accounting theory and practice is not based on complicated mathematics; it is based on *logic* and uses basic terminology, fundamental concepts, and relatively straightforward procedures. Applying the logic of accounting requires only the most basic math skills: addition, subtraction, multiplication, and division. Once the terminology, concepts, and procedures of accounting are mastered, accounting practices are not as difficult to understand as some people tend to believe. The important point is that accounting is a means to an end (a profitable or efficient operation) and not an end in itself.[1]

Who Manages the Accounting System?

Top-level managers are ultimately responsible for the financial status of the property, but, since the general manager is extremely busy with a wide range of responsibilities, staff (advisory) personnel are needed to manage the accounting system. Small properties may employ a staff **bookkeeper** (someone who records and classifies business transactions) and/or hire an outside accountant to design and manage the accounting system. Large properties require a division of several people headed by a **controller** to account for and summarize the results of the numerous transactions that take place in a hotel or restaurant. Regardless of property size, accounting personnel must possess specialized technical knowledge and skills and must have experience and objective judgment.

Individuals unfamiliar with accounting activities often believe that a controller is simply a glorified bookkeeper. However, there are many important differences between the two. Bookkeepers conduct only one part of the overall accounting function. The controller supervises the work of bookkeepers and also interprets accounting data. Because the controller's job is more demanding than a bookkeeper's, it requires more training.

The controller oversees the development of systems for recording, classifying, and summarizing financial information. In addition, the controller may also design and monitor internal controls, prepare forecasts and coordinate the budgeting process of the property, conduct cost and feasibility studies, prepare tax returns, analyze the results of operations, and advise management.

Who Uses Financial Information?

The users of financial information are classified as internal and external users. In hotels and restaurants, all managers are internal users of financial statements. These managers use financial statements and reports to analyze and control revenues and expenses and to manage the financial position of the business. External users include:

- Owners and investors—Owners include stockholders, partners, and proprietors. Investors are potential owners. The primary concern of owners is the past, present, and future profitability of the business. Dividends to the stockholders and increases in ownership to partners and proprietors depend on the profitability of the business.

- Creditors and lenders—Short-term creditors want to know that there are sufficient assets (resources of value) that could be converted to cash to repay loans made to the business. Long-term lenders are more interested in current and future profits available to the hospitality operation that can be used to make future loan payments.

- Government agencies—A business pays many different taxes to various government agencies—federal, state, and local—that want to ensure that they collect the proper amount of tax. Some of the taxes are: income taxes, payroll taxes, sales taxes, property taxes, hotel occupancy taxes, and alcoholic beverage taxes.

- General public—Community pride and growth is often fostered by successful hospitality properties in the area. The general public has an economic interest in the success of any business that provides jobs.

Accounting Principles and Practices

As noted previously, accounting is the language of business, and it must be widely understood to be useful. Uniformity in accounting terminology and in methods of recording financial transactions helps make accounting more widely understood. This uniformity has evolved largely through the efforts of the American Institute of Certified Public Accountants (AICPA). This organization has been instrumental in developing generally accepted accounting principles used in the United States.

Generally Accepted Accounting Principles (GAAP)

For almost every profession there are guidelines and rules to ensure that members carry out their responsibilities according to accepted standards. In the field of accounting, these standards are known as **generally accepted accounting principles (GAAP)**.

The application of generally accepted accounting principles ensures that business transactions are recorded and financial statements are prepared according to consistent accounting procedures. This consistency allows internal and external users of financial statements to make reasonable judgments about the overall financial condition of a business and the success of business operations from period to period. Some of the generally accepted accounting principles that hospitality managers should know are discussed in the following sections.

Unit of Measurement. Money is the standard medium of exchange in virtually every nation. Therefore, accountants use the prevailing monetary unit to record the results of business transactions. For businesses in the United States, the common unit of measurement is the U.S. dollar. A common unit of measurement permits the users of accounting data to compare current and past business transactions. Imagine the difficulties that would arise if the accounting records of a hospitality operation recorded food purchases in terms of the British pound and food sales in terms of the U.S. dollar!

Historical Cost. The principle of historical cost states that the value of merchandise or services obtained through business transactions should be recorded in terms of actual costs, not current market values. For example, assume that a truck having a market value of $15,000 is purchased from a seller for $12,800. The amount recorded as the cost of the truck is $12,800. As long as the truck is owned by the business, the value (cost) shown in the accounting records and on the financial statements will be $12,800.

Going Concern. The principle of going concern (also known as *continuity of the business unit*) requires financial statements to be prepared under the assumption that the business will continue indefinitely and thus carry out its commitments. Normally, a business is assumed to be a going concern unless there is objective evidence to the contrary. The principle of going concern can be used to defend the use of historical costs in the presentation of financial statements. Since the assumption is that the business will not fail in the immediate future, the use of market values would not be appropriate unless the principle of conservatism applies.

Conservatism. The principle of conservatism guides the decisions of accountants in areas that involve estimates and other areas that may call for professional judgment. However, it is important to stress that this principle applies only when there is uncertainty in reporting factual results of business transactions. The principle of conservatism provides accountants with a practical alternative for situations that involve doubt. When doubt is involved, the solution or method that will not overstate assets or income should be selected.

Objectivity. The principle of objectivity states that all business transactions must be supported by objective evidence proving that the transactions did in fact occur. Obtaining objective evidence is not always a simple matter. For example, a canceled check serves as objective evidence that cash was paid. However, it is not evidence of the reason for which the check was issued. An invoice or other form of independent evidence is necessary to prove the reason for the expenditure. When independent evidence is not available to document a business transaction, estimates must be made. In these cases, the choice of the best estimate should be guided by the principle of objectivity.

Realization. Under the realization principle, revenues resulting from business transactions are recorded only when a sale has been made *and* earned, when a hotel receives cash from a guest served in the dining room, for example. The results of the transaction are recorded to the proper accounts.

However, according to the principle of realization, if a hotel receives cash for services that have not yet been earned, the transaction cannot be classified as a sale. For example, if a hotel receives an advance deposit of $500 for a wedding banquet to be held two months later, the cash received must be recorded—but the event cannot be classified as a sale. This is because the business has not yet earned the revenue; services have not been performed or delivered.

Matching. The matching principle states that all expenses must be recorded in the same accounting period as the revenue that they helped to generate. When expenses are matched with the revenue they helped to produce, external and internal users of financial statements can make better judgments about the financial position and operating performance of the hospitality business. There are two accounting methods for determining when to record the results of a business transaction: cash accounting and accrual accounting.

Cash accounting. The cash accounting method records the results of business transactions only when cash is received or paid out. Small businesses usually follow cash accounting procedures in their day-to-day bookkeeping activities. However, financial statements prepared solely from cash accounting sources may not necessarily comply with generally accepted accounting principles. If expenses are recorded on the basis of cash disbursements, expenses will not necessarily match the revenue that they helped to generate. This may occur for any number of reasons.

For example, assume that each month a new accounting period for a particular restaurant begins. During each month, the restaurant follows the principle of realization and records revenue only as sales are made and earned. The restaurant also records expenses only as cash payments (which include payments by check) are made to various suppliers and vendors. Cash accounting will not ensure that expenses will match the revenue generated during the month because many expenses will be incurred during each month but not paid until the following month. These expenses include utility bills, laundry bills, and telephone bills that the restaurant may not even receive until the first week of the following month.

The Internal Revenue Service generally will accept financial statements prepared on a cash accounting basis only if the business does not sell inventory products and meets other criteria. Since food and beverage operations sell inventory products, these establishments must use the accrual method.

Accrual accounting. To conform to the matching principle, most hospitality operations use the accrual method of accounting. Accrual accounting adjusts the accounting records by recording expenses that are incurred during an accounting period but that (for any number of reasons) are not actually paid until the following period. Once the adjusting entries have been recorded, financial statements and reports for the accounting period will provide a reasonable basis for evaluating the financial position and operating performance of the hospitality business.

Consistency. There are several accounting methods that determine certain values used as accounting data. For example, there are several methods for determining inventory values. Deciding which accounting method to use is the responsibility of the property's high-level managers. The generally accepted accounting principle of consistency states that, once an accounting method has been adopted, it should be followed consistently from period to period. In order for accounting information to be comparable, there must be a consistent application of accounting methods and principles. When circumstances warrant a change in the method of accounting for a specific kind of transaction, the change must be reported along with an explanation of how this change affects other items shown on the operation's financial statements.

Uniform Systems of Accounts

While generally accepted accounting principles ensure that accountants carry out their responsibilities in accordance with accepted standards, uniform systems of accounts standardize formats and account classifications and guide accountants in the preparation and presentation of financial statements. Standardization permits users of financial statements to compare the financial position and operational performance of a particular property to similar types of properties in the hospitality industry. For new businesses entering the hospitality industry, a uniform system of accounts serves as a ready-made accounting system that can be quickly adapted to the needs and requirements of the business.

A uniform system of accounts also serves as an instructional handbook because it identifies and explains many of the **line items** that may appear on the financial statements of a particular kind of business. Some line items may not apply to every kind of property in the industry, but accountants can easily adapt a uniform system to meet the individual needs of their properties by deleting or adding line items as necessary.

The idea of a uniform system of accounts is not new or unique to the hospitality industry. The *Uniform System of Accounts for Hotels* was first published in 1926 by a group of hoteliers who had the foresight to recognize the value of such a system to the hotel industry. Although there have been several revised editions since 1926, the fundamental format of the original uniform system survives as testament to the success of the system in meeting the basic needs of the industry. The ninth revised edition, now titled the *Uniform System of Accounts for the Lodging Industry*, was published in 1996.[2]

Following the lead of the lodging industry, the National Restaurant Association published the *Uniform System of Accounts for Restaurants* in 1930. Its objective was to give restaurant operators a common accounting language and to provide a basis upon which to compare the results of their operations. This uniform accounting system has been revised several times, and today many restaurant operators find it a valuable accounting handbook.[3]

There are also uniform systems of accounts for clubs, hospitals, condominium operations, and conference centers. The uniform accounting systems for the hospitality industry are continually revised to reflect changes in acceptable accounting procedures and changes in the business environment that may affect hospitality accounting. They now enjoy widespread adoption by the industry and recognition by banks and other financial institutions, as well as the courts.

Hotels, motels, restaurants, and other segments of the hospitality industry benefit from adopting the uniform system of accounts appropriate for their operations. Perhaps the greatest benefit provided is the uniformity of recording business transactions. This uniformity allows local, regional, or national statistics to be gathered, alerting the industry to threats and/or opportunities of developing trends. In the past, accounting firms serving the hospitality industry have been instrumental in standardizing reporting procedures. Today, Smith Travel Research collects and publishes statistical data on hotels. Statistical data on restaurants and private clubs is compiled by the National Restaurant Association and the Club Managers Association of America, respectively. Exhibits 1 and 2 show what happens to the average revenue dollar in the lodging and food service industries. Exhibit 3 lists a number of important sources of information for the major segments of the hospitality industry.

Accounting Tools

Some managers believe they are experts in the physical levels of production and service and prefer to leave accounting to the controller. They may reason, for example, that they have enough work to do and that the subject is too difficult and specialized. However, a fact of business life is that a manager must be able to apply the basics of managerial accounting.

Exhibit 1   Revenue and Expense Distribution Ratios to Total Revenue for U.S. Hotels

Full-Service Hotels

Revenue		Expenses	
Rooms	68.4%	Departmental	41.3%
Food	18.5%	Undistributed	26.9%
Beverage	5.0%	Management Fees	2.8%
Other Food & Beverage	2.0%	Fixed Charges	19.4%
Telephone	2.6%	Pre-Tax Income	9.6%
Minor Operated Depts.	2.0%		
Rentals & Other Income	1.5%		

Limited-Service Hotels

Revenue		Expenses	
Rooms	95.5%	Departmental	27.0%
Telephone	2.0%	Undistributed	26.4%
Minor Operated Depts.	.9%	Management Fees	3.0%
Rentals & Other Income	1.6%	Fixed Charges	20.6%
		Pre-Tax Income	23.0%

Total Lodging Industry

Revenue		Expenses	
Rooms	73.7%	Payroll	22.1%
Food & Beverage	20.5%	Departmental	16.7%
Telephone	2.5%	Undistributed	26.9%
Minor Operated Depts.	1.8%	Fixed Charges	19.8%
Rentals & Other Income	1.5%	Management Fees	2.7%
		Pre-Tax Income	11.8%

Source: *1996 HOST Report,* Smith Travel Research.

Managerial accounting systems provide financial information to managers at all organizational levels. Financial information is used to develop operating plans (for example, an operating budget), to assess how well the operation is doing (an income statement can be used for this purpose), and to make operating decisions. Detailed information about managerial accounting systems cannot be presented in this chapter. However, several basic accounting tools (operating budgets, income statements, balance sheets, and ratio analysis techniques) will be introduced.

Operating Budgets

Wise managers understand the need to plan for the future. To help do this, they use operating budgets, which are formal plans indicating the property's estimated

Exhibit 2   The Restaurant Industry Dollar

	Full Service Restaurants (Average Check Per Person Under $10)	Full Service Restaurants (Average Check Per Person Over $10)	Limited Service Fast Food Restaurants
Where It Came From			
Food Sales	87.2%	76.5%	96.4%
Beverage Sales (alcoholic)	12.8	23.5	3.6
Where It Went			
Cost of Food Sold	28.2	26.8	31.2
Cost of Beverages Sold	3.5	6.6	0.9
Salaries and Wages	29.9	28.5	24.4
Employee Benefits	3.8	4.4	2.7
Direct Operating Expenses	6.7	7.3	7.4
Music and Entertainment	0.3	0.7	0.1
Marketing	3.5	2.6	5.3
Utility Services	3.0	2.5	2.7
Restaurant Occupancy Costs	5.8	5.3	6.4
Repairs and Maintenance	1.7	2.0	1.6
Depreciation	2.1	2.1	1.7
Other Operating Expense/(Income)	0.4	(0.2)	(2.1)
General and Administrative	3.3	4.5	5.7
Corporate Overhead	1.8	1.5	1.9
Interest	0.6	0.6	1.0
Other	0.2	0.5	0.1
Income Before Income Tax	5.2%	4.3%	9.0%

Source: National Restaurant Association, *Restaurant Industry Operations Report*, 1997.

revenue and expenses. The purpose of the budget is to state how to achieve the maximum financial benefits from available resources.

The annual operating budget acts as a profit plan for the property, addressing all revenue sources and expense items. Annual budgets are commonly divided into monthly plans. These monthly plans become standards against which management can evaluate the actual results of operations. Thus, the operating budget enables management to accomplish two of its most important functions: planning and control.

The budget process requires a closely coordinated effort involving all supervisory and management personnel. Each manager responsible for a functional area within the property should participate in the budget process. When managers are given real input into the budget process, they often become more motivated to

Exhibit 3   Major Hospitality Statistical Publications

Publication	Industry Segment	Firm
Trends—Worldwide	Lodging	PKF Consulting
Trends—USA	Lodging	PKF Consulting
Clubs in Town and Country	Clubs	PKF Consulting
Directions		Coopers & Lybrand
The HOST Report	Lodging	Smith Travel Research
Restaurant Industry Operations Report	Restaurant	National Restaurant Association

implement the property's profit plan and are less likely to adhere blindly to budget numbers that they feel are imposed upon them.

The accounting division normally supplies department managers with statistical information from which they can project sales volume and revenue and estimate expenses for their areas of responsibility. The accounting division is also responsible for coordinating the budget plans of individual department managers. The controller then combines these plans into a comprehensive operating budget for the general manager's review.

The general manager and the controller review the departmental budget plans. If additional adjustments are required, they meet with the appropriate managers to identify how the adjustments will be made. If major adjustments are made, the effects of such changes on the budgets of other departments and/or the total budget package are carefully analyzed. After reviewing the final budget report with department managers, the general manager and the controller present the operating budget to the owners of the property. If the budget is not satisfactory, elements requiring change are returned to the appropriate department managers for review and revision.

To ensure that adequate time is available for preparing the operating budget, a schedule should be set and closely followed. Exhibit 4 presents a sample schedule that could be used by properties whose fiscal year coincides with the calendar year.

Budgets take time and cost money to prepare, but, done properly, they are management's primary hedge against the uncertainty of the future and an important tool in planning and control. Once developed, the budget becomes a road map to achieving profit goals and a benchmark against which actual operating results can be compared. For example, if the budget plan suggests a specified income level and certain dollar (or percentage) limitations on expenses, it will be possible to compare actual income/expense levels (from the income statement) with the operating budget. Realistically, almost all budgeted revenue and expense items will differ from actual results of operations because no budgeting process is perfect. However, significant variances should be analyzed, and managers should follow through with appropriate corrective actions.

Exhibit 4   Timetable for Operations Budgeting

Who	What	When
General Manager, Controller, Department Heads	Budget planning meetings.	October 1–31
Department Heads	Preparation of departmental budget plans.	November 1–9
Accounting	Consolidation of departmental budget plans.	November 10–19
General Manager, Controller	Preparation of the General Manager's Budget Report.	December
Owners	Review and approval of the General Manager's Budget Report.	December

Income Statements

The operating budget indicates the ideal financial picture of an operation, that is, its situation if nothing goes wrong. Typically, at the end of each month, the accounting division develops an income statement, which indicates *actual* income and expense levels. Because this statement reveals the bottom line (net income for a given period), it is one of the most important financial statements used by managers to evaluate the success of operations. It is also an important measure of the effectiveness and efficiency of management.

In the case of a restaurant, the income statement pertains to the entire property. Exhibit 5 presents a sample income statement for a small restaurant corporation.

Most hotel income statements are a consolidation of the income or expenses reported on departmental statements. Exhibit 6 presents a sample income statement for a full-service hotel. Amounts shown on the hotel income statement for the rooms division were drawn from the rooms department income statement illustrated in Exhibit 7. Exhibit 8 shows a breakdown of administrative and general expenses that are summarized on the hotel income statement.

While there are some obvious differences between the forms used by lodging and restaurant properties (many relating to differences in terminology), the basic purposes for and uses of the statements are exactly the same.

Balance Sheets

The balance sheet provides important information regarding the financial position of a hospitality business *on a given date*. The phrase *on a given date* carries an entirely different meaning from "for a period of time." A balance sheet dated December 31,

Exhibit 5   Sample Income Statement for a Small Restaurant

Deb's Steakhouse, Inc.
Statement of Income
For the Year Ended December 31, 19X2

REVENUE		
Food Sales	$120,000	
Liquor Sales	50,000	
Total Revenue		$170,000
COST OF SALES		
Food	42,000	
Liquor	11,000	
Total Cost of Sales		53,000
GROSS PROFIT		117,000
OPERATING EXPENSES		
Salaries and Wages	55,000	
Employee Benefits	7,900	
China, Glassware, and Silverware	300	
Kitchen Fuel	900	
Laundry and Dry Cleaning	2,100	
Credit Card Fees	1,500	
Operating Supplies	5,000	
Advertising	2,000	
Utilities	3,800	
Repairs and Maintenance	1,900	
Total Operating Expenses		80,400
INCOME BEFORE FIXED CHARGES AND INCOME TAXES		36,600
FIXED CHARGES		
Rent	6,000	
Property Taxes	1,500	
Insurance	3,600	
Interest Expense	3,000	
Depreciation	5,500	
Total Fixed Charges		19,600
INCOME BEFORE INCOME TAXES		17,000
INCOME TAXES		2,000
NET INCOME		$ 15,000

Source: Raymond Cote, *Understanding Hospitality Accounting I,* 4th ed. (East Lansing, Mich.: Educational Institute of the American Hotel & Motel Association, 1997), p. 69.

Exhibit 6 Sample Income Statement for a Hotel

Hotel DORO, Inc.
Statement of Income
For the year ended December 31, 19X2

Schedule A

	Schedule	Net Revenue	Cost of Sales	Payroll and Related Expenses	Other Expenses	Income (Loss)
Operated Departments						
Rooms	A1	$ 897,500		$ 143,140	$ 62,099	$ 692,261
Food and Beverage	A2	524,570	$ 178,310	204,180	54,703	87,377
Telephone	A3	51,140	60,044	17,132	1,587	(27,623)
Other Operated Departments	A4	63,000	10,347	33,276	6,731	12,646
Rentals and Other Income	A5	61,283				61,283
Total Operated Departments		1,597,493	248,701	397,728	125,120	825,944
Undistributed Expenses						
Administrative and General	A6			97,632	66,549	164,181
Marketing	A7			35,825	32,043	67,868
Property Operation and Maintenance	A8			36,917	24,637	61,554
Energy Costs	A9				47,312	47,312
Total Undistributed Expenses				170,374	170,541	340,915
Income Before Fixed Charges		$1,597,493	$ 248,701	$ 568,102	$ 295,661	$ 485,029
Fixed Charges						
Rent	A10					28,500
Property Taxes	A10					45,324
Insurance	A10					6,914
Interest	A10					192,153
Depreciation and Amortization	A10					146,000
Total Fixed Charges						418,891
Income Before Income Taxes and Gain on Sale of Property						66,138
Gain on Sale of Property						10,500
Income Before Income Taxes						76,638
Income Taxes						16,094
Net Income						$ 60,544

Source: Raymond Cote, *Understanding Hospitality Accounting II,* 3d ed. (East Lansing, Mich.: Educational Institute of the American Hotel & Motel Association, 1997), p. 138.

19X2, shows the financial position of the business *on December 31, 19X2,* not for the month of December or any other period of time. The balance sheet is like a snapshot of the financial condition of the business. The exposure captures just one moment of the business's financial condition.

Hospitality managers have a more direct and immediate need for information on income statements but, at the same time, find balance sheets useful for conveying

Exhibit 7   Rooms Department Income Statement for a Hotel

Hotel DORO, Inc.		
Rooms Department Income Statement		
For the year ended December 31, 19X2		**Schedule A1**
Revenue		
Room Sales		$900,000
Allowances		2,500
Net Revenue		$897,500
Expenses		
Salaries and Wages	$120,000	
Employee Benefits	23,140	
Total Payroll and Related Expenses		143,140
Other Expenses		
Commissions	2,500	
Contract Cleaning	5,285	
Guest Transportation	10,100	
Laundry and Dry Cleaning	7,000	
Linen	11,000	
Operating Supplies	11,125	
Reservation Expenses	9,950	
Uniforms	2,167	
Other Operating Expenses	2,972	
Total Other Expenses		62,099
Total Expenses		205,239
Departmental Income (Loss)		$692,261

Source: Raymond Cote, *Understanding Hospitality Accounting II,* 3d ed. (East Lansing, Mich.: Educational Institute of the American Hotel & Motel Association, 1997), p. 132.

financial information to creditors and investors. Understanding how the statement is used to reveal the financial position of a business is the key to understanding the logic behind the sequence of categories that appear on the statement. The major categories that appear on the balance sheet are:

- Assets
- Liabilities
- Equity

Simply stated, assets represent anything a business owns that has commercial or exchange value. Liabilities represent the claims of outsiders (such as creditors) to assets. And equity represents the claims of owners to assets. On every balance sheet, the total assets must always agree (that is, balance) with the combined totals of the liabilities and equity sections. Therefore, the very format of the balance sheet reflects the fundamental accounting equation:

$$\text{Assets} = \text{Liabilities} + \text{Equity}$$

Exhibit 8   Administrative and General Department Expense Statement for a Hotel

Hotel DORO, Inc. Administrative and General Department Statement For the year ended December 31, 19X2		Schedule A6
Salaries and Wages	$85,718	
Employee Benefits	11,914	
Total Payroll and Related Expenses		$ 97,632
Other Expenses		
Credit Card Commissions	14,389	
Data Processing Expense	7,638	
Dues and Subscriptions	3,265	
Human Resources Expense	3,743	
Insurance—General	6,614	
Operating Supplies	9,784	
Postage and Telegrams	4,416	
Professional Fees	4,136	
Uncollectible Accounts	1,291	
Traveling and Entertainment	4,250	
Other Operating Expenses	7,023	
Total Other Expenses		66,549
Total Administrative and General Expenses		$164,181

Source: Raymond Cote, *Understanding Hospitality Accounting II,* 3d ed. (East Lansing, Mich.: Educational Institute of the American Hotel & Motel Association, 1997), p. 135.

Exhibit 9 illustrates a balance sheet of a hotel corporation. Exhibit 10 illustrates a balance sheet of a small restaurant corporation.

Ratio Analysis Techniques

Financial statements issued by hotels and restaurants contain a considerable amount of information. A thorough analysis of this information requires more than a simple read of the reported figures and facts. Users of financial statements need to be able to make the figures and facts reveal aspects of the property's financial situation that might be overlooked. This is accomplished through ratio analysis. A ratio mathematically expresses a significant relationship between two figures and is calculated by dividing one figure by the other.

Ratios are useful only when compared against useful criteria. Useful criteria against which to compare the results of ratio analysis include: (1) the corresponding ratio calculated for a prior period, (2) other properties and industry averages, and (3) planned ratio goals. Users of ratio analysis must be careful when comparing two different properties because the accounting procedures used by the properties may differ and their ratios may not be comparable.

Exhibit 9   Sample Balance Sheet for a Hotel

Hotel DORO, Inc.
Balance Sheet
December 31, 19X2

Schedule C

ASSETS

Current Assets		
Cash—House Banks	$ 3,500	
Cash—Demand Deposits	55,000	
Total Cash		$ 58,500
Marketable Securities		25,000
Accounts Receivable	41,216	
Less Allowance for Doubtful Accounts	1,020	40,196
Inventories		11,000
Prepaid Expenses		13,192
Total Current Assets		$ 147,888
Property and Equipment		
Land	850,000	
Building	2,500,000	
Furniture and Equipment	475,000	
Total	3,825,000	
Less Accumulated Depreciation	775,000	
Total	3,050,000	
Leasehold Improvements (net)	9,000	
China, Glassware, and Silver (net)	36,524	
Total Property and Equipment		3,095,524
Other Noncurrent Assets		
Security Deposits	1,000	
Preopening Expenses (net)	3,000	
Total Other Assets		4,000
Total Assets		$3,247,412

LIABILITIES

Current Liabilities		
Accounts Payable	$ 13,861	
Current Portion of Long-Term Debt	70,000	
Federal and State Income Taxes Payable	16,545	
Accrued Payroll	11,617	
Other Accrued Items	7,963	
Deposits and Credit Balances	3,764	
Total Current Liabilities		$ 123,750
Long-Term Debt		
Mortgage Payable	2,125,000	
Less Current Portion	70,000	
Total Long-Term Debt		2,055,000
Total Liabilities		2,178,750

SHAREHOLDERS' EQUITY

Common Stock, par value $1, authorized and		
issued 50,000 shares	50,000	
Additional Paid-In Capital	700,000	
Retained Earnings (Schedule B)	318,662	
Total Shareholders' Equity		1,068,662
Total Liabilities and Shareholders' Equity		$3,247,412

Source: Raymond Cote, *Understanding Hospitality Accounting II*, 3d ed. (East Lansing, Mich.: Educational Institute of the American Hotel & Motel Association, 1997), p. 352.

Exhibit 10   Sample Balance Sheet for a Small Restaurant

Deb's Steakhouse
Balance Sheet
December 31, 19X2

ASSETS

Current Assets

Cash	$34,000	
Accounts Receivable	4,000	
Inventories	5,000	
Prepaid Expenses	2,000	
Total Current Assets		$ 45,000

Property and Equipment

	Cost	Accumulated Depreciation	
Land	$ 30,000		
Building	60,000	$15,000	
Furniture and Equipment	52,000	25,000	
China, Glassware, Silver	8,000		
Total	150,000	40,000	110,000

Other Assets

Security Deposits	1,500	
Preopening Expenses	2,500	
Total Other Assets		4,000
Total Assets		$159,000

LIABILITIES

Current Liabilities

Accounts Payable	$ 11,000	
Sales Tax Payable	1,000	
Accrued Expenses	9,000	
Current Portion of Long-Term Debt	6,000	
Total Current Liabilities		$ 27,000

Long-Term Liabilities

Mortgage Payable	40,000	
Less Current Portion of Long-Term Debt	6,000	
Net Long-Term Liabilities		34,000
Total Liabilities		61,000

OWNER'S EQUITY

Capital, Deb Barry—December 31, 19X2		98,000
Total Liabilities and Owner's Equity		$159,000

Source: Raymond Cote, *Understanding Hospitality Accounting I,* 4th ed. (East Lansing, Mich.: Educational Institute of the American Hotel & Motel Association, 1997), p. 76.

Ratio analysis can help owners, managers, and creditors evaluate the financial condition and operation of a hotel or restaurant. However, ratios are only indicators; they do not resolve problems or actually reveal what the problems may be. At best, when ratios vary significantly from past periods, budgeted standards, or industry averages, they indicate that problems may exist. When problems appear to exist, considerably more analysis and investigation is necessary to determine the appropriate corrective actions. A full discussion of ratio analysis is beyond the scope of this chapter. However, the following paragraphs introduce common operating ratios analyzed by restaurant and hotel managers.

There are several ways to express ratios. A common way is to use a percentage. For example, a food cost percentage results when cost of food sold is divided by food sales. Using appropriate figures from Exhibit 5, the food cost percentage for Deb's Steakhouse for 19X2 can be calculated as follows:

$$\text{Food Cost Percentage} = \frac{\text{Cost of Food Sales}}{\text{Food Sales}}$$

$$= \frac{\$42{,}000}{\$120{,}000}$$

$$= .35, \text{ or } 35\%$$

In this example, food costing $42,000 is sold for $120,000. That is, for every dollar of food sold, 35 cents was required to cover the costs of food sales. Food cost percentages are often calculated on a daily basis. Most food and beverage managers separate food income and costs from beverage income and costs to more closely monitor these important revenue centers. If this is not done, food or beverage income may be too low or expenses too high without the manager being able to isolate the specific problem.

A second way to express a ratio is to use *per-unit* information. For example, an average breakfast check may be calculated for a meal period by dividing the total breakfast sales by the number of breakfasts served. Another way to express a ratio is to use a turnover rate. For example, seat turnover for a meal period can be determined by dividing the number of customers served by the number of dining room seats available.

Operating ratios useful to hotel managers relate revenue or expenses to total revenue. For example, using figures from Exhibit 6, rooms net revenue at the Hotel DORO ($897,500) is divided by the total revenue figure ($1,597,493) to yield the percentage amount of approximately 56 percent. This means that room sales accounted for 56 percent of the total revenue taken in by the Hotel DORO during the year 19X2. Administrative and general expenses for the year 19X2 were $97,632. These expenses can be expressed as a percentage of total revenue by dividing $97,632 by $1,597,493. The ratio result yields a percentage amount of approximately 6 percent. This means that for every $1 of revenue generated during the year, 6 cents went to cover administrative and general expenses.

Revenue and expense ratios can also be calculated from figures on departmental income or expense statements. These ratios are useful for control purposes when the ratio results are compared to budgeted or planned ratio goals. There are literally hundreds of operating ratios that can be calculated. Exhibit 11 suggests over 200 of them.

The Role of Accounting in Control

What is control? Some people think that the management task of control merely involves physical activities such as locking up money in a safe, limiting access to keys, using a perpetual inventory system for expensive items, and so forth. While these tasks are part of control, an effective control system is much broader in scope. It actually involves five steps:

1. Establish ideal standards indicating what things would be like if nothing went wrong. For example, the food and beverage manager may determine that a 35 percent food cost in the coffee shop is a realistic goal. (That is, of all the income generated by sales in the coffee shop, 35 percent of this income will be used to pay for food used to generate the income.)

2. Assess actual costs. At this point, accounting procedures come into focus. Pre-established, acceptable accounting procedures must be used to determine actual food costs. The food and beverage manager must work with the accountant to determine how to collect information about applicable costs. The report of actual costs is typically presented in the income statement in a restaurant operation or in records generated in support of that document in a hotel operation with more than one food service outlet.

3. Compare standard costs with actual costs.

4. If the comparison reveals a variance between what costs are and what they should be, corrective action is required to bring costs closer to the planned standard cost level. At this point, physical actions such as securing income, limiting access to food storage areas, and keeping perpetual inventory are implemented.

5. Evaluate the extent to which the corrective actions have been effective. This evaluation must look at both the specific problem (such as high food costs) and related areas (such as marketing concerns if food costs are lowered by reducing portion sizes).

Managerial Accounting

Managerial accounting is the branch of accounting that uses various techniques and concepts to process historical and forecasted information for planning and control decisions. Data generated by the accounting system must be analyzed and interpreted if it is to be useful. Hospitality managers can use a variety of analytical techniques and reports for controlling and planning operations.[4]

Internal Controls

A small owner-operated hospitality business often restricts its recordkeeping and control systems to those required by governmental agencies and creditors. Since the owner handles all incoming cash and makes all payments, his or her presence

Exhibit 11   Operating Ratios Useful in Analysis

CERTAIN OPERATING RATIOS USEFUL IN ANALYSIS	% of Total Revenues	% of Depart. Revenues	% of Depart. Total Cost	% Change from Prior Period	% Change from Budget	Per Available Room	Per Occupied Room	Per Available Seats	Per Cover/Guest	Per Square Foot	Per Full-time Equiv. Employee	% of Total Salaries & Wages	Per Unit Produced or Used
Total Revenues				•	•	•	•				•	•	
Rooms													
Revenue	•			•	•	•	•				•		
Salary, Wages & Burden		•	•	•	•	•	•					•	
Other Expenses		•	•	•	•	•	•						
Departmental Profit		•		•	•	•	•						
Food													
Revenue	•			•	•	•	•	•	•	•	•		
Cost of Sales		•	•	•	•				•				
Salary, Wages & Burden		•	•	•	•			•	•			•	
Other Expenses		•	•	•	•				•				
Departmental Profit		•		•	•			•	•	•	•		
Beverage													
Revenue	•			•	•	•	•	•	•	•	•		
Cost of Sales		•	•	•	•								
Salary, Wages & Burden		•	•	•	•			•				•	
Other Expenses		•	•	•	•								
Departmental Profit		•		•	•			•		•	•		
Minor Departments													
Revenue	•			•	•								
Cost of Sales		•		•	•								
Salary, Wages & Burden		•		•	•							•	
Other Expenses		•		•	•								
Departmental Profit		•		•	•								
Administrative & General													
Salary, Wages & Burden	•			•	•	•	•					•	
Other Expenses	•			•	•	•	•						
Departmental Total Cost	•			•	•	•	•						
Marketing													
Salary, Wages & Burden	•			•	•	•	•					•	
Other Expenses	•			•	•	•	•						
Departmental Total Cost	•			•	•	•	•						

(continued)

Exhibit 11 *(continued)*

CERTAIN OPERATING RATIOS USEFUL IN ANALYSIS	% of Total Revenues	% of Depart. Revenues	% of Depart. Total Cost	% Change from Prior Period	% Change from Budget	Per Available Room	Per Occupied Room	Per Available Seats	Per Cover/Guest	Per Square Foot	Per Full-time Equiv. Employee	% of Total Salaries & Wages	Per Unit Produced or Used
Property Operation & Maintenance													
Salary, Wages & Burden	•			•	•	•	•					•	
Other Expenses	•			•	•	•	•						
Subtotal Maintenance	•			•	•	•	•						
Energy Cost	•			•	•	•	•						•
Departmental Total Cost	•			•	•	•	•						
House Laundry													
Salary, Wages & Burden	•			•	•	•	•					•	•
Other Expenses	•			•	•	•	•						•
Departmental Total Cost	•			•	•	•	•						•
Food & Beverage (or Outlets)													
Revenue	•	•		•	•	•	•						
Salary, Wages & Burden		•		•	•							•	
Other Expenses		•		•	•								
Departmental Total Cost		•		•	•								
Total Other Expenses	•			•	•	•	•						
Payroll Burden Items	•			•	•						•	•	
Total Salary & Wages	•			•	•	•	•				•		
Capital Expenses													
Property Taxes	•			•	•	•	•			•			•
Insurance	•			•	•	•	•						•
Rent/Lease	•			•	•	•	•						
Interest	•			•	•	•	•						•
Management Fee	•			•	•	•	•						
Debt Service	•			•	•	•	•						•
FF&E Reserve/Replacement	•			•	•	•	•						

helps ensure smooth and efficient operations. However, as an operation increases in size or becomes multi-unit, managers increasingly need timely and accurate reports and analysis systems to control and manage the business.

Internal controls are those procedures and methods adopted by the manager to safeguard the assets of the business, to ensure proper accountability, and to promote efficient operations. Internal control begins with an organization plan that clearly establishes lines of communication and levels of authority and responsibility throughout the operation. A good organization plan separates recordkeeping of assets from the actual control of assets. Additionally, the responsibility for related transactions should be separated so the work of one person can verify that of another. For example, an accounts receivable clerk should not both receive payments (control of assets) and post those payments to the accounts receivable register (recordkeeping of assets). These related transactions should be separated so that one person receives the payments and another person posts the records.

Internal controls require forms and procedures that measure the efficiency and effectiveness of the employees and provide accounting information that, when analyzed, will help identify problem areas. These controls must also be cost-effective. The potential cost savings of a particular control must outweigh the cost of implementing and continuing the control procedure.

Another element in a sound system of internal control is the effective selection, training, and supervision of personnel. The hospitality operation must have policies that define employee skill levels, education, and job responsibilities.

In addition to checks and balances inherent in a well-designed system of paperwork controls (such as pre-numbered guest checks and sales tickets) and correct use of cash registers, internal control also includes the following areas:

- Comparative statistical analysis
- Planning and forecasting sales and the cost of goods sold
- Departmental budgeting controls
- Predetermined standards and evaluation reports
- Properly designed and secured storage areas
- A system for the continuous review and evaluation of the entire internal control system

No internal control system is foolproof. However, a soundly designed and well-maintained system may reveal areas where fraudulent conversions could occur.

Other Managerial Accounting Techniques

There are many managerial accounting systems other than those dealing with control and budgeting. In fact, the only constraints on managerial accounting systems are logic and the usefulness of the information generated. Important managerial accounting techniques are cost analysis, cost-volume-profit analysis, and cash budgeting.

Cost Analysis. Managers constantly face situations in which the knowledge of costs helps them make decisions. Knowing how a particular cost relates to changes in sales volume helps managers compare actual costs and predetermined standard costs. With a knowledge of different types of costs, hospitality managers are able to select the costs relevant to a particular decision.

Cost, considered as an expense, is the reduction of an asset to ultimately increase revenue. Costs include cost of food sold, labor expense, supplies expense, utilities, marketing expense, rent expense, depreciation expense, insurance expense, and many other expenses incurred by a hospitality business as reflected on its income statement. Profitability planning requires that management examine how costs are affected by changes in sales volume (occupancy). In this context, costs can be seen as *fixed*, *variable*, or *mixed* (partly fixed and partly variable).

Fixed costs are costs that remain constant in the short run, even though occupancy may vary. Common examples of fixed costs are salaries, rent expense, insurance expense, property taxes, depreciation expense, and interest expense. Variable costs are costs that change in relation to changes in the volume of business. When a hotel is full, variable costs are at their maximum; when a hotel is empty (for example, during the off season), these costs are at a minimum or, theoretically, at zero. If variable costs are strictly defined as costs that vary in exact proportion to total sales, few, if any, costs are truly variable. However, several costs come close to this definition and may legitimately be considered variable costs. Examples of such variable costs are: the cost of food sold, the cost of beverages sold, some labor costs, and the cost of supplies used in production and service operations.

Mixed costs are costs that contain both fixed and variable cost elements. These costs are sometimes referred to as *semi-variable* or *semi-fixed* costs. For example, expenses incurred by a resort's telephone, golf course, or tennis operation have a fixed cost portion that is independent of the amount of guest usage. Costs incurred by these operations also contain a variable portion that is assumed to vary with the amount of guest usage. Although in practice the variable element of a mixed cost may not be directly proportional to usage or sales volume, this assumption is generally accepted.

Cost-Volume-Profit (CVP) Analysis. An important tool used to set specific profit objectives is cost-volume-profit (CVP) analysis. CVP analysis expresses (in either graphic or equation form) the relationships between costs, sales volume (occupancy), and profits. This profitability planning tool enables hotel managers to determine the level of occupancy necessary to achieve a specific amount of profit for operations. CVP analysis can also be used to determine the break-even point for a hotel—the level of occupancy at which total revenue equals total costs. In addition, CVP analysis can be used to determine the amount of profit (or loss) that can be expected at any occupancy level.

Cash Budgeting. Cash budgeting is extremely helpful in managing the property's cash flow. A cash budget helps ensure that the operation has enough cash to pay bills when due and, during periods of excess cash, that the excess is invested wisely. Cash budgeting differs from operational budgeting in that it shows when cash is collected and when expenses are paid. The operating budget shows sales when they are earned (not when cash is received) and expenses when they occur (not when they are paid). It is very possible for a hospitality operation to show a profit in the operating budget and on the income statement, but still not have enough cash to pay bills when due.

Routine Activities of the Accounting Division

The routine work of the hotel or restaurant accounting division falls into three categories: revenue, expenses, and payroll. Accounting functions in hotels are more complicated than those in restaurants, so this discussion will focus primarily on hotels. Keep in mind, however, that many of the principles discussed here apply to restaurants as well as hotels.

Revenue Accounting

When charges for a hotel guest are incurred, these charges must be entered into the guest folio. These transactions must usually be authorized by a source document—a guest check from a restaurant, for example. In a manual system, the guest check is hand-carried to the front desk when the charge is posted to the guest folio. Computerized point-of-sale (POS) systems electronically transmit charges from their point of origin (in this case, the restaurant) to the front desk.

All charges sent to the front office cashier, either manually or by computer, must also be posted in the guest ledger (containing all the accounts of people staying at the hotel) or the city ledger (the accounts of local businesspeople, credit card accounts of people not residing in the hotel, and unpaid accounts of departed guests). As with folio entries, posting in the ledger may be done by hand or by computers that accomplish this work in a fraction of the time.

At the close of each day, the night auditor recaps the type and amount of business done by each department. Sources of information include cashier reports from each department producing revenue and data from the city and guest ledgers.

The night auditor starts with the food and beverage recap. Working with cashiers' reports from the hotel's restaurant(s) and with register readings, the night auditor compiles a complete record of food and beverage sales for the day. The next step is to complete the rooms revenue. The night auditor posts all room charges to the guest accounts while working in conjunction with the night front desk agent (who must prepare a report). The night auditor also posts any late charges that come in after the front office cashier has left duty. Once all room and late charges are posted, the night auditor compares machine totals with individual reports. Any discrepancies must be checked and corrected.

Having compiled and audited the day's revenue from each department of the hotel, the night auditor turns over all data to the auditor. Once the auditor has compiled, checked, and certified all revenue data from the previous day, he or she completes a daily occupancy and gross revenue report. This report informs the manager of the day's activities. It is a vital tool, since it provides a complete picture of the operation. Data from this report will be discussed by the manager with department heads and other members of the staff. The exact form of the report depends upon the individual manager or the chain.

With the morning reports out of the way, the accounting division turns its attention to recording the revenue figures in the books. The net revenue figures for each department, taken from the daily revenue report, are posted in the sales journal. At the end of the month, the departmental totals of the sales journal are posted to the ledger. The remaining step is to transfer figures from the ledger to the monthly financial statements.

Expense Accounting

The second category of accounting work involves handling expenses. All purchases by the property must be certified, recorded, and paid. Larger hotels have a purchasing agent, and all purchases are made through this office; however, most properties are not large enough to require such a position. In other cases, purchases are made by individual department heads with the approval of the manager. In most cases, the manager's approval is merely a formality, since the goods have already arrived and may be in use. Ideally, the manager trusts the integrity of department managers and knows they will always obtain approval before entering large orders. In properties using a purchase-order system, the manager approves every expenditure before it is made. A purchase-order system provides close control over expenses, but it also involves much more paperwork than other systems. Which system is used depends entirely on the management policy of each property.

A simple purchase might move through the accounting channels like this: A department head places an order and an invoice arrives in the accounting office. It is stamped when received and then sent to the appropriate department head who initials the invoice to signify that the goods have been received, that they are in order, and that the charge is correct. The invoice is then returned to the accounts payable clerk, who posts the invoice to a purchase voucher. The clerk checks additions and extensions and routes the invoice to the auditor, who charges the purchase to the appropriate expense account. From here, the invoice is sent to the manager for approval, then returned to the accounts payable clerk, who distributes the figures. That is, the clerk checks the proper category and lists the account number and the amount of the purchase. At the end of the month, the amounts are totaled, allowable discount (if any) is calculated, and the voucher is sent to the auditor who writes a check that is sent to the purveyor. The voucher is entered in the voucher register and the check in the check register. The check and voucher registers are closed to the ledger. At the end of the month, the ledgers are totaled and the financial statements are prepared.

For food and beverage, this procedure is altered somewhat. The invoice arrives with the food or beverage. The steward and/or receiving clerk check(s) all foods and beverages for quantity, quality, and price before accepting them. The steward signs the invoice and forwards it to the accounting office, which performs the necessary changes, distributions, and postings.

Purchasing is discussed in greater detail later in this chapter.

Salary and Wage Accounting

The third principal area of work in accounting involves the preparation and payment of salaries and wages. The payroll clerk sets up an individual earnings record and fills out a time card for every employee. Federal tax forms must be filed and notation of any deductions (insurance, bonds, charities, and so forth) must be made. During the payroll period, the clerk makes up the payroll recap sheet, which lists all employees by departments. On the 15th of the month, the time cards are pulled and compared with the time books kept by department heads.

Today, computerized time check systems are available that automatically record hours worked, pay, withholding taxes, benefits, and so forth for each employee. These systems can also tally labor cost and related information by position, shift, department, and so forth, so that this information can be used for labor control purposes. Some units will even complete required governmental tax withholding and other forms.

Properties without computerized systems must either complete payroll records manually or send basic information (hours worked and pay data) to outside bookkeeping agencies or banks for machine processing and totaling of payroll information.

Purchasing

As noted previously, a purchasing agent is often part of the accounting staff at large hospitality properties, though each department head is often responsible for his or her own purchases in a small property. Like all members of the accounting division, purchasers are there to assist other staff members who must use products to be purchased. For example, the chef and/or food and beverage manager must make the final decision about the need for and quality of food products to be used, although the purchasing department may make suggestions.

Lodging and food service operations must purchase a wide variety of products, supplies, and services in the course of daily operations. The purchasing process is complex and multi-faceted, and its proper functioning is vital to the success of the restaurant or hotel. A property cannot provide the best possible products and services or reach its financial goals unless the purchaser does a good job.

Good purchasing systems will have written procedures that are approved by management and adhered to by all those involved. It is also important to have purchase specifications covering at least the expensive and high-volume purchase items. A testing committee under the direction of management and supervised by the purchasing agent is also useful. Every price or transaction either should be verified in writing through the routine use of a system that secures competitive prices or should be the result of a system of negotiated prices.

Purchasing involves a wide range of activities, such as:

- Assessing the quality and quantity of items that are needed
- Selecting suppliers and arranging deliveries
- Negotiating prices, expediting (following up on late deliveries and other problems), and arranging for payment terms
- Maintaining records, controlling inventories, and inspecting products

Insider Insights

Stephen Rushmore, MAI, CRE, CHA
President
Hospitality Valuation Services
Mineola, New York _____

My career in the hospitality industry led me to discover a unique product niche that I have developed into a major service organization used by hotel owners, lenders, and operators.

After attending the Cornell hotel school as an undergraduate and the University of Buffalo's business school as a graduate student, I was hired by Stephen W. Brener of Helmsley-Spear, a large real estate firm in New York City. Steve's Hospitality Division was a full-service hotel consulting firm with a definite real estate orientation. It specialized in hotel brokerage, management, and consulting. I worked in the consulting area, which gave me experience in market-feasibility studies and appraisals.

After taking several of the introductory appraisal courses required to become a member of the Appraisal Institute, I was surprised to learn there was virtually no body of knowledge devoted to the valuation of hotels and motels. Most of the national hotel accounting firms valued hotels as businesses with no consideration for the real estate, and most real estate appraisers valued hotels as real estate with no consideration for the businesses. With my educational training in the business of operating hotels and my real estate experience at Helmsley-Spear, I developed a unique hotel valuation procedure that accounts for both the business and real estate components.

Two years of research and hundreds of hours of time went into producing my first book, *The Valuation of Hotels and Motels*. This text quickly became the bible on hotel valuation when it was published by the Appraisal Institute. As author of a definitive work on a very specialized, technical subject, I soon started receiving inquiries from a variety of hotel investors looking for accurate, well-documented appraisals.

In 1980 I established Hospitality Valuation Services (HVS) as the only appraisal firm specializing exclusively in the valuation of hotels and motels. With a secretary, a computer, and a small office outside New York City, I created what became known as an economic study and appraisal. Until this time, hotel developers had to first contract with a hotel accounting firm to obtain a market feasibility study to interest lenders in making a mortgage. Once the financing was approved, an appraisal was then ordered from a real estate appraisal firm to justify the amount of the loan. Since HVS had both the market feasibility and appraisal expertise, it was able to combine both studies into a single report, saving a considerable amount of time and money in the development process. The economic study and appraisal immediately became the industry standard and HVS rapidly grew to an organization of over 60 professionals with offices in New York, San Francisco, Miami, and London.

Today, HVS offers more than just hotel market studies and valuations. It is a full-service hotel consulting firm with expertise in such areas as operational

(continued)

Insider Insights *(continued)*

reviews, litigation support, asset management, management contract and franchise negotiations, and staff planning.

To achieve its standing in the industry, HVS had to compete with several older, more established hotel consulting firms. Some of the factors giving HVS a competitive advantage and contributing to its success are summarized as follows:

- HVS professionals have college degrees in hotel administration. It is easier to teach a hotel expert the real estate business than to teach a real estate expert the hotel business.

- HVS believes that there is no substitute for quality. The client must always receive the very best.

- HVS stays on the cutting edge of technology. I continue to write books, publish articles, develop software, and create improved procedures for evaluating hotels.

- HVS always plans for the future. I always have a one-, three-, and five-year plan complete with goals and objectives. These plans can be altered at any time, but you must know where you are heading in life in order to make progress.

- Successful businesses require constant marketing. HVS markets itself by demonstrating its knowledge and expertise in the area of hotel valuations.

- HVS was built by people willing to put in the extra effort to satisfy the client, conduct the research, write the article, and be the very best in what they do. Not many businesses succeed on a 40-hour week.

The success of HVS has spawned related ventures with similar ties to the hospitality industry. HVS-associated entities actually own and operate hotels, assist others with asset management, provide investment banking and brokerage services, conduct executive searches, and consult in the health care area. This diversification not only creates synergy among these entities, but broadens everyone's professional perspective and experience.

My future goals include continued product development and looking for and then controlling unique niches. The hospitality industry has so many opportunities for those with new ideas and the drive to succeed.

- Obtaining information, studying the needs of the property, and estimating trends of future product availability, prices, and so forth

Objectives of Effective Purchasing

The goal of the purchasing process is to obtain the right product from the right supplier at the right price at the right time. It is, however, much more difficult to attain this end than to state it.

The Right Product. Generally speaking, the right product is the one that represents the greatest value to the property. The term *value* relates to concerns for both the cost and quality of items being purchased. Quality is the suitability of a product for its intended use. The wise purchaser is able to match the desired quality with the intended use to obtain the best value for the purchase dollar expended.

Purchasers record quality requirements on a purchase specification form. Exhibit 12 shows a sample form that outlines the criteria used to help develop specifications for products. Once developed, the form is given to all suppliers who can provide the product, allowing them to quote prices for comparable products.

The Right Supplier. Some hospitality managers believe that items should be purchased from the supplier with the lowest prices. In fact, there are other important concerns: The supplier must be honest and fair. He or she must know the product and the buyer's needs. Meeting quality and quantity requirements consistently is important, as is providing helpful information about products that the operation now uses or may use in the future.

Suppliers who care about their customers' needs, easing problems with deliveries, invoices, and back orders, are most likely to continue a mutually profitable business relationship with clients.

The Right Price. Price is an important consideration in all purchasing decisions. Quality (suitability for intended use) has already been noted and is integral to any discussion about purchase price. An experienced purchaser looks for ways to reduce purchase price without sacrificing minimum quality requirements. For example, the purchaser can:

- Reduce costs involving delivery, scheduling of payment, degree to which services are required, and so forth through negotiation. The purchaser can also take advantage of a supplier's wish to sell overstocked products, to break into new markets, or to increase sales during highly competitive times. It may also be possible to take advantage of special promotional discounts.

- Purchase products in larger quantities (with possible lower per-unit costs), pay cash if savings can result, or use competitive bidding procedures.

- Venture into creative price agreements. For example, perhaps selling prices can be based on a specified percentage markup above the wholesale price.

The Right Time. Sometimes prices fluctuate. When possible, wise purchasers buy larger quantities during times when prices are increasing and smaller quantities when prices are decreasing.

Many properties use a minimum-maximum inventory system to determine the number or amount of items that should be kept on hand. Under this system, a **par level** (the quantity of a product required to sustain normal operations) is established. Par level equals the **lead-time quantity** plus the **safety stock level** of any given product. The lead-time quantity is the number (or amount) of items that will be used between the time an order is made and the time it arrives on the property. The safety stock level is the number of purchase units (that is, normal size shipping containers such as cases, drums, and so on) needed in case of emergencies, spoilage, or unexpected delays in delivery. When the inventory level of an item reaches the minimum quantity, additional supplies must be ordered.

Exhibit 12　Purchase Specification Format

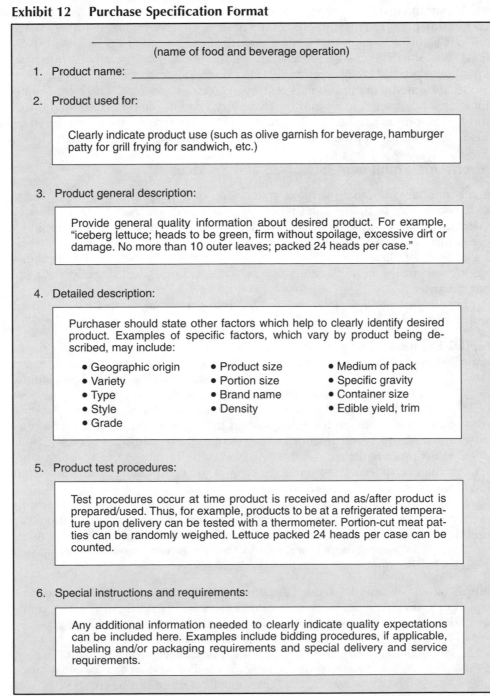

_____
(name of food and beverage operation)

1.　Product name: _____

2.　Product used for:

> Clearly indicate product use (such as olive garnish for beverage, hamburger patty for grill frying for sandwich, etc.)

3.　Product general description:

> Provide general quality information about desired product. For example, "iceberg lettuce; heads to be green, firm without spoilage, excessive dirt or damage. No more than 10 outer leaves; packed 24 heads per case."

4.　Detailed description:

> Purchaser should state other factors which help to clearly identify desired product. Examples of specific factors, which vary by product being described, may include:
>
> - Geographic origin
> - Variety
> - Type
> - Style
> - Grade
> - Product size
> - Portion size
> - Brand name
> - Density
> - Medium of pack
> - Specific gravity
> - Container size
> - Edible yield, trim

5.　Product test procedures:

> Test procedures occur at time product is received and as/after product is prepared/used. Thus, for example, products to be at a refrigerated temperature upon delivery can be tested with a thermometer. Portion-cut meat patties can be randomly weighed. Lettuce packed 24 heads per case can be counted.

6.　Special instructions and requirements:

> Any additional information needed to clearly indicate quality expectations can be included here. Examples include bidding procedures, if applicable, labeling and/or packaging requirements and special delivery and service requirements.

Source: Jack D. Ninemeier, *Planning and Control for Food and Beverage Operations*, 4th ed. (Orlando, Fla.: Educational Institute of the American Hotel & Motel Association, 1998), p. 154.

Maximum quantity is the greatest number of purchase units that should be in stock at any time. The maximum quantity must not exceed available storage space and must not be so high that large amounts of cash are tied up in unnecessary items. The shelf life of an item also affects the maximum quantity of purchase units; some products may deteriorate if stored too long before use.

As the amount of product in inventory decreases to par level, additional quantities must be ordered to rebuild the inventory level to the predetermined maximum. Computers are being used more and more frequently to establish or calculate quantities of products to purchase.

Purchasing Equipment, Supplies, and Services

Hotels and restaurants must make purchasing decisions involving major items such as ovens or computers and relatively minor items such as table napkins or business forms.[5] In other instances, purchasers may be involved in obtaining services from outside contractors for such things as pest control or maintenance of office equipment. Buyers usually deal with a distributor (a go-between who obtains products from the manufacturer) but may occasionally deal directly with the manufacturer.

Equipment purchases can be divided into three major categories—capital equipment, supplies, and services—that bear separate discussion here.

Capital Equipment. Capital equipment purchases are, simply put, "big ticket items." They are usually items that the property expects to use for a year or more. Some examples include walk-in refrigerators, guestroom furniture, and computers.

A buyer's main concern in purchasing capital equipment is to determine how well the item fulfills the function for which it is intended. For example, suppose the front office wants to buy a computer system to help staff keep records. The purchaser must not only find an affordable system, but one that does what the front office staff wants it to do and one that will be easy to learn to use. In addition, purchasers must consider the expected life span of the equipment and the projected downtime needed for routine maintenance or repair.

Suppliers generally offer warranties and provisions for servicing the equipment they sell. A good buyer will include these items in the cost considerations for capital equipment. Also, discounts are frequently offered for large or expensive orders, prompt payment, and other related factors. Buyers should ask suppliers about these discounts when they discuss purchases.

Supplies. Supplies can be defined as consumable or disposable products such as paper cups, soap, and business forms. Purchasers will typically deal with a number of distributors to keep these many small items in stock. For example, a restaurant or food and beverage division in a hotel may have different suppliers for table linens, china, flatware, dishwashing soap, and guest check forms. In addition, each of these suppliers will generally offer the same kind of product at a variety of price ranges and levels of quality. The purchaser must determine an acceptable cost and quality level for the operation and then compare items of similar quality to find the needed item at the right price.

The level of quality needed in supplies is determined by how the product will be used. Items used in front-of-the-house areas where guests will see them may be purchased largely for their appearance. For example, pink linen table napkins might be chosen because they match the dining room's china and create a pleasing effect for guests. By the same token, back-of-the-house items are generally chosen on the basis of their utility. The kitchen staff probably will not care what color the garbage bags are as long as the bags are strong enough to hold the garbage securely.

Services. Hospitality operations are increasingly using outside contractors to supply some services. Examples include pest control, office machine maintenance, and bank deposit pick-up. As a result, purchasers are often required to find companies that will provide these services at a satisfactory price.

When negotiating with service contractors, purchasers need to consider such questions as these:

- Will the contractor consider the property's individual needs?

- What equipment or supplies will the contractor use? Smelly chemicals or noisy, disruptive equipment will probably not be acceptable to guests.

- How will services be scheduled? Will the contractor offer services only at specified times, or will he or she be on call to handle problems that may arise at any time?

- How will the effectiveness of the contractor's services be monitored?

Miscellaneous Purchases. Buyers frequently must handle a number of other purchases not included in the three main categories just discussed. Vending machines, candy and tobacco, periodicals, and electronic games are all items that a hospitality operation may provide and that would involve purchasing staff.

Food Purchasing

Although poor preparation may destroy the quality of a good product, good preparation practices cannot put quality into an inferior product that should not have been purchased in the first place. The control of food costs begins at the time of purchase. No set of controls can bring back lost profits that occur through poor buying or dishonesty in buying.

The cost of food supplies accounts for about a quarter of the food sales dollar. Experience has shown that a good purchasing system can reduce food costs by 5 percent or more without reducing the quality of food supplies that are used.

The open market method of food purchasing is used by at least 90 percent of all restaurant and hotel operations. This method requires purchasers to obtain price quotations based on specifications from one or more purveyors on a daily, weekly, or monthly basis. These quotations can be obtained from weekly market lists, over the phone, or as the result of negotiated prices. The order is then placed with the purveyor submitting the best quotation.

The arrival of large restaurant and hotel chains ushered in changes in the usual open market buying methods. Large operators can make use of their concentrated buying power to make long-term contracts with national food distributors. Large multi-unit operators also take advantage of *cost-plus* arrangements (that is, supplies are purchased at cost plus a negotiated percentage). They buy directly from packers or at public produce auctions. They may also have their own private label merchandise, which is rather risky unless the volume is large and the buyer knows how to operate financially with the packers.

An effective food buyer:

- Understands how a kitchen works and what happens during food production

- Knows about market buying techniques and food distribution systems, and where to look for market trends

- Is alert to new markets and products and realizes that weather and politics can affect food supplies and prices

- Works effectively with the food service staff to develop product specifications and to perform butchering and yield tests to support the purchase specifications

- Maintains good working relations with chefs, purveyors, and department heads

- Knows about accounting controls and systems and understands the mechanics of purchase orders, invoices, receiving sheets, and credit memoranda

All food purchases should be based on the food service operation's actual need, which is determined by menus, parties actually booked or expected to be booked, and records showing the number/amount of items normally consumed by the operation. As noted previously, most good operations establish a minimum and a maximum stock level. Generally, no more than a 90-day supply of anything is purchased without the approval of the general manager.

The operation should have a good internal control system run by an alert controller and an involved manager. When the purchasers and suppliers know that they are being checked, they will do a better job than if there were no internal controls in place.

Ethics and Supplier Relationships

Purchasers should make buying decisions based on what is best for the property. A system of ethics ensures that other factors do not enter into the decision. Many operations regulate such things as acceptance of gifts and meals, purchasing for personal use, and showing favoritism to a specific supplier. Successful purchasers must be very knowledgeable as well as honest, fair, and protective of the interests and resources of the hospitality operation.

Both the purchaser and supplier need to win in the business relationship. This cannot occur if, for example, the purchaser does not honor appointments, makes suppliers wait for meetings, shares prices with other suppliers in the hopes that costs can be reduced, and so forth. The buyer must be able to interact effectively with salespeople and recognize that they are partners rather than adversaries in the food service operation. It is always best for the purchaser to think about how he or she would like to be treated if the purchaser/salesperson roles were reversed.

Endnotes

1. For a more complete discussion of the accounting function in hospitality businesses, see Raymond Cote's *Understanding Hospitality Accounting I*, 4th ed. (East Lansing, Mich.: Educational Institute of the American Hotel & Motel Association, 1997).

2. *Uniform System of Accounts for the Lodging Industry*, 9th rev. ed. (East Lansing, Mich.: Educational Institute of the American Hotel & Motel Association, 1996).

3. *Uniform System of Accounts for Restaurants*, 7th ed. (Washington, D.C.: National Restaurant Association, 1996).

4. For a more complete discussion of managerial accounting tools and techniques, see Raymond S. Schmidgall's *Hospitality Industry Managerial Accounting*, 4th ed. (East Lansing, Mich.: Educational Institute of the American Hotel & Motel Association, 1997).

5. This discussion is taken from William B. Virts, *Purchasing for Hospitality Operations* (East Lansing, Mich.: Educational Institute of the American Hotel & Motel Association, 1987), Chapter 17.

Key Terms

bookkeeper—A staff member at a small property who records and classifies business transactions.

controller—The head of an accounting division at a large property; accounts for and summarizes the results of business transactions.

generally accepted accounting principles (GAAP)—Guidelines and rules to ensure that members of the accounting profession carry out their responsibilities according to accepted standards.

journal—An accounting document used to record business transactions.

lead-time quantity—The number (or amount) of items that will be used between the time an order is made and the time it arrives on the property.

line items—Specific categories of sales or expenses tracked on an accounting statement or budget.

par level—The quantity of a product required to sustain normal operaitons.

safety stock level—The number of purchase units (that is, normal size shipping containers such as cases, drums, and so on) needed in case of emergencies, spoilage, or unexpected delays in delivery.

Review Questions

1. What functional differences exist between a hotel bookkeeper and a controller?

2. What is accrual accounting?

3. What is a uniform system of accounts? Explain its value in a hotel operation.

4. Is it necessary for all department managers to be familiar with financial information? Why or why not?

5. What is meant by the sentence, "Budgets are a hotel's road map"?

6. How does the balance sheet differ from the income statement?

7. What are the distinctions between fixed and variable costs? Give several examples of each.

8. Would you advocate institution of a purchase order system in all hotels and restaurants? Why or why not?

9. What does the term "managerial accounting" mean?

10. If you were writing the job specification for food buyer, what specific knowledge and qualities would you include?

Internet Sites

For more information, visit the following Internet sites. Remember that Internet addresses can change without notice. If the site is no longer there, use a browser to look for additional sites.

Associations

American Hotel & Motel Association (AH&MA)
http://www.ahma.com

The Educational Foundation of NRA
http://www.restaurant.org/educate/educate.htm

The Educational Institute of AH&MA
http://www.ei-ahma.org

Hospitality Financial & Technology Professionals
http://www.hftp.org

Hospitality Information Technology Association
http://www.hita.co.uk

International Hotel & Restaurant Association
http://www.ih-ra.com

National Restaurant Association (NRA)
http://www.restaurant.org

Chapter 13 Outline

The Mission of the Human Resources Division
Hiring the Best Employees
    Recruitment
    Selection
    Wages, Salaries, and Benefits
Retaining Employees
    The Turnover Problem
    Orientation
    Training and Development
    Career Development
    Employee Relations
    Relocation
    The Role of Discipline
Creating the Climate for Productivity
    Evaluating Employee Performance
Recordkeeping
Quality Assurance Programs
Human Resources Internationally

13

The Human
Resources Division

THE HUMAN RESOURCES (sometimes called personnel) function is handled in a number of ways throughout the industry, often depending on the size of the property. Large operations and multi-unit companies, for example, may have a human resources division that coordinates recruitment, hiring, training, career development, and so forth. At other, smaller properties, the human resources division may have fewer staff members—sometimes only a human resources director—and more limited duties. At very small properties, the general manager or his or her designee typically undertakes all or some of the human resources functions.

Whether human resources activities are conducted by a single manager or an entire staff, most people would agree that the key to successful management in any hospitality operation—no matter how large or small—is the quality of its human resources. All of the activities discussed in this chapter, whether they are performed by a human resources division or by a variety of staff members in a number of departments, must be addressed if the operation is to succeed.

The human resources division must be aware of the important role it plays in the major management functions:

- Planning—Managers set the organization's long-range goals through planning. Planning procedures may include long-range strategic planning, regular operating procedures planning, and daily activities planning. The human resources division plays an advisory role in all phases of operations planning.

- Organizing—Organizing establishes the flow of authority and communication among employees. The human resources division helps maintain this flow. Organizing dictates the number of jobs and the tasks involved in those jobs needed to accomplish goals. The human resources division must be thoroughly familiar with the property's job needs in order to fill slots as they become available and to suggest new positions as the company expands.

- Coordinating—Coordinating brings individual and group goals together to meet the organization's objectives. The human resources division helps managers coordinate the type and the number of employees needed to attain organizational goals.

- Directing—Directing involves a wide array of activities: motivating, training, overseeing, evaluating, and disciplining subordinates. The human resources division may handle all or some of these duties.

Insider Insights

Vincent H. Eade
Assistant Professor
Harrah College of Hotel Administration
University of Nevada
Las Vegas, Nevada

The hospitality industry has taken a quantum leap forward in recent years in its approach to and understanding of human resources management. Lodging and food service operators have realized the impact this discipline can have. Thus, personnel departments and specialists, now known as human resources managers, have risen from the designation of "paper-shufflers" to administrators of the most valuable asset an organization can have: its employees. Career opportunities in human resources areas are increasing at an astonishing rate as more hospitality industry employers turn to human resources departments and legal guidance relating to employment laws. Due to the ever-changing nature of this field, students may find more unique employment opportunities in human resources management than in any other field.

The term *human resources management* implies three inherent concepts. First, employees are *human* beings; no longer should workers be subjected to the dehumanizing concept that they are nothing more than payroll liabilities. Employees are people with social as well as economic needs. Therefore, perhaps the greatest need in the workplace is to care for and nurture our "human" workers. Second, employees are a *resource*. As with any resource, effective control can yield rewarding results. This does not suggest that employees should be treated well so that they will be more productive. Rather, employers should treat employees well because it is the proper approach. Finally, these human resources must be properly *managed*. Each supervisor, then, must understand the concepts emanating from the human resources department for the management concept to work. Therefore, human resources management is everyone's responsibility.

Students interested in human resources management should take courses that will help them understand the basic industry components and jobs. The following courses will also help lay a solid foundation: labor-management relations or industrial relations, personnel administration, employee compensation and benefits, organizational behavior, employee development, communications or public speaking, employment law, foreign languages, and business ethics. A special internship in a human resources department and actual work experience in such an area is ideal.

Once in industry, graduates can pursue a career in a number of specialized areas within the human resources management spectrum. Some examples include:

- *Labor Relations.* This is an especially important field in the United States due to the proliferation of unions and employment laws. Employers must be familiar with, and develop an expertise in, such laws as the Americans with Disabilities Act, the Fair Labor Standards Act, the National Labor Relations Act, the Civil Rights Act of 1964 and 1991, the Pregnancy Discrimination Act

(continued)

Insider Insights *(continued)*

of 1978, the Employee Polygraph Protection Act, the Immigration Control and Reform Act, and the Consolidated Omnibus Budgetary Reform Act. Labor relations specialists also handle internal employee grievances as well as external charges filed with a union or a government agency.

- *Wage and Benefits Administration.* Wages and health care are primary employee concerns, and employers now rely on human resources specialists to develop competitive economic packages. More and more companies have created pension, savings, and retirement accounts for their employees.

- *Training.* Larger organizations have specialists who are responsible for orientation and initial as well as ongoing training programs.

- *Safety/Loss Control.* An unsafe work environment can result in needless and costly worker compensation claims. Numerous hotels and restaurant chains have staff employees who focus on accident and claims prevention and management.

- *Incentive Programs.* Hotel chains such as Marriott and Stouffer have given their human resources departments the responsibility of creating and managing employee incentive programs. Employee newsletters, employee assistance programs, bonus programs, and service awards are just a few examples of incentive programs.

- *Personnel Administration.* The flow of application forms and maintenance of personnel records is another human resources management function that requires excellent logistical and administrative skills.

In summation, human resources management has come of age. Its contributions to an organization are immeasurable. Career paths offer unique challenges and growth potential. Students interested in employee development will find a rewarding career opportunity in human resources management.

- Controlling—Controlling helps ensure that procedures help attain organizational objectives. Controlling requires performance standards, performance assessment, and a comparison between performance standards and actual performance to determine whether or not any corrective action is needed. All of these tasks are human resources functions.

- Evaluating—Evaluating determines whether the property's goals established in the planning process are met. Evaluation measures employee performance and training effectiveness and helps to establish new or revised organizational objectives. While employees are evaluated by their supervisors, the human resources division helps develop evaluation criteria and keeps records of employee evaluations.

In spite of its key role in the organization, however, the human resources division has only recently received the recognition and support from ownership and management it so richly deserves. Several developments have helped underscore the importance of the human resources division in recent years. These developments include the growth of individual properties and chain companies, a decreasing labor supply, and the increasing strength of organized labor.

The Mission of the Human Resources Division

The mission of the human resources division or those staff members involved in human resources functions should be to:

- Attract, develop, train, and maintain qualified management and staff for the hospitality property

- Minimize losses by reducing labor charges, liability, and employee turnover

- Monitor the entire property to ensure that property policy and standards are met by each department head

- Make sure the property complies with state and federal laws governing employment

The old saying that "people make the difference" has never been truer than in today's competitive market. If a property wishes to employ the best possible staff, it must identify, screen, and select the best possible applicants. Staff planning and career management programs must be implemented. The property must constantly look to the future and, in so doing, show a continuing concern for employees, even though positions may be eliminated, combined, or otherwise changed as internal and external conditions warrant. The human resources division provides advice about these vital matters to help managers make the best decisions possible for the property.

Hiring the Best Employees

The success or failure of any operation relies on two basic factors: the products and the people providing them. In the hospitality business, these elements are often one and the same. Without staff members who are skilled in serving guests, the hotel or restaurant can never be successful. Human resources management helps ensure quality control.

Recruitment

Hospitality executives agree that two of their toughest challenges are finding good property locations and recruiting good employees. Overall high employment and a shrinking pool of traditional workers, for example, have led to fierce competition among all industries to hire employees.

Employers are finally showing some genuine creativity in developing new and improved means of finding people, hiring them, and keeping them on the payroll. To attract management and staff to the property, the human resources division continues traditional recruiting efforts such as advertising in newspapers and magazines, working with colleges and their placement offices, and using external employment agencies and/or in-house job-posting systems. New recruiting tools include brochures, tray liners, bag stuffers, table tents, signs, and banners, all detailing opportunities with the property and designed to attract good employees. Properties may also offer financial rewards to employees for referring people for jobs if the people are hired and stay with the property for a stipulated period of time. One program offers up to $500 to any non-profit organization that refers an employee who stays on the job one year. Some properties methodically contact former employees who left voluntarily, in an attempt to attract some of them back to the property. Many hotels and restaurants have discovered that a location that is excellent for attracting guests is a very poor location for finding employees. As a result, some companies bus employees to work, at company expense, for distances of up to 60 miles. A few very innovative properties use their marketing departments in the recruitment process.

Enlightened properties are meeting the worker shortage challenge by providing improved working conditions, better training programs, and more appealing advancement opportunities. Indeed, the hospitality industry is truly selling careers, not just jobs. AH&MA's Educational Institute, for example, has a variety of programs outlining career opportunities in the lodging industry.

These approaches may not, in and of themselves, solve the industry's employee recruitment problem. Charles Bernstein, former editor of *Nation's Restaurant News*, advises managers that they can help alleviate the employment crisis by recognizing employee achievement.

Non-Traditional Employees. Entry-level positions in the hospitality industry have traditionally been filled by high school students seeking their first jobs and college students looking for a way to defray their educational expenses.[1] However, the number of 18- to 24-year-olds has been shrinking in recent years and will continue to do so as the industry enters the twenty-first century. To supplement this dwindling labor source, hospitality managers are now considering so-called non-traditional employees—older people, immigrants, disabled people, and others.

Recently, McDonald's devoted at least one national television commercial to the recruitment of older workers. Part-time employment may appeal to retirees for a number of reasons; relief from boredom or the need to augment Social Security or a pension are chief among these. Older workers forced into early retirement or laid off as a result of plant closings may also be willing to enter the work force again, providing they are taught the necessary new skills. Homemakers seeking part-time employment after raising families may also be attracted to jobs that used to be filled by younger people.

While U.S. immigration laws place certain restrictions on hiring immigrants, many are eligible and eager for work. Immigrants may have good job skills but little facility in speaking English. An entry-level position allows them a chance to gradually enter mainstream American life and to improve both language and employment skills on the job.

Physically disabled people have made great progress in the workplace in recent years. Entry-level employees who use wheelchairs have proven they can handle clerical and desk jobs, answer telephones, and offer information to guests quite efficiently. Many hotels and restaurants already accommodate disabled guests with specially designed entrances and exits that could also be used by disabled workers.

Mentally disabled people have often found work in back-of-the-house areas in the hospitality industry, and they typically perform repetitive tasks more willingly and with lower turnover rates than average workers. As the labor pool of traditional workers dwindles, some properties are discovering that mentally disabled workers can perform front-of-the-house duties as well.

Selection

While department or division heads typically make the final selection of a potential employee, human resources staff must screen candidates to be sure they have the required job skills, knowledge, and attitude for serving guests. Without a human resources staff to help screen candidates, quick hiring—and quick firing—may occur, forcing up job turnover rates and decreasing operational efficiency.

Staff look for employees who enjoy hospitality work because they will be more reliable, capable, and willing to make a long-term commitment to the property. To select the best employees, the human resources division must conduct interviews, administer tests, and ensure that laws affecting hiring procedures are followed.

Staffing Tools: Job Descriptions and Job Breakdowns. Before anyone can be hired to fill a position, the human resources division must know what skills and training the position requires.[2] Job descriptions and breakdowns thus become important tools for human resources staff.

A job description outlines specific information about the job, such as duties, materials, and equipment needed to perform those duties, how the job relates to other positions within the property, and working conditions. A sample job description for a barperson is shown in Exhibit 1.

A job breakdown is developed from a job list (see Exhibit 2). The job list enumerates the tasks involved in a particular job, and the job breakdown—too long and involved to include here—outlines how each of those tasks should be performed.

Job descriptions and breakdowns usually include a summary of the employee's duties and responsibilities. They help the human resources staff explain to potential employees what the job entails, provide a basis for developing job performance standards, and play an important role in training later on.

Usually, job descriptions and breakdowns are generated in the department or division in which the job is performed. For example, the housekeeping department would write the job descriptions and breakdowns for its personnel. It is up to the human resources division to find individuals suitable for those positions.

Interviewing. Interviews are the core of the employee selection process. Human resources staff members may interview prospective employees initially. A second, follow-up interview, again with a human resources staff member or a division or department manager, may also be conducted. In other instances, the division manager or general manager may do all the interviewing.

Generally, the interview should focus on work attitudes, skills, and employment history. In addition, interviewers should look for important personal qualities that mark the successful hospitality employee: an ability to get along with

Exhibit 1   Sample Job Description—Barperson

Job Summary:

Keeps bar supplied, maintains clean linens and assists bartenders as much as possible.

Work Performed:

1. Carries supplies and equipment, such as liquors, fruit, ice, glasses, linen and silverware from storeroom to the bar.
2. Slices and pits fruit.
3. Fills ice bins and crushes ice for frappes.
4. Washes fixtures, mops floors, and sweeps carpet in the bar area.
5. Washes and dries bar glasses and utensils.
6. Replaces empty beer kegs with full ones.
7. Helps in setting up service bar and portable bars for catered parties.
8. Carries debris to waste containers.
9. May mix simple drinks under the supervision of the bartender.

Equipment Used:

Hand truck	Furniture polish	Polishing cloths
Glass washer	Broom	Vacuum cleaner
Soap solution	Mop	Metal polish
Bar polish	Ice buckets	

Relation to Other Jobs:

Promotion from: Dishwasher, Yardperson
Promotion to: Cellarperson, Bartender, Server, Assistant Bartender
Transfer from and to: Busperson

Job Combination:

The duties of this job may be combined or included with those of Porter, Dishwasher, Bartender, Cellarperson.

Special Qualifications:

This is usually a beginning job in a club for which experience is not required.

others, an ability to handle oneself with people, an interest in the property, and a desire to learn. Personal appearance and grooming are also important, especially for employees who will work in front-of-the-house areas.

It has often been stated that a smaller, well-trained, quality staff will always be much more productive and efficient than a larger, less qualified group of employees. The hospitality industry is fast becoming the proving ground for that theory. Properties are becoming much more selective in their hiring procedures even as the labor pool shrinks. More and more job candidates are being tested before or during the interviewing process. It would appear that properties know their

Exhibit 2   Sample Job List—Morning Shift Room Attendant

Date: xx/xx/xx

JOB LIST

Position: Housekeeping Room Attendant

Tasks: Employee must be able to:

1. PARK in designated area.
2. WEAR proper uniform.
3. PUNCH in.
4. PICK up clipboard and keys.
5. MEET with supervisor.
6. OBTAIN supplies.
7. PLAN your work.
8. ENTER the room.
9. PREPARE the room.
10. MAKE the beds.
11. GATHER cleaning supplies.
12. CLEAN the bathroom.
13. DUST the room.
14. CHECK/REPLACE paper supplies and amenities.
15. CLEAN windows.
16. INSPECT your work.
17. VACUUM the room.
18. LOCK the door and mark your report.
19. TAKE breaks at designated times.
20. RETURN and restock cart.
21. RETURN to housekeeping with clipboard and keys.
22. PUNCH out.

new employees will have to be thoroughly trained and so are seeking employees who can absorb the training and achieve a high level of performance quickly.

In addition to skills examinations, such tests as the Human Factors Personnel Selection Inventory and the Employee Attitude Inventory can help screen out candidates with undesirable traits—dishonesty, violence, and drug abuse, for example—as well as measure burnout and dissatisfaction levels.

Some hospitality operations also use computers to help interviewers screen candidates. Prospective employees are asked to respond to computer-generated questions before being interviewed, and the responses help human resources personnel screen candidates.

Employment Laws. In recent years, federal and state legislation such as affirmative action programs and fair labor laws have changed the way staff are recruited and selected.

The Civil Rights Act of 1964 has done much to increase the importance of the human resources division in the hospitality industry. Among many things, this law requires employers to make judgments about a job candidate or employee based only on business necessity. Often, the human resources division has a full-time job just making sure that all actions affecting employees are based on business necessity or **bona fide occupational qualifications (BFOQ)**. The human resources division must make line managers aware of their responsibilities to all applicable federal and state laws affecting training, promotion, and transfer. If an employee files charges alleging discrimination, the human resources division investigates each allegation, determines its merit, informs managers whether there is just cause for the claim, and provides necessary documentation.

The Immigration Reform and Control Act of 1986 requires employers to make certain that no illegal aliens are hired and provides for stiff penalties for violation of the law.

The most recent employment law, and one of the most comprehensive, is the Americans with Disabilities Act (the ADA), which went into full effect in 1992. Title I of the ADA deals with the employee, while Title III deals with physical facilities.

Title I makes it illegal to discriminate against a qualified disabled person in the job application process and in the hiring, promoting, and discharging of employees. The ADA does not require employers to hire unqualified disabled people, but does require the employer to make some reasonable changes to accommodate an otherwise qualified disabled person in the workplace. The definition of disabled includes people with dyslexia, the AIDS virus, head trauma, and arthritis. Also included are recovering alcoholics, but not current users. Disabled people can now sue businesses for job discrimination. Basically, the ADA is designed to force employers to consider more qualified disabled people for jobs.

Title III details the requirements for physical access to the workplace and to public accommodations. Hotels and restaurants are directly affected, and many existing operations have been forced to make "reasonable physical changes" to comply with the law. All new construction must comply 100 percent. Some of the areas of concern are the number of parking spaces, accessibility of ramps, the widening of doors to accommodate wheelchairs, special provisions in bathrooms, the change from doorknobs to levers, and the size of bathrooms.

Other laws that affect the hospitality industry include various anti-discrimination statutes, the Fair Labor Standards Act, the National Labor Relations Act, the Equal Pay Act, the Civil Rights Act of 1964 as amended in 1972, and more. All of these laws regulate what can and cannot be done to and with an employee. The human resources division helps to keep the property from violating these laws.

Exhibit 3 offers a 15-point quiz about the Equal Employment Opportunities Act and indicates some of the matters human resources staff must consider when hiring new employees.

Exhibit 3   Equal Employment Opportunities Act Test

Instructions: Circle "T" for "True" or "F" for "False." For either true or false, depending on the circumstances, draw a circle between the "T" and the "F."

1. Administering general aptitude tests prior to hiring is an acceptable procedure. T F
2. Requesting an arrest record on an application form is not permitted.   T   F
3. An employer may refuse to hire an individual on the grounds that he or she is not a U.S. citizen. T   F
4. An employer must accommodate the religious needs of his or her employees with regard to the Sabbath. T   F
5. An employer may refuse to hire a woman because the job is "too strenuous" for her. T   F
6. A restaurant operator may refuse to hire waitresses because management assumes that customers prefer waiters. T   F
7. If supervisory training is made available to members of one sex, it must be made available to members of the other. T   F
8. If a job requires lifting of more than 60 pounds, it is safe to confine recruiting to men only. T   F
9. It is legal to have a policy to require a woman to start maternity leave two months before delivery. T   F
10. If a group of men paid $5.00 an hour is performing the same work as a group of women whose pay rate is $4.50, the men's pay must be reduced to $4.50. T   F
11. A pay differential between older (40-65) workers and younger ones is permitted on the assumption that older workers as a group are less productive. T   F
12. Help-wanted ads may be placed in classified columns headed "Male" and "Female." T   F
13. Asking for photographs from job applicants before employment does not in itself violate the law. T   F
14. A company may have a policy of not hiring females with pre-school children. T   F
15. It is unlawful to mention race or religion on an application form. T   F

KEY: 1-T or F. (The answer is generally false; however, it may be true if the test is validated.) 2-T. 3-F. 4-T or F. (This answer is generally true; it is false, however, if the employee's work cannot be done by another employee of substantially similar qualifications during his or her absence on the Sabbath. The employer has the burden of proving that undue hardship would result from accommodating the employee's religious needs.) 5-F. 6-F. 7-T. 8-F. 9-F. 10-F. (The women's pay must be raised to $5.00 if they perform with equal skill, effort, and responsibility and the jobs are performed under the same working conditions.) 11-F. 12-T or F. (The answer is generally false; it is true, however, if sex is a BFOQ [bona fide occupational qualification].) 13-F. 14-F. 15-T.

Wages, Salaries, and Benefits

Wages, salaries, and benefits concern everyone. The human resources division must help provide consistency and continuity in wage and salary administration programs, not only because state and federal laws require it, but also because it makes good business sense. In addition, the human resources division must ensure that pay complies with the federal Fair Labor Standards Act, which identifies exempt and non-exempt employees. If employees are eligible for raises on their employment anniversary date, the human resources division identifies those employees and makes recommendations to the proper managers.

As a result of the shrinking labor pool, properties are emphasizing the need to develop new, high-profile compensation and benefit programs designed to make jobs more attractive and to keep employees on the payroll.

Employees in many hospitality operations are not unionized. Human resources staff in a non-union property must help ensure that property pay rates and benefits are comparable to those in unionized operations. The property must make sure it complies with federal law, that no one is paid less than the applicable minimum wage, and that eligible individuals receive overtime. Miscellaneous concerns such as those dealing with meals, lodging, and uniforms are often addressed by the human resources division.

Employees are very concerned about the **fringe benefits** offered by their property. Human resources staff members also monitor the benefits program to see that it is competitive within the local industry and that it meets the needs of the employees. Today, benefits range from medical, dental, and disability insurance to leaves of absence and wage-related benefits such as holidays, sick leave, and vacation leave.

Compensation and Benefits Laws. All phases of the benefits program must be controlled by the human resources division to ensure that employees are eligible for the benefits they receive, that laws are obeyed, and that accurate records are maintained. Unemployment compensation is provided in most states to protect individuals who have lost their jobs through no fault of their own. State laws provide for a percentage of salary to be paid to these individuals while they are unemployed. The human resources division is an integral part of this system: (a) it provides the state with background information required to establish the candidate's eligibility for compensation, and (b) it protects the property against erroneous claims.

Workers' compensation programs may also be available to provide an income for employees who are injured on the job. The human resources division monitors this program both to benefit the employee and to help protect the property from fraudulent or erroneous claims. The condition of the employee should be monitored to permit him or her to return to work as soon as possible and to reduce the amount of lost productivity due to a work-related injury. Human resources officials in some properties are responsible for, and/or work with security personnel in, providing periodic reviews of the property to maintain a safe environment for the guests and employees.

Some recent changes in compensation and benefits laws greatly affect lodging and food service operations. Most important are the Consolidated Omnibus Budget Reconciliation Act (COBRA), the Tax Reform Act of 1986 (TRA 86), and the Family and Medical Leave Act of 1993 (FMLA). COBRA legislation requires that employers allow employees to stay in the medical coverage program (at the employee's expense) up to 36 months after termination. TRA 86 establishes very stringent new non-discrimination rules that regulate eligibility for medical and life insurance.

The FMLA states that any private-sector employer of 50 or more employees during each working day of 20 or more workweeks in the current or previous calendar year is subject to the FMLA.[3] An employee is eligible for leave and related benefits if he or she has been employed by a covered employer for at least one year and worked 1,250 hours for that employer in the previous year. Not eligible for coverage in some cases are employees who earn among the highest 10 percent of salaries paid by the company.

Covered employers must let eligible employees take unpaid leaves of absence or a series of leaves totaling 12 weeks to care for a newborn, newly adopted, or newly placed foster child or because of a serious health condition of the employee or the employee's spouse, child, or parent. These leaves can be taken in any 12-month period. Employers may require employees to use their paid vacation, personal, or sick leave as part of the 12-week period.

During a leave, the employer must maintain an employee's health insurance coverage. When the leave ends, the employee is entitled to return to his or her old job or to a similar one, without losing any benefits accrued before the leave began. The FMLA does not require accrual of benefits during the leave.

Another recent addition to the list of benefits provided by some hospitality industry properties is the 401(k) retirement benefit vehicle. Until a few years ago, retirement benefits were rare at the executive/managerial level and just about non-existent at other employment levels. The 401(k), widely used in other industries, has gained ground in the hospitality industry as a means of providing retirement benefits.

Retaining Employees

Fighting turnover and retaining good employees has been one of the major concerns of the hospitality industry in recent years and will continue to be important as the labor pool of traditional employees shrinks. Good orientation, training, and career development programs and effective employee relations can help keep good employees at the property. In addition, the human resources division can help smooth relocation of employees and ensure that the property has a fair and equitable disciplinary procedure.

The Turnover Problem

The philosophy of many managers has been: high employee turnover is characteristic of the food service and lodging industry, so accept it and learn to live with it. Fortunately, times and attitudes are changing. The modern, positive approach is that turnover can be reduced and the potential savings in this area could represent big profits. Exhibit 4 indicates some of the cost considerations in hiring and training.

As noted previously, human resources staff must provide turnover information to managers and advise them about the extent and potential causes of the problem. Exit interviews provide an excellent means of identifying problems that may contribute to the turnover rates. Progressive management also relies on the

Exhibit 4   Cost Factors in Hiring and Training

Selection and Placement:

Advertising for new employees
Employment agency fees
Brochures, booklets, exhibits
Prizes and awards to employees for encouraging their friends and neighbors to apply for resort jobs
Public relations activities that aid recruiting
Application blanks, printing and processing
Interviewing, screening, and final interview
Medical exams
Reference checking
Testing
Travel expenses of candidates for interviews

On-the-Job Costs:

Setting up payroll records, completing forms, etc.
Identification badges
Orientation
Job training
Increased cost of productivity
Increased cost of supervision
Increased frequency of accidents
Higher cost of damage to equipment, spoilage, errors, etc.

Separation Costs:

Exit interviews
Severance pay
Additional Social Security and unemployment insurance costs
Clerical costs of separation forms

Source: Chuck Y. Gee, *Resort Development and Management*, 2d ed. (East Lansing, Mich.: Educational Institute of the American Hotel & Motel Association, 1988), p. 230.

human resources staff for advice on developing policies and practices that will enhance employee morale and productivity while reducing turnover.

Turnover figures for the industry are somewhat suspect, but they do provide a reasonably clear picture of the size of the problem. It is not unusual to find turnover rates above 200 percent and as high as 400 percent for some job categories. One company in the fast-food industry experienced these turnover rates recently:

- Hourly restaurant personnel—190 percent

- Hourly office/clerical personnel—63 percent

- Restaurant management personnel—32 percent

This company is one of the most progressive in the industry and strongly emphasizes the human resources function.

If only mediocre or below-average workers created all the statistics, turnover would be easier to accept. However, such is not the case. Good workers also quit. Good workers quit most often, they say, because opportunities for advancement are limited. They also cite lack of recognition from management, dislike of management, boredom, and inadequate salary and benefits.

While some degree of turnover is unavoidable and probably desirable, it is nevertheless expensive. Using only actual out-of-pocket expenses to recruit, hire, and train new employees, industry executives estimate that turnover costs $170 per person at the hourly level and $4,000 per person at the managerial level.

While this turnover cost may not seem too high at first glance, its yearly drain on a large food chain's profits can be dramatic. For example, suppose a chain with 900 units averages 15 hourly workers and one manager per unit. According to the turnover rates listed previously (190 percent for hourly workers and 32 percent for managers), each unit would have to budget training for 28.5 hourly employees and .32 managers each year. That amounts to $4,845 (28.5 × $170) for hourly workers and $1,280 (.32 × $4,000) for managers. These are not huge sums, of course, but multiply those costs by 900 units (the total number in the chain), and they add up to over $5.5 million that could have gone to the bottom line of the company's profits.

Orientation

First impressions are often lasting impressions. The property's orientation program (or lack of one) is one of the first impressions that employees receive of the property. All too often, employees begin work without being introduced to the property's goals or its complexities. It may be weeks or months before they learn this information on their own. Such a situation should be avoided. New employees feel a strong need for security and social acceptance. The human resources division can and should play a major role in welcoming new employees to the organization.

A properly developed orientation program will help foster motivation, promote early success, and prevent employee problems initially and in the future. The program may last one or several days and should be tailored to the property's needs. It may be conducted by human resources staff, the division or department manager, or the general manager—or all of these. Employees generally receive an employee handbook during their orientation. An orientation program might address such topics as:

- An introduction to the job and property including the history, organization, and goals of the property
- Wage concerns including paydays, shift differentials, deductions, and frequency of pay reviews
- Benefits
- Working conditions including hours, uniforms and identification cards (if required), parking, meals, and procedures for reporting absences
- Human relations on the job
- A tour of the property including introduction to all staff, location of smoking and break areas, staff restrooms, and cafeterias

- A review of fire and safety procedures, conduct regulations, and grievance procedures
- A question and answer period

Exhibit 5 shows a sample orientation activities list.

Essentially, an orientation program opens lines of communication among employees, their fellow workers, and managers. Often the human resources division will help keep those lines of communication open through in-house newsletters, bulletin boards, memos, and so forth.

Training and Development

Training and development takes many forms in the hospitality industry and is becoming increasingly sophisticated. Career development programs, management training activities, training seminars for hourly employees, orientation programs at all organizational levels, career counseling, and miscellaneous workshops are examples. The Educational Institute of the American Hotel & Motel Association, for example, provides college and university textbooks, videotapes, and computer software covering all subjects important to the hospitality industry. Other professional associations also provide training programs.

In spite of these efforts, training is probably the most misunderstood function within the industry. Until recently, employees were trained by following an experienced staff member and learning required knowledge and skills on the job. Today, training has become much more complex. Most people want to get ahead and know that the only way they can do so is to be properly trained.

There are almost as many different ideas on management training as there are properties. Some properties rely solely on on-the-job training (OJT) approaches and do not allow trainees any other time to develop or test their knowledge and skills. Other properties require individuals to complete a comprehensive training program before they are allowed to assume management functions. The best method probably lies somewhere between these extremes.

The influx of many more non-traditional workers requires that both skills and attitude training be more intense than in the past. Video is playing a major role in both training and development. Even the chains, with all their resources, are finding this new training a real challenge.

Management trainees are an investment in a property's future. Most large companies have management trainee programs. But it is risky to promote a trainee into a responsible position without properly monitoring his or her success during the training program. The human resources division monitors trainees to ensure that they are not just used as ready labor to fill staffing vacancies.

Skills training has always been important for hospitality employees, but in today's world it is doubly important. Throughout the hospitality industry, the buzzword is *service*. Advertising focuses on it, books are being written about it, guests are demanding it, and property after property promises it. If the goal of providing superior service is to be achieved, the industry will need excellent personnel who are well trained. Providing these employees is the greatest challenge the human resources division faces.

Exhibit 5   Sample Orientation Activities Checklist

New Employee Orientation Checklist

Name of New Employee: ————————————————   Position: ——————————————

Department: ——————————————   Supervisor: ———————————————————

Date Hired: ——————————————

Instructions—Initial and date when each of the following is completed.

Part I—Introduction

- ☐ ——— Welcome to new position (give your name, find out what name the employee prefers to be called, etc.)
- ☐ ——— Tour of resort
- ☐ ——— Tour of department work area
- ☐ ——— Introduction to fellow employees
- ☐ ——— Introduction to trainer
- ☐ ——— Explanation of training program
- ☐ ——— Review of job description
- ☐ ——— Explanation of department

Part II—Discussion of Daily Procedures

- ☐ ——— Beginning/ending time of workshift
- ☐ ——— Break and meal periods
- ☐ ——— Uniforms (responsibilities for, cleanliness of, etc.)
- ☐ ——— Assignment of locker
- ☐ ——— Employee meals (if any)
- ☐ ——— Parking requirements
- ☐ ——— First aid and accident reporting procedures
- ☐ ——— Time clock or "sign-in log" requirements
- ☐ ——— Other (specify)
- ☐ ———

Part III—Information About Salary/Wages

- ☐ ——— Rate of pay
- ☐ ——— Deductions
- ☐ ——— Pay periods
- ☐ ——— Overtime policies
- ☐ ——— Complete all payroll withholding, insurance, and related forms
- ☐ ——— Other (specify)

Part IV—Review of Policies and Rules

- ☐ ——— Safety, fires, accidents
- ☐ ——— Maintenance and use of equipment
- ☐ ——— Punctuality
- ☐ ——— Absenteeism
- ☐ ——— Illness
- ☐ ——— Emergencies
- ☐ ——— Use of telephone
- ☐ ——— Leaving work station
- ☐ ——— Smoking/eating/drinking
- ☐ ——— Packages
- ☐ ——— Vacations
- ☐ ——— Other (specify)
- ☐ ———

Exhibit 6   Training with Job Breakdowns

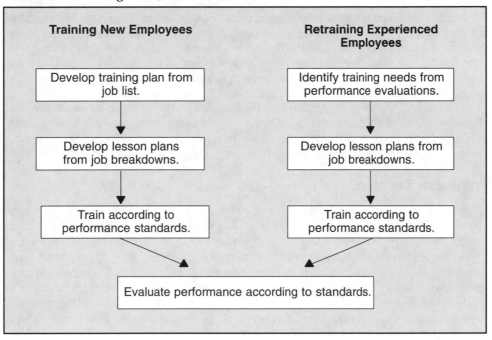

One way to promote quality service is to use job breakdowns to develop performance standards. Job breakdowns, as noted previously, list all job tasks and how they should be performed. Once a list of tasks is completed, the department or division personnel can then develop *job performance standards* (a certain level of quality) for each of those tasks.

To be most effective, performance standards must be observable and measurable. For example, telling employees to be pleasant when greeting guests is too general a performance standard. A more measurable and observable standard would be to require that employees smile pleasantly when they greet guests. Once job performance standards are in place, they provide a basis and focus for employee training, which may be conducted by human resources staff or by division or department personnel. Exhibit 6 illustrates how training of new employees and retraining of experienced employees hinges on job breakdowns and performance standards. Job performance standards also become the basis of employee job performance evaluations, which will be discussed later in this chapter.

The human resources department must monitor all training to ensure that employees are capable and understand the job, and that the department has taken the time and effort to train them properly. Most hotels and restaurants realize that their success lies, in part, in making certain that all employees understand their roles in the organization. Therefore, they are investing in programs to train employees not only in what to do, but also in why to do it.

Career Development

Properties are beginning to realize that if they wish to attract and retain high-caliber individuals, they must provide more than just paychecks and benefits. They must provide advancement and/or skills development programs that will enable employees to advance within the company. Career development programs are becoming more popular within the industry, and the human resources division helps develop and monitor these programs.

There are so many opportunities for success in the hospitality industry that choosing the best course of action is often confusing to both management and employees. The human resources staff can help by counseling employees and providing them with information that will enable them to make decisions about their future.

Employee Relations

Employee relations is a very broad subject, covering everything from employee contests to proper disciplinary action to assisting an employee who has had a tragedy in the family. Staff members in the human resources division interact with and represent all levels of management and non-management staff. Employees must have ready access to the human resources division and feel free to voice their concerns and opinions. Frequently, there is a direct correlation between the success of the hotel or restaurant and the attitude of the employees toward the property. If the human resources director understands the property's goals, the division will be a key element in the success of the hospitality operation. The human resources division can help foster mutual respect between employees and managers, which allows everyone to be proud of his or her association with the organization.

It has been said that 80 percent of one's problems lie in 20 percent of one's misunderstandings, and this is very true in the hospitality industry. The human resources division must represent management to the employees, but it must also communicate information upward to management and laterally to all other divisions. At unionized properties, the **grievance process** is a vital area of communications. It is extremely important to settle a grievance as quickly as possible and at the lowest level in the organization. To accomplish this, the property needs an efficient, well-understood grievance procedure; the human resources director often creates, monitors, and supervises it. It should be noted that, while grievance procedures are emphasized in union operations, a good grievance procedure is also a great asset in non-union operations.

Relocation

During the last 20 years, more and more hospitality managers in the United States have been relocated. Relocation is on the rise for two reasons. First, the tremendous growth of the hospitality industry is forcing the recruitment of managers from all possible sources (including other properties). Second, internal growth has created the need to transfer and relocate management personnel within company operations. The human resources division has become largely responsible for relocating and transferring employees once the decision to do so has been made. Human resources staff members help develop relocation policies and explain those policies to individuals facing relocation. The human resources director should be able to handle problems caused by relocation, such as those concerning the timing of the move and the starting date of the affected employee. Many human resources divisions supply new managers and their families with detailed information about the company, property, and geographical area to which they are being assigned.

The Role of Discipline

Disciplinary action, although negative in its connotation, can have a very positive effect on an employee's performance if used properly. Disciplinary action should be used to modify inappropriate behavior. Under no circumstances should it be used merely as revenge against an employee. The human resources division itself does not discipline employees. It can, however, act as the conscience of the property, to ensure that all employees are disciplined equally and fairly. This concern has become even more important in recent years. Employers who use disciplinary action unequally may be subject to grievances or even to a charge of unfair labor practices. All disciplinary procedures should be submitted in writing and a progressive disciplinary program followed.

Termination. When disciplinary action fails to correct undesirable behavior, it may become necessary to terminate employment. Recent labor laws have focused on termination of employees because, over the years, many businesses (including some hotels and restaurants) fired employees indiscriminately based on personality, background, and appearance, but not necessarily on business necessity. In today's labor market, a property can lose a great deal of money because of lawsuits, attorney's fees, and/or lost time spent in dealing with improperly handled termination matters. An effective human resources division can save the property thousands of dollars by helping to ensure that individuals leave the property voluntarily or are terminated with just cause.

Creating the Climate for Productivity ─────────────

Today's competitive marketplace requires managers to focus on productivity. Hospitality managers must evaluate an individual's achievements and the quality of his or her work. The lodging and food service manager has sometimes settled for mediocrity, both in service and product, but the hospitality industry can no longer afford this. The profit squeeze has been on for some time. Increasing income has been difficult; keeping costs from rising has been impossible. In searching for methods to increase profit potential, the industry must focus on employee productivity. Discussions on productivity are part of nearly every conference, convention, and seminar.

Many hospitality professionals believe that efficiency rates are much lower for the hospitality industry than for other businesses. Unfortunately, productivity rates have actually declined slightly in recent years. Thus, while the industry is raising wages and increasing fringe benefits, it frequently receives no additional productivity from its staff, and sometimes it receives less.

Insider Insights

Yvette F. Thuring
General Manager
Hotel Oro Verde
Puerto Vallarta, Mexico

Tourism represents an important industry in Mexico. In the beach destinations it is often the only source of income for the inhabitants, who are therefore very vulnerable to the economic conditions of the town and the surrounding counties.

It's a special challenge to manage a successful, profitable resort hotel in Mexico today. One must have flexibility and good marketing strategies to adapt to the sudden changes in the demands of tour operators, airlines, and individual travelers. Stiff competition between national and international hotels has turned destinations like Puerto Vallarta into buyer's markets.

Corporate management must let individual managers react quickly to changing conditions and try new strategies. It is important that managers be able to make quick decisions that will yield immediate, favorable results, especially in areas involving marketing and cost-cutting measures.

In Mexico, wages, along with the social benefits and taxes, represent a large percentage of the total costs of hotel operation. The variation in room occupancy during the off-season and in tough economic times requires careful consideration of staff scheduling needs.

Maintenance and cleaning activities, for instance, cannot be decreased at any percentage of room occupancy in a beach hotel because of the wear and tear caused by surrounding conditions. Guests expect high standards of quality and service from an international resort hotel. Therefore, during the slow season, staff size must be decreased with great care. Managers must make careful study of positions that can be temporarily eliminated during the off-season. And sometimes we require management and administrative employees to take on the duties of more than one position during the slow season.

If a general manager wants to take unconventional operational measures or put aggressive marketing strategies into practice, he or she requires the assistance and cooperation of an efficient, flexible, and company-minded staff. A team! Not only on paper, in the introduction leaflet, or in the hotel mission statement, but also in everyday operations. A manager cannot delegate team-building. Teamwork has to be wanted, prepared for, looked after, cared for, and pushed by the head of the operation. Hierarchy, customs, and social backgrounds may be obstacles, but should by no means prevent team members from working together effectively.

Undertaking such a task is neither easier nor more difficult for a female boss than it is for a male boss. Maybe a female boss tends to promote a woman more easily than a male boss would. There is no doubt that impulsive decisions have to be well controlled to avoid the "typical woman" accusation. But, from my experience, it is clear that the respect one gains as a professional, having a clear leadership, and cultivating human relationships make it possible to build a team under any circumstances or in any country.

The acceptance within the organization for a female executive depends, on one hand, on the executive's own personality, and, on the other, on the backing of the corporate office.

The human resources division must be involved in creating the climate that will encourage increased productivity. In the long run, the very future of the industry rests on its ability to do so.

Evaluating Employee Performance

Employee performance evaluations or performance reviews, as they are sometimes called, can help increase productivity by drawing out the great potential within all employees. To be most effective in tapping that potential, however, the evaluation must help motivate the employee to do better. One way to help motivate employees is to offer them information about which tasks they perform well and which tasks they need to work on.

Job breakdowns and performance standards, as discussed previously, can provide this kind of specific information during employee performance evaluations. Using a point system—for example, three points for excellent work, two points for adequate performance, and one point for those areas that need improvement—managers can rate employees on each task they perform. The job performance standards will provide the criteria for determining how well the employee performs any given task.

This kind of evaluation system allows an employee to identify which tasks he or she needs to do better and, more important, indicates *how* to do those tasks more efficiently. By identifying tasks that the employee does well, the system also prevents the evaluation from becoming wholly negative, which might discourage the employee.

Recordkeeping

In addition to all its other duties, recordkeeping is an extremely important function of the human resources division. State laws require employers to maintain accurate and timely personnel records regarding, among other things, participation in benefit programs, amount of reported tips, accident/safety matters, grievances, withholding taxes, and more. Computerized recordkeeping systems are being used more frequently, requiring human resources staff to develop ways to use the computer's capabilities to full advantage. One way is to store data from candidates and employees. This allows quick recall of information as needed. Many hotel companies such as Marriott, Westin, and Hyatt have turned to computers in their properties to keep track of applicants and current employment records. Labor turnover analysis is another prime concern for most properties, and the computer immediately makes available information that may help reveal why people are leaving an organization.

Quality Assurance Programs

One of the most significant management trends dating from the mid-1980s has been to introduce some form of quality assurance into the operation of hospitality properties. A major premise is to instill a sense of responsibility for job performance in every employee. Quality assurance seeks the maximum commitment of every employee to "taking care of the customer" and empowers the employee to make decisions for the benefit of his or her customer. In simple terms, each employee understands exactly who his or her customer is. Employees who deal directly with guests know that the guests are their customers. But behind-the-scenes employees also learn that they have "customers." For example, the cook in the kitchen works for the server (the cook's customer), who in turn works for the restaurant guest. The houseperson delivering clean linens and supplies to guestroom floors has customers, too; the room attendants are his or her customers. Once employees understand these worker-customer relationships, they can then discuss how to best serve the customer.

Quality assurance programs simplify the organizational structure and eliminate layers of supervisory staff by taking decision-making to the lowest possible organizational level. Supervisors can concentrate on providing training and other resources to employees, thus ensuring that the employees have the right tools to work effectively and serve the customers. When employees feel direct responsibility for their efforts, job satisfaction increases.

Responsibility for administering the quality assurance program usually falls to the human resources division. As with many of the hotel's programs, the human resources division must receive full commitment to the program from all departments and all levels of the organization if the program is to succeed. Once assured of complete management commitment, employees can become decision-makers, and the program will more likely achieve the desired results.

Human Resources Internationally

Hotel chains and companies are becoming international entities as they expand beyond their own national borders. Concurrently, much of the world's work force has become increasingly mobile. People from developing countries seek work in the industrialized areas of the world. In Europe, hotels have never employed as many people of different nationalities at one time as they do today. People from other continents have moved to Europe in record numbers. This influx has provoked profound changes socially, politically, and in the workplace. Multiculturalism is on the verge of becoming the rule, not the exception. It presents new challenges to the human resources division, which is responsible for assembling multicultural employees into a productive staff with high morale and a talent for service.

International chains face special problems in the human resources area. Each country into which an international chain expands has a different set of laws and regulations concerning work permits, health programs, wages, job security, and so on. The primary challenge is to the human resources division at chain headquarters since it must be completely familiar with the laws and regulations of each country into which the chain expands. The director of human resources in each hotel will administer the human resources program, but will depend heavily on the region or chain headquarters for updates and new rules, regulations, and policies.

Earlier in this chapter, the duties and responsibilities of the human resources division in an American hotel were covered in considerable detail. Internationally, the duties and responsibilities are generally the same. Activities related to recruitment,

Insider Insights

David Jones
Vice President
Shangri-La Hotels
Hong Kong ———————————————————————

A great deal has been said about how growth in the Pacific Rim will make Asia the focal point of the next century. While there is little question of the growing economic impact of the region, few North Americans understand or appreciate the contrasts within Asia.

An understanding of the differences in cultures from one Asian country to another, and also of the differences in how business is done in Asia versus North America and even Europe, will be essential in working with Asia and within it. The most common mistake North Americans make is assuming all Asians are alike and basing their expectations on one stereotype. Nothing could be more offensive to the Asian businessperson with whom you are dealing.

So much has been made of Japanese success that it is common to depict theirs as the typical Asian culture. The fact is, however, even within Asia, the Japanese are treated differently. Hotels throughout the rest of Asia do as much as they can to separate Japanese travelers from all others at Japanese request. This includes supplying special Japanese menus, having Japanese restaurants run by Japanese in hotels, employing Japanese nationals as sales staff purely to secure Japanese business, and employing as many Japanese-speaking staff as possible in guest contact areas. The influence of the Japanese is evident in all of Asia, but not the integration; Japan remains separate.

The future of Asia in the next century will be shaped by a number of other key players. These are the four dragons (Hong Kong, Korea, Taiwan, and Singapore) and China, the giant neighbor to the north. Each of these countries has tremendous economic potential and will be factors in the hospitality industry as destinations and as outbound markets for business and leisure travel. Therefore, North Americans will have to become more aware of how the cultures and business practices of these countries differ from Japan's as well as from one another's. It is important to note that North America has been very influential in the development of Korea and Taiwan, while the United Kingdom has greatly influenced Hong Kong and Singapore. Taiwan, in fact, has the largest surplus of U.S. dollars of any country in the world including Japan. American cars are commonplace in Korea and Taiwan, yet far less of the population can speak English than in either Hong Kong or Singapore.

China is an incredible sleeping giant that makes up one-third of the world's population. Although China remained isolated from the rest of the world during the Cultural Revolution, its spread of influence in all of Asia is immense. The Chinese population outside of China is a major factor in every other Asian country, particularly in the business community. Those whose families left China generations ago still feel strong ancestral ties to China. This has been especially evident in recent years with the re-opening of relations between countries such as Taiwan, Singapore, Malaysia, and Indonesia, which has resulted in a major

(continued)

Insider Insights *(continued)*

increase in outbound travel back to China. The continued economic success and increased level of higher education within the four dragons has raised incomes and also the cost of labor, which has made China an extremely important source of workers for labor-intensive industries. This, combined with the more open attitude of government to capitalistic ways and the incorporation of Hong Kong into China in 1997, puts all the ingredients for success into place. These points are crucial for North Americans to understand because the Chinese are very different from the Japanese in culture and business practice.

Understanding the diversity of each of these countries is essential because each has a strong sense of national pride. However, many customs that have been influenced by the Chinese and Japanese carry throughout the region. These customs determine how business is done and are vastly different from all of the Western world. Probably the most significant is the intense work ethic. It can best be summarized as "work before self." Most North Americans understand the attitude of work before pleasure, but this is much different: it is an unconditional commitment to work success and the personal rewards that go with it. It's probably most noticeable in Japan and the four dragons, but carries throughout the region where Chinese ethics have influence. An important driving force in this work ethic is a materialistic view of success: "The one with the most toys wins." This has led many Japanese businesspeople to purchase hotels and other real estate at far more than they are worth. On the other hand, the Chinese prefer to negotiate and always compare how well one did in getting a bargain than another. This is another important difference to understand when doing business with a Japanese versus a Chinese.

A second important ideological concept that differentiates Asian business ethics from those in the Western world is that of "face." In a nutshell, it simply means you can *never* directly tell an Asian that he or she is wrong, or you risk giving him or her a major loss of "face," which in turn will make you the loser. North Americans, on the whole, are very self-critical and are receptive to constructive criticism. They are also accustomed to personal evaluations and individual performance goals. These tools do not easily adapt to the Asian "face" ideology. Therefore, to accomplish the same objectives, you must approach management issues from an entirely different direction. This is particularly important in directing employees and motivating them to achieve a targeted result.

The third custom that differentiates Asian business practices from those of North America is that of "respect for the elders." The concept applies not only to the senior person in chronological terms, but also in terms of status on the corporate ladder. It is simply not acceptable to go against the wishes of the elders, as they are seen to know best; whether you personally agree is irrelevant. This is very different from the North American approach that challenges senior staff members to listen to and involve others in the decision-making process. It also makes the sales approach method of asking for the business much more difficult because it is viewed as improper to question the decisions of others. Modifying the sales effort to a more public relations-oriented approach where the customer's status level is nurtured is important.

(continued)

Insider Insights *(continued)*

   North Americans have always viewed Asia as very mysterious, largely because of a lack of understanding of important differences in some of the basic principles of doing business and a lack of education about the region's culture and geography. The globalization of the hospitality industry through the increased international ownership of hotels and hotel companies, especially by Asians, has made the entire world smaller. Therefore, it is imperative that we all do more to adapt to and understand the contrasts in Asia instead of imposing our own ideological concepts and stereotypes.

---

selection, interviewing, wage and salary administration, compensation and benefits laws, training, quality assurance, turnover analysis and reduction, and employee relations are performed in hotels around the world. Techniques, laws, and wages and salaries will vary from region to region, but hotels the world around still strive to increase productivity and provide quality and service to the guest. Regardless of country, the importance of the human resources division is at an all-time high in the hospitality industry.

Endnotes

1. Parts of the discussion in this section are taken from Chuck Y. Gee, *Resort Development and Management*, 2d ed. (East Lansing, Mich.: Educational Institute of the American Hotel & Motel Association, 1988), p. 230.

2. Parts of the discussion in this section are taken from Stephen J. Shriver, *Managing Quality Services* (East Lansing, Mich.: Educational Institute of the American Hotel & Motel Association, 1988), pp. 277–278.

3. This discussion is based on Sean A. Mulloy and Mary C. Crotty, "Making Sense of Family Leave," *Lodging Magazine*, March 1993, pp. 13–16.

Key Terms

bona fide occupational qualifications (BFOQ)—A provision of the Civil Rights Act that requires employers to use business necessity as the standard in making judgments about job candidates.

fringe benefits—Employment benefits such as medical, dental, and disability insurance; holidays; sick leave; and vacation leave.

grievance process—Formal procedure that employees follow to voice complaints about job conditions or treatment by supervisors and/or co-workers.

Review Questions

1. What is the mission of the human resources division?

2. What factors and events have led to the greatly increased importance of the human resources division?

3. Can hotels and restaurants hire non-traditional employees? If yes, in which departments? If no, why not?

4. What tools are used in the selection process? Describe them.

5. What effect has government legislation had on the recruitment and selection of employees?

6. What role does human resources play in the area of wages, salaries, and benefits?

7. In what ways does a safety program have both humanitarian and economic aspects?

8. Why is turnover so expensive? What approaches can hospitality employers take to reduce turnover?

9. What recently enacted employment and benefits laws affect the hospitality industry? What effects do these laws have?

10. What role does the human resources division play in creating a climate conducive to productivity?

Internet Sites

For more information, visit the following Internet sites. Remember that Internet addresses can change without notice. If the site is no longer there, use a browser to look for additional sites.

Associations

American Hotel & Motel Association (AH&MA)
http://www.ahma.com

Hospitality Information Technology Association
http://www.hita.co.uk

The Educational Foundation of NRA
http://www.restaurant.org/educate/educate.htm

International Hotel & Restaurant Association
http://www.ih-ra.com

The Educational Institute of AH&MA
http://www.ei-ahma.org

National Restaurant Association (NRA)
http://www.restaurant.org

Hospitality Financial & Technology Professionals
http://www.hftp.org

Society for Human Resource Management
http://www.shrm.org

Employment Laws and Applications

Links to Government Agencies and
Legal Interpretations
http://www.yahoo.com/Govern-
ment/Law/Employment_Law

OSHA Regulations
http://www.osha.gov

U.S. Department of Labor
http://www.dol.gov

Sexual Harassment Policy; Index of
Sexual Harassment Issues
http://www.yahoo.com/Soci-
ety_and_Culture/Crime/Crimes/
Sex_Crimes/Sexual_Harassment

Americans with Disabilities Act
http://www.usdoj.gov/crt/ada/ada-
hom1.htm

Job Accommodation Network
http://janweb.icdi.wvu.edu

Chapter 14 Outline

Security: A Continuous Concern
Physical Security
 External Security
 Internal Security
Employee Practices and Procedures
 The Accounting Division
 The Human Resources Division
 The Engineering Division
 The Rooms Division
 The Food and Beverage Division
 The Marketing and Sales Division
The Guest's Role
Administrative Controls
 Inventory Control
 Key Control
 Other Control Considerations
Safety
 The Safety Committee

14

The Security Division

IN THE HOSPITALITY INDUSTRY, change is the name of the game, and security is a prime illustration of that statement. For years, the security function received little respect, attention, or funding. The 1980s changed this perception drastically.[1] Most hotel and restaurant executives today rank security with sales, profits, and service in its value to the property.

What brought about such a radical change in management's attitude toward the security division? In part, a number of changes on the American scene. A rising urban crime rate did not bypass the hospitality industry. As violent crime increased everywhere, incidents occurred in hotels and restaurants, receiving plenty of media play and affecting business as a result. Fire disasters in hotels in Las Vegas, Houston, Puerto Rico, and Westchester, Connecticut, received national attention and heightened guests' concerns about fire safety. An increasing number of court cases held bars liable for crimes committed by intoxicated patrons. White-collar and employee theft increased—not only in the hospitality industry, but in many other businesses as well. International terrorism led to questions about how safe domestic travel had become.

As these and other security-related incidents occurred more frequently, Americans responded. More single women traveling alone demanded heightened protection of their accommodations. People became more likely to sue as a result of injuries—either real or imagined. Potential hotel guests and restaurant patrons became more security-conscious and more frequently wanted to know what hotels and restaurants were doing to protect their guests.

The S in security began to loom like a huge dollar sign in the minds of hotel and restaurant managers. Today, for example, meeting planners will not simply ask about alarms, systems, and procedures; they will demand that the alarm system be demonstrated and the emergency procedure manual be reviewed before booking rooms. Several large companies even supply portable smoke detectors to their executives when they travel.

Further evidence of growing concern is supplied by a recent VPI Business Traveler Survey. For the first time, respondents cited nine specific safety and security factors that affect their choice of which hotel to stay in. These features were ranked so highly by the respondents that free cable TV, free newspaper, family restaurants, low price, bathroom amenities, and free continental breakfasts were knocked out of the top 20 selection criteria. A quick glance at Exhibit 1 reveals that sprinkler systems, deadbolt door locks, parking area lighting, bright hallway lighting, chain locks, and peepholes all ranked among the top 20 criteria affecting hotel choice.

Exhibit 1   Factors Affecting Hotel Choice

Rankings		Percent
1.	Cleanliness	96.4
2.	Comfortable mattress and pillows	96.0
3.	Good-quality bath and wash towels	93.2
4.	Good lighting for reading/working	92.3
5.	Well-maintained furnishings	88.7
6.	No surcharge on long distance calls	88.5
7.	Friendly service	85.5
8.	Sprinkler systems	84.3
9.	Deadbolt locks	84.2
10.	Good reputation	82.6
11.	On-premises parking	82.5
12.	Convenient to business	82.2
13.	Free local telephone calls	80.1
14.	Parking-area lighting	79.7
15.	Bright hallway lighting	79.4
16.	Desk/worktable in room	78.3
17.	Non-smoking rooms	76.9
18.	Chain locks	75.2
19.	Wake-up calls	70.8
20.	Peepholes	70.7

Source: VPI Survey in *Hotel & Motel Management* (New York: Harcourt Brace Jovanovich, July 6, 1992).

In the broadest sense, the aims of the security division are to protect the property's assets, and to protect guests, employees, and any personal property that is lawfully on the premises.

Security: A Continuous Concern

For the hospitality industry, maintaining security is an all-encompassing endeavor, not limited to the security division. Matters relating to the physical plant, staff, and operations in general affect the protection of the property's assets and its guests and employees. Anything less than a property-wide view of security and the resolution and disposition of security problems leads to inefficiency, needless expense, and great potential for harm to employer and guests.

The security division is an integral part of an operation. The security division should help prevent loss through patrols, parcel inspections, spot-checks of departing delivery trucks, security system monitoring, fire safety inspections, and so forth. Security staff should assist other departments in investigation, detection, and apprehension when such action is warranted by the circumstances.

The security manager is a full-fledged member of the management team and maintains close contact with all management staff. In addition to knowing about protection measures, the security manager should understand property operations, should be profit-oriented, and should use modern supervisory techniques. He or she should know about all ordinances governing security, should know how to deal with law-enforcement personnel, and should be diplomatic and tactful in dealing with guests and employees.

The security manager should be watchful of fire safety, prowlers and burglaries of guestrooms, prostitutes and confidence men operating on the premises, drunken or disruptive guests, and guests who steal or from whom things are stolen. Furthermore, security investigates accidents for which the property may be liable. This important task determines the legitimacy of the claim. It also allows the division to take corrective action so similar accidents do not occur in the future.

The hospitality industry recognizes that good security not only protects the guest and the property, it also helps increase profits and improve operating efficiency for both hotels and restaurants. A sound, properly conceived security program concentrates on four interrelated areas to achieve the best security possible: (1) physical security, (2) employee practices and procedures, (3) administrative controls, and (4) safety. All security measures should be operationally and economically feasible. They must not harm good labor relations nor keep employees from performing their work efficiently. The number one goal must be *preventing* security problems rather than detecting, apprehending, and prosecuting those responsible for the losses.

Physical Security

Physical security literally begins at the property line. It involves the protection of the building and grounds and the building's contents. It covers such diverse aspects as layout and design, lighting, alarms, closed-circuit television, and storage facilities.

External Security

A property located on a landscaped plot must consider installing **perimeter protection** and exterior lighting. The grounds must be protected against trespassers and vandals. If parking facilities are provided for guests, automobiles must be safe from theft and burglary. Outdoor swimming pools must be protected to prevent both vandalism and accidents.

The principal means of perimeter protection are fences, shrubbery, and alarms. As a practical matter, fences or shrubs of sufficient height and thickness are best suited to hotels and can even enhance the property's appearance. Swimming pools are best protected by fences with gates that are locked when the pools are closed. Both the grounds in general and parking areas in particular need to be well-lighted at night.

A property that occupies all or part of a city block is confronted with different problems than the property on a landscaped plot. The city, not the property, has control over after-hours exterior lighting. The doors leading from the sidewalk to the property constitute the property's perimeter protection. Local safety statutes or ordinances may require that a certain number of safety exits be available. Nonetheless, the fact that a door must be available does not mean that it cannot be locked and fitted with an alarm to prevent unwanted entry and exit.

Internal Security

Layout and Design. Inside the property, layout and design have important security implications. The locations of work areas—the front office cashier, the head cashier, the human resources office, the controller's office, the receiving dock, the various storerooms, lockers, and refrigerators, the employees' locker rooms, the timekeeper's office (where the employee time clock is kept), the executive offices, housekeeping, and the laundry—will affect security efforts. In hotels, the design of the lobby, the front desk, the space in which safe deposit boxes are located, and the timekeeper's office all affect physical security. So does the basic design of the guest floors in relation to the restaurants and bars.

Alarms are part of security. Until recently, a large number of hotels and restaurants had no robbery or burglar alarms. Consequently, areas in which substantial sums of money were handled or in which guests' valuables were kept were extremely vulnerable. In motels, a large number of television sets were stolen because alarms were not used.

Virtually all properties today have fire alarms, but not all alarms are audible throughout the building. Even with the finest alarm system available, the property needs various emergency plans and a staff trained to carry them out. Plans should cover such things as fires, riots, terrorist attacks, hurricanes, and other natural disasters. If the alarm sounds, guests need instructions and reassurance to prevent panic. Management should disseminate the emergency plans to all staff members and periodically conduct emergency drills. The safety—and, often, the survival of both guests and employees—depends on how well the staff carries out the emergency plan.

Communications Systems. Effective security often requires quick action. Alarms indicate that some emergency—a fire, for example—is in progress. Many properties, however, augment their alarms with communications systems. These may be pagers, beepers, two-way radios, and so forth. Such devices allow personnel in any area of the property to contact security staff quickly.

Closed-Circuit Television and Cameras. Hotels and restaurants are considered private property but are open to the public. Because of the property's public nature, unwanted visitors—prostitutes, burglars, vagrants, muggers, and so forth—may be able to enter public areas rather freely. However, the property has a right and a duty to protect guests from unwanted visitors, especially in guestrooms and adjacent corridors. These areas are not considered public areas.

Closed-circuit television and time-lapse cameras can discourage undesirables from entering the hotel and can be particularly effective as protection for the front office cashier. The most effective deterrent, however, is a staff well-trained by security personnel to spot suspicious people or activities and to report them immediately.

Storage Facilities. The storage facilities for negotiables, valuables, and important records are a part of physical security. The mere presence of a lock does not necessarily

In-room safes add a measure of security.

mean that adequate protection is being provided. Safes and file cabinets provide varying degrees of protection against burglary, vandalism, and fire.

Many properties have safe deposit boxes or even in-room safes in which guests' valuables may be stored. Individual state laws determine the property's liability for the loss of valuables stored in such containers; usually this liability is limited, but managers should be aware of statutes in their own areas.

Managers should develop and monitor safe deposit procedures for their property and carefully train employees to comply with the procedures. Managers should require an immediate report of unusual incidents, and maintain accurate, up-to-date records.

Employee Practices and Procedures

The best security systems will not work without employee cooperation. Security tips that involve many different divisions of the property are listed in Exhibit 2. Each individual division, however, has special security responsibilities. The

Exhibit 2   Checklist of Procedures to Help Protect Hotel Guests

Using all or any combination of these procedures may be effective:

- The front office clerk can provide information to guests about checking valuables in the hotel safe at time of registration. The clerk might tactfully say, "The hotel accepts responsibility only for guest valuables deposited in its office safe; please let us serve you in this way," or give the guest a card with a similar message printed on it.

- Bellpersons can give the guests a card with applicable security information when luggage is brought to the room. They can also ensure that the lock and deadbolt system is working correctly (including those on connecting doors, if any).

- A tent card containing a security message can be placed in a conspicuous place in the room by the housekeeper.

- Hotels with turn-down service can use cards placed on pillows which read, "Please bolt your door before retiring to ensure your privacy and security."

- A decal can be placed on each room's hall door at eye level to remind guests about security concerns.

- Guests placing requests for wake-up calls can be reminded to bolt the door.

- Peepholes can be used on room doors to allow guests to view visitors before opening the door.

responsibilities of individual divisions in security functions are outlined in the following sections.

The Accounting Division

Internal control begins with an organization plan that clearly establishes lines of communication and levels of authority and responsibility throughout the operation. A good organization plan separates recordkeeping of assets from the actual control of assets. Additionally, the responsibility for related transactions should be separated so the work of one person can verify that of another. Related transactions should be separated so that one person receives the payments and another person posts the records.

Internal controls require forms and procedures that measure the efficiency and effectiveness of the employees and provide accounting information that, when analyzed, will help identify problem areas. These controls must also be cost-effective.

Another element in a sound system of internal control is the effective selection, training, and supervision of personnel. The hospitality operation must have policies that define employee skill levels, education, and job responsibilities.

In addition to checks and balances inherent in a well-designed system of paperwork controls (such as pre-numbered guest checks and sales tickets) and correct use of cash registers, internal control also includes the following areas:

- Comparative statistical analysis

- Planning and forecasting sales and the cost of goods sold

- Departmental budgeting controls

- Predetermined standards and evaluation reports

- Properly designed and secured storage areas

- A system for the continuous review and evaluation of the entire internal control system.

Good purchasing systems have written procedures that are approved by management and adhered to by all those involved. It is also important to have purchase specifications covering at least the expensive and high-volume purchase items. A testing committee under the direction of management and supervised by the purchasing agent is also useful. Every price or transaction either should be verified in writing through the routine use of a system that secures competitive prices or should be the result of a system of negotiated prices.

All food purchases should be based on the food service operation's actual need, which is determined by menus, parties actually booked or expected, and records showing the number/amount of items normally consumed. Most good operations establish a minimum and a maximum stock level. Generally, no more that a 90-day supply of anything is purchased without the approval of the general manager.

The operation should have a good internal control system run by an alert controller and an involved manager. When purchasers and suppliers know that they are being checked, they will do a better job than if there were no internal controls in place.

The Human Resources Division

Properly screened and oriented employees play an important role in maintaining a safe and secure property. The human resources staff usually has the first contact with potential employees and therefore plays a large role in the screening and orienting process.

State and federal privacy laws may restrict the kinds of questions that interviewers can ask job candidates or the kind of screening checks they can conduct. It is important, then, that the human resources division develop hiring procedures with an attorney to avoid violations of these laws. Where lawful, the human resources division may consider such measures as:

- Criminal conviction checks

- Background checks through private investigators

- Submitting fingerprints to law enforcement agencies for checks

- Polygraph (lie detector) tests

- Honesty exams

- Credit checks

- **Bonding**

- Department of Motor Vehicles checks

In addition, employers sometimes (again, where lawful) state on the job application that falsifying information will result in immediate dismissal. They may also ask for the job candidate's authorization to review job performance records from former employers. In some regions, the state gambling commission or local unions set standards for job applicants and provide applicant certification.

While smaller properties may not be able to conduct extensive screening checks, operations of all sizes should have an application form. Information on the form should be verified. The form also provides the basis for the interview with potential employees. Human resources staff should note discrepancies between information obtained on the form and that gathered during the interview. Staff should also note unexplained gaps in an applicant's work record and try to get those gaps explained during the interview. Finally, staff should document the reason for rejecting a job candidate. Comments, however, should not be derogatory.

When applicants are hired, human resources personnel often ask for identification proving that employees are who they say they are. Such identification should be requested *only* after the employee has been hired to avoid charges of age discrimination.

Human resources staff who train employees have an opportunity to stress the importance of everyone's security responsibility. New employees should be made thoroughly familiar with all security communications systems and emergency procedures.

The human resources division may be responsible for making sure that keys, uniforms, or any other property issued to employees are returned when the employees leave the property.

In recent years, employers in virtually all industries across the nation have been concerned about the possibility of employee alcohol and drug abuse. State and federal laws may restrict or prohibit certain procedures designed to uncover substance abuse (locker searches, for example). However, all properties should have a written policy regarding abuse and may consider obtaining legal counsel when such abuse is discovered.

The Engineering Division

The engineering division should give high priority to maintaining and repairing security devices and systems. Specially colored work orders or "security priority" stamps can be used to highlight security-related maintenance and repairs. Copies of these work orders should be sent to the security division.

At some properties, engineering personnel may be called on in emergencies. In such cases, a radio system that can dispatch emergency messages to engineering staff right away is useful.

Engineering personnel also play an important part in **key control**. The division should develop and maintain good control procedures for guarding key blanks and key-making machines. Only those with proper authorization should have access to blanks and machines. Inventories of keys and blanks should be conducted periodically. Requests for new keys should come only from authorized personnel in writing. These requests should be kept on file.

Tools and other engineering equipment with home use or resale value should be issued only through a check-out procedure. Conducting occasional, unscheduled inventories of tools and equipment may help uncover problems.

The Rooms Division

Personnel in the rooms division play an important and varied role in security. For example, front desk personnel should never give room keys out on request without asking for identification and ensuring that the person making the request is the guest registered to that room. Front desk personnel are often the first to spot suspicious circumstances or guest activities and should be encouraged to report these situations to the security staff. In some cases, the front desk controls nighttime access to the property. The front desk may become a command center in the event of an emergency such as a fire or flood, with the PBX operator facilitating emergency communications. The front desk also plays an important role in asset protection. Regular procedures for handling checks and credit cards should be developed to help the property reduce payment loss.

Uniformed service personnel are also involved in security. They may advise guests to lock valuables such as citizens band radios or tape players in the trunks of their cars when they check in. Car valets should make sure keys are protected. Door attendants should attach receipts to and move luggage and other articles to a secure area where guests can retrieve items. Bellpersons may instruct guests about security devices, fire escapes, emergency phone numbers, and so forth when they room guests.

Housekeepers should work closely with security personnel to define their role in maintaining property security. For example, a procedure should be developed for housekeepers to report suspicious circumstances or guests to security personnel. The housekeeping department should maintain good key control. Housekeepers should be instructed never to leave keys on top of cleaning carts or other places where they could be stolen easily. Some properties may require that master keys be signed in and out and that all keys be locked up when not in use. Housekeepers should collect any keys left in guestrooms, secure them, and turn them in in a timely manner.

Housekeepers should not allow anyone to enter a room without showing his or her room key. Often properties require that housekeepers refer anyone requesting entrance to a room to the front desk where proper identification can be verified.

Checking in-room security devices is another important job of housekeepers. Faulty deadbolt locks, window latches, fire alarms, and the like should be reported immediately.

Housekeeping staff also need to protect their own equipment. Linens and other supplies should be kept in locked storage areas. Keys to these areas should be strictly controlled. A good inventory system which includes unannounced checks can help deter theft.

The Food and Beverage Division

The food and beverage division often implements procedures to guard against theft of food, beverages, and division equipment. **Cash bars** for special functions, for example, pose special problems. The amount of alcohol must be measured exactly so that the guest's bill is accurate. Some properties sell tickets that can be exchanged for drinks in order to verify the amount of alcohol consumed. Periodic checks by supervisors may also help ensure that alcohol consumption is properly monitored. A procedure for moving the alcohol from storage areas to the bar and back to storage should also be in place.

Food preparation can be monitored by numbered guest checks. Only food listed on the guest checks should be prepared. When checks are voided, they should be retained and the reason for voiding stated on the check. Using duplicate guest checks allows checks in the preparation area to be compared with checks collected at the cashier's area. Discrepancies can be noted and investigated.

A precheck register can also monitor food sales and preparation. Servers use the precheck register (which is like a cash register without a cash drawer) to identify their own orders by depressing a certain key. They then enter items guests wish to order. For example, if a guest orders spaghetti, a key labeled *spaghetti* is pushed and that item and its price automatically appears on the check. The precheck register tallies the total food sales made by a particular server, and this total can be compared with the totals on that server's guest checks. Discrepancies then become the server's responsibility.

Another security measure used by some food and beverage divisions is garbage raking. Garbage is stored in an area or container that can be raked. Raking can uncover utensils and equipment thrown away accidentally or intentionally placed in the garbage to be retrieved later.

The Marketing and Sales Division

The marketing and sales division keeps a close eye on guest concerns including security and safety issues. Personnel in this division can pass along concerns to proper staff members so that the property can address these concerns.

In addition, the public relations staff in the marketing and sales division plays an important role in maintaining the property's image in the event of an emergency or accident. Some properties develop a public relations manual. This manual, developed with legal counsel, offers guidelines for dealing with the media in case of a major incident.

The Guest's Role

Now that the employees' role in security has been outlined, a closer look at guest considerations is in order. Guests may be victims or perpetrators of accidents or crimes. Whatever the case, the results can work against the property's best interest.

In addition to keeping guests safe for moral, ethical, and humane reasons, there is an economic reason: Juries today often make huge awards to guests in many cases. As a result, property liability insurance rates have skyrocketed.

Property owners and managers must be certain that every protective security device is in perfect working order and that staff has exercised reasonable care in protecting guests from any hazards to their safety and well-being. In the well-publicized Connie Francis case, for example, a faulty lock on a sliding glass door led to an award of nearly $1.5 million for the harm Ms. Francis suffered. Guests have been accidentally burned by flaming dishes at tableside. Some of these guests have sued and won huge damages. As a result, many dining rooms have eliminated tableside flaming, and many lawyers strongly advise restaurants and hotels against the practice. Guests have also sued restaurants because they found some foreign substance in the food. Swimming pool diving boards are another potential source of lawsuits. Guests suffering injuries have sued and won cases with damages. As a result, the Sheraton Corporation banned diving boards in all its swimming pools on the advice of legal counsel.

Liability suits resulting from liquor sales are increasing and are among the most costly in the hospitality industry. States control the sale and consumption of alcoholic beverages, and laws therefore vary across the nation. However, there has been increased national concern over alcohol abuse. Accidents and deaths involving drunken drivers, and the efforts of Mothers Against Drunk Driving (MADD) and other organizations, have caused a majority of states to pass dram shop acts. These laws place liability for a drunken driver's actions on the establishment where the driver consumed the alcohol. As a result of awards in these cases, insurance has become either unobtainable or unaffordable for many restaurants and hotels. To promote the security of guests, a number of hospitality establishments have banned happy hours and are conducting alcohol awareness programs for the staff and supporting community campaigns urging responsible drinking.

The problem of the guest who steals from the hotel is serious. Guests steal for several reasons. Some consider themselves souvenir hunters, but they do not restrict stealing to keys or ashtrays. Others take things as a matter of convenience (for instance, a bath towel in which to wrap a wet bathing suit). Some steal for home use or for the purpose of resale and profit. Yet others, called *skips*, simply leave the property without paying. Hotels are particularly vulnerable to thefts because virtually everything found on the premises can be used in a private home. Many people are neither deterred nor embarrassed by a name on a towel or a logo on china, glass, or silverware. As a result, except for the professional thief who seeks a buyer for stolen wares, third parties are not involved, and detection and apprehension of thieves virtually never happens.

While some items in guestrooms may have to be written off as expendable, such measures as providing hangers that are not readily adaptable to home use and plastic bags for wet bathing suits and dirty laundry will help reduce losses at least partially chargeable to convenience. Proper orientation, alertness, and cooperation among front desk personnel, bellpersons, housekeepers, and security personnel can help reduce losses generated by professional thieves. Mechanically securing pictures and wall hangings and using electronic devices (such as alarms that indicate unauthorized unplugging) to protect televisions and radios are additional precautions.

Administrative Controls

Security control systems also play a role in a comprehensive security program. However, they must be viewed in their proper context. Controls will not necessarily prevent employee thefts; they will discourage some and make it easier to fix responsibility when losses do occur. Controls are necessary, but they cannot be so restrictive that, in monetary terms, the loss of efficiency exceeds the loss of assets.

Employee theft in retail business establishments in this country is considerably greater than most people realize and is a serious drain on a business's profitability. Employees need to clearly understand that a variety of activities can constitute stealing. For example, unauthorized use of washers and driers for personal laundry is a form of stealing. So is punching a time card for a friend who arrives late, leaves early, or is absent. The housekeeper who removes hotel property from the premises and the worker who eats hotel restaurant food on the job in violation of property rules are guilty of theft. The reception agent who accepts a "gratuity" for making a room available is working against a hotel's best interests as surely as the purchasing agent or buyer who accepts kickbacks from vendors. Directly or indirectly, all of these factors will eventually show up as a reduction of profits.

Reliable estimates place the amount of employee theft at 2 percent of retail sales. Specific figures for the hospitality industry are not available, but applying the 2 percent figure to the industry overall results in an annual cost of nearly $5 billion. This figure may be exaggerated, but even sliced in half to $2.5 billion, the point is clear: Security measures to guard against employee theft need to be improved drastically.

The fast-food segment of the industry is especially vulnerable to employee theft because all sales are handled in cash, and, usually, more than one employee accepts cash and operates the register(s). Because of this cash on hand, late hours of operation, and a sometimes isolated location, fast-food corporations have established elaborate security procedures that have been fairly successful in reducing robbery losses. Every major fast-food corporation has a security department plus an internal audit department which devotes a portion of its time to security throughout the corporation.

Full-service restaurants and hotels have much less cash around than fast-food operations because of the widespread use of credit cards and traveler's checks, but they are not immune to employee thefts of cash. Both restaurants and hotels face the problem of credit card fraud by guests or employees.

Inventory Control

One obvious form of control is the inventory, which should be taken regularly. When inventories are taken, they should be supervised by a representative of the controller's office. It is possible, though, that merely taking frequent inventories offers a false sense of security. Food and beverages provide an excellent illustration. Many operations take these inventories on a monthly basis. If a shortage occurs, management learns of it within a relatively short time; however, management does not necessarily learn the source of the problem—whether it is, for example, the result of collusion between the vendor's driver and the receiving clerk or an in-house theft.

Key Control

Inventories are not the only important controls. Sometimes, controls over hotel keys are lax—grand masters (keys which open all doors in the hotel) are issued to people on the basis of status rather than need; floor masters are made available where section masters would suffice; and far too many people can simply walk up to the reception desk, ask for a room key, and get it without question.

While these situations may be typical of some operations, many hotels now use electronic and other card key systems which provide greatly increased security for the guests. Under one method, the guest registers and is given a plastic card the size of a credit card. Guestroom doors have a doorknob but no keyhole. Instead there is a slot. By inserting the plastic card into the slot, the guest unlocks the door. Only one duplicate of the plastic card is made, which is kept by the front desk agent who inserts it into a master console. When the console receives the duplicate card, it "instructs" the lock on the guestroom door to accept only the identical card issued to the guest.

If a guestroom card is inserted into a guestroom slot for which it is not intended, a signal flashes in the control center to alert security personnel. The door will not unlock, and security personnel will be on the way to investigate. When the guest checks out, the lock combination is changed by memory circuit and new plastic cards with new combinations are issued to the next guest.

The electronic card key system is one of the fastest growing technology-related amenities in the lodging industry. In the years between 1985 and 1988, use of this new feature increased by 300 percent. A number of companies manufacture these systems, and they are becoming more sophisticated each year. With the newer systems, an entire hotel can re-key its rooms in a couple of hours. Compared with manual re-keying, this system saves thousands of dollars in labor and materials costs annually, while providing greater guest security.

In spite of the increase in electronic card key systems, less than 50 percent of the nation's hotels today have such a system in operation. However, most new and major refurbished properties are equipped with these systems, so the day is coming when lost or stolen keys are no longer a major security problem.

Other Control Considerations

The protection of front office, restaurant, and bar cash banks when not in use between shifts is important; it is equally important to fix responsibility when shortages occur. The control of cash register tapes is important to the hotel's security since the tapes may provide evidence of fund tampering if any occurs. And beware of the cashier whose bank invariably balances to the penny.

Controls must be exercised over procedures as well as over assets. Bar stock should not be replenished on the basis of anything less than a written requisition submitted by the bar manager, and there should be a valid reason behind every food requisition signed by the executive chef. Controls must be considered for the protection of linens, housekeeping supplies, china, glassware, silverware, laundry supplies, tools, furniture and furnishings, office equipment, and even executive office telephones when direct long-distance dialing is available.

The hotelier and restaurateur must recognize the importance of preventive control. Catching the cook who steals food products is commendable. From a profit and loss point of view, however, it is more important to prevent the theft in the first place. If the key to a liquor storeroom has been misplaced or stolen, it is far more intelligent to have the engineering staff change the lock cylinder than it is to leave it alone in the hope of detecting and apprehending a thief.

Safety

Safety, as it affects the well-being of employees and guests, is an important part of security. Like other security considerations, safety is the responsibility of all employees. Many properties may want to encourage a team approach to safety by:

- Developing a system for instructing each new employee on the details of the job
- Fostering employee pride in performing jobs the right—and safe—way
- Discouraging employees from taking shortcuts that may shave time off certain jobs but result in safety risks
- Relating accidents and injuries to human error
- Instructing employees to ask questions to ascertain safe work procedures
- Encouraging employees to report safety hazards and to suggest safety innovations
- Stressing the importance of reporting all injuries, no matter how minor
- Checking from time to time to see that employees are working safely

The Safety Committee

Even small properties can involve employees more fully in safety concerns by forming a safety committee. The committee might consist only of managers and supervisors to begin with. Meetings (every month is usually sufficient) to discuss safety concerns should be well planned, and minutes should be taken. The committee may consider such things as accidents and hazards, unsafe work practices, and solutions to safety problems. Outside experts—insurance company safety engineers, local inspectors, fire department representatives, and so forth—may be called in to provide safety information. Committee members may also want to review films, posters, or other materials to help heighten employee safety awareness or plan a property safety campaign. A safety self-inspection program could also be developed.

Endnotes

1. Some of the discussion in this chapter is taken from *Security and Loss Prevention Management* by Raymond C. Ellis, Jr., and the Security Committee of AH&MA (East Lansing, Mich.: Educational Institute of the American Hotel & Motel Association, 1986). For a more detailed discussion of security issues and the law, readers may consult Jack P. Jefferies, *Understanding Hospitality Law,* 3d ed. (East Lansing, Mich.: The Educational Institute of the American Hotel & Motel Association, 1995).

Key Terms

bonding—An insurance agreement in which an agency guarantees payment to an employer in the event of a financial loss due to the actions of an employee.

cash bar—A beverage setup at a special function (such as a banquet) where guests pay for their own beverages.

key control—A security system involving procedures that restrict keys to guest-rooms, work areas, and storage areas to authorized personnel and/or guests.

perimeter protection—Fences, shrubbery, alarms, lighting, and other particulars that help guard a property surrounded by a landscaped area. For a property that occupies all or part of a city block, the doors leading from the sidewalk to the property constitute the property's perimeter protection.

Review Questions

1. What are some of the factors that led to the greatly increased importance of the hotel security division?

2. What measures can a hotel take to help ensure its internal security?

3. How can the human resources division assist the security division?

4. In what ways does the engineering division need to cooperate with the security division?

5. Why, in addition to moral, ethical, and humane reasons, is there a vital economic reason to keep guests safe?

6. Why is key control so vital in today's hotels? Describe methods used to control keys.

7. Is employee theft a problem in the hospitality industry? If so, what areas of the industry are most vulnerable?

8. In what ways does the food and beverage division assist in the security function?

9. In what ways is guest theft a problem in hotels and motels?

10. How do security concerns for a suburban hotel differ from those of a center city hotel?

Internet Sites

For more information, visit the following Internet sites. Remember that Internet addresses can change without notice. If the site is no longer there, use a browser to look for additional sites.

Associations

American Hotel & Motel Association (AH&MA)
http://www.ahma.com

The Educational Foundation of NRA
http://www.restaurant.org/educate/educate.htm

The Educational Institute of AH&MA
http://www.ei-ahma.org

Hospitality Financial & Technology
Professionals
http://www.hftp.org

Hospitality Information Technology
Association
http://www.hita.co.uk

International Hotel & Restaurant
Association
http://www.ih-ra.com

National Restaurant Association (NRA)
http://www.restaurant.org

Society for Human Resource
Management
http://www.shrm.org

Part V

A Look into the Future

Chapter Outline

Lodging Operations at the Turn of the Century
What to Look for in the Next Century
    Changing Channels of Distribution
    Consolidation
    Globalization
    Technology
    Branding/Marketing
    Product and Market Segmentation
    Finance
    Interval Ownership
    Supply Segments
    Other Trends
Business or Art?
Food Service in the Twenty–first Century

Conclusion

A Look into the Future

CHANGE HAS ALWAYS BEEN A FEATURE of the hospitality industry, but never has change been more fast-paced than in the past few years. To keep up with these changes, hoteliers and restaurateurs must anticipate trends in the industry before they occur. But predicting the future is no easy task. Predictions must come from studying developing trends and from educated guesses of industry experts. Sometimes these predictions conflict.

While experts differ over the direction certain trends in the industry will take, some common themes emerge in this chapter that are important to note. Technological advances have already affected the industry profoundly and will continue to do so. Large companies will become increasingly international in their outlook. This will affect the economies and labor forces of all nations. Chains and management companies will continue to consolidate, and this will pose major challenges for independent operations with fewer economic resources seeking to compete in the market of the future. All these changes will require more aggressive, forward-thinking management.

In compiling this look into the future, we have drawn on the expertise, experience, and thinking of three industry leaders, each of whom has given serious thought to the future of the hospitality industry. The three panel members are: Mr. John Norlander, recently retired President and CEO, Carlson Hospitality World Wide; Dr. Bjorn Hanson, Industry Chairman-Hospitality, Coopers & Lybrand; and co-author Tom Lattin.

Lodging Operations at the Turn of the Century

In the third edition of *The Lodging and Food Service Industry*, we predicted:

- Hotels will be viewed more as businesses than real estate investments.

- Tomorrow's hotel industry leaders will be experienced, successful hotel operators.

- U.S. hotel chains will focus primarily on domestic brand conversions and international development of value-oriented properties. Mexico, South America, Western Europe, and Eastern Europe will be flying the flags of U.S. brands.

- New domestic hotels will not appear in any significant numbers until the second half of the 1990s. They will have more equity and less debt.

- The owners of future hotels will be more active than passive and will be predominantly owner-operators.

- The physical configuration of tomorrow's hotels will be different from hotels as we know them today.

- Average room rates will increase faster than inflation, and room revenue will rise as a percentage of total revenue.

- Food and beverage revenue as a percentage of total revenue will decrease.

- Rooms profit as a percentage of rooms revenue will increase.

- Telephone department and other revenue will increase in both actual dollars and as a percentage of revenue.

- Administrative & General expenses will decrease as a result of (1) lower franchise royalties, more franchise competition, and performance-driven franchise fees; and (2) lower credit card commissions as bank debit cards become more popular.

- However, these economies will be somewhat offset by higher security costs as guest security and life safety become higher priorities for hotel owners.

- There will be fewer independent management companies.

- U.S. financial institutions will gradually sell off their hotel assets but with substantial equity requirements.

- Hotel franchise companies will increase franchise benefits to include assistance with finance, disposition, and acquisition.

- More independent properties will become franchises.

- Consolidation will continue, conversions will accelerate, and more major lodging companies will be attracted to time-sharing.

A brief analysis of the industry today substantiates that we compiled a very respectable record in our projections of future trends.

What to Look for in the Next Century

Each member of the panel, acting independently, submitted his forecast of events to look for in the coming century. Only trends on which there was a consensus have been included in this chapter.

Changing Channels of Distribution

In recent years, we have looked at the changing channels of distribution and thought about the shift from individually owned hotels to chain operations, to central reservation systems, to travel agents, and then to airline global distribution systems. Now, we will see something much more significant in the next leap of distribution channels. Nicholas Negroponte, the author of *Being Digital* (Knopf, 1995), has posited that, in the future, we will each have our own "smart agent": an electronic butler that will know more about us as individuals than we seem to know about ourselves.

This electronic agent will remember all the details we frequently forget, such as addresses, phone numbers, corporate travel policies, birthday and anniversary dates, and preferences in airplane seating on various airline configurations. In the not-too-distant future, we will be able to turn to our computer to set up a business meeting in a distant city. The database smart agent will then search the Internet for airlines serving the pair cities, our preferred times of arrival and departure, our preferred restaurants and, even, menus. The resulting data will be offered as a series of choices, and merely by "point and click," we can order the trip and confirm it. This means that the Internet will become a significant new channel of distribution. The necessary technology already exists. All that we need is the time and interest to organize such a system. This is the direction of new channels of distribution; all airlines, travel agents, and hospitality providers will be participating in one form or another.

Consolidation

Mergers, acquisitions, and consolidation will be a trend fueled by the explosive growth in the number of public lodging companies (now approaching 50), the benefits of scale, and the likely stability of access to capital from the capital markets to existing successful companies rather than from IPOs (initial public offerings).

We have seen some form of consolidation in the U.S. hotel industry for the past 40 years as chains have formed and now represent 75 percent of the industry. At the same time, the number of rooms has doubled (from 1.5 million to over 3 million) and is still growing. Consolidation will continue in the United States because Wall Street will press for more and more efficiencies as the normal business cycles continue and the current euphoria over this "new" hospitality business subsides. In the next ten years, we will see faster change of the same type in both Europe and Asia. Europe has not experienced the same growth of product or chains, but it has begun. The various restrictions that have been the norm—whether government controls, corporate ownership structure, or simply availability of appropriately priced sites—will be overcome to some degree by the need to affiliate so Europe can properly present its products to the new global customer in Asia and elsewhere around the world. The deregulation of airlines in the United States certainly had its effect on the hospitality business during the past ten years. We can expect a similar effect in both Europe and Asia over the next ten years.

Consolidation does not mean that only U.S. hospitality firms will be the survivors. We have seen European and Asian interests acquire some of the U.S. brands while other firms and brands have been created in both Europe and Asia. However, the U.S. firms have a head start because the United States is still the leader in marketing and technology. As we see the increasing impact of technology on marketing in the hospitality industry, we will again see the U.S. companies taking a leadership position.

Globalization

What does globalization mean? Two things. First, the breaking-down of barriers to travel as the developing world opens its doors not only to tourism, but also to corporate investments that it has long avoided in an effort to support local businesses.

It is now pretty clear that foreign investment can make products and services in all industries more available and less costly for the local populace. This means that every company needs to structure its internal and external processes to incorporate a wide variety of cultures. Indeed, Radisson's name for its work with strategic partners in each corner of the globe is "Global Power with Local Presence."

Second, the developing economies are not only producing more goods, but also more consumers. The middle class is growing faster elsewhere in the world than it is in Europe and the United States. With India having 250 million in its middle class (albeit at a lower average income) and China and the rest of Asia growing their economies at 7+ percent per annum, we are seeing the creation of millions of new consumers. One of the first luxuries these consumers want is travel. Only the basics of food, housing, and the initial investments in hard goods take precedence. By the year 2004, 40 percent of cross-border airline travelers will be from Asia. That's globalization. Our industry must be ready and able to market to them.

These emerging middle-class travelers will be strongly interested in visiting the United States; thus, inbound U.S. travel will potentially accelerate dramatically over the next decade. The travelers will originate from China, India, Eastern Europe, Mexico, and South America. We are also likely to see increasing travel from Asia, Latin America, and Western Europe.

Outbound U.S. travel has the potential to increase, especially because of the demographics of the baby boomers. They are approaching peak ages for travel, and they tend to value experiences over assets. Having acquired home, car, and college education for the children, they have both the desire and the finances to travel.

Technology

It will be the technological developments over the next ten years that will really change the way we do business. The American Hotel & Motel Association (AH&MA) is already working closely with the technology industries to set new standards. Two examples are the Windows Hospitality Specification group and AH&MA's Hospitality Industry Technology Interface Standards group (HITIS).

Each of the major hospitality companies already has an untold wealth of information about its customers, but it is not organized in a manner that makes it possible to use successfully. This will be done through database marketing and the standardization of technology that will allow interfacing within companies and between industries.

Videoconferencing is developing rapidly. It is evolving from an enhancement of a teleconference to a substitute for face-to-face meetings as users become more experienced with technology, as a younger technology-oriented generation gains influence, and as cost continues to decrease even as quality improves. Currently, videoconferencing has the potential to displace approximately 2 percent of business travel. There is a limit to the level of displacement because of the desire and need for relationship building. In fact, relationship management is another emerging "technology." However, in the next decade the 2 percent displacement may well increase to 5 or 6 percent.

As we mentioned, the Internet will become a substantial distribution system for the lodging industry. Online booking, auctions of available rooms, greater and more easily available information at the user's convenience, low cost, and other factors will result in growth of reservations from less than 1 percent today to 10 or 15 percent in the next decade. Current distribution costs of 7 to 9 percent will decrease steadily.

Branding/Marketing

As globalization continues, branding will become more important, not less. The farther a consumer intends to travel from home, the more he or she will want to use a branch with which he or she is comfortable. Consolidation of brands will help to make this happen.

Branding is actually marketing. Globalization will increase the need for branding, and branding will increase the need for solid marketing through technology. Global brands will be able to afford the technology and will have the ability to access the data to build the requisite databases to market globally. Few, if any, individual properties will be able to compete.

There will always be a place for the unique hotel and the niche chain, but the bulk of business will go to the brands that master the strategies of globalization, consolidation, marketing, and technology.

Product and Market Segmentation

Although we will see a reduction of companies through consolidation, we will most likely see a proliferation of brands. There will be a richness of niche markets. The paradox is that the giants will best be able to serve these markets because they will be able to afford and best use the new technology of database marketing.

Finance

Relative occupancy and rate stability will be a by-product of Wall Street's embrace of the lodging industry. There are over 20 analysts following and publishing research on companies and industry fundamentals. Although there will be peaks and troughs in industry performance, the extreme fluctuations that we saw in years 1979 and 1990 will be reduced because of high quality, widely distributed industry research identifying the potential of overbuilding, or other industry-induced opportunities and threats.

Public debt is likely the next phase of capital market involvement in the lodging industry. Debt is more stable in its availability and often follows public equity to an industry.

Franchise and management fees will continue to drop.

Public ownership of hotels will continue to be led by the REITs. Insurance companies will invest in REIT shares rather than in physical assets.

Interval Ownership

Highly respected lodging companies including Hilton, Hyatt, Marriott, and Disney have raised the visibility and creditability of interval ownership, also called

Insider Insights

Ted J. Balestreri
President
The Sardine Factory Restaurant
Monterey, California _____

It's fascinating to speculate about the twenty-first century. That's why science fiction writers are able to sell so many books. But for restaurateurs, future planning—or forecasting—is serious business. In our highly competitive industry, an inability to plan for the future can mean the difference between success and failure.

Let's take a look at the foods that will be served in homes and restaurants in the future. Mention of the twenty-first century evokes futuristic, high-tech images, but chances of the food supply changing radically are unlikely. It won't be for lack of technical know-how, though. Research for the space program has produced a variety of dehydrated foods as well as formulas for completely nutritious "predigested" liquid meals. The nature of the human race makes it unlikely that this technology will be used. Most people enjoy consuming a variety of foods and meals eaten in a relaxed atmosphere. Food consumption fulfills a psychological as well as a physiological need. We all know that dining out has become an essential social outlet in American society. Liquid nutrition or encapsulated foods would eliminate one of our necessary pleasures.

Biotechnology will probably have the most far-reaching effect on the twenty-first century food supply. For example, seasonal foods such as strawberries and asparagus may be available year-found, thanks to the biosynthesis of plants.

The most publicized branch of biotechnology, however, has been genetic engineering—the process of transferring a specific gene from one living organism to another. Genetic transfer can produce faster-growing, leaner, and more disease-resistant animals. Cattle production is the obvious application, but this process can also improve dairy, baking, and brewing products. Food irradiation will also be more widely used in the next century.

As America's search for low- and non-calorie ingredients continues, fat substitutes will have a great impact on such products as margarine, mayonnaise, ice cream, yogurt, cheese, and butter. Seafood and poultry consumption will continue to rise. As fish consumption grows, new technologies for seafood production will emerge. Aquaculture will grow in importance and expand to species such as shrimp and saltwater finfish. The result will be a more constant supply of higher-quality seafood.

How about the machinery that will be used in the restaurants of the future? Industry experts predict that, at fast-food restaurants, machines will flip hamburgers, bag french fries, spread pizza dough, fry chicken, bake biscuits, stuff burritos, and deliver drive-through orders to cars. Furthermore, they will perform these tasks in about half time and at approximately half the cost that human workers require.

In the future, there will challenges, and competition will be more intense. However, if we learn from past mistakes and prepare for tomorrow's challenges, I predict an exciting and unlimited future for the food service industry.

time share. It will continue to strengthen and will become increasingly fashionable with all the major chains. The public markets will bless time share as a serious long-term industry. "Combination" resorts and properties will emerge in which there is a mixture of regular hotel rooms, time share, and condominiums all in one location sharing services, infrastructure, and amenities.

Supply Segments

Extended Stay has the potential to become a major segment. Small site requirements, low project cost, high margins, and simplicity of management contribute to its appeal for developers and investors. For travelers, this concept shares much with the entire limited-service concepts introduced in the early 1980s: offer a product and service targeted to the needs of specialized travelers or travelers with a special need at a lower price, and there likely will be strong market acceptance.

Deluxe/Luxury hotels have the potential to substantially outperform the industry. High development cost, greater complexity of marketing and management, difficulty in many markets of acquiring affordable competitive sites, the reality that new projects have much higher investment bases than for existing hotels (often resulting in lower returns on new projects), the limited number of deluxe/luxury brands, and other factors portend favorably for current owners of deluxe/luxury hotels.

Conference centers in new forms, especially with more efficient designs (for example, fewer gross square feet per available room), will likely emerge as technical training needs increase at the same time that organizations need to reinforce corporate culture training in the face of alternative office concepts (the virtual office, hoteling, just-in-time offices, telecommuting, and so on).

Resorts may well have the best future of all. Based on demographic data and tourism trends, this segment will potentially outperform all other segments. The *National Travel Monitor* reports on an emerging trend that will have a positive effect on one portion of the resort segment: namely, the all-inclusive resort. The *Monitor* declares that all-for-one is now a pricing strategy. There is an emerging preference for inclusive pricing (for example, one price for accommodations, meals, beverages, entertainment, and even recreation) as more consumers embrace a defensive strategy in vacation planning.

Other Trends

New hotels will be built in the next century as they have been in this century, but they will differ somewhat in general concept. The new hotels will be either smaller niche hotels or huge hotels. The emphasis will be on rooms. The food and beverage functions will be leased to outside operators. Well-known restaurant brands will locate in the hotels. The food court concept that both Holiday Inn and Choice Hotels introduced will be adopted by comparable brands. Hotels will employ fewer employees per room than they do currently.

There will be fewer hotel companies with only a handful of major players. In almost every case, these major players will own the brand, the management, and the real estate.

Cruise ships are actually floating resort hotels, and, in the future, will seriously compete for lodging industry guests. The *National Travel Monitor* reports that, to date, only 6 percent of Americans have taken a cruise. However, 60 percent now express an interest in taking a cruise during the next two years. The cruise industry is well on the way to preparing for these new customers. Each of the major cruise lines has one or more new, gigantic cruise ships, each of which will accommodate over 3,000 passengers. While the number of hotel companies operating cruise ships can now be counted on the fingers of one hand, this number could double in the next decade.

Business or Art?

Currently, public companies are being created because of the ready access to capital. Growth must be fueled by capital, and, now that Wall Street is enamored with the industry, public companies will find it easier to access the capital markets than private and small companies can—and at a lower cost of capital. This will change the industry. It will be run more as a business than as an art form. The structure of the company may become more important than the guest services. This will be risky, because the guest will measure the services' value from his or her point of view, not Wall Street's. In the next business downcycle, this may be a problem for those companies structured primarily as investment vehicles. Those that marry service and investment structure the best will have the best chance to survive. It is possible, but it is not necessarily natural.

Customer satisfaction is still the key. Occupancy and demand were up in 1997. Where will they be in 2005? Already, in 1997, after only two or three years of "good business," customers were seeing their measure of "value for money" drop. Fewer than 53 percent consider the value excellent or very good. This percentage has decreased steadily each year since 1993 (per D.K. Shifflet & Associates). The consumer is more sophisticated in his or her lodging decisions, and has increasing expectations that must be met. Chains need to examine what guests will pay for and what amenities they will expect as standard.

One thing is certain: industry leaders will find no shortage of challenges facing them in the twenty-first century.

Food Service in the Twenty-first Century

With the new century rapidly approaching, industry executives, consultants, and the trade press are all involved in forecasting the future. To compile our projections, we have drawn from all three sources. In this chapter's Insider Insight, Ted Balestreri, past president of the National Restaurant Association, shares his thoughts. In its published report, *Foodservice 2005, Satisfying America's Changing Appetites*, McKinsey & Company identify business models that will lead the field, while *Restaurants and Institutions* magazine selects a winner for several models.

McKinsey & Company predict that, from 1995 to 2005, consumer food expenditures will have grown by $100 billion or about 2.9 percent annually, and that the food service industry will capture 100 percent of these dollars.

Who will get the business? The report identifies five business models that have demonstrated abilities to respond to driving consumer trends, maintain low cost/high efficiency operating structures, reduce prices faster and further than their competition, and still offer the value their customers demand. The five models are:

1. *Traditional limited-menu quick-service chains*

   Here, sales are expected to reach $93 billion by the year 2005.

   Restaurants and Institutions says that McDonald's will reign number one in 2005.

2. *Quick service restaurants geared toward "home meal replacement"*

   This segment should achieve 13.5 percent annual growth and triple sales to $8 billion.

   Restaurants and Institutions predicts that Boston Market will lead the pack in 2005.

3. *Full-service chains*

   This segment is expected to grow 5.1 percent annually to sales of $46 billion by 2005.

   Restaurants and Institutions believes the winner here will be Friday's Hospitality Worldwide with its main concept, TGI Friday's, plus Friday's American Bar, Italianni's, and Front Row Sports Grill.

4. *Contract Food Service Management*

   This model will grow 2.7 percent annually to $49 billion by 2005 with primary growth coming from colleges and universities, recreation venues, sporting events complexes, and schools.

   Restaurants and Institutions predicts that Sodexho Marriott Management will lead in this category.

5. *Supermarkets*

   Sales should grow 11.8 percent annually to a total of $28 billion by 2005. The consultants believe that the best bet for this model will be prepared foods, and that the retailers will outsource most meal preparation, if not all.

   Restaurants and Institutions does not select a clear winner, but does select The Vons Companies, Inc.'s Fresh and Ready concept as an excellent model for others to follow.

The food service industry is nearly unanimous in the belief that managers represent the ultimate key to success. We asked a panel of food service industry executives to describe the Food Service Manager of the Twenty-first Century. Consensus was achieved on a number of points. The manager:

- Will need to be computer proficient.
- Will oversee a much more diverse, multi-ethnic work force.

- Must be a better time manager.
- Must create more ways to employ persons with handicaps.
- Will have a high commitment to employee career development.
- Will serve consumers who are more knowledgeable in nutrition.
- Will need a greater knowledge of ingredient and nutritional content.
- Will need better teaching and training skills.
- Must be oriented to the latest technology.

We conclude this look into the future with these projections:

1. The food service industry will have the largest employee count of any industry in the nation.
2. Globalization will accelerate.
3. Franchising will be the primary method of doing business in the industry.
4. Mergers, acquisitions, and consolidation will accelerate.
5. Environmental concerns will create a greater emphasis on waste management and recycling.

Appendix

Periodicals

Lodging and food service trade journals offer the latest information and advice about the hospitality industry. Professionals in the hospitality field rely, in part, on trade publications to help them stay current in this fast-paced industry. These publications also make important reading for hospitality industry students who want to keep up with the latest trends and changes, especially in the job market. Most schools offering hospitality management courses subscribe to some or all of the following publications. Students should ask the librarian at their school for a list of current periodicals.

Annals of Tourism Research (quarterly)
Beverage World (monthly)
Briefing: The Restaurateurs' New Digest (monthly)
Canadian Hotel & Restaurant (monthly)
Club Management (monthly)
CKC Report: The Hotel Technology Newsletter (10 times/year)
Cornell Hotel and Restaurant Administration Quarterly
        Cornell University
FIU Hospitality Review (quarterly)
        Florida International University
Food Management (monthly)
The Foodservice Distributor (monthly)
Hospitality Law (monthly)
Hospitality Education and Research Journal (three times/year)
        Council on Hotel, Restaurant and Institutional Education
Hotel & Motel Management (17 times/year)
Hotel & Resort Industry (monthly)
Hotel & Travel Index (quarterly)
Hotels (monthly)
International Journal of Hospitality Management (quarterly)
Journal of Travel Research (quarterly)
        University of Colorado
Lodging Magazine (monthly except August)
        American Hotel Association Directory Corporation
Lodging Hospitality (monthly; twice in November)
Lodging Outlook (monthly)
Nation's Restaurant News (weekly)
Restaurant Business (18 times/year)
Restaurant Hospitality (monthly)
Restaurant Management (monthly)
        (formerly *Independent Restaurants*)

(continued)

Periodicals *(continued)*

Restaurants and Institutions (biweekly)
Restaurants USA (monthly except July)
   (formerly *NRA News*)
      National Restaurant Association
Sales and Marketing Management (monthly)
The Service Edge (monthly)
Washington Report (bimonthly)
      American Hotel & Motel Association

Index